T0295889

MODELS OF RISK PREFERENCES

RESEARCH IN EXPERIMENTAL ECONOMICS

Series Editors: R. Mark Isaac and Douglas A. Norton

Recent Volumes:

Volume 7:	Emissions Permit Experiments, 1999
Volume 8:	Research in Experimental Economics, 2001
Volume 9:	Experiments Investigating Market Power, 2002
Volume 10:	Field Experiments in Economics, 2005
Volume 11:	Experiments Investigating Fundraising and Charitable Contributors, 2006
Volume 12:	Risk Aversion in Experiments, 2008
Volume 13:	Charity With Choice, 2010
Volume 14:	Experiments on Energy, The Environment, and Sustainability, 2011
Volume 15:	New Advances in Experimental Research on Corruption, 2012
Volume 16:	Experiments in Financial Economics, 2013
Volume 17:	Experiments in Macroeconomics, 2014
Volume 18:	Replication in Experimental Economics, 2015
Volume 19:	Experiments in Organizational Economics, 2016
Volume 20:	Experimental Economics and Culture, 2018
Volume 21:	Experimental Law and Economics, 2022

RESEARCH IN EXPERIMENTAL ECONOMICS VOLUME 22

MODELS OF RISK PREFERENCES: DESCRIPTIVE AND NORMATIVE CHALLENGES

EDITED BY

GLENN W. HARRISON
Georgia State University, USA

and

DON ROSS
University College Cork, Ireland
University of Cape Town, South Africa
Georgia State University, USA

SERIES EDITORS

R. MARK ISAAC
Florida State University, USA

and

DOUGLAS A. NORTON
Florida State University, USA

United Kingdom – North America – Japan
India – Malaysia – China

Emerald Publishing Limited
Emerald Publishing, Floor 5, Northspring, 21-23 Wellington Street, Leeds LS1 4DL.

First edition 2023

British Library Cataloguing in Publication Data
A catalogue record for this book is available from the British Library

ISBN: 978-1-83797-269-2 (Print)
ISBN: 978-1-83797-268-5 (Online)
ISBN: 978-1-83797-270-8 (Epub)

ISSN: 0193-2306 (Series)

CONTENTS

ABOUT THE EDITORS

Glenn W. Harrison is University Distinguished Professor, C.V. Starr Chair of Risk Management & Insurance and Director of the Center for the Economic Analysis of Risk, Maurice R. Greenberg School of Risk Science, J. Mack Robinson College of Business, Georgia State University. His current research spans risk management & perception, experimental economics, behavioral econometrics, behavioral welfare economics, and development economics.

Don Ross is Professor in the School of Society, Politics, and Ethics at University College Cork, Professor in the School of Economics at the University of Cape Town, and Program Director for Methodology at the Centre for the Economic Analysis of Risk at Georgia State University. His current research focuses on experimental studies and theoretical modeling of risk and time preferences in humans and other animals, gambling disorders and policy, economic methodology, the economics of road transport networks in Africa, and the metaphysical implications of science.

LIST OF CONTRIBUTORS

Glenn W. Harrison	Maurice R. Greenberg School of Risk Sciences and Center for the Economic Analysis of Risk, Robinson College of Business, Georgia State University, USA; School of Economics, University of Cape Town, South Africa
Morten I. Lau	Department of Economics, Copenhagen Business School, Copenhagen, Denmark; Department of Economics, Durham University, Durham, UK
Brian Albert Monroe	School of Economics, University of Cape Town, South Africa
Don Ross	School of Society, Politics and Ethics, University College Cork, Ireland; Center for the Economic Analysis of Risk, Robinson College of Business, Georgia State University, USA; School of Economics, University of Cape Town, South Africa
J. Todd Swarthout	Department of Economics, Andrew Young School of Policy Studies, Georgia State University, USA; Center for the Economic Analysis of Risk, Robinson College of Business, Georgia State University, USA
Nathaniel T. Wilcox	Department of Economics, Walker College of Business, Appalachian State University, Boone, USA
Hong Il Yoo	School of Business and Economics, Loughborough University, Loughborough, UK
Hongming Zhao	Department of Economics, Durham University, Durham, UK

INTRODUCTION

Glenn W. Harrison and Don Ross

The insights of behavioral economics have directly influenced policy in recent decades, and have started to influence the way in which welfare economics is used to design and evaluate policy. The need to provide guidance for policy design premised on behavioral patterns, and evaluate existing or new policy, has generated a "derived demand" for better descriptive models of behavior as well as better ways to understand relevant normative standpoints. This volume brings together contributions to that challenge, with a focus on behavior with respect to risky choices.

In Chapter 1, Glenn W. Harrison and Don Ross develop a philosophically consistent approach to behavioral welfare economics. They call their approach the Quantitative Intentional Stance (QIS), based on the Intentional Stance (IS) of Dennett (1971, 1987). For Dennett, there are complementary styles of scientific explanation that he calls "stances," and the one he calls the IS is the stance most generally applicable in cognitive and behavioral science. It also happens to be close to how economists have historically constructed their explanations and models, which makes it an ideal basis for linking the modeling of descriptive behavior toward risk with the modeling of normative evaluations of this behavior. The observer, or normative policy-maker, forms priors about the (risk) preferences and (risk) perceptions of the agent being evaluated, and the choice environment the agent faces, using the best models that her evidence allows. Then the observer forms priors about how those preferences and beliefs should affect choices over risky prospects, and contrasts those expected choices with observed choices. Sometimes the agent makes the choices "expected" by the observer given her priors over preferences, beliefs, and how they should affect choices, and sometimes they are different. The former then constitute welfare gains for the agent, and the latter constitute welfare losses for the agent.[1]

All of this imposes a burden on the economist to generate rigorous models of risk preferences and risk perceptions, which is why there is the derived demand for more care being given to the descriptive side of the structural modeling of risk.

Models of Risk Preferences: Descriptive and Normative Challenges
Research in Experimental Economics, Volume 22, 1–6

ISSN: 0193-2306/doi:10.1108/S0193-230620230000022007

Harrison and Ross contrast their QIS with existing approaches toward behavioral welfare economics in the economics literature, some of which err because they conflate the economist's technical concept of welfare with wider understandings of well-being that do *not* admit of technical specification. This raises the question of how policy-makers, and agents themselves, should regard the normative force of the economist's technical analysis. Answers to this question are highly context-sensitive, but some guidelines are provided for identifying frequently relevant contextual features. Harrison and Ross also directly answer a wide range of questions about the QIS that arise from those looking for easier solutions to the challenges of behavioral welfare economics, explaining the dangers of various short-cuts.

A first step at reconsidering the structural descriptive evidence about risk preferences is taken in Chapter 2 by Nathaniel T. Wilcox. He considers a popular meme, according to which everyone exhibits a specific type of bias in the way they process risky probabilities: that they overweight the extreme outcomes, and underweight outcomes in between. This presumption arose from early statements of Original Prospect Theory by Kahneman and Tversky (1979), and in later statements of Cumulative Prospect Theory (CPT) by Tversky and Kahneman (1992). To an economist, a model of risk preferences does not normally come with specific functional forms or parameter values for those functions as parts of the model, but in some parts of psychology that is common. Many people believe that CPT *requires* this particular mix of optimism and pessimism in the face of risk. Economists take the view that the general validity of the way that CPT explains risky choices should not stand or fall on particular patterns of probability weighting.

In that spirit, Wilcox elegantly lets the data speak on the matter, by careful experimental design as well as careful econometric evaluation of the observed data. He designs a battery of choice tasks over risky prospects that allow a wide range of utility functions and probability weighting functions to play a role in explaining choices for each individual, and ensures that the resulting data should have high power for the inferences to then come. And in the econometric evaluation he completely avoids taking a stance on the functional form of either the utility function or the probability weighting function. He also avoids pooling behavior over individuals. Even with conditioning on observable characteristics of individual subjects, pooling prevents the data from revealing the full heterogeneity of behavior at the individual level.

The methodological drive to model behavior at the individual level is more significant than it might seem. What if one third of the subjects in a sample overweighted the worst outcomes in the battery, one third overweighted none of the outcomes, and one third overweighted the best outcomes in the battery? Pooling data from these three cohorts, and assuming their choices are all determined by one specific probability weighting function, the observer would be led to find support for the meme when, by construction, there is none at the individual level. Of course, one might just wag a finger at such inferences, chiding that the average of a distribution of choices by many individuals should never be assumed to apply exactly to *every* choice by *every* individual, or even *any* choice by *any* individual ... except that one would be wagging fingers at a vast literature! The heterogeneity that Wilcox documents with respect to probability weighting is convincing testimony to the dangers of pooled estimation.

In Chapter 3, Glenn W. Harrison and J. Todd Swarthout pick up these themes, and set about evaluating what fraction of risky choices are best characterized descriptively by CPT in a controlled lab setting, where the initial empirical insights underlying CPT arose. In contrast to Wilcox in Chapter 2, they assume popular, flexible functional forms from the literature. Consistent with Wilcox, they stress the need to estimate risk preferences at the level of the individual. Hence, they design and conduct experiments with hundreds of subjects, each making a large number of choices over risky prospects that allow CPT to play a role. Their approach is to estimate several models of risk preferences for each individual: an Expected Utility Theory (EUT) model, a Dual Theory (DT) model, a Rank-Dependent Utility (RDU) model, a Disappointment Aversion (DA) model, and a CPT model. They allow the DT and RDU models to employ a particularly flexible probability weighting function, mindful in their priors of the heterogeneity in probability weighting that Wilcox demonstrates so thoroughly. And their choice battery includes many choices in a gain frame, a loss frame, and a mixed gain-loss frame, as required to identify the core parameters of CPT. Of course, although not "of course" to much of the extant CPT literature, all choices involved real monetary rewards.

Their striking finding is that CPT performs poorly when the risky prospects are set up to give it the most favorable chance of explaining behavior. The clear modal model accounting for behavior is RDU, with EUT solidly in second place. The root of the poor performance of CPT is easy to identify: local asset integration by subjects when faced with losses out of an endowment, whether or not that endowment was provided by the experimenter or earned in some prior task. If an individual has a $60 endowment and faces a prospect of losing $20 from that, does she evaluate the net gain of $40 or does she evaluate the gross loss of $20? CPT assumes the latter, at least under plausible assumptions about what "the" reference point for this subject is. But if she locally integrates the loss of $20 with the endowment of $60 and just evaluates the net gain of $40, CPT is "dead in the water" in terms of what differentiates it from RDU and EUT. Here, it is important to recognize that RDU and EUT are *not* nested within CPT, as commonly and casually claimed.

The data of Harrison and Swarthout, as well as their detailed cautions about short-cut models that allegedly find evidence for the beloved loss aversion parameter of CPT, should provide a rich starting point for consideration of further evaluations of CPT. Apart from DA, existing models of "endogenous reference points" provide no useful *operational* guidance for estimation. So perhaps we need more operational guidance from theory on what the reference point of CPT might be. And even with the large battery of choices each subject made, estimating all of the moving parts of CPT poses serious econometric challenges which Harrison and Swarthout urge others to take up with Bayesian Hierarchical

Models that use pooled behavior solely to provide weakly informative priors with which to tease apart those moving parts at the level of the individual. In our own work, we simply do not bother with CPT any more, since it is a needless and ill-motivated distraction for the behavioral welfare economist. If advocates of CPT ever take the incentivized data and econometric demands more seriously, we are of course open to reconsider that judgment.

In Chapter 4, Morten I. Lau, Hong Il Yoo, and Hongming Zhao consider a different aspect of risk preferences if they are to be used to make normative evaluations, their stability over time. They start from a recognition that "stability" can mean several things. It might mean unconditional stability over time, even as characteristics and "states of nature" change, or it might mean conditional stability given values for those characteristics and states.[2] And it might mean that some population exhibits stability over time, even if individuals do not, or it might mean that individuals exhibit stability over time. They use panel data from influential longitudinal lab experiments previously applied to estimate CPT risk preferences by Glöckner and Pachur (2012) and Murphy and ten Brincke (2018). Their econometric approach extends a random coefficient approach to estimation of risk preferences developed by Harrison, Lau, and Yoo (2020) to consider CPT, rather than just EUT and RDU.

CPT posits three possible "pathways" to explain the risk premium. One is aversion to variability of outcomes, one is pessimism with respect to better outcomes, and one is a special aversion to losses. One of the core findings of Lau, Yoo, and Zhao is that none of the three pathways to the risk premium in CPT seems to be stable over time, no matter what definition of temporal stability is used. A second core finding is that temporal stability varies with the model of risk preferences adopted. For example, for their data and models, they conclude that EUT exhibits temporal stability even if CPT does not, even when applied to the same data. One can always point to cautions about sample sizes, payoff scales, econometric specifications, and other methodological attributes of the comparisons, and Lau, Yoo, and Zhao do this carefully. But it is apparent that temporal stability of some kind[3] is needed in order to undertake normative evaluations of policies to be applied in the future, so further attention to these issues is needed.

Finally, in Chapter 5, Brian Albert Monroe takes up a subtlety in the application of the QIS of surprising significance for welfare evaluations. In an early application of the QIS by Harrison and Ng (2016) subjects were asked to make a series of binary choices over risky lotteries, to allow inferences about the risk preferences of each individual. Those inferences were, in turn, to be used as priors in the normative evaluation of insurance purchase decisions that the same subjects made in a separate task. A key step in the evaluation was to initially determine if the risk preferences of each individual were better characterized by EUT or by RDU, and then to use the estimates[4] for EUT *or* RDU for that individual when evaluating the insurance choices by that individual. An individual was assumed to be characterized by EUT unless their choices over the risky lotteries exhibited statistically significant evidence of probability weighting, using appropriate tests and various significance levels. In large part, this initial step of "typing" the individual as EUT or RDU was undertaken to make the point that the normative evaluation of insurance choices depends on the *type* of risk preference as well as the *level* of risk aversion.

Monroe explains that there are two potential problems with this approach. The first problem is that subjects who are judged to be better characterized as EUT decision-makers could just be extremely noisy RDU decision-makers. And there is no reason to expect that the "noise" in question here affects inferences in some simple additive, linear manner that might wash out when making normative evaluations. The second problem is that declaring somebody to be better characterized as an EUT decision-maker, and then using their EUT estimates for normative evaluation, is actually saying that they are a RDU decision-maker with *exactly* estimated parameters for their probability weighting function.[5] This is not the same thing as saying that they are "sufficiently noisy" in terms of probability weighting that one cannot reject a null hypothesis that they exhibit no probability weighting at all.

What is remarkable, and skillfully demonstrated in numerical simulations by Monroe, is that these seemingly subtle steps in the descriptive characterization of risk preferences can have a significant impact on normative evaluation. The impacts are most pronounced on the inferred size of the welfare gain or loss, rather than the sign of the welfare effect, but that is not the main methodological point. The important lesson from Monroe, already adopted in later studies[6] with reference to his arguments, is to just use the RDU model for every subject when undertaking the normative evaluations of welfare. One can still usefully use the classification of risk preference type, by whatever means one wants, to help understand the sources of welfare gains and losses, but one should not use the special case of EUT when an individual is better characterized for *normative* purposes as RDU and EUT is nested in RDU. The clear exception here is if the policy-maker or analyst has a well-motivated and explicit reason to maintain EUT as the normative metric for evaluating choices, in which case every subject's risk preferences should be characterized by the EUT model, even if the RDU model does a better job for *descriptive* purposes.

Taken as a whole, the contributions here constructively make the case that structural insights into risk preferences are needed in order to make rigorous normative evaluations of risky choices. They also clearly flag remaining challenges in undertaking these normative evaluations.

NOTES

1. The key to the confident statement here is that if the QIS has been rigorously applied in a Bayesian inferential procedure, there is nothing more than anyone could relevantly know about the choice situation, at least in isolation from possible general equilibrium effects as unintended consequences.
2. See Andersen, Harrison, Lau, and Rutström (2008).
3. In fact it is temporal *predictability* of risk preferences that is needed, but that can just be viewed as stability conditional on evolving characteristics that affect risk preferences.
4. By "estimates" we mean point estimates as well as estimates of standard errors and covariances, which were incorporated in the normative evaluation using bootstrap procedures.

5. And, of course, that those exact values imply zero probability weighting consistent with EUT.

6. For example, Gao, Harrison, and Tchernis (2023) and Harrison, Morsink, and Schneider (2022).

REFERENCES

Andersen, S., Harrison, G. W., Lau, M. I., & Rutström, E. E. (2008). Lost in state space: Are preferences stable? *International Economic Review*, *49*(3), 1091–1112.

Dennett, D. (1971). Intentional systems. *The Journal of Philosophy*, *68*(4), 87–106.

Dennett, D. (1987). *The intentional stance*. Cambridge, MA: MIT Press.

Gao, X. S., Harrison, G. W., & Tchernis, R. (2023). Behavioral welfare economics and risk preferences: A Bayesian approach. *Experimental Economics*, *26*, 273–303.

Glöckner, A., & Pachur, T. (2012). Cognitive models of risky choice: Parameter stability and predictive accuracy of prospect theory. *Cognition*, *123*(1), 21–32.

Harrison, G. W., Lau, M. I., & Yoo, H. I. (2020). Risk attitudes, sample selection and attrition in a longitudinal field experiment. *Review of Economics and Statistics*, *102*, 552–568.

Harrison, G. W., Morsink, K., & Schneider, M. (2022). Literacy and the quality of index insurance decisions. *Geneva Risk and Insurance Review*, *47*, 66–97.

Harrison, G. W., & Ng, J. M. (2016). Evaluating the expected welfare gain of insurance. *Journal of Risk & Insurance*, *83*(1), 91–120.

Kahneman, D., & Tversky, A. (1979). Prospect theory: An analysis of decision under risk. *Econometrica*, *47*, 263–291.

Murphy, R. O., & ten Brincke, R. H. W. (2018). Hierarchical maximum likelihood parameter estimation for cumulative prospect theory: Improving the reliability of individual risk parameter estimates. *Management Science*, *64*(1), 308–326.

Tversky, A., & Kahneman, D. (1992). Advances in prospect theory: Cumulative representations of uncertainty. *Journal of Risk & Uncertainty*, *5*: 297–323.

CHAPTER 1

BEHAVIORAL WELFARE ECONOMICS AND THE QUANTITATIVE INTENTIONAL STANCE

Glenn W. Harrison and Don Ross

ABSTRACT

Behavioral economics poses a challenge for the welfare evaluation of choices, particularly those that involve risk. It demands that we recognize that the descriptive account of behavior toward those choices might not be the ones we were all taught, and still teach, and that subjective risk perceptions might not accord with expert assessments of probabilities. In addition to these challenges, we are faced with the need to jettison naive notions of revealed preferences, according to which every choice by a subject expresses her objective function, as behavioral evidence forces us to confront pervasive inconsistencies and noise in a typical individual's choice data. A principled account of errant choice must be built into models used for identification and estimation. These challenges demand close attention to the methodological claims often used to justify policy interventions. They also require, we argue, closer attention by economists to relevant contributions from cognitive science. We propose that a quantitative application of the "intentional stance" of Dennett provides a coherent, attractive and general approach to behavioral welfare economics.

Keywords: Behavioral economics; welfare economics; behavior toward risk; revealed preference; normative economics; cognitive science

Models of Risk Preferences: Descriptive and Normative Challenges
Research in Experimental Economics, Volume 22, 7–67

ISSN: 0193-2306/doi:10.1108/S0193-230620230000022001

One theme lies at the heart of a rigorous evaluation of policy using the insights of behavioral welfare economics: how to judge if some policy is encouraging good choices or bad choices. One approach, which drives the nudge movement and some randomized evaluations, is to assume that judgment away, and simply assert that some change in an *observable* must be good regardless of special features of the preferences and beliefs of individuals. Isn't it obvious that people should save more, eat fewer fatty foods, drink less wine, and take up insurance? The only appropriate answer to this for an economist is "no." Demand for these behaviors depends on preferences and beliefs, and hence the expected consumer surplus (CS) they deliver is also conditional on preferences and beliefs. Further, no realistic economics that recognizes heterogeneity of preferences and beliefs, and identifies a welfare enhancing policy conditional on those preferences and beliefs, tells us that such policies would be welfare-enhancing *on average* if applied *unconditionally*.

Revealed preference theory (RPT), the various axiomatizations of which are reviewed by Chambers and Echenique (2016), minimizes the inferential gap between agents' observed behavior and ascribed goals by treating preferences as summaries of actual choices. As emphasized by Binmore (2009), under RPT it is simply an *error* to regard preferences as *causes* of choices, or as *explaining* them. The motivation for this is not philosophical commitment to behaviorism about "mental states," but reflects the value to the economist, for the sake of theoretical power, of treating all processes that generate common utility outcomes for an agent as an equivalence class. This raises problems for normative analysis, however, because it seems to leave no room for treating any individual choices as reflecting *error*. In effect, every choice that the agent makes is assumed to make her no worse off. Such an idealization makes it impossible *a priori* for the economist to offer any advice about prospective choices that would be potentially superior with respect to the agent's subjective welfare.

Behavioral welfare economics seeks to bridge this gap. One obvious way to do this, which is common in the literature, is to simply abandon RPT, and directly model preferences as hypothesized psychological states that cause choices. The theorist is then free to suppose that different psychological processes have varying welfare consequences, and that an agent can profit from the economist's advice whenever her choices result from less-than-optimal such processes. But this approach has major costs. It makes welfare economics conditional on strong psychological assumptions that must be expected to vary from case to case, even across choices that are identical with respect to outcomes. Thus, it directly undermines the kinds of generalizations economists care about both descriptively and normatively. The psychological assumptions in question are often, necessarily, pure conjectures. Where they are based on psychological experiments, they are hostage to inferential methods in psychology that are heavily criticized, have produced many post-publication retractions by journals, and are rejected by most economists when applied in their own discipline (Ortmann, 2021; Yarkoni, 2022). Appeals to hypothesized brain states based on neuroimaging studies involve yet more egregious violations of econometric best practice with respect to both identification and estimation (Harrison, 2008; Harrison & Ross, 2020). Worst of all where unified science is concerned, as we discuss, interpretation of preferences (and beliefs) as inner states of agents that cause chosen behavior is now rejected outright by the majority of the relevant experts on the issue, cognitive scientists.

The challenge for behavioral welfare economics, then, is to find a way of remaining within the broad ambit of RPT – that is, deriving preferences (and beliefs) directly from observed behavior – but with a richer set of modeling techniques that avoid idealizing each and every choice as optimal for the agent. These requirements generate a derived demand for thinking carefully about the methodologies of behavioral welfare economics, and that requires economists to think more deeply about the methodology and philosophy of their subject. In this respect thought experiments and laboratory experiments stand as ideal places to begin this long, slippery path. One major risk we face, and that is tragically illustrated by what currently passes for behavioral economic policy, is that the new behavioral economics causes us to forget the old welfare economics: see Atkinson (2001, 2009, 2011), who eloquently reflects on "the strange disappearance of welfare economics." In the words of Homer Simpson (season 5, episode 22), "every time I learn something new, it pushes some old stuff out of my brain."

We argue that this challenge can be met systematically, generally, and with available tools, by recognizing a body of work in cognitive sciences that seems to have been constructed with economists in mind (though of course it wasn't). We refer to "the intentional stance" developed by Dennett (1971, 1987).

In Section 1, we briefly review the descriptive evidence on behavior toward risk, as we see it. Section 2 reviews broad approaches toward behavioral welfare economics by economists. Section 3 is then a statement of the proposed application of the intentional stance to behavioral welfare economics, which we refer to as the Quantitative Intentional Stance (QIS). Section 4 reviews several approaches toward behavioral welfare economics by philosophers. Section 5 concludes.

1. THE DESCRIPTIVE EVIDENCE, AS WE SEE IT

Our focus here is on the descriptive evidence about risk preferences, but the general issues that the QIS is intended to address also require attention to time preferences and subjective beliefs, at the very least. And since these interact with the evaluation of risky choices anyway, we also briefly cover them.

1.1 Theoretical Context

The notion of a risk premium is one of the core concepts that different theories of risk preferences agree on. Expected Utility Theory (EUT) assumes that aversion to variability drives a risk preference, where variability can be much more than just variance. Rank-Dependent Utility (RDU) complicates this assumption with the additional idea that probability optimism or pessimism can augment, positively or negatively, any risk premium due to aversion to variability. And Cumulative Prospect Theory (CPT) is based on a hypothesized psychological mechanism on top of these, where sign dependence relative to some reference point affects risk preferences. All of these models agree on the *concept* of a risk premium, and just decompose it differently. In general, since the utility function under each model will differ, the models will not agree on the *value* of the risk premium. Harrison and Swarthout (2023) review the comparative evidence for these models.

Important extensions to these basic constructions include considerations of downside risk aversion that differs from the loss aversion of CPT, and is related to literature on "higher order risk preferences"; considerations of "regret" or "disappointment" that can arise from contemplation of realized outcomes; intertemporal risk aversion toward variability of outcomes over time; and allowance for multivariate risk aversion, including connections between foreground and background risk.

Principal theories of time preference include exponential, hyperbolic, and quasi-hyperbolic discounting. The differences can best be understood by thinking of the lender of money as assigning some cost to not having liquidity for a time period. Exponential discounting assumes a constant variable cost of being without the loaned funds with respect to time and no fixed cost; hyperbolic discounting assumes a declining variable cost with respect to time and no fixed cost; and quasi-hyperbolic discounting assumes a fixed cost and a constant variable cost.[1] An alternative approach from psychology is to view the perception of time horizon as subjective: if the agent perceives time units contracting as the horizon gets longer, declining discount rates will arise. Andersen, Harrison, Lau, and Rutström (2014) review these models, and provide evidence for them.

Virtually all theories of time preference assume an *additive* intertemporal utility function, in which utility over time is a discount factor-weighted sum of utility for each distinct period. In this respect, the alternative theories behind the discount factor tend to agree. This seemingly technical assumption, however, has dramatic implications for behavior toward risk: it implies that agents are neutral toward risk *over time*, even if they are averse to risk *at a point in time*. In other words, agents might be averse to risk resolved at a point in time, but must then be neutral to risk resolved *over* time. A restrictive corollary of this additivity is that atemporal risk preferences and time preferences are formally "tied at the hip," in the sense that the intertemporal elasticity of substitution *must* be equal to the inverse of relative risk aversion. This corollary sits uncomfortably with everyday observations and the stylized aggregate data, forcing problematic calibrations in macroeconomic models. A simple resolution of this impasse is to allow non-additive intertemporal utility functions, such that interactions between atemporal responses across time periods matter to the agent. Andersen, Harrison, Lau, and Rutström (2018) review the theory.

The static theory of subjective beliefs is dominated by Subjective Expected Utility (SEU), which assumes that agents behave as if satisfying the Reduction of Compound Lotteries (ROCL). The effect is that non-degenerate subjective belief distributions can be replaced by the weighted average belief, and then EUT applied as usual. It is noteworthy that SEU does not assume that the subjective belief distributions that agents hold satisfy Bayes' rule when updated over time, despite Savage (1954, 1962a, 1962b) being a staunch advocate for both Bayes' Rule and SEU. Bayes' Rule generates a separate model of (dynamic) risk perception, which may or may not be applied with SEU. Relaxations of ROCL that still assume that the agent has a well-defined subjective belief distribution characterize uncertainty, and models of decision-making that do not assume a well-defined subjective belief distribution characterize ambiguity: see Harrison (2011b) for an exposition.

1.2 Experimental Evidence

There are various methods for eliciting and estimating risk preferences, reviewed by Harrison and Rutström (2008). Unfortunately some of the methods in use have well-known weaknesses and biases. One of the most flexible is to ask the agent to make a series of unordered binary choices over risky lotteries, where each lottery typically has between 1 and 4 outcomes. This method provides enough flexibility to allow for estimation of risk preferences at the level of the individual. For normative analysis, recognizing the heterogeneity of risk preferences across individuals is critical. Moreover, heterogeneity here refers to much more than the risk premium: it also refers to the *type* of risk preferences. It makes a significant difference for the normative evaluation of insurance products if the agent is an EUT or RDU decision-maker. In general, these models will imply different utility functions, and it is the utility function that is used to calculate the Certainty Equivalent (CE) of polices to manage risk (e.g., Harrison & Ng, 2016).

There is overwhelming evidence that laboratory and field samples demonstrate heterogeneity with respect to which models of risk response describe their choice patterns. Harrison and Ross (2016, p. 401) summarize a selection of their own studies, conducted in both developed and developing countries, which find that substantial proportions of subjects in all samples exhibit behavior best characterized by EUT. At the same time, in all of these studies we observe somewhat larger proportions presenting choice patterns better modeled by RDU. This classification refers to estimated models at the level of the individual: comparable classifications arise if one uses mixture models over data that are pooled over individuals, as proposed by Harrison and Rutström (2009). There is seldom any evidence for Dual Theory, which proposes the special case of RDU in which utility functions are linear, so that the entire risk premium derives from probability weighting.

There is actually very little evidence for CPT in controlled, incentivized experiments. This may come as a shock to some. Harrison and Swarthout (2023) provide an extensive literature review, which finds that most reported evidence for "loss aversion" is actually evidence for probability weighting. Very often there is evidence of probability weighting over choices between two gain-frame lotteries, and that is literally reported as evidence for CPT. The context always makes it clear that it is *evidence for* RDU, and is *consistent with* evidence for CPT, but that distinction is all too often glossed.

Harrison and Swarthout (2023) also report evidence of (at least local) asset integration in the laboratory, which is *fatal* for the empirical adequacy of CPT. In a nutshell, this explains why they find so little support for CPT in a "three horse race" that includes EUT and RDU; Dual Theory never gets out of the gates, by the way. Harrison and Ross (2017) review further evidence, and consider the implications for welfare assessment of the conjecture that the many reported "two horse race" victories of CPT over EUT were really wins for RDU in disguise, where the successes of CPT stemmed from its allowance for probability weighting rather than "utility" loss aversion relative to an idiosyncratic reference point.

Harrison and Swarthout (2023) further stress that there are two pathways for the loss aversion meme that "losses loom larger than gains." The usual way in which CPT models loss aversion comes from Tversky and Kahneman (1992, p. 309), who popularized the functional forms we often see using a CRRA specification of utility over money m: $U(m) = m^{1-\alpha}/(1 - \alpha)$ when $m \geq 0$, and $U(m) = -\lambda[(-m)^{1-\beta}/(1 - \beta)]$ when $m < 0$, where α and β define the curvature of some "basic utility function" that captures the "intrinsic value of outcomes and satisfies usual regularity conditions" (Wakker, 2010, p. 239), U is some "overall utility function," and λ is the celebrated loss aversion parameter for utility. Here, we have the assumption that the degree of utility loss aversion for small unit changes in money is the same as the degree of loss aversion for large unit changes: the same λ applies locally to gains and losses of the same monetary magnitude around 0 as it does globally to any size gain or loss of the same magnitude. This is not a criticism, just a restrictive parametric turn in the specification compared to Kahneman and Tversky (1979). However, even if the basic utility functions for gains and losses are linear, and conventional loss aversion is absent ($\lambda = 1$), differences in the *decision weights* for gains and losses could induce the same behavior as if there were utility loss aversion emanating from λ. This is called "probabilistic loss aversion" by Schmidt and Zank (2008, p. 213). Imagine that there is no probability weighting on the gain domain, so the decision weights are the objective probabilities, but that there is some probability weighting on the loss domain. Then one could easily have losses weighted more than gains, solely from the implied decision weights.

Another critique of EUT that has arisen in experimental settings is the so-called calibration critique popularized by Rabin (2000). This is the concern that "small stakes risk aversion," supposedly common in lab experiments, implies implausibly large "high stakes risk aversion" under EUT. The point was originally made by Hansson (1988), and has been viewed as an indirect rationale for wanting to consider (utility) loss aversion from CPT as playing an important role in decision-making over low stakes. However, the general experimental literature on risk aversion does not support the theoretical premise of the calibration critique: that premise depends on observing the *same person* facing small stakes lottery choices over a range of wealth levels. Cox and Sadiraj (2006) proposed an elegant design to implement this test, building on the ability to vary "lab wealth" for a given subject. Evidence from university undergraduates in the United States indicates that the premise is simply false for that population (Harrison, Lau, Ross, & Swarthout, 2017), although evidence from representatives of the adult Danish population shows that the premise is valid for the range of lab wealth considered (Andersen et al., 2018). In the latter case, there are alternative assumptions about the degree of asset integration between field wealth and lottery prizes that allow one to readily reconcile small stakes risk aversion with plausible high stakes risk aversion, and these assumptions appear to apply to the Danish population.

There is much less evidence for "hyperbolicky" discounting than conventionally assumed. Prior to Coller and Williams (1999), there were very few experiments that provided designs that allowed one to infer monetary discount rates rigorously. This might seem like a simple point, but prior literature typically generated annualized discount rates in the hundreds or thousands of percent (and typically chose not to report them as such, for obvious reasons). Another important insight, often neglected completely, has been to correct for the effect of diminishing marginal utility on inferences about utility discount rates drawn from choices between "smaller, sooner" amounts of money and "larger, later" amounts of money. Modest levels of diminishing marginal utility generate first-order changes in inferred discount rates (Andersen, Harrison, Lau, & Rutström, 2008a). Variations in designs allow one to test Exponential discounting of money against all major alternatives, and Exponential discounting clearly characterizes the data best in such settings (Andersen et al., 2014). Nor is there any evidence for the alleged "magnitude effect," whereby elicited discount rates appeared to be lower for higher stakes (Andersen, Harrison, Lau, & Rutström, 2013).

There have been important advances in the manner in which subjective beliefs can be elicited. One strand of literature concerns the estimation of subjective *probabilities* over *binary* events, using incentivized scoring rules and corrections for the effect of risk aversion on reports (Andersen, Fountain, Harrison, & Rutström, 2014). Another strand tackles the more challenging problem of inferring whole subjective belief *distributions* for *continuous or non-binary* events (Harrison, Martínez-Correa, Swarthout, & Ulm, 2017). In the latter case, one can directly make statements about the level of "confidence" that individuals have in their beliefs. The application of these *incentivized* methods has not yet been widespread in behavioral economics.

2. METHODOLOGIES OF BEHAVIORAL WELFARE ECONOMICS FROM ECONOMISTS

There is a large, general literature on behavioral welfare economics, including Bernheim (2009, 2016), Bernheim and Rangel (2008, 2009), Bernheim and Taubinksy (2018), Manzini and Mariotti (2012, 2014), Rubinstein and Salant (2012), Salant and Rubinstein (2008), and Sugden (2004, 2009). A general concern with this literature is that although it identifies the methodological problem well, it does not yet provide clear guidance to practical, portable, rigorous welfare evaluation with respect to risk preferences as far as we can determine. That is what the approach by Harrison and Ng (2016, 2018) and Harrison and Ross (2018), described in Section 3, seeks to do.

2.1 Nudges and Boosts

A principal source of interest in behavioral economics has been its advertised contributions to policies aimed at "nudging" people away from allegedly natural but self-defeating behavior toward patterns of response thought more likely to improve their welfare. Leading early promotions of this kind of application of behavioral studies are Camerer, Issacharoff, Loewenstein, O'Donoghue, and Rabin (2003) and Sunstein and Thaler (2003a, 2003b). Grüne-Yanoff and Hertwig (2016) have distinguished nudging, which is based on the heuristics-and-biases branch of behavioral economics research associated with Kahneman, Slovic, and Tversky (1982), from policies aimed at "boosting," which apply the simple heuristics research program of Gigerenzer, Todd and the ABC Research Group (1999) and Hertwig, Hoffrage, and the ABC Research Group (2013).

Nudging and boosting are contrasted as follows. Nudges aim to change a decision-maker's ecological context and external cognitive affordances in such a way that the decision-maker will be more likely to choose a welfare-improving option without having to think any differently than before. Boosts aim to supplement cognitive processes with heuristics that are viewed as reliable guides, despite glossing some information and avoiding computationally intensive algorithms, to produce good inferences, choices, and decisions when applied in the appropriate ecological contexts. An alternative way to define boosting builds on the role that "scaffolds" play in aiding cognition (Clark, 1998; Dennett, 2017). Access to the internet or experts, for example, might be expected *a priori* to make individuals more literate on facts that affect their cognition, as better inputs to their "cognitive production function."[2]

An additional contrast between nudges and boosts is that a nudge would normally be expected to have effects only on the specific behavior to which it is applied, and only in the setting that the nudge adjusts. A boost, on other hand, to the extent that it alters standing cognitive capacities and associated behavioral propensities across ranges of structurally similar choice problems, might be hoped to generate "rationality spillovers" discussed by Cherry, Crocker, and Shogren (2003). Furthermore, boosting might plausibly capacitate people with defenses against non-benevolent nudging by narrowly self-interested parties, such as marketers and demagogs (de Haan & Linde, 2018).

Nudging is open to the charge that it is manipulative. Its defenders point out that if people are naturally prone to systematic error, then any scaffolding built by any institution unavoidably involves manipulation, so the manipulation in question might as well be benevolent. Of course, as stressed above, what is actually "benevolent" is typically conditional on some unobserved preference or belief ascribed to the decision-maker. How this ascription might occur is the deeper question, addressed in Section 3.

Boosting, by contrast, involves endowing decision-makers with enhanced cognitive capacities by teaching them more effective decision principles, which they can choose to apply or not once they have been enlightened. Thus, boosting avoids manipulating the agents to whom the policies in question are applied, and is to that extent less paternalistic. But boosting unavoidably raises the question of what are more "effective" decision principles.

2.2 Randomized Evaluations in Search of "What Works"

One of the slogans that burdens most behavioral economic policy studies, and the focus on randomized evaluations, is the claim that they are only interested in "what works."[3] It is hard to imagine a less informative, and more dangerous, slogan. The core problem is that it characterizes approaches that only look at observables.

The problem with just looking at observables is that they tell us nothing about the virtual variables that are of interest in welfare evaluation. For that we need to make inferences about expected CS, and for that we need to know about the preferences that people bring to their choices, such as risk preferences and time preferences. We also need to know about the subjective beliefs that people bring to their choices. The reason for the recurrent focus on observables is easy to discern and openly discussed: a desire to avoid having to take a stand on theoretical constructs as maintained assumptions. We will discuss the general grounds for such abstinence from theory in Section 3. The same methodological precept guides the choice of statistical methods, but that is another story about modeling costs and benefits. One can fill in these blanks in our knowledge about virtual preferences and beliefs with theories and guessed-at numbers, or with theories and estimated numbers, as stressed by Leamer (2010) and Wolpin (2013). But one has to use theory to make conceptually coherent statements about preferences and beliefs, and then undertake welfare evaluations.

Advocates of randomized evaluations portray the tradeoff here in overly dramatic fashion: either one uses the methods that avoid these theoretical constructs, or one dives deep into the shoals of full structural, parametric modeling of behavior. This is a false dichotomy. The missing middle ground becomes apparent when empirical puzzles emerge, leading to casual theorizing and even more casual appeal to loose behavioral inferences, documented by case studies in Harrison (2011a).

In any event, randomized evaluations can be wonderful tools for gathering information about the cost-effectiveness of alternative policies toward some given goal, but are silent on the real question of the net welfare consequences of those policies.

2.3 Behavioral Welfare Analysis Using "Frames"

Bernheim and Rangel (2009, 2018) and Bernheim (2009, 2016) present an approach to behavioral welfare economics that recognizes the methodological challenge of evaluating welfare when one is concerned that choices might reflect mis-framing, weakness of will, or other psychological "disturbance" factors. They propose that one develop two frames with which to ask a question bearing on financial choices, where two conditions are met, and are couched here in terms of a financial literacy application:

1. Each frame is *a priori* presumed to generate actions that have the same welfare consequences for the individuals.
2. One frame is simple and transparent to understand, so *a priori* does not require any significant degree of literacy to assess, while the other frame asks the respondent to bring some degree of such literacy to bear.

Both conditions rely on *a priori* judgments. There is nothing wrong with this, but of course the conditions are open to empirical assessment when one gets to specific applications, and priors may vary on the extent of their validity.[4] The application of these ideas in Ambuehl, Bernheim, and Lusardi (2014, 2017, 2022) and Ambuehl, Bernheim, Ersoy, and Harris (2018), reviewed in Bernheim (2016, p. 51ff), provide such an instance.[5]

The application in each case is the same, and tests comprehension of the concept of compound interest as it affects intertemporal choices between a smaller, sooner (SS) amount of money and a larger, later (LL) amount of money. This is a canonical task for the elicitation of time preferences: see Coller and Williams (1999) for an extensive review of the older literature and clean experimental implementation of this task. To illustrate, consider these two statements, which very slightly paraphrase those actually used:

A. You will receive $88 in 72 days.
B. We will invest $22 for you at 3% interest, compounded daily, for 72 days.

Subjects are then asked, in response to one of these statements, to say "What is the present amount that is equivalent?" Responses are elicited using an Iterative Multiple Price List (iMPL) procedure developed by Andersen, Harrison, Lau, and Rutström (2006), and can be assumed for present purposes to lead subjects to reveal their true answer in an incentive compatible manner.

If subjects exhibit financial literacy they "should" give the same answers in response to statements A and B, since we observers know that the amount of money in B will end up being $88 in 72 days. If the answers to A and B differ, then we have identified a financial literacy gap, and it is asserted that we can take the absolute value of the difference in valuations as a measure of the welfare loss from that gap. Since the present value amounts are stated in deterministic form, this welfare loss is in the form of a certainty equivalent. In effect, here, the observed choice is a willingness to exchange the LL amount mentioned or implied by statement A or B for the SS amount stated in the response elicited by the iMPL procedure.

Now consider whether statements A and B meet the conditions required for inferences about welfare loss due to financial illiteracy.

One immediate concern is that statement B might be interpreted, from a conversational perspective, as already providing the answer: surely it is $22. The interpretation is that you have been asked what amount of money today would generate the implied $88 in 72 days, and this must be a "trick question" because the statement already tells you that it was $22. Of course, we analysts are expecting subjects to tell us the present discounted amount that is equivalent to $88 in 72 days, where the discount rate need not be the same as the interest rate, but that is just one interpretation of the question. One might expect, if inspecting the raw data, to see some respondents simply say $22 in this instance.

Another, more subtle, interpretive issue concerns the information about a 3% interest rate. A subject might reasonably presume that this is taken to be the market (borrowing and lending) interest rate for this question. Then, we know from the Fisher separation theorem that we cannot recover estimates of discount rates due to censoring (see Coller & Willams, 1999). All that we would recover is the subject's knowledge of the interest rate, which is again included in statement B, hence we would again expect a spike of responses at $22.

Extending this point, the mere mention of interest rates might affect responses differently for statement B compared to statement A. In effect, statement B offers a cognitive scaffold that could be expected to change the response compared to statement A, where there is no such explicit scaffold mentioned. Thus what is claimed to be the welfare effect of literacy might just be the welfare effect of having access to a more specific[6] scaffold, and that is ambiguous as a theoretical matter.

Finally, any difference between responses to statements A and B might simply reflect an inability to apply the principle of compound interest in evaluating statement B, to arrive at the implied $88 correctly. A subject might understand what compound interest is, and just not be able to do the math on the spot, even with a calculator provided. The issue here is whether one labels any difference in present value responses a welfare-significant failure of literacy with respect to the concept of compound interest or a welfare-significant failure of the capability of applying the correct concept. And the focus throughout Ambuehl et al. (2014, 2017, 2018, 2022) is on the effect of an intervention to improve decision-making, whether or not it is literacy or capability that is driving the effect.

One overarching concern here is that to apply the method of Bernheim and Rangel (2009, 2018), one must find frames that convince readers that they meet the two conditions noted earlier, and this is not likely to be an easy task across domains. Their method is not, in this sense, a general method.

Our concern about generality in this approach can itself be generalized. All economically interesting choice in humans and other intelligent social animals relies on complex networks of scaffolding.[7] Consequently, the frames methodology makes welfare assessments parasitic on an indefinite number of theories of these myriad exogenous influences that structure choice. We are glad that cognitive anthropologists and others are working hard on such theories and on the fascinating empirical findings that underpin them (see Caporael, Griesemer, & Wimsatt, 2014). But importing them into welfare analysis undermines economic generalization in the same way as do flavors of behavioral economics that implicitly collapse the field into the psychology of valuation: they fracture the equivalence classes on which economists and policy-makers depend. The classes in question in economics are selected by reference to *outcomes*, not generative mechanisms or enabling conditions. Of course, we want to know about such mechanisms and conditions to be confident that a recommended policy doesn't accidentally interfere with their operation. But we seek welfare specifications that are robust against measurable heterogeneity, not specifications that simply splinter in response to it. The frames approach does not so much rescue welfare economics as supplant it by mixed applications of other sciences. Furthermore, being mixtures, such models tend to lack *any* unifying disciplinary foundations. Every experimental design becomes a fresh adventure in *de novo* identification.

2.4 Identifying the Inner Utility Function

Many who view RDU or CPT as a better descriptive model of risk preferences nonetheless view EUT as an appropriate normative model of risk preferences. This raises an important practical issue: if all you have before you as an observer is someone exhibiting RDU or CPT behavior, how do you recover the utility function you need to undertake normative evaluations?

One approach is to simply impose EUT on the estimation of risk preferences that are observed, and use the utility function that is then inferred. This approach is used, for purposes of exposition, by Harrison and Ng (2016).

Bleichrodt, Pinto, and Wakker (2001) maintain that EUT is the appropriate normative model, and correctly note that if an individual is an RDU or CPT decision-maker, then recovering the utility function from observed lottery choices requires allowing for probability weighting and/or sign dependence. They then implicitly propose using *that* utility function to infer the CE using EUT. This is a radically different normative position than the one proposed by Harrison and Ng (2016, p. 116).

Some notation will help. Let $RDU(x)$ denote the evaluation of an insurance policy x in Harrison and Ng (2016) using the *RDU* risk preferences of the individual, including the probability weighting function. They calculate the *CE* by solving $U^{RDU}(CE) = RDU(x)$ for *CE*, where U^{RDU} is the estimated utility function from the *RDU* model of risk preferences for that individual. But Bleichrodt et al. (2001) evaluate the *CE* by solving $U^{RDU}(CE) = EUT(x)$ where $EUT(x)$ uses the U^{RDU} utility function in an *EUT* manner, assuming no probability weighting. This is normatively illogical. The logical approach here would be to estimate the "best fitting *EUT* risk preferences" for the individual from their observed lottery choices, following Harrison and Ng (2016), and then use the resulting utility function U^{EUT} as the basis for evaluating the *CE* using $U^{EUT}(CE) = EUT(x)$, where $EUT(x)$ uses the same U^{EUT} function used to evaluate the *CE*.

2.5 Modeling Mistakes

Another way to undertake normative evaluations is to develop a structural model of mistakes, and consider the effects on behavior of removing those mistakes. The issue here is whether the modeled behavior is indeed reasonably classified as a mistake or not, and from whose perspective. Behavioral economists have not been shy to quickly label any "odd behavior" as due to the first heuristic that comes to mind, rather than dig deeper. Harrison (2019, section 5.2) provides a critical review of structural models of this kind applied to health insurance and income annuity choices.

An example in which the modeled "mistake" could obviously be due to a simple risk preference is instructive of the dangers of this approach. Handel (2013) exploits a natural experiment in which a large firm changed health insurance options from an active choice mode to a passive mode where the previously selected choice was the default choice in later years unless action was taken. This change allowed inferences about the role of "inertia" in insurance plan choice. The behavior of new employees, who needed to make an active choice when previous employees were faced with passive choices, provides potential insight into the significance of inertia, assuming comparability of other characteristics between the two employee groups. In addition, some passively enrolled employees faced dominated choices over time as insurance parameters changed, and their sluggishness in the face of these incentives provides indicators of inertia. Atemporal risk preferences are assumed to be distributed randomly over the population sampled, and to be consistent with EUT. Individuals know their own risk preferences, but these are unobserved by the analyst.[8] In keeping with other observational studies of health insurance, the distribution of claims was simulated using sophisticated models akin to how an actuary would undertake the task, and individuals were assumed to know the risks they faced exactly.

Since the focus is on "inertia" over time, an important behavioral omission is the implicit assumption that individuals are *intertemporally risk neutral*. Hence, whatever the implied *atemporal* risk aversion from the random coefficient estimation, individuals in this model are unable to exhibit inertia in choices due to intertemporal risk aversion. This is quite separate from the assumption that "consumers are myopic and do not make dynamic decisions whereby current choices would take into account inertia in future periods" (Handel, 2013, p. 2662). Those assumptions have to do with sophistication with respect to the effect of current consumption on future consumption, akin to "rational addiction" models. Intertemporal risk aversion is just a taste for not having variability in claims risks over time, and that can be met simply by choosing the same plan year over year. Just as one is willing to pay a risk premium in terms of expected value (EV) to reduce atemporal risk aversion, the willingness to put up with lower *expected value* plans can be seen as a risk premium to reduce intertemporal risk aversion. This has fundamental implications for the resulting welfare analysis (pp. 2669–2679). The story here is that

> consumers enroll in sub-optimal health plans over time, from their perspective, because of inertia. After initially making informed decisions, consumers don't perfectly adjust their choices over time in response to changes to the market environment (e.g., prices) and their own health statuses. (p. 2669)

Another story, equally consistent with the observed choices and EUT, is that consumers simply have a preference for avoiding intertemporal risk in the health plan lotteries they choose.

Another approach is to use structural models of noisy decision-making to infer a measure of lost welfare by finding the least such noise that can rationalize observed behavior. This exercise should always be undertaken when one allows for standard errors on preference parameters, since that is another source of noise. However, the popular Fechner or Tremble models of noisy decision-making are a part of the hypothesized economics. The Fechner model, for example, assumes that the agent can evaluate the EU (or RDU) of two lotteries, that the agent can take the difference in the EU (or RDU), but that when making a choice the agent inflates or deflates that difference by some amount. In the extreme, the deflation collapses to a zero difference between the EU (or RDU) of the two lotteries, such that the agent is indifferent between the two and always selects one option with a probability of ½. In the extreme, the inflation expands the economic significance of any difference in EU (or RDU) such that the agent behaves as if strongly motivated to select the option with the highest EU (or RDU) with near certainty, no matter how small the initial pre-inflation difference in EU (or RDU). This is a story about how sensitive an individual is to differences in EU (or RDU) in terms of how those differences translate into probabilities of choosing the more attractive lottery.[9]

These piecemeal adjustments, however, fail to drill down to a foundational level, for more general re-orientation on the problem raised by choice errors for estimating welfare. In developing our more general approach to behavioral welfare economics in Section 3, we take advantage of the extensive work in cognitive science, over many decades, of distinguishing functional responses to ecological and strategic problems faced by agents from noisy processes. Much of the work in question has been inspired by practical issues in artificial intelligence (AI). The designer of a programmable robot with a narrow intended application can try to get noise close to zero. The designer of a system intended to be relatively flexible and autonomous cannot; she must accept noise, and learn to theoretically control and contain it, as a side-cost of making a system able to recognize problems coming from the world as being the same or similar even if they vary significantly in the processes and conditions that generate them. In AI, this is known as "the frame problem" (see Ford & Pylyshyn, 1996; Pylyshyn, 1987). It is logically isomorphic to the challenge faced by the welfare economist who seeks to discover and design effective policies.

2.6 Reduced Form Inferences

Townsend (1994) initiated a major stream of research by studying the response of household consumption to income shocks. Examining data from villages in rural India, he found that "household consumptions are not much influenced by contemporaneous own income, sickness, unemployment, or other idiosyncratic shocks, controlling for village consumption (i.e., for village level risk)" (p. 539).[10] Under certain, strong assumptions, evidence that consumption remains "stable" over time in relation to relative volatility of income indicates that there are likely to be only small welfare gains, if any, from "social insurance" schemes.

Because of the influence of this approach, it is worth noting the explicit methodological position that motivated it. Townsend (1994) was well aware of the long list of mechanisms and institutions that might provide informal insurance, noting family transfers among villages, informal credit markets, plot and crop diversification, and animal sales. And rigorously documenting this type of long list has occupied him in later work in rural Thailand: see Samphantharak and Townsend (2010). However, Townsend (1994, p. 540) argues that

> [...] in studying one market or institution only, the researcher may miss smoothing possibilities provided by another. For example, transfers may be small or missing, but this may not leave the family vulnerable if credit markets function well. [Hence this study] presents a general equilibrium framework which overcomes the problem of looking at risk-sharing markets or institutions one at a time. Specifically, the general equilibrium model inevitably leads the researcher to focus on outcomes, namely, consumption and labor supply, so that all actual institutions of any kind are jointly evaluated.

One concern with this position is that a general equilibrium structure is used to generate "reduced form" results which are then empirically evaluated, without the economist being able to go back and verify the structure.

Chetty and Looney (2006, p. 2352) note, with citations, that "the presumption that consumption fluctuations give a measure of the welfare costs of risks, and therefore the value of additional insurance, remains prevalent."[11] However, Baily (1978) had much earlier identified an important trade-off between the factors causing benefits from consumption smoothing (higher risk aversion) and the factors causing costs of smoothing consumption in the design of optimal unemployment insurance. Focus on the latter: in a world of complete and perfect markets, these costs are low. Absent these imaginary markets, it is often presumed that private or informal insurance mechanisms at the individual, household, village, state, or national level somehow act as if providing "full insurance" against consumption variability. Or in the debate over the roles of social *versus* private insurance, that private insurance serves to do what social insurance proposes doing. However, the logic proposed by Baily (1978) implied that evidence of consumption smoothing in Townsend (1994) might just be evidence of *extremely* high risk aversion and *inefficient* risk management options. As long as the demand for risk reduction is high enough, even wasteful risk management schemes will be tolerated. A review of the vignettes from the *Portfolios of the Poor* financial diaries, by Collins, Morduch, Rutherford, and Ruthven (2009), tells of the myriad, costly risk management schemes needed to understand "how the world's poor live on $2 a day." Chetty (2006) and Chetty and Looney (2006) show precisely how this logic applies to understand the identification issues that plague the conclusions from Townsend (1994) about the potential welfare gains to households from social insurance.

3. BEHAVIORAL WELFARE ECONOMICS WITH THE QIS

Economists have long realized that *if one assumes some risk preferences*, it is possible to make normative statements about the observed demand for certain products in which risk plays a critical role. For example, Feldstein (1973) proposed that, on average, US households carried too much health insurance. Armed with estimates of a measure of risk aversion, a price elasticity of demand for health care, the (gross) price change induced by lower insurance coverage, and the decrease in health care quality induced by lower insurance coverage, he estimated that the CE of the EUT loss from reduced insurance coverage would be more than offset by the gain from reduced purchases of lower-priced health care. His estimate of risk aversion was derived (p. 274) from casual introspection about what he regarded as a plausible risk premium for a hypothetical bet of a 50:50 chance of ±$1,000.[12] The challenge is to go beyond just assuming some risk preference and to utilize risk preferences that have some claim to be appropriate for the agent being evaluated.

Harrison and Ng (2016, 2018) and Harrison and Ross (2018) estimate the best descriptive model of risk preferences for individuals, and use these estimates to make normative evaluations of the insurance and investment product choices of their laboratory subjects. They justify this method by appeal to a leading interpretation of preferences in cognitive science.

It is unlikely that most people choosing insurance contracts or investment funds attempt to compute internally represented optima, either from EUT or RDU bases, and then make computational errors that could be pointed out to them. This echoes a point made by Infante, Lecouteux, and Sugden (2016) when they complain that behavioral welfare economists typically follow Hausman (2011) in "purifying" empirically observed preferences. Infante et al. (2016) argue that purification reflects an implicit philosophy according to which an inner Savage-rational agent is trapped within a psychological, irrational shell from which best policy should try to rescue her. They provide no general theoretical framework within which they motivate their skepticism about "inner rational agents." However, such a framework is available from cognitive science.

Long ago, Aristotle distinguished between four kinds of what translators render as "causation": material, efficient, formal, and final causes. Most contemporary philosophers are reluctant to fracture the concept of causation. But Aristotle's distinctions can readily be updated as referring to different *principles of explanation*. If I explain a change in the price of pizza in Cork by analyzing changes in prices of inputs and demand elasticities from data, then I appeal to efficient "causation." If my explanation adverts to equilibrium in an applied Bertrand model, then Aristotle would see me as giving a formal explanation. And if my story has recourse to a regulator who has intervened to break up a local pizza cartel, I am in the domain of final "causation." The interpretation of Aristotle is of course not what we are interested in here. We mention him in order to make the point that it has long been recognized that explanations are typically *partial* and *jointly complementary*. An economist might publish a whole study that just focuses on one of the types of explanation and mentions the others only in footnotes. This does not imply that the relegated explanations are false.

Someone might object that we should see the different explanations as stepping-stones along the path to a "complete" explanation. But it is not clear what that might mean in practice. What would a "complete explanation" of pizza prices look like? Would it have to include a general equilibrium model of the global economy? Would it involve a chemical analysis of what makes some cheeses but not others suitable for melting on pizza crust? Economists do not aspire to complete explanations. No sensible scientist does.

The modern extension of Aristotle's general point to the cognitive and behavioral sciences has been fleshed out by Daniel Dennett (1971, 1987). He calls complementary styles of explanation "stances." In cognitive and behavioral science, he argues that we find coherent literatures that make use of three stances, which he calls "physical," "design," and "intentional." If we carry these distinctions into economics, then as in the case with Aristotle we get some semantic awkwardness. For reasons best reserved for a philosophy of science setting, we think that the "physical" stance should more accurately be called the "mechanism" stance, even in its home domain of Dennett's applications. The "design" stance is suitably named for use in biological ecology and evolutionary theory, where Dennett applied it, but this would cause confusion in economics and trip over the fact that economists use the word "design" – in the concept of "mechanism design" – in a way that does not map neatly onto what Dennett means. We think that if the "design stance" were renamed the "selection stance," it would still be a good label for Dennett's motivating cases, but also avoid muddying waters in economics.

We will focus here on the intentional stance, which can comfortably keep its name in our context. We mention the others only to help readers understand what a stance is. Instead of defining them, we will illustrate them by reference to economic applications. Suppose an economist wants to predict comparative trade volumes between countries. She would be advised to use a gravity model, which focuses on the micro-scale processes – operational ranges of trucking firms, shared transport infrastructures, cultural and social underpinnings of business networks – through which physical movements of goods and services are implemented. This is an instance of a mechanism stance. But she might be more interested in the strategic and policy-sensitive aspects of international trade. In that case she would control for geographical distance (i.e., control for what the gravity model highlights) in a modernized Ricardian, Heckscher-Ohlin, or political economy model. Here, her focus is on factors that select for relative dispositions to form trade links implemented by varying transport and business mechanisms across cases treated as equivalence classes in the model. Here, she adopts a selection stance. This does not imply rejecting her colleague's gravity modeling; the two imagined economists address different aspects of the same general cluster of phenomena, international trade patterns. The alternative stances are not reflections of subjective hunches about what "really" matters. Each is characterized by rigorously developed families of models and easily identified, distinct, literatures.

Now suppose that further down the corridor in the Economics Department, a third colleague is trying to predict which interest group lobbies in a country will support or reject a newly negotiated trade deal awaiting legislative ratification. She will focus most directly on the utility functions of different firms, labor unions, and subnational governments. Her explanations will be based on the intentional stance.

3.1 The Intentional Stance

Dennett (1971, 1987) provides a rich account of the relationships between beliefs, preferences and propositional attitudes[13] that provides a rigorous foundation for behavioral welfare economics. He argues[14] that the *attribution of preferences and beliefs involves taking an intentional stance toward understanding the behavior of an agent. This stance consists in assuming that the agent's behavior is guided by goals and is sensitive to information about means to the goals, and about the relative probabilities of achieving the goals given available means*. The intentional stance is a product of cultural evolution. It arose and persists because of the importance of coordinated expectations in an intensely social species with massive behavioral heterogeneity due to large brains that support sophisticated learning. Beliefs, preferences, goals, and other propositional attitudes do not have counterparts at the level of brain states. They instead index relationships between target agents, environments, and interpreters trying to explain and anticipate the target agents' behavior (including their communicative behavior). The welfare economist attempting to determine what people regard as subjectively preferable is in the same situation as all people in all social contexts all the time: she seeks accounts of her targets' lattices of propositional attitudes, with particular emphasis on preferences and beliefs about probabilities, that the targets would endorse themselves. She is *not* trying to make inferences about anyone's "latent" states or states that are hidden in brains until someone with a neuroimaging scanner comes along.

Dennett's analysis of propositional attitudes is a scientifically inspired *revision* to everyday "folk psychology." Most people, when they express *their own* preferences and beliefs, take themselves to be publicly reporting private facts about themselves. A major conceptual reform on which cognitive scientists have gradually converged[15] over the past four decades is that this is a *useful illusion*. It arises because people are socially and culturally obliged to take the intentional stance toward *themselves*, and to self-attribute networks of propositional attitudes that others can understand and use as input for coordination. Because this self-interpretation is continuous, except in times of crisis or major life-course discontinuities, its specific elements for a person become habitual and non-reflective. "I am a lover of unspoiled places," reports the environmental activist in response to an open-ended range of social prompts she encounters from day to day, which are made relevant by her various activist activities and arguments. Because no conscious deliberation is involved in these reports, she takes them to reflect direct "inner perception" of feelings and valuations that must be "in her brain," if she lives in a modern scientific culture, or "in her heart," if her culture's metaphysic of the self is traditional or partly mystical. But there is no such literal process as "inner perception" of propositional attitudes (Dennett, 1991; Lyons, 1986; Schwitzgebel, 2011). The most direct evidence comes from developmental psychology. Children learn to adopt the intentional stance toward others, and *then* apply it to themselves (McGeer, 2001). They can tell plausible narrative stories about others before they can produce fragments of autobiography. Furthermore, early autobiographical narratives are typically generated by parental encouragement and *correction* (McGeer, 2002), which would make no sense if they were reports of inner perceptions.

The folk psychological view of beliefs and preferences as inner, private states has encouraged the widespread idea that people form expectations about one another's behavior and communications by "mindreading" (Nichols & Stich, 2003). This idea will be familiar to economists from the standard stylized psychological stories that often accompany models of extensive-form games in which players infer utility functions of other players from observed play. However, Zawidzki (2013) musters evidence that accurate mindreading cannot be carried out in real time except among very closely entangled agents, and that the evolution of mindreading mechanisms could not have been supported by the natural selection of cortex. Zawidzki (2013) convincingly shows that people mainly achieve coordination (to the extent that they do) by *mindshaping* – that is, by influencing one another to conform their preferences and beliefs to narrative models that can easily be socially recycled. Mindshaping is not mere mindless imitation that an economist could model only using something like a replicator dynamics. It is more accurately conceived as high-speed bargaining with a strong strategic dimension. Ross and Stirling (2021) offer a general, formal framework by which game theorists can model it.

The recognition that inner propositional attitudes apprehended by introspection are useful illusions has led some theorists to conclude that they are *mere* illusions, as noted earlier. With application to the design and interpretation of economic lab experiments, this is basically the view urged by Chater (2018), who argues that behavioral scientists should cease to use the concepts of preference and belief in theoretical generalizations. Sugden (2018) also advances some arguments that seem to imply this position. A more common view among both philosophers and cognitive scientists is that Dennett's account of propositional attitudes amounts to instrumentalism about them. This idea emphasizes both the "illusory" and the "useful" parts of "useful illusion." "Instrumentalism" about the scientific use of a concept is the word used in philosophy of science when the concept in question is thought to not designate anything that objectively exists in the world, but to be a helpful tool for constructing theory. The original home of the idea was in philosophies of physics according to which there are no real atoms, essential though the concept of an atom is to theory in physics and chemistry.

Instrumentalism is familiar to any economist, even if she is not acquainted with the philosophers' word for it. It is the hugely influential philosophy of economics promoted by Milton Friedman (1953), and many followers over the years. Friedman argued that literal utility and production functions are operated only by economic modelers, not by the actual economic agents they model. Economists use these concepts because they generate good predictions of individual and firm behavior, according to Friedman; but because the concepts have no counterparts in extra-theoretical reality, economists should not regard assumptions cast in terms of them as making any empirical commitments that could be tested against data.

Friedman's instrumentalism finds no support among specialists in economic methodology.[16] One of many bases for objection is that it implies that economists never explain any empirical facts, and should not attempt to do so. Similarly, if the intentional stance is a form of instrumentalism, but is the correct account of beliefs and preferences, then no models in cognitive science that invoke these concepts could ever explain anything. Dennett has thus made various reluctant forays over the years into general philosophy of science (which is not his field) to try to ward off associations with instrumentalism. Ladyman and Ross (2007, chapter 4) show that Dennett's efforts have not been entirely successful, but that Dennett provided a clear pathway, which they complete by applying some technical resources from computational information theory.

We avoid getting into these deep philosophical waters here. Instead, we gloss the issue informally as follows. According to the intentional stance, beliefs, preferences, and other propositional attitudes are virtual or interface elements of reality. They denote systematic, recurrent patterns that arise in the relationships between brain-powered organisms and their external environments, particularly including, in the case of humans and other highly intelligent animals, social environments.[17] Being virtual is not a way of being fictional; it is a way of being real. Propositional attitudes are scientifically studied, and empirical claims about them are true or false. We need merely acknowledge that these claims are not, in general, decided by facts about brains. It is worth drawing attention here to another example of a type of virtual object, money. There has never been a shortage of pop-philosophical claims to the effect that "money isn't real." But that opinion deserves to be called "the silly stance." Thinking that facts about beliefs and preferences must ultimately boil down to facts about brains is like thinking that facts about a country's money supply must ultimately boil down to facts about its printing presses and mints. They don't; but there are still plenty of facts about money.

The intentional stance implies that propositional attitudes are states of entire intentional systems (e.g., a person), not states of inferred *parts* of systems. Economists still often use the expression "latent states," borrowed from a transition period in psychological theory when post-behaviorists had restored mental states to scientific status, but supposed that they must ultimately all reduce to hidden brain states that awaited identification by a future neuroscience. This use by economists should be discontinued as invoking obsolete psychology.[18] The holistic nature of intentional stance description of agent behavior allows for error, but also complicates it: as stressed by Hey (2005), the "behavioral error" stories that we append to our structural models are part of the economics.[19]

Ross (2014) argues that this marks a fundamental basis for the distinction between economics and psychology. The intentional stance does not deny that brains are information processors, or that such information processing is a crucial *part* of the causal vector that supports attribution of propositional attitudes to people. The intentional stance simply denies that these important brain states should be *identified* with beliefs and preferences, or that brain processes should be modeled as inferences that have beliefs and preferences as conclusions. Psychologists are professionally interested directly in these processes, and in how they influence decisions. Economists, by contrast, are concerned with this only derivatively. If a system of incentives will lead various people, through heterogeneous sets of psychological *along with* social, institutional, financial and technological processes, to all make the same choices, then the people form, at least for an analysis restricted to that choice, an equivalence class of economic agents. But it is a strictly empirical matter when this heterogeneity with respect to processes will and won't matter economically. Economists, like all scientists, seek generalizations that support out-of-sample predictions. Different data-generating processes tend to produce, sooner or later, different data, including different economic data. Economics is thus crucially informed by psychology in general, as is sociology and anthropology, while not collapsing into the psychology of valuation as some behavioral economists have urged (e.g., Camerer, Loewenstein, & Prelec, 2005).

Applying this understanding of mind and agency to the applications to insurance in Harrison and Ng (2016), we assume the intentional stance to make sense of the experimental subjects' overall behavioral patterns, and use the risky lottery choice experiment as a relatively direct source of constraint on the virtual preference structures we assign when we perform welfare assessment of their insurance contract choices. The more precisely we specify the contents of propositional attitudes, especially in quantitative terms, the less weight in identification will rest on "inboard" elements of data-generating processes relative to external aspects of the agents' overall behavioral ecologies (i.e., cognitive scaffolds). This somewhat subtle point is of crucial methodological significance. Biological brains, with their dynamic, highly distributed, and essentially analog processing architectures, face strong limits, relative to digital representational technologies, on the extent to which they can stably discriminate between magnitudes. If a theorist conceives of beliefs and preferences as brain states, therefore, then the levels of precision assignable to these states will fall short of the discriminations that matter to theory, particularly in such domains as finance and insurance. But of course people *can* make these finer discriminations, by reading written numbers and using computers. They do not need to store stable quantitative representations "in their heads" (as the common metaphor puts it) when the representations in question are stored on paper or in external data files.

It might be objected here that subjects can only be attributed beliefs and preferences about quantitative and mathematical representations they actually understand. This is basically correct, but the simple statement hides much complexity. People learn to understand mathematical expressions by using them. As everyone who has taught mathematics or statistics to students knows, people can typically respond behaviorally to distinctions before they can correctly write them down or code them. Where normative consulting interactions are concerned, the financial or actuarial advisor can play a crucial pedagogical role. Of course this opens scope for concerns about paternalism, which we address later. The key point for now is that the intentional stance does not require the attributor of preferences and beliefs to stick to those that a naïve subject could apply to themselves.[20] Experimental treatments[21] might provide evidence that attention to certain informational patterns induces a significant number of subjects to act as if they were stochastically closest to being EU optimizers; evidence about other subjects might indicate patterns of probability weighting, as in RDU. These patterns therefore enter into a fully informed analyst's specification of the subjects' beliefs and preferences.

3.2 An Illustrative Application

Armed with some rigorous basis for assessing the benefit or harm to an individual from some experimental treatment, how do we make it operational? One general recommendation is to use Bayesian methods. The reason that this recommendation is general is that integrating economic theory with experimental data entails the systematic pooling of priors with data, and that is what Bayesian methods are designed to allow. And, critically, we view the attribution of preferences and beliefs that is central to the QIS as exactly akin to forming priors *about the agent*, and then pooling them with observations *of the agent* to make (normative and descriptive) inferences.

For economists, a canonical illustration of the need to pool priors and data is provided by the evaluation of the expected CS from observed insurance choices. Even if we limit ourselves to EUT, the gains or losses from someone purchasing an insurance product with known actuarial characteristics depend on their (atemporal) risk preferences. If we have priors about those risk preferences, then we can directly infer if the observed purchase choice was the correct one or not, as illustrated by Feldstein (1973). Here the word "correct" means consistent with the inferred EUT risk preferences for the individual making the choice we evaluate normatively. The same point extends immediately to non-EUT models of risk preferences, such as RDU. From a Bayesian perspective, this inference uses estimates of the posterior distributions of individual risk preferences to make an inference over "different data" than were used to estimate the posterior.[22] Hence, these are referred to as *posterior predictive distributions*.

In the simplest possible case, considered by Harrison and Ng (2016), subjects made a binary choice to purchase a full indemnity insurance product or not. The actuarial characteristics of the insurance product were controlled over 24 choices by each subject: the loss probability, the premium, the absence of a deductible, and the absence of non-performance risk. In effect, then, these insurance purchase choices are just re-framed choices over risky lotteries. The risky lottery here is to not purchase insurance and run the risk of the loss probably reducing income from some known endowment, and the (very) safe lottery is to purchase insurance and deduct the known premium from the known endowment.

The same subjects that made these insurance choices also made choices over a battery of risky lotteries, and a Bayesian model can be used to estimate individual risk preferences for each individual from their risky lottery choices.[23] The task is then to infer the posterior predictive distribution of welfare for each insurance choice of each individual. The predictive distribution is just a distribution of unobserved data (the expected insurance choice given the actuarial parameters offered) conditional on observed data (the actual choices in the risk lottery task). All that is involved is marginalizing the likelihood function for the insurance choices with respect to the posterior distribution of EUT model parameters from the risk lottery choices. The upshot is that we predict a *distribution* of welfare for a given choice by a given individual, rather than a *scalar*.[24] We can then report that distribution as a kernel density, or select some measure of central tendency such as the mean or median.

Fig. 1 displays several posterior predictive distributions for insurance purchase choices by one subject. For choice #1 the posterior predictive density shows a clear gain in CS, and for choice #4 a clear loss in CS. In each case, of course, there is a distribution, with a standard deviation. The predictive posterior distributions for choice #13 and choice #17 illustrate an important case, where we can only say that there has been a CS gain with some probability.

This example allows us to illustrate how one can undertake *adaptive* welfare evaluation during an experiment, following Gao, Harrison, and Tchernis (2023; section 3.C).[25] Some of the subjects in this experiment gain from virtually every opportunity to purchase insurance, and sadly some lose with equal persistence over the 24 sequential choices. Armed with posterior predictive estimates of

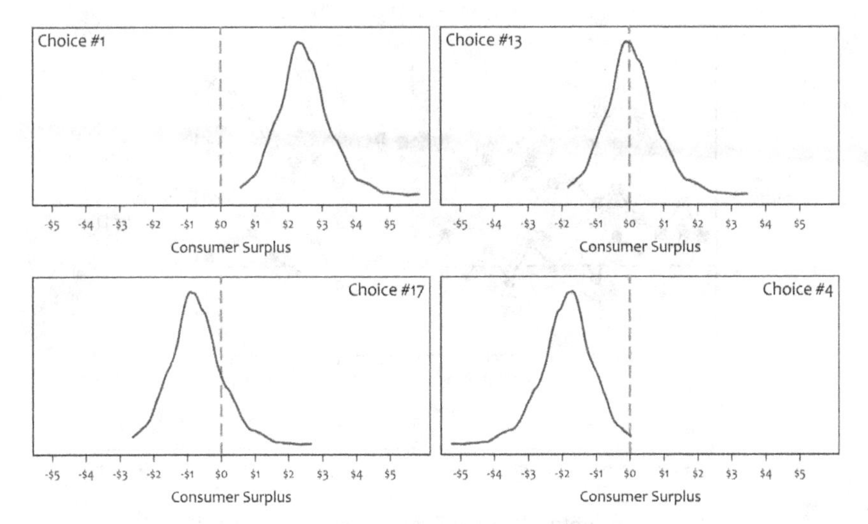

Fig. 1. Posterior Predictive Consumer Surplus Distribution for Each of Four Insurance Purchase Choices by One Subject.

the welfare gain or loss distribution for each subject and each choice, can we adaptively identify *when* to withdraw the insurance product from these persistent losers, and thereby avoid them incurring such large welfare losses? Important recent research by Caria et al. (2020), Hadad, Hirshberg, Zhan, Wager, and Athey (2021), and Kasy and Sautmann (2021) considers this general issue. The challenges are significant, from the effects on inference about confidence intervals, to the implications for optimal sampling intensity, to the weight to be given to multiple treatment arms, and so on.

Assume that the experimenter could have decided to stop offering the insurance product to an individual at the mid-point of their series of 24 choices, so the sole treatment arm was to discontinue the product offering or continue to offer it.[26] The order of insurance products, differentiated by their actuarial parameters, was randomly assigned to each subject when presented to them. Fig. 2 displays the sequence of welfare evaluations possible for subject #1, the same subject evaluated in Fig. 1. The two solid lines of Fig. 2 show measures of the CS: in one case the average gain or loss from the observed choice in that period, and in the other case the cumulative gain or loss over time. Here, the average refers to the posterior predictive distribution for this subject and each choice. Since this is a distribution, we can evaluate the Bayesian probability that *each* choice resulted in a gain or no loss, reflecting a qualitative Do No Harm (DNH) metric enshrined in the *Belmont Report* as applied to behavioral research.[27] This probability is presented in Fig. 2, in cumulative form, by the dashed line and references the right-hand vertical axis.

Although there are some gains and losses in average CS along the way, and the posterior predictive probability of a CS gain declines more or less steadily toward 0.5 over time, the DNH probability is always greater than 0.5 for this subject. And there is a steady, cumulative gain in expected CS over time. These outcomes reflect

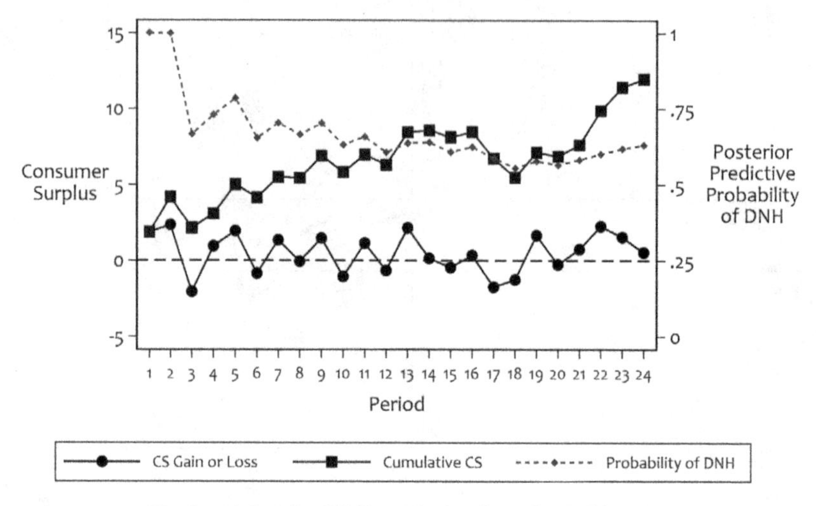

Fig. 2. Adaptive Welfare Evaluations for Subject #1.

a common pattern in these data, with small CS losses often being more than offset by larger CS gains. Hence one can, and should, view these as a temporal series of "policy lotteries" which are being offered to the subject, if the policy of offering the insurance contract is in place (Harrison, 2011b). In this spirit, we can think of the probabilities underlying the posterior predictive DNH probability as the probabilities of positive or negative CS outcomes, given the risk preferences of the subject. The fact that the EV of this series of lotteries is positive, even as the probability approaches 0.5, reflects the asymmetry of CS gains and losses in quantitative terms and the policy importance of such quantification. For now, we might think of the *policy-maker* as exhibiting risk neutral preferences over policy lotteries, but recognizing that the evaluation of the purchase lottery by the subject should properly reflect her risk preferences.

Consider comparable evaluations for four individuals from our sample in Fig. 3. Subject #5 is a "clear loser," despite the occasional choice that generates an average welfare gain. It is exactly this type of subject one would expect to be better off if not offered the insurance product after period 12 (or, for that matter and with hindsight, at all). Subject #111 is a more challenging case. By period 12, the qualitative DNH metric is around 0.5, and barely gets far above it for the remaining periods. And yet the EV of the policy lottery is positive, as shown by the steadily increasing cumulative CS. This example sharply demonstrates the "policy lottery" point referred to for subject #1 in Fig. 2.

The remaining subjects in Fig. 3 illustrate different points: that we should also consider the time and intertemporal risk preferences of the agent when evaluating the policy lottery of not offering the insurance product after period 12. Assume that these periods reflect non-trivial time periods, such as a month, a harvesting season, or even a year. In that case the temporal pattern for subject #67 encourages us to worry about how patient subject #67 is: the cumulative CS is positive by the

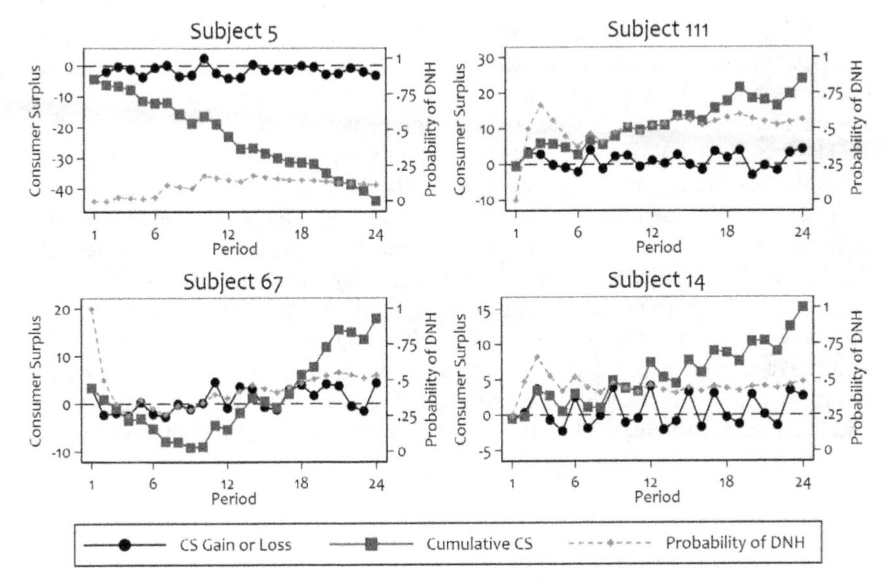

Fig. 3. Individual Adaptive Welfare Evaluations for Four Subjects.

end of period 24, but if later periods are discounted sufficiently, the subjective present value of being offered the insurance product could be negative due to the early CS losses.[28] Similarly, consider the volatility *over time* of the CS gains and losses faced by subject #14, even if the cumulative CS is positive throughout. In this case, a complete evaluation of the policy lottery for this subject should take into account the *intertemporal* risk aversion of the subject, which arises if the subject behaves consistently with a non-additive intertemporal utility function over the 24 periods.

Applying the policy of withdrawing the insurance product after period 12 for those individuals with a cumulative CS that is negative results in an aggregate welfare gain of 108%, implicitly assuming a classical utilitarian social welfare function (SWF) over all 111 subjects.

One general lesson from this example is that we now have the descriptive and normative tools to be able to make adaptive welfare evaluations about treatments during the course of administering the treatment. How one does that optimally is challenging, but largely because we have not paid it much direct attention in economics. Optimality here entails many tradeoffs, and not just those reflecting the preferences of the instant subject.[29] Our focus here is on the partial equilibrium impact on the *welfare* of each and every individual.[30] This is often confused by economists as trying to evaluate social welfare, a different concept altogether, although ideally concepts that are related to each other in subtle ways. Hence, when we report an average of individual welfare effects descriptively, that is not to impose a utilitarian SWF, but just to describe our calculations in a familiar manner. The role of formal general equilibrium welfare evaluations is to account for some of the interactions between agents, and second-best constraints, that affect the evaluation of policy. Just as the numerical models evaluating general equilibrium welfare effects have been extended over the years to include imperfect competition, scale economies, trade barriers that are not *ad valorem* tariffs, and so on, eventually they could be extended to incorporate richer models of behavior in stochastic policy settings.[31] That is not our immediate focus.

The other general lesson from this case study is the difficulty of making decisions during the instant experiment when the inferences from the experiment have some, presumed welfare implications for *individuals outside the instant experiment*.[32] If we had truncated these experiments adaptively as suggested, would we have been able to draw reliable statistical inferences about the treatment in a way that would influence future applications of the treatment? The only way to evaluate these issues, particularly with multiple treatment arms, is to undertake them in safe laboratory settings in which subjects literally have nothing to lose, and study the implications of "throwing data away" in accordance with such adaptive rules. Then be Bayesian about deciding how much to learn from that for the field.

3.3 Issues in the Application of the QIS

3.3.1 Is Rationality Being Assumed?

Dennett has often[33] characterized the basic posture of the intentional stance as assuming that an agent is rational, assessing her circumstances, and then posing the question, "What should we expect her to do in light of her rationality and her circumstances?" Glossed at such a high level of generality, this looks identical to twentieth century "neoclassical" economic methodology as most influentially described by Lionel Robbins (1935). Is this not precisely the methodology against which behavioral economics is generally taken to be a corrective strategy?

Part of the answer to this implied objection, on which we have been focusing so far, is that the QIS counsels measuring the agent's "circumstances" very carefully and exactly, based on empirical evidence and particularly on experimental manipulation. But every behavioral economist agrees, in contrast to Robbins, that the rationality of any actual agent is necessarily "bounded" in the sense of Simon (1955). We must assume that the target is rational in the *broad* sense required for agency: that there is a systematic relationship between her behavioral patterns over the time frame about which we seek generalizations, and the information that empirical evidence suggests she registers and tracks. We should *not* assume – and Dennett has never suggested that any inquirer using the IS should assume – that her expectations are "rational" in the ideal sense of reflecting all information that is *in principle* available, or that she makes no errors of inference. These bounds on a given agent's rationality must also be identified empirically.

Crucially, however, the QIS emphasizes that we should not attempt such identification by studying the agent individually and in isolation. Her preferences and beliefs will be those that people regarded as approximate equivalence classes by her social reference network would attribute to her and would expect her to attribute to herself, conditional on specifics of the decision setting. According to the IS, *there is no "deeper" fact of the matter about what she prefers and believes.*

This strongly licenses the method of identifying response functions – or, more specifically, utility functions and probability weighting functions – by estimating models that include covariates sufficient for specifying the expected *social* model of the target agent. We gain powerful evidence about the information her "society" expects her to attend to when she makes choices by studying the information scaffolds that the society in question affords her. Societies are full of structure, hierarchies, and biases. They expect people with different demographic profiles to respond differently from one another, and these different profiles will consequently tend to rely on different scaffolding packages for many problems of interest to economists. For example, we might hypothesize that it is easier for women than for men, statistically, to get pediatric information and to assess its value. Economists, like other social scientists, tend to be *most* interested in launching studies precisely where they find these variations.

In everyday choices, relevant scaffolds will typically be quite general. For example, an adult in a modern society is expected to be able to understand, and pay at least some attention to, the daily news in the mass media, public notices and signs, and conventions for estimating and applying everyday magnitudes. In a workplace or hobby setting, expectations and the scaffolding that sustains them will be more extensive, and more tightly standardized, within relatively narrow domains. The economist's model of participants in a finance experiment will differ depending on whether her subject pool is drawn from the general population or from the banking and accounting professions. She might be described as modeling the latter as "more rational," within the context of the experiment, than the former. The relevant sense of "rationality" here is what Vernon Smith (2007), drawing on Hayek, calls "ecological rationality." This usage involves substantial transformation of the concept of rationality. The economist does not treat her banker subjects as less likely to make *logical* errors, or less likely to be emotionally biased or cognitively lazy, than her subjects from the general population. She just expects them to be better informed, and to be more likely to accurately apply the information they have. Thus the "rationality" in the concept of ecological rationality is not what the philosophical decision theorist means by that word.

For deep reasons we discuss in Section 4, we are doubtful about the value to economists of any concept of "rationality" that is intended to be fully general. We regard the phrase "rational agent" as including a redundant adjective. Economists study choices under incentives, so *all* of their subjects (including, sometimes, non-human ones) are agents. The IS, and following it the QIS, apply wherever agency does. Beyond that common threshold, different capacities of different agents to solve problems are mainly a function of the different scaffolding kits they are expected to use. People, but not rats or elephants, can read text; bankers, but not most other people, can compute compound interest rates without special support from the experimenter.

To summarize the answer to the question, then: the economist deploying the QIS *assumes* agency, and *expects* variation in ecological rationality that she must do empirical work to identify and estimate. She makes no special assumptions about "general" rationality, an idea she can and should avoid altogether.

3.3.2 Are We Assuming Some True Risk Preference?

No, we are instead assuming some prior belief is being formed about the risk preferences of the agent whose behavior is being evaluated. Thinking of these as priors rather than some "assumed truth" has important implications, quite apart from being consistent with the QIS, and also opens the way to developing ways to better inform the choice of priors for behavioral welfare economics.

The value of viewing these QIS attributions as priors, and employing a Bayesian approach, derives from the methodological need for normative analysis of risky choices to have estimates of risk preferences from choice tasks *other than the choice task one is making welfare evaluations about.*[34] In settings of this kind, it is natural to want to debate and discuss the appropriateness of the risk preferences being used. In fact, the need for debate and conversation becomes more urgent when, as here, we infer significant losses in expected CS, and significant foregone efficiency. How do we know that the task we used to infer risk preferences, or even the models of risk preference we used, are the right ones? The obvious answer: we do not. We can only hold prior beliefs about those, and related questions. And when it comes to systematically examining the role of alternative priors on posterior-based inference, one wants to be using Bayesian formalisms.

Saying that we view these as priors is not an invitation to then claim that the welfare evaluation is arbitrary. It is recognizing what economists of a wide range of methodological persuasions have been doing for many decades and just formalizing it. The analogy to the nudge literature is apt. Proponents of nudges correctly stress that when we adopt some choice architecture for decision-makers, and have priors over the effect of that architecture on their behavior, we have simply replaced one existing choice architecture with another. That is, some choice architecture is required, and will be used anyway, so why just assume that historical accident has generated a normatively attractive architecture? Another analogy comes from the classic *Specification Searches* of Leamer (1978): many of the *ad hoc* methods used by econometricians are clumsy attempts to use priors, so why not recognize that and do it explicitly and elegantly with Bayesian methods?

There are immediate reasons why one would want to use Bayesian estimates of risk preferences for the type of normative exercise illustrated in our extended example in Section 3.2. One obtains more systematic control of the use of priors over plausible risk preferences, and the ability to make inferences for every individual in a sample.

However, there are also more general reasons for wanting to adopt a Bayesian approach, to make explicit the role for priors when making normative evaluations. A related, general reason for a Bayesian approach derives from the *ethical* need to pool data from randomized evaluations and non-randomized evaluations, discussed by Harrison (2021). The motivation for randomized control trials in many areas, such as surgical procedures, derives from non-randomized evidence accumulated in widely varying circumstances, such as the health and co-morbidities of the patient. These data are evidently not inferred from "clean beakers," but they are often *completely discarded* when designing a randomized test of the procedure. This practice reflects the notion of "clinical equipoise," which holds that one should initiate and apply the randomized procedure as if none of the prior non-randomized evidence had existed at all. The counter-argument is just to view those prior data as justifying what is actually observed: someone thinking *a priori* that some new procedure is worth testing. That is not, by construction, a completely diffuse prior at work, so one should formally reflect that fact. The ethical issue takes on urgency when patients or parents of patients are being asked to submit to 50:50 chances of a procedure that these priors suggest is inferior. Of course, such equipoise might be justified by a social objective of arriving at a general conclusion more quickly, for the benefit of all potential patients, despite the expected cost to the instant patient; we would disagree with the implied tradeoff, but we see the logic.

3.3.3 Are We Assuming Stable Risk Preference?

To conduct normative evaluation of insurance decisions in our extended example we needed to make the explicit and necessary assumption that there is a set of risk preferences of an individual that we can identify in a risky lottery task, and that we can apply as priors in an insurance task, so as to infer expected welfare changes from insurance choices. If risk preferences are not stable *over time*, is there a risk of normative evaluation being based on "stale" preferences? If risk preferences elicited in one domain are not stable *across domains*, how do we know that they are appropriate for another domain?

Even though these are relevant concerns, we argue that they are second order, simply because there are no other assumptions that one can make *if the objective is normative evaluation*. Now that we have demonstrated the QIS method based on that assumption, however, it is entirely appropriate to engage in debate over the strength or weakness of our prior and potential alternative priors for risk preferences that might be used. This is where the ongoing discussion of these, and related, descriptive characterizations of risk preferences have a legitimate role: helping us navigate among the various priors we might use. In our first attempt at applying the QIS method in the laboratory, the risky lottery choice task and the insurance decisions are made contemporaneously, implying that there is no serious issue of temporal stability that arises in this instance. And the financial-outcome frame of the risky lottery choice task is close to the financial-outcome frame of the insurance purchase task, so we also don't anticipate a serious issue of domain specificity in this instance. But what can we say in general?

Consider the issues raised by any instability of risk preferences over time. Temporal stability of preferences can mean three things, and can be defined at the aggregate level for pooled samples or for individuals.[35] Our concern is with individuals, and this is arguably a more demanding requirement.[36] One interpretation of temporal preference stability is that risk preferences are *unconditionally stable* over time. This means that the risk preference parameter estimates we obtain for a given individual should predict the risk preference parameters she would use in the future when she makes the decision that we are normatively evaluating, no matter what else happens in her life. This is the strongest version of a "temporal stability of preferences" assumption, and will presumably be rejected for longer and longer gaps between elicitation of the risk preferences and normative evaluation of the decision.[37]

A second interpretation of temporal preference stability is that risk preferences are *conditionally stable*. This interpretation assumes that risk preferences might be state-dependent and a stable function of states over time, but there could be changes in the relevant states over time. This interpretation implies that the risk preference parameter estimates for a subject might depend on her age, for example, and that particular "state" changes in thankfully predictable ways. Of course, this predictability presumes that we have a decent statistical estimate of the effect of age on risk preferences, but it is plausible that this could be obtained. If the states are readily observable, such as age, conditional stability is perhaps a reasonable prior to have for normative evaluation.

A third interpretation is that risk preferences might be state-dependent and the states are not observable, or that the risk preferences are themselves stochastic. In this instance there are stochastic specifications, which in turn embody hyper-priors, that let us say something about stability (e.g., that the unobserved states are fixed for the individual, or that the stochastic variation in preference realizations follows some fixed, parametric distribution).[38]

3.3.4 What About Source-dependent Risk Preference?

Domain specificity of risk preferences involves systematically examining the role of alternative priors over the risk preferences from various possible domains on posterior-based inference about the specific domain of the financial decisions we aim to normatively evaluate. This again implies we should use Bayesian techniques.

Imagine one was designing a field experiment, say in rural Ethiopia, in which various interventions for a health insurance product were to be used to improve the welfare of households. Assume that this health insurance product focused on acute conditions, with significant mortality risk. The only priors on risk preferences you have come from university students who participated in laboratory experiments in the United States. Should you go ahead and design interventions that, conditional on the risk preferences of the university students, lead to expected welfare losses for the same students, of the kind we have demonstrated? We suggest that, ethically speaking, you should not.

Now imagine you have been able to conduct comparable incentivized artefactual field experiments with risky lottery choices in Ethiopia with a sample from the target population of rural Ethiopian households that allow you to infer risk preferences over financial outcomes. These are obviously better priors for the risk preferences needed to undertake the eventual normative inference about the health insurance decisions, and should be used. In this case we would completely discard the priors from students in the United States. Next, imagine that you have been able to conduct artefactual field experiments over some risky health outcomes in Ethiopia that allow you to infer risk preferences. Assume that these health outcomes refer to morbidity risks, not mortality risks, but to real outcomes nonetheless.[39] Clearly the domain of risk preferences here is closer than the risk preferences defined over money because they were elicited in the context of health choices. However, because we know that eliciting risk preferences over health risks is not as reliable, would you now attach *zero weight* to the risk preferences over money by similar Ethiopians? Probably not.

What this discussion shows is that it is simplistic to attempt to make a general statement about the validity of preferences for a reference risk preference elicitation task and a different task that is the target of normative evaluation, since it depends entirely on the timing, context, and domain of the two tasks. However, the statistical methods that we have at our disposal (Bayesian analysis) merely demand that we are able to define a diffuse or an informed prior in one task or domain, to do normative evaluation of choices in another domain, without having to require that the elicited risk preferences are "perfectly valid" for the choice task that we want to make normative statements about.

3.3.5 But Can't I Just See What Works?

This question comes up a lot, often also in the guise of the question, "does it have to be this hard?" in the sense of requiring so much theory and structural modeling of preferences, beliefs and constraints. The response is to question what can be inferred about welfare directly from observed behavior without some implicit or explicit theory of motivation. Then the structural modeling that some theory requires just has to be done, recognizing that some theories require more or less structure.

A recent debate between Sunstein (2021) and Sugden (2021) illustrates this divide, where the context is commentary by Sunstein (2021) on a critique of the nudge movement in Sugden (2018):

> Sunstein's response to this critique is one that I have heard from many behavioural economists. It is, as he says, "brisk" [...]. In rough paraphrase: "We all know that the criteria we use are conceptually problematic, but the cases we are dealing with are too important for us to be held back by abstract problems. It's so obvious that people are making errors that we don't need a definition of error. The effects on people's welfare are so clear-cut that we don't need a definition of welfare. Wake up and smell the coffee." I have to say that I find this response frustrating. My critique addresses what behavioural welfare economists have actually written about the concepts of preference, welfare, error and bias when explaining how they reach their policy recommendations. Was that not supposed to be taken seriously? (Sugden, 2021, p. 420)

We hasten to add that we share some of Sunstein's briskness when it comes to many of the commentaries on behavioral welfare economists by philosophers. They often demand analytically complete theories which, even if we could all eventually be brought to agree on, would be extravagantly demanding of data. But the importance of the "inner rational agent" critique of Sugden (2018) and Infante et al. (2016) cannot be doubted or waved aside because it is inconvenient.

3.3.6 How Much Structure Is Needed?

It is popular to come up with "reduced form" surveys or experiments to elicit risk preferences, and to many researchers it seems like a lot of work to elicit choices over lotteries, and then also to have to engage in structural estimation, before even getting to the task of real interest. A short response might be, "that's life." A longer response recognizes that these are what are often called "nuisance parameters," in the sense that they are not the primary focus of interest, and that there is an opportunity cost of every extra task added to a design. One of the advantages of Bayesian Hierarchical Models (BHM) is that one can make informed inferences at the level of the individual without every lottery choice in a large battery being asked. In our own work it is now common to construct a battery of 80 to 100 lottery pairs, and then randomly select 20 or 30 for each subject to complete, following Gao et al. (2023, section 3.A). These efficiencies are particularly important in field applications.

Three qualifications are important. First, one cannot just have some measure of risk preferences that might be (linearly) correlated with the minimal structure needed to evaluate the expected CS. One needs to know the relevant parameters of some utility function, at a bare minimum, and of course any stochastic error around any point estimates of parameters. Responses to Likert scales that positively correlate with the propensity to bungy-jump need not apply.

Second, there may be settings in which one wants to ensure that the estimated risk preferences allow inferences about specific axioms. A core instance in our work is the ROCL axiom. This axiom is assumed in EUT, RDU, and CPT, but is often a central focus of skeptical attention. One example is when there is a compound risk of non-performance of an insurance contract (e.g., Harrison & Ng, 2018), or there is basis risk in index insurance contracts (e.g., Harrison, Morsink, & Schneider, 2022). Another general example is when one wants to consider how uncertainty aversion, as distinct from risk aversion, affects inferences whenever there are subjective belief distributions (e.g., Harrison, 2011b, section 4). In these cases, we always want to ensure that each subject faces a certain number of paired binary choices that allow direct inference from choice patterns to the extent of ROCL violation.[40]

The third qualification has to do with the difference between *atemporal* risk aversion and *intertemporal* risk aversion. The former refers to risk over outcomes that are to be received by a subject at a point in time, often immediately in controlled experiments.[41] The latter refers to risk over outcome streams that are time-dated. In general there is no theoretical need for one type of risk aversion to imply anything about the other: see Andersen et al. (2018) for theoretical results and experimental evidence. There are important field settings in which both are needed to undertake normative evaluations (e.g., annuities and other retirement options). So the general point is that "enough structure" is needed to properly undertake the instant normative evaluation. We appreciate that this entails even more tasks than just one to elicit atemporal risk preferences.

A related point is that one might often need priors over time preferences as well as risk preferences, and indeed priors over subjective beliefs as well as preferences.

Our experience is that *all* attempts to find short-cuts to eliciting these preferences and beliefs end in inferential misery. As Mencken once said, "there is always a well-known solution to every human problem – neat, plausible, and wrong." Given the intellectually parlous state of behavioral welfare economics, and its potential value, now is not the time to look for short-cuts.

3.3.7 Why Just EUT and RDU?

In general, we agree that other models of risk preferences should be considered. There seems to be enough support for RDU as the most empirically important alternative to EUT, once the lack of controlled laboratory evidence for CPT is accepted. We view the various "regret theory" models of Bell (1982), Fishburn (1982), and Loomes and Sugden (1982, 1987), as well as the "disappointment aversion" models of Bell (1985), Gul (1991), and Routledge and Zin (2010), as particularly worthy of attention.[42]

For now, we take the agnostic view that the risk preferences we have modeled as best characterizing the individual are those that should be used, in the spirit of the "welfarism" axiom of welfare economics. Even though the alternatives to EUT were originally developed to relax axioms of EUT that many consider to be normatively attractive, it does not follow that one is unable to write down axioms that make those alternatives attractive normatively. For instance, consider inverse-S probability weighting in an RDU setting, which leads the decision-maker to place greater weight on the probabilities associated with the best and worst outcomes. This might be a reasoned heuristic for recognizing that "tail probabilities" are known to be inferred less reliably, and are more reliant on parametric forms for probability distributions being correct. In fact, it characterizes one approach to "actuarial prudence" in the calculus of risk management. In terms of decision theory, it may be viewed as one way to extend the reasoning from the "small worlds" of Savage to his "large worlds" (Binmore, 2009).

3.3.8 Why Ignore Loss Aversion?

We do not ignore loss aversion. Instead, as noted in Section 1.2, we just do not find enough evidence in controlled experiments to justify using CPT models that define it as such. In many of our experiments, not all, we have been careful to use a risk lottery battery that allows one to estimate a CPT model if desired, but more recently do not see the point having reviewed the data. Given that, and recognizing that "zombie parameters" walk among us, we do nonetheless have a position on how loss aversion should be viewed from the perspective of the QIS, and review that below in Section 4.2.

3.3.9 But There Is No Single, Correct Way to Elicit Risk Preferences

It is true that there are many alternative ways to elicit risk preferences, even if we restrict attention to those that involve incentivized choices. Although we are content, as practicing applied economists, with the methods we use (binary choice over a randomly ordered battery of lotteries), we see no need for anyone to try to define a single "correct" way to elicit risk preferences, and do not even know how to define a sensible metric to use to undertake that race and seek to determine a winner. More strenuously, we do not see the existence of different risk elicitation methods as a reason to pause using one that meets certain criteria, just because there are others under consideration. These are, after all, just priors. The fact that there are several elicitation methods for these priors does not make the priors *arbitrary*. Rather, it makes them *conditional* on the elicitation methods, and that is all.

3.3.10 What About Subjective Probabilities?

We have focused attention on "small world" settings with objective probabilities, since there are enough conceptual issues to sort out in that setting. But we completely agree that the very next step must be to extend the approach to when we must also make inferences about subjective probabilities. The reason is that poorly-calibrated subjective probabilities, or failures to update subjective beliefs consistently with Bayes' Rule, are *a priori* likely to be an important source of welfare losses in many policy-relevant settings.

We believe that the next step will be to utilize additional tasks to directly elicit subjective relative likelihoods over events, which can then be used to make inferences about RDU models that separately identify the subjective belief that is then subject to probability weighting. The theoretical framework to do this was developed by Machina and Schmeidler (1992, 1995), assuming one could do so without making any assumptions about risk preferences or probability weighting.[43] One would also need to have a task to identify the utility function and probability weighting function, using objective probabilities, as they also propose, but that is by now standard fare for experimental economists.

3.3.11 What About Social Welfare?

Our approach has been to generate priors about the preferences and, if necessary, subjective beliefs of the individual[44] in order to evaluate two or more risky prospects that the individual has to make a choice over. The evaluation might reflect an EUT or RDU model of risk preferences. Each evaluation results in a comparison of CE, which is the expected CS of choosing one prospect rather than other prospects. The descriptive models of EUT or RDU predict that the individual will choose the prospect with the highest CS. Normative models just tabulate the CS of the observed choice, which may or may not be the prospect with the highest CS. All of this is undertaken for one individual.

Over a sample of individuals, we can then build up a distribution of welfare effects of observed choices. Some elements of this distribution may be positive, some might be zero, and some might be negative. If an individual makes a number of choices, it is therefore possible for an individual to accrue some positive welfare effects, some zero welfare effects, and some positive welfare effects of those choices. A central component of this evaluation of the distribution of welfare effects is to start with priors over the risk preferences and, if necessary, subjective beliefs of each individual. This can be called a "bottoms up" approach to behavioral welfare evaluation.

The final step in this approach is to describe the distribution. One might look at the average, one might look at quartiles, and one might look at measures of variability such as standard deviation, skewness or even kurtosis. These are just descriptions, and should not be confused with social welfare evaluations. To be sure, some social welfare evaluations might be the same, numerically: for example, taking the unweighted average also reflects a classical utilitarian SWF.

An alternative approach is to start with a SWF defined over *final, non-risky* outcomes, and then allow for risk to be associated with those outcomes. The arguments of the initial SWF in economics are typically utility-based evaluations of final outcomes by individuals. Adler (2012, 2019) provides a careful exposition of this approach, which we do not take up here. We have many problems with the treatment of risk being "added on" as a last step, but they take us too far astray for present purposes.

4. DISTINGUISHING WELFARE FROM WELL-BEING

4.1 Well-being and Reflective Rationality

An unusual feature of economics, among the academic disciplines, is that it is subject to a swollen, and endlessly replenished, hostile literature that attacks the whole enterprise. This is not a recent phenomenon; it dates from the historical origins of modern economics (Coleman (2002), and is closely entangled with, though not identical to, hostility to markets (Ross, 2012)). Generalized anti-economics often gives pride of place to a range of epistemological arguments, intended to cast doubt on economists' claims to knowledge and to status as scientists. This literature consequently receives persistent attention from philosophers of economics. Notwithstanding these abstract debates, which reach far beyond our scope here, it is obvious that their volume and frequency is fueled by resentment and anxiety about the role of economists and economics in designing and promoting public and corporate policies. Recent and explicit examples are Applebaum (2019) and Berman (2022).

We set aside debates about whether the basic logic of mainstream normative economics reflects ideology, which one of us has reviewed directly elsewhere (Ross, 2012). A less polarized, but equally dense, body of contestation is about whether normative economics claims an overly expansive domain of influence, implicitly or explicitly promoting a narrow and particular set of values that drive out those championed by non-economists, and professionally explored by moral philosophers, sociologists, and political scientists from outside the "rational-choice" tradition in that discipline. Marglin (2008) provides a sympathetic review of this perspective by an economist. We comment on these debates here because many behavioral welfare economists argue that their special alertness to psychology offers a path for correction of the alleged normative imperialism of traditional welfare economics.

Like much of the economist's special lexicon, the word "welfare" has both everyday and technical meanings that diverge. In professional economics, welfare is an efficiency measure, referring to quantitative comparisons between ratios of marginal gains in preference satisfaction from outputs and marginal sacrifices of preference satisfaction associated with opportunity costs of inputs. Such welfare can be individual or social, and there is of course a vast literature on different approaches to welfare aggregation. Work that compares these methods *can* be purely technical, but very often is not, because alternative ways of defining social welfare are often motivated normatively by reference to implications for distribution across individuals or groups. This creates constant tension between welfare as a technical efficiency concept and an everyday use of "welfare" that treats it as equivalent to "general well-being." Economists frequently fuel this tension by using rhetoric that implies that if there is consensus among economists that policy *X* delivers more marginal welfare per input unit of cost than alternative policy *Y*, then *X* should "automatically" be chosen by whichever agents control the choice in question. This suggests that economics should govern policy in general, and triggers backlash and resistance.

We do not begin to have space here to review arguments about the entangled complex of mathematical, philosophical, political, and psychological elements that critics combine and re-combine into comprehensive normative views about the authority and social role of welfare economists. We instead simply summarize conclusions of Ross and Townshend (2021) and Ross (2023) that review arguments we consider most pertinent.[45] We number the claims for subsequent convenience of reference.

1. Comparative states of general human well-being are too multifaceted, cross-culturally variable, and resistant to full description without use of normatively inflected narratives, to be reduced to or decidable by any quantitative efficiency measure. So welfare in its technical sense is not equivalent to general well-being. The most sophisticated literature on general well-being is produced by some philosophers, such as Tiberius (2010), Williams (1981, 2006), and Nussbaum (1997). This kind of work does not reach scientifically testable conclusions, and does not aspire to do so. Economists have no special expertise, as economists, in assessing the relative merits or soundness of this literature as a whole, or of specific instances of it.
2. Economists best promote clarity of their own work by restricting use of "welfare" to technical interpretations that admit of specifications that can be identified in realistically obtainable empirical data.
3. Because economists are not experts in general human well-being, they should manifest the attitude that Keynes (1936, reprinted 1963, p. 373) recommended when he famously urged them to adopt the posture of "humble, competent people, on a level with dentists." The meaning of Keynes here is not vague: what he specifically advised economists against was advocating sweeping reforms of individual or social values.[46]
4. In a broadly liberal society, public administrators should be seen as agents who aim to promote the welfare of principals, that is, the body of citizens, whom they are hired to serve. They should act to promote welfare, not general well-being, because the latter activity would unavoidably impose their special philosophical opinions about what is best for people in general on citizens with conflicting such opinions (Dowding & Taylor, 2019).
5. Economists who are humble experts on welfare are appropriate consultants for public administrators in broadly liberal political and social orders. When

an economist's advice is not followed by a government, her response that efficiency is being traded off for something else may be true, but does not justify, in principle, a claim that injustice has been allowed.

These five claims complement a pair of closely linked corollary opinions on the general philosophy of economics.

First, we think that economists should be much more cautious than most are in rendering judgments about "rationality." One conclusion of Robbins (1935) that has stood the test of time is that what economists *properly* mean by "rationality" in their professional work is consistency of agents' ends with means, and among ends, for some assignment of agency roles and across some time interval. This is a far narrower idea than what anyone other than economists, and certainly the philosophers cited above, mean by "rationality." Just as economists have no special expertise as assessors of well-being in general, they have no special expertise as assessors of rationality "in general." Most economists, we suggest, have always acknowledged this in treating alternative distributional allocations consistent with Kaldor–Hicks–Scitovsky improvements as matters of "ethics," to be modeled by a social choice theory that they have never claimed to monopolize, but share with philosophers and political theorists.

But, second, we also have a skeptical attitude to that literature. Consider one of its best products, the magisterial and technically careful critical review by Adler (2012). The main literatures on which he relies are technical welfare economics and philosophical decision theory. The goal of the enterprise is a manual for governing a community of members, each of whom is held to, and expects others to be held to, the decision theorist's standard of general rationality. One representative implication is Adler's conclusion that although most people are, *as a matter of empirical fact*, risk averse, ideally rational agents are risk neutral; therefore the set of best SWFs that should be operated by public administrators should be applied *as if* citizens aimed to maximize their EV. Another implication is that citizen's preferences over "remote" outcomes outside their control space, for example, concerning the collective well-being of distant future generations, should be ignored (Adler, 2012, pp. 174–181). By contrast, we think that economists assessing welfare should be sensitive to all actual preferences they find, including preferences about risk and about "remote" matters. Adler's disagreement with us here can, we suggest, be diagnosed as follows. He assumes that a liberal society is the best kind of society for promoting general well-being, and that general well-being can be assessed within a framework that assumes general rationality. Thus "illiberal" preferences about people unconnected with the preference-holder, and "irrational" preferences such as risk aversion, should be ruled out of the domain of a SWF.

It is a biographical fact about us, the present authors, that we are liberals. As political participants, we encourage others to be liberals, or at least to support the liberal policies we prefer. But we do not see this as any of our business *as (humble) economists*. Furthermore, we claim enough expertise in philosophy of economics to hold as a professionally informed opinion that general well-being and general rationality cannot be reduced to a technical decision theory that makes preference-consistency the decisive element of methodology for assessing value. When, on evenings and weekends, we want to contemplate the best forms of private and political life, we find more interesting guidance from writers such as Tiberius, Williams, and Nussbaum than from analysts like Adler. In our view, philosophical decision theorists and architects of "top-down" SWFs mis-apply the economist's technical tools to the philosopher's discursive, narrative job. In consequence they invite the kind of backlash against excessive ambition to regulate all of society that fuels anti-economics.

In light of these remarks, our suggestion that "welfare" be restricted to "technical interpretations that admit of specifications that can be identified in realistically obtainable empirical data" might be misinterpreted. We certainly do *not* mean by this that changes in welfare should be identified with changes in "material" outcomes. The point of behavioral experimentation is to apply the techniques of quantitative welfare estimation to conditions that otherwise lack metrics for assessment. For example, Harrison, Morsink, and Schneider (2022) criticize other economists, specifically Matsuda, Takahashi, and Ikegami (2019), for understanding the "direct" benefits of insurance as consisting in actual payouts received by policy-holders, implying that purchasers of insurance who suffer no redeemable damages have made investments that turned out badly *ex post*. This is clearly confused. Of course people often get convinced to buy insurance policies that reduce their welfare for reasons related to actuarial odds and price. But stable insurance markets exist because reduction of risk is itself welfare enhancing in cases where no claim against a policy is made. Part of the gain is that the policy-holder frees resources for consumption or investment that would otherwise be tied up in self-insurance or self-protection. But another part of the gain is typically psychological: relief from aversive feelings of anxiety. The behavioral welfare economist is not advised by the QIS to try to identify the second element by scanning subjects' brains or measuring their cortisol levels. But it can be estimated from willingness to pay *if* an experiment is administered in which the subject's understanding of the terms of the transaction is effectively promoted by careful design.

So what *do* we have in mind when we say that there are aspects of well-being that are not aspects of welfare, and that can only be addressed by qualitative philosophical reflection? It is crucial to our point that we *cannot* point to specific kinds of circumstances that apply predictably across contexts. Where we *can* point to such targets, a behavioral welfare economist can set out to design an experiment for measuring them. But we can imagine comparing two communities in which preferences are satisfied comparably efficiently, but where almost anyone who is culturally external to both communities would regard one as enjoying a wiser or ethically better way of life. We stress that we do *not* think that such judgments can be expressed on generally agreed metrics – that is exactly half of our point. So we should not expect philosophical reflections on such cases to produce arguments that would settle the case for any soundly thinking observer.

The *other* half of our point, however, is that it is arrogant and churlish of an economist to insist that reflections are useless if they cannot establish such definitive conclusions, that is, cannot turn the judgment about well-being into a judgment about welfare after all. The best substitute for argument here is just to orient skeptics toward some best cases of narrative reflection and hope they see the point. But we can supplement this with a practical argument. If an economist insists that everything of value must be reducible in principle to measurable welfare, then she invites anti-economic cultural backlash. In fact, though we can think of some economists who are inclined to rattle humanistic sensibilities in this way in off-hours pontification, the institutionalized sub-discipline that truly embodies the error is another group of philosophers, those who construct technical theories of general rationality and then insist that a best life must conform to such theories.

Thus, we defend a conception of the welfare economist's brief as being identification of feasible Kaldor–Hicks–Scitovsky improvements,[47] given structurally specified subjective, heterogeneous utilities within fields of interacting agents, to be identified empirically from observed choice behavior in the lab and the field, modeled using the QIS.

4.2 Paternalism

Sugden (2004, 2009, 2018) develops a framework for normatively evaluating agents' outcomes under alternative institutional arrangements in a way that privileges their autonomy as choosers (i.e., their consumer sovereignty) without depending on their specific preference orderings, and thus without requiring their preferences to even be consistently ordered, let alone fully EUT-compliant. According to Sugden (2004, 2009), agents are made better off to the extent that their *opportunity sets* are expanded, and worse off to the extent that their *opportunity sets* are contracted.[48] Against this standard, "pure" boosts will typically make agents better off and "pure" nudges will typically make them worse off.

This idea is indeed attractive as a way of addressing normative questions in circumstances where welfare analysis in the technical sense is not possible due to substantive preference reversals.[49] Thus, for example, this approach can generate recommendations in cases where the method of Bernheim (2009, 2016) and Bernheim and Rangel (2009, 2018) would find Pareto indifference and therefore yield no guidance. But we should not abjure ever doing standard welfare analysis merely because it cannot be undertaken in every context. In both the Harrison and Ng (2016, 2018) case and in the situation presented to Harrison and Ross (2018) by their consulting client, the complications arise from the existence of preferences that violate EUT but are nevertheless well-ordered. Arguably, this is the standard situation where relevant utilities are defined over expected monetary values that are risky.

A pre-behavioral theory of welfare that assumes that all choices by agents optimize their SEU faces no concerns about paternalism. In that setting, the welfare analyst who gives policy advice is, where each individual's welfare is concerned, merely transmitting the agent's own revealed preferences, and can do this with high confidence because the power of the full set of Savage axioms, when these are applied to a set of observations with reasonable dispersion on the

Marschak–Machina triangle (Machina, 1987), typically imposes tight constraints on all unobserved (including future) choices by the agent.

However, the very point of a behavioral approach is based on *rejecting* the general applicability of the assumption that no observed choices are errors. Once we acknowledge that people often make choices that are inconsistent with one another from the perspective of an SEU model, we seem to face the choice between *either* throwing up our hands and pronouncing the agent's utility function to be undiscoverable or finding grounds for regarding some of her choices as errors. The behavioral welfare economist is committed to the second approach except in cases where she has good independent evidence that the individual subject has in fact lost her agency.

Loss of agency might occur from extreme cognitive impairment or because she has been completely captured by coercive agents who struggle with one another for control of her. Implications of cases of the first kind are discussed in Ross (2023, pp. 97–99). The second kind of case may initially look like it could only arise in a *Matrix*-type science fiction setting, but in fact is essentially the view of some traditions in sociological theory that minimize agency and view individuals as captives of power dynamics in networks. The behavioral welfare economist, however, predicates her work on the view that most people at least often exercise agency, but also often make mistaken choices. This confronts her with two problems: she must justify identifying errors in other agents' behaviors that they seem not to have spotted themselves, and she needs acceptable grounds for recommending policy interventions that implicitly correct the choices of people who typically are not explicitly asking to be set straight. In other words, the behavioral welfare economist needs a principled position on paternalism.

The traditional ideal in economics is to avoid paternalism. Referring back to our discussion of welfare and rationality immediately above, this sets the economist apart from philosophers and legal scholars such as Adler (2012) who advocate discarding preferences over remote contingencies, and discarding preferences that fail to meet their tests for general rationality, when selecting objectives for policy designers. We must not give the impression that these theorists enjoy consensus about the standard of general rationality. Buchak (2013) has excited considerable discussion amongst philosophers in arguing that general rationality enjoins conforming to the axioms of RDU, with flexible parameters on risk preferences, rather than EUT.[50] But as economists we prefer to stand aloof from such debates, taking the view that public policy officials should do their best to satisfy the preferences they actually find, rather than try to optimize the general well-being of ideally rational counterparts of actual people.

This gulf with respect to grand objectives should not obscure practical affinities. Our welfare economist who applies the QIS is not motivated to worry about choice consistency because she thinks it is required by general rationality. However, her aim is to infer patterns from observed choices and extend these out of sample, a task which necessarily must gain leverage from such consistency as she finds. Furthermore, her Bayesian inferential methods, relying on demographic and other circumstantial covariates about agents and populations, imply that her efforts to avoid paternalism will lead her to frustration *to the extent that* choices of individual agents are governed by *idiosyncratic* parameters. An important example of such a parameter is the λ parameter for idiosyncratic reference-dependent loss aversion in CPT. We gain illustrative traction on the economist's paternalism problem, under the QIS, by contrasting our attitude to CPT with that of Buchak (2013), who is uninhibited about paternalistically separating the rational from the irrational. Insofar as loss aversion is based on λ, it must undermine consistency across (loss, gain and mixed frame) contexts under any set of decision axioms. Therefore, Buchak argues that policy-makers or advisors should seek to correct for CPT preferences, just as they might feel justified in correcting revealed preferences for smoking *if and where* such preferences turned out to be crucially conditioned on scientifically false beliefs about effects of smoking propagated by tobacco companies and their captured experts.

We argued in Section1 that there is little empirical basis for regarding utility functions that include λ as descriptively important. But this is strictly a contingent matter. There obviously *might be* some agents who find loss of whatever assets they happen to acquire so painful that they would require extravagant compensation to part with them. Such a case is the most natural psychological analogue to λ. These kinds of sentiments are *exactly* the kind that an anti-paternalist should take care to respect; "Shake off your pain and be rational!" is as literally paternalistic an attitude as it is possible to have. By contrast, *probabilistic* loss aversion that results from subjective probability weighting, which Buchak (2013) promotes as typically recommended by general rationality, is the kind of case where the welfare economist following the QIS may find her anti-paternalist commitments leading to ambiguity.

We agree with Buchak (2013) that rank-dependent risk preferences make sense as heuristics. But this is not because they can be rendered *technically* "rational" in philosophical decision theory. It is rather because of some features of the social world inhabited by strategic agents. This world abounds with scaffolding built by self-interested parties whose manipulations are obscured. Furthermore, such parties (e.g., advertisers, politicians, and clickbait artists) typically exploit a general epistemic limitation: marks who only encounter their ploys from time to time will typically have sparse observations from the tails of distributions of game outcomes.[51] In such a world, it is a sensible policy to behave as if tails of distributions on outcome event spaces are fatter than available direct evidence suggests, particularly on the downside. Advisors should not make it their general policy to steer their clients away from such heuristics.

However, under *some* circumstances clients are poorly served by failure to encourage closer alignment between subjective and objective probabilities. The case reviewed in Harrison and Ross (2018) is a crisp example. In this instance, we as economists had a direct client, a retail investment bank. It aimed to discourage its customers from inefficient churning of assets in their portfolios, where "inefficient" was defined by the bank in terms of expected wealth at retirement age. This objective was identified by reference to declared goals of a majority of customers. Of course, it cannot be inferred from this that any *particular* customer's pattern of behavior had been inefficient. The client bank sought to boost customers' knowledge of stock behavior through an educational intervention it would make available to them on a voluntary basis. The bank also wished to avoid wasting customers' time by specifically promoting the boosting intervention to customers who wouldn't be expected to benefit from it. Thus the bank proposed to entangle the boosting intervention with selective nudging for a subset of customers. Our task was to identify that subset, based on a population-level model informed by risky (lottery) choice experiments *with individual-level estimations* and a simulated investment task, involving real and salient monetary rewards, conducted with a random sample of customers. The model of course included demographic covariates. Based on the experimental data, we distinguished between subjects whose patterns of lottery choices were best modeled by EUT from subjects whose patterns of lottery choices were best modeled by RDU. We then compared the results of individual-level estimation of the lottery choice data with outcomes from the simulated stock market investment choices. We aimed to identify characteristics of customers who would, statistically, be likely to enjoy welfare improvements if they were nudged to be boosted by the bank's educational intervention.

In deciding how to advise our client, issues of paternalism arose in two places.

First, we could assume or not assume that customers preferred to have more money rather than less at the end of the investment history. We assumed that they preferred more money. Arguably, this was not a genuine "choice" on our part; in the absence of this assumption we would not have been able to address our client's question at all. But the choice could be supported by empirical facts: the portfolio products we simulated in the investment task were modeled on actual portfolios explicitly advertised to individuals and households as devices for maximizing their expected monetary wealth at retirement. This knowledge clearly belonged in the priors for any Bayesian model of the study population. In principle, the prior could have been undone by behavioral observations that our subjects atemporally preferred less money to more, though of course that would have been extremely surprising, to put it mildly.

Second, and more interestingly, we had to decide whether to base welfare estimations on EUT models for EUT-conforming subjects and RDU models for RDU-conforming subjects, or on CS calculations that "imposed" EUT on all subjects. We opted for the first approach, based on considerations about paternalism. We found that against this rubric RDU-conforming subjects suffered significant welfare losses from their investment choices relative to their EUT-conforming counterparts.[52] Thus, we recommended nudges toward boosting for customers whose choice patterns indicated that they were best characterized as RDU-conforming, and no nudging for customers whose choice patterns suggested that they were best characterized as EUT-conforming.

Why did we suppose it would be unacceptably paternalistic to model all subjects' welfare outcomes on the basis of EUT? Again, we defend this decision on empirical grounds reflected in our priors as modelers of welfare. There is empirical evidence that many pension funds underweight stocks in portfolios, given historical equity premia, relative to the weighting they would operate if they thought their representative client was an expected utility maximizer with a utility function linear in money (Gomes & Michaeldes, 2005). RDU preferences over financial investments, in any given sample, might reflect disutility from anxiety some people feel during periods of market retrenchment, and our priors recognize this possibility. It would be paternalistic to over-ride such heuristic preferences. On other hand, subjects might reveal RDU preferences that reflect concerns about strategic exploitation and mis-apply these in circumstances, such as buying standard portfolios from well-regulated retailers, where incentives of manipulative brokers would work in the *opposite* direction to the intent of the intervention we were studying.[53] Our client's boost intervention, by providing customers with richer information about historical distributions of asset prices than customers might otherwise access, might lead them to detect and correct such errors – of course that is precisely the assumption and motivation for the intervention.

We were not advising our client on whether to offer the boosting intervention. We were advising them on who to nudge and who not to nudge. As Sugden (2018) argues, *any* nudge is paternalistic to some extent if it suggests that the nudgee devote time and cognitive resources to attending to a boosting effort before the nudgee has full information about the potential value to them of the boost. This should simply be acknowledged. We do not think it is efficient for a welfare economist to generally try to reduce nudging elements of recommended measures to zero; such a fanatical policy would almost certainly lead to net welfare losses. The key difference between applied behavioral welfare economics following the QIS, and alternative approaches such as those we criticized in Section 2, is that the economist following the QIS does not try to distinguish, *a priori*, behavior that reveals "true" or "purified" or "serious" preferences from behavior that reveals "defective" or "impulsive" or "myopic" preferences, and base welfare estimations only on the former. The fully conscientious behavioral welfare economist includes *all* information about policy clients' behavioral records in her priors. When her posterior settles on a model that identifies some choices as errors, she ideally designs independent tests of the relevant error specification. The QIS tells us to design policy suggestions on the basis of the *best* model of client agency that realistically obtainable data allows. It does not tell us to try to discover the "true" model of the latent rational agent, because there is no such thing.

It is noteworthy in this context that the version of behavioral welfare economics promoted by Bernheim and Rangel (2009, 2018) grew from their earlier work on justifying interventions to help people overcome addictions (2004). Identifying the preferences of addicts from the intentional stance is unusually challenging because the typical addict's pattern of choices is highly ambivalent. Addicts often spend resources to try to establish commitments against future addictive consumption *while also* spending resources on drugs or gambling. Many economic models of addiction, following the lead of Schelling (1978, 1980, 1984), consequently model addicts as two-agent communities forced to bargain with one another. Paternalism with respect to the single *person* is then unavoidable if the policy-maker sides with the interests of one agent, who is trying to quit, against the other agent, who wants to keep the dopamine spikes rolling.

The way to take this seriously as a problem of paternalism is not to search ingeniously for ways of re-framing the technical model so as to avoid having to say that one is ignoring an internal agent. On any modeling, we have paternalism if an economist ends up telling a person who wants to go the bar that he should not "for your own good." If the economist is a friend of the advisee she might ethically think she should intervene in her role as friend rather than in her role as economist. But if she has studied the social statistics on the kinds of scaffolding regulations that actually work to control relapses in addicts, something that *is* within her professional purview, she will find good empirical reason to emphasize the addict's autonomy and responsibility: only self-management rules that addicts construct for themselves,[54] typically with support from family and friends, tend to successfully produce stable outcomes of either abstinence or controlled consumption (Ross, 2020). The most useful contribution of the welfare economist here is to identify policies that minimize the number of people who become caught in addictive ambivalence in the first place. She should focus on optimal taxation of addictive goods that are allowed to be produced because addiction is a side-consequence of their production (e.g., alcohol and painkillers), while studying prospects for banning goods that are profitable to producers only if they are sold to addicts (e.g., cigarettes and digital slot machines). Once a person is addicted, the appropriate expert for her to consult is a clinical counselor, not a welfare economist.

Similarly, welfare economists who study consequences of financial behavior should not be viewed as individual investment advisors with the whole population as clients. Investment advisors benefit from understanding economics of markets, but they operate mainly in the role of applied psychologists, not economists (Ross, 2023). In the case we are using as an example, Harrison and Ross (2018), though we estimated agents' risk preference types at the individual level, we did not design a separate policy for each individual subject. However, ideal it might be for the welfare economist's work to be taken up as input by waiting squads of investment counselors, such an approach is very expensive to scale up in real institutional settings. Our policy advice was based on statistical facts about actual people rather than representative agents, but the basis of the advice *was* statistical. We recommended nudging all RDU-conforming customers. Thus, the policy almost certainly involved recommending nudges for some subjects who did not need them.

It is conceptual confusion to regard *that* as representing paternalism. All corporate and government policies are based on population-scale statistics. For example, no doubt there are some drivers who are so careful and whose reaction times are so quick that they would never have accidents if they ignored stop signs. No one is being paternalistic to these drivers by not trying to identify them so they can be exempted from the law that all must do what the signs say. Policies are very seldom intended to optimize the welfare of each individual taken one at a time. They usually have, as a crucial objective, coordinating expectations among people who lack specific individual-scale models of one another.

This is why we resist approaches to welfare, such as that of Adler (2012), based on SWFs. A SWF is intended to aggregate individual preferences in such a way as to ensure that no individual's welfare is over-ridden simply because her preferences are statistically unusual. This may be ethically admirable, but it is too data-hungry to be a feasible ambition. At the same time, Adler (2012) and other SWF theorists advocate ignoring "remote" preferences, that is, preferences that mainly concern consequences for people other than the preference-holder (e.g., people living in the distant future or people living in distantly connected geographical or normative communities). The point here is not that SWF theorists think that policy-makers should ignore the future or the well-being of foreigners; it is that they don't think that policies in these areas should be based on individual preference aggregation. The distinction expresses liberal individualism, indeed atomism: remote preferences are considered unacceptably meddlesome and "bossy." Adler (2012) works hard, and carefully, to identify methods for uncovering potential Pareto improvements based on SWFs, but he is skeptical, indeed scathing, about the value of Kaldor–Hicks–Scitovsky improvements, because in the absence of commitment devices that ensure that compensating transfers will actually be made, the efficiency is merely hypothetical.

Our strongly contrasting view is that identifying potential Kaldor–Hicks–Scitovsky improvements is the distinctive core activity of welfare economists.[55] We suggest that the QIS embeds this way of understanding efficiency in a coherent philosophical and methodological package. The view of preferences and beliefs as constructed from the intentional stance through mindshaping processes[56] directly challenges the atomist view of societies as "adding up" sets of individuals with fully pre-formed and complete propositional attitudes latent in their psychologies. We are highly skeptical of a view of administrators as people hired to promote rigorous liberalism as a best universal ethic for maximizing well-being. In complex societies made up of individuals and sub-communities with heterogeneous preferences and beliefs, institutions and rules play vital *coordinating* functions. This activity takes intentional-stance profiles of people as it finds them, but it is highly dynamic; because networks of intentional-stance profiles are constructed to mediate mutual expectations and stabilize bargaining spaces, they adapt to and co-evolve with institutional and legal structures. Underlying welfare economics in every society is continuous cultural evolution of values, as Binmore (2005) emphasizes. Thus, the need for efficiency analysis never ends – windows for improvement are passing phenomena, many of which are grasped and many of which are wasted.

The welfare economist's concern to keep paternalism in check is an expression of liberalism. It is a *fact* about the history of mainstream economic theory that it has evolved from the outset within a broadly liberal ethical frame (Ross, 2012). But liberalism is a mansion of many rooms. The version according to which the first duty of the policy-maker is to safeguard the sovereignty of atomic individuals is one tradition in liberal philosophy, and it expresses itself in programs for welfare management such as Adler's. Another tradition emphasizes instead the role of government as an agent hired by a democratic principal – citizens – that should avoid promoting an independent conception of the good. It does this not by blocking out all information except non-remote individual preferences, but by being open to influence from any coalition of interests. Restricted by a constitution that is hard to amend, it tinkers with rules and institutions so that complex networks of bargainers can evolve by their own dynamics. In effect, it uses the rule of law to stabilize a policy market, similar in structure to the markets for goods and services that it also enables. In case some readers are unconvinced that this second conception, the one we defend as a sound ethical basis for behavioral welfare economics, is truly liberal, we will just point out here that its leading visionary theorist is Hayek (Ross, 2011). That is a reliable enough anti-paternalist brand for us. The core of our effective anti-paternalism is the Keynesian humbleness we urged on applied economists in Section 4.1: the economist's job is to identify social inefficiencies for general consideration, not to try to effect ideological reforms. Such reforms are often morally salutary or even morally urgent, but they are not the professional business of the economist.

5. CONCLUSIONS

The path that leads to the QIS for behavioral welfare economics is summarized in six steps.

First, we begin from the recognition that an agent's welfare cannot be identified by naïve RPT, that is, by assuming that the agent *always* chooses what is best for her. The agents that most interest economists, people, make choices that are inconsistent over time. Sometimes that can be accommodated by recognizing that a natural person who lives a full lifespan is a sequence of agents. With respect to the features economists use to define agency, no one is the same agent at 20 and 70 years old. But human inconsistency of choice is more pervasive and "instantaneous" than that. We must allow that many human choices are errors. Estimations of welfare must identify and discount these errors.

Second, one way to reduce proportions of choices to be treated as errors is to impose a strong model of general individual rationality. Then the analyst can count as errors any choices that fall short of this standard. This approach has a deep history in philosophy, which in its modern form has its roots in Kant's conception of practical reason. It is now best represented by the enterprise of analytic decision theory, which economists readily recognize because it shares its technical foundations with EUT. But economists should reject this approach. One reason to reject this approach is that, like the other parts of analytic philosophy, it seeks an unreachable objective. Just as there will always be counterexamples to every attempted philosophical analysis of knowledge, so there will always be counterexamples to every attempted philosophical analysis of general rationality. Welfare economics is a practical enterprise intended to guide policy-makers and administrators. We will not make progress in this by endlessly constructing, puncturing, and patching technical specifications of general rationality. The other reason to reject this approach is that, because of its radical individualism, this tradition effectively amounts to a project of trying to work out what a single agent should do if she wants to earn the sobriquet "rational." That is not the welfare economist's project. The welfare economist's typical project is to identify policies and structures that are inefficient at the social, statistical level. Reforms at this level inevitably produce winners and losers. In recognition of this, economists should self-consciously maintain Keynesian humbleness. Our job is to be experts on efficiency, not to re-engineer our societies. If an economist's society needs fundamental reform for moral reasons, she could go out to the barricades with everyone else who shares her convictions, but leaving her economist's hat at home.

Third, another popular way to try to reduce the proportion of choices to use as the "real" evidence for welfare optima is to try to identify psychological mechanisms that tend to generate choices that undermine a chooser's welfare. Then choices that are predominantly produced by these mechanisms can be regarded as "anomalies" to be corrected in theory, and nudged against in practice. This has been the dominant approach in behavioral welfare economics. The deep problem with it, as recognized by a few "insiders" to economics such as Ken Binmore, Nick Chater, and Robert Sugden, is that it rests on a naïve conception of psychology. Most human behavior is not mechanically caused by mechanisms that are latent within, or even "supervene on," their brains. Welfare is characterized in terms of preference satisfaction. Preferences cannot be identified from choice behavior independently of specifying beliefs. The most promising, and increasingly dominant, approach in cognitive science emphasizes that preferences and beliefs are social constructions used to make people mutually comprehensible to one another and to coordinate their expectations so they can make shared policies – sometimes cooperatively, and sometimes competitively, but always within arenas of institutional constraint. Saying that preferences and beliefs are social constructions is not a way of saying that they are unreal. It is rather to say that they are virtual kinds of objects. Modern societies teem with such real objects, money being an example very familiar to economists. Preferences and beliefs are identified in everyday contexts by a "folk" intentional stance. Like all folk models, this incorporates many myths that scientific study does not ratify. Cognitive scientists make progress from a scientific intentional stance, meaning one that survives the filtering processes of collective rigor about observability across cases.

Fourth, economics is fundamentally quantitative. This does not reflect a view to the effect that careful qualitative reflection is uninformative. Economists should have deep respect for an older philosophical tradition, which we associate with Aristotle but which has many superb contemporary practitioners, of articulating more and less wise ways for humans to aim to live. Such reflections gain their power and reasonableness precisely by being highly sensitive to nuances of historically and culturally specific cases. This makes them valuable for individuals or densely connected communities, but less useful for policy-makers and administrators who must rely on statistical generalizations.[57] Economists should not be committed to quantitative methods because they want to be as respected as physicists. That motivation unquestionably did motivate many of our iconic predecessors, but humble Keynesians should treat that as an embarrassing quirk in tribal history. Economics is quantitative because what we study are statistical patterns in sets of observed choices. We take a special *quantitative intentional stance* with respect to behavior that is based on choice. We do not identify "choice" with any psychological mechanism. We regard behavior as "chosen" if it can be influenced by changes in incentives. That is also identifiable by statistical evidence. Blinking is not chosen behavior because people will not stop doing it no matter how much you pay them. Physiologically similar winking is chosen behavior, and we have the statistical evidence to assure us of this. Far more of our fathers and grandfathers winked at their female colleagues at their offices than our contemporaries do. Everyone knows why this changed, without our having to know anything about processing details in any heads.

Fifth, the basic engine for identifying choice patterns is Bayesian inference. Crucial to this methodology is that everything we think we know to be relevant, and everything we observe, is included in priors. In this sense, the approach is the opposite to methods that deliberately exclude choices thought to be irrational on philosophical grounds, or that result from purported mechanisms that the subject would disown when thinking at her best. Of course, we can only include in priors what we can represent in a single model. So models must be structural. The aim is to identify the production function for a subject's welfare, so we can ask under what conditions the function in question outputs the highest *flow* of utility. Best methodology is thus to estimate at the level of the individual, even when our ultimate focus is on social efficiency, that is, potential Kaldor–Hicks–Scitovsky improvements.

Sixth, while rejecting simple-minded RPT that allows for no errant choices, the QIS is very much in the *spirit* of RPT. That is, it understands utility functions as summaries of observed choices, conditioned on beliefs. This "contemporary" RPT has been discussed in the leading economic methodology literature for some years; highlights are Binmore (2009), Hands (2013), and Ross (2014, 2023). Ross (2014) refers to the methodological program as "neo-Samuelsonian": it is "Samuelsonian" because, like the intentional stance, it ascribes preferences in order to describe observed behavior, and it is "neo" because it goes well beyond the original weak axiom of revealed preference and applies to finite sets of choices.

We agree with Leamer (2012) that economics is fundamentally a policy science. Like medical and engineering academics, its practitioners, even when they are not directly serving specific clients, choose the domain to which they apply their theory, mathematics, and statistics, on concerns about efficiency.[58] Nothing is efficient or inefficient in economics except with respect to values of inputs and outputs, and it is the realm of practical pursuits that sets these values. This is not a narrow conception of economics. It applies to many transactions that do not take place in markets mediated directly by exchanges of money. The practical pursuits that establish values might be those of fish, bees, elephants, or humans.[59] But at least in the background to everything that economists professionally think about is someone's welfare. Therefore, it is as important as can be that we conceptualize and measure welfare with great care.

NOTES

1. The quasi-hyperbolic model assumes a rather strange fixed cost, a constant *percentage* of the principal. One can write down models that assume that the fixed cost is a scalar amount of money, or a scalar level of utility.

2. Hence, boosts need not rely on the use of heuristics. The key distinction between an algorithm and a heuristic has to do with the knowledge claim that they each allow one to make. If an algorithm has been applied correctly, then the result will be a solution that we know something about. For example, we may know that it is a local optimum, even if we do not know that it is a global optimum. Heuristics are lesser epistemological beasts: the solution provided by a heuristic has no claim to be a valid solution in the sense of meeting some logical criteria. In the computational literature, if not some parts of the psychological literature, heuristics are akin to "rules of thumb" that simply have good or bad track records for certain classes of problems. The track record may be defined in terms of the speed of arriving at a candidate solution, or the ease of application. Harrison (2008, section 4.2) provides more discussion of the role of heuristics in decision-making, particularly their crucial role in "behaviorally plausible" homotopy, or path-following, algorithms.

3. This expression is widely used, but examples might be of value in case one doubts that it is so common. Karlan and Appel (2011, p. 5) state that "... at the end of the day, even Sachs and Easterly could agree on the following: Sometimes aid works, and sometimes it does not. That can't be all that controversial a stand! The critical question, then, is which aid works. The debate has been in the sky, but the answers are on the ground. Instead of getting hung up on the extremes, let's zero in on the details. Let's look at a specific challenge or problem that poor people face, try to understand what they're up against, propose a potential solution, and then test to find out whether it works. If that solution works – and if we can demonstrate that it works consistently – then let's scale it up so it can work for more people. If it doesn't work, let's make changes or try something new." And the U.S. Department of Education maintains a "What Works Clearinghouse" at https://ies.ed.gov/ncee/WWC.

4. This is the approach adopted in Ambuehl, Bernheim, and Lusardi (2014), to view one of the frames as revealing true, virtual valuations. In Ambuehl, Bernheim, and Lusardi (2017) this position was qualified, allowing that there might be some normative metric that does not lead one to accept that either frame represents the true, virtual valuation. The example provided is when subjects exhibit quasi-hyperbolic discounting in response to both questions, with exponential discounting *a priori* deemed to be normatively attractive and quasi-hyperbolic discounting deemed *a priori* to be normatively unattractive. In this case, they claim, both responses might be "contaminated" by the "passion for the present" one expects from quasi-hyperbolic responses. They then present a formal result that essentially says that if the responses to statements A and B are equally contaminated, then as one takes the *limit of the difference between the responses as that difference goes to zero*, a first-order approximation to a valid welfare measure can be obtained. But that says nothing about whether the difference between the responses that are non-zero, or not close to zero, have any valid interpretation, unless one wants to invoke stringent path-independence assumptions from welfare economics (see Boadway & Bruce, 1984, p. 199 or Harrison, Rutherford, & Wooton, 1993). The bulk of responses of interest are decidedly non-zero, and not close to zero, as illustrated in Ambuehl, Bernheim, Ersoy, and Harris (2018, Fig. 1, p. 16).

5. An application of the same methodology to retirement savings plans is provided by Bernheim, Fradkin, and Popov (2015).

6. We say "more specific" to stress that literacy is also scaffolding.

7. Literacy is itself a general scaffolding architecture, which provides people who can read with access to more specific elements of scaffolding such as technical or popular investment manuals.

8. This might cause identification problems if the "nonfinancial attributes," to use the expression of Handel and Kolstad (2015), also varied across all plan choices, but three PPO plans had no differences in these attributes: hence their variations in "financial attributes,"

such as deductible, coinsurance, and out-of-pocket maxima, could be used to identify atemporal risk preferences. The presumption is that individuals do not subjectively believe that these attributes differ across these PPO plans.

9. Measures developed by Alekseev, Harrison, Lau, and Ross (2018) to implement this idea for models of risk preferences are, methodologically, similar to the Critical Cost Efficiency Index (CCEI) of Afriat (1972), which is used to evaluate the degree of consistency with the Generalized Axiom of Revealed Preference (GARP). The CCEI relative cost measure is defined on the unit interval, and its complement shows what proportion of monetary value an agent should be allowed to waste in order to rationalize her choices by some utility function. While GARP provides qualitative statements, Alekseev et al. (2018) put more structure on the estimation procedure and provide quantitative evidence of welfare costs from observed choices. This approach can be applied to any model of risk preferences that admits of one or other model of noisy choice.

10. This conclusion was qualified in some villages for those that did not own land.

11. The subsequent literature on full or partial insurance, inferred from such correlations, continues. For example, Blundell, Pistaferri, and Preston (2008) conclude from US data that there is "some partial insurance of permanent shocks, especially for the college educated and those nearing retirement [and that there is] full insurance of transitory shocks except among poor households" (p. 1887).

12. Feldman and Dowd (1991) updated these calculations with later, improved estimates of the moving behavioral parts. Their estimates of risk aversion came from econometric estimates in the health insurance literature based on comparable observational data and survey questions.

13. Philosophers group statements identifying beliefs, desires, preferences, hopes, fears, wishes, and their boundless counterparts and conjugates across human languages, as all being about *propositional attitudes*. The point of this terminology is that all of these verbs refer to views that a user of language can take to an actual or hypothetical state of affairs in the world. For example, one person might *believe that* Acme stock will crash, while a holder of the stock *fears that* this is so and another investor who has shorted it both *hopes* that the stock will fall and *prefers* to say things that encourage others to affirm the belief. The word "proposition" here signifies that the relevant "state of affairs" (i.e., the fate of Acme stock) is not a *linguistic* item, because a unilingual speaker of English could share the above attitudes with a unilingual speaker of Tagalog or Mandarin. The most difficult and perennial problems in applied logic arise from complexities in propositional attitude *reports*. Metaphysically, their status is bound up with what it is to be or have a mind. That is, a "mind" is often said by philosophers to be a delimited entity or process that can truly be said to express and behaviorally respond to propositional attitudes. This claim is practically central to identifying the theoretical subject matter of cognitive science, and to the goals of AI research. A few philosophers doubt that propositional attitudes, and therefore minds, can ever be proper objects of scientific study, and urge that they should ultimately be explained away. The philosopher Alex Rosenberg (1992), for example, argues that economics can never be good science as long as its theory makes ineliminable reference to preferences and beliefs. A main career objective of Dennett, on whose ideas we rely, has been to cleanly integrate study of propositional attitudes and their uses into the general scientific worldview, thereby answering sceptics such as Rosenberg. A critical survey of the debate for economists is provided by Ross (2005).

14. The origins of debates about propositional attitudes in philosophy, described above, might lead a reader to suppose that Dennett's arguments must be *a priori*. In fact, they are almost exclusively empirical, drawn from details in the uncontroversial success of some scientific research programmes based on the intentional stance, such as the main streams of human developmental psychology, cognitive ethology, and the "deep learning" (or "connectionist") branch of AI.

15. The relevant literature here is vast. Hood (2012) reviews evidence up to a decade ago, and Spivey (2020) draws on more recent developments.

16. Mäki (2009) reviews the history and critiques of Friedman's instrumentalism.

17. No highly intelligent animals are asocial, with the possible exception of a few species very recently descended from intensively social ancestors.

18. There are important uses of the word "latent," in statistics, that don't carry these connotations. We are not, for example, advising anyone to stop talking about latent indices. Linguistic theorists use the word in yet another way that isn't threatened by changes in prevailing psychology. Instances of such polysemy abound in the history of science. Wilson (2006) refers to cases where more than one discipline technically co-opts the name of the same pre-scientific concept as "wandering significance." He demonstrates the importance of such histories by documenting instances where unregulated interactions between rival semantic anchors produced unintended consequences for the evolution of theories and experimental traditions.

19. To add complication, they interact directly with the stochastic specifications that attend to sampling errors in the econometrics, and hence inferences about preferences: see Wilcox (2008, 2011) for a masterful review in the case of risk preferences.

20. The discussion here is crucial to answering the common objection heard from some behavioral economists, and external critics of economic theory, that people do not or cannot perform the "mental computations" that most microeconomic models specify. The discussion simultaneously shows why the right answer to such critics is *not* to join Gul and Pesendorfer (2008) in asserting that psychological processing is *a priori* irrelevant to economists. It is relevant exactly and only when it makes an economic difference, and this is an empirical matter to be assessed from one application to another.

21. For example, the informational treatment of Harrison and Ross (2018) with respect to investment decisions, or the various informational treatments of Harrison, Morsink, and Schneider (2020) with respect to index insurance decisions.

22. The usual application in Bayesian modeling is to additional out-of-sample instances of the same data used to estimate the posterior. A typical example would be to predict choices by one of our subjects if she had been offered a new, different battery of choices over risky lotteries.

23. Details are provided in Gao, Harrison, and Tchernis (2023). A Bayesian hierarchical model was used in which informative priors for the estimation of individual risk preferences were obtained by assuming exchangeability with respect to the risk preferences of other individuals in the sample. A relatively diffuse (weakly informative) prior was employed to estimate the risk preferences of the representative agent, and the posterior distribution from that estimation was used as the informative prior for estimation of individual risk preferences.

24. If one was using point estimates from a traditional maximum likelihood approach, or even point estimates from one of the descriptive statistics of a posterior distribution (e.g., mean, median, or mode), then the inferred welfare measure would be a scalar.

25. Harrison, Morsink, and Schneider (2020) provide a number of examples of the evaluation of *non-adaptive* treatments.

26. A more sophisticated "targeting" policy might use the information from the first 12 insurance choices to adaptively determine the actuarial parameters that might lead each subject to make better decisions in the remaining 12 choices.

27. See Teele (2014) and Glennerster (2017) for discussion of the *Belmont Report* and some aspects of the ethics of conducting randomized behavioral interventions in economics. Even when randomized clinical trials were not adaptive, or even sequential in terms of stopping rules, it was common to employ termination rules based on extreme, cumulative results (e.g., the "3 standard deviations" rule noted by Peto, 1985, p. 33).

28. This point has nothing to do with whether the subject exhibits "present bias" in any form. All that is needed is simple impatience, even with exponential discounting. Berry and Fristedt (1985, chapter 3) stress the importance of time discounting in sequential "bandit" problems in medical settings.

29. And this lesson is on top of the lessons from a well-known medical case study, reviewed by Harrison (2021), about the normative basis of experimentation at all based on prior evidence from *non-experimental* environments.

30. We stress the welfare impact. Many economists confuse impact evaluation with welfare evaluation, arguing that surely the observable impact being measured must matter for welfare. Even when statistical circumstances are ideal, impact evaluation constitutes at best an intermediate input into the welfare evaluation of interventions. That intermediate input is valuable, but should not be confused with the final product, a proper cost-benefit analysis (Harrison, 2014).

31. See Harrison, Rutherford, and Tarr (1997) for discussion of the role of these modeling extensions in the context of a welfare evaluation of the Uruguay Round of multilateral trade reform, and Harrison (2011b) for a review of "policy lotteries" that have been evaluated with computable general equilibrium models. A key feature of those evaluations for practical welfare economics is the ability to explicitly calculate sidepayments required by the Kaldor–Hicks–Scitovsky Compensation Criteria, allowing for the distortionary effects of sidepayments that are not "lump sum." For applications in climate policy, tax policy, and trade policy, respectively, see Harrison and Rutherford (1999), Harrison, Jensen, Lau, and Rutherford (2002), and Harrison, Rutherford, and Tarr (2003).

32. This tradeoff has long been felt keenly in the literature on sequential clinical trials in medicine: see Armitage (1985).

33. For example, in Dennett (1987, p. 17), "Here is how it works: first you decide to treat the object whose behavior is to be predicted as a rational agent; then you figure out what beliefs that agent ought to have, given its place in the world and its purpose. Then you figure out what desires it ought to have, on the same considerations, and finally you predict that this rational agent will act to further its goals in the light of its beliefs. A little practical reasoning from the chosen set of beliefs and desires will in most instances yield a decision about what the agent ought to do; that is what you predict the agent will do."

34. To be strict, we should say "other than directly, naively inferred from the choice task one is making welfare evaluations about." We discuss the notion of structural models of mistakes in Section 2.5.

35. The relevant characteristic of stability can also vary with the inferences being made. For some inferences we only care about the *ranking* of individuals in terms of risk premia, and for some inferences we care about the *level* of the risk premia for individuals. We assume the latter for our purposes here.

36. There are very few data collected on any forms of stability at the individual level. Most of the evidence concerns averages or distributions over individuals.

37. Chuang and Schechter (2015) review the literature and suggest low correlations of risk preferences over time. Harrison, Johnson, McInnes, and Rutström (2005) find evidence of unconditional stability over five or six months for average levels of risk aversion. Andersen, Harrison, Lau, and Rutström (2008b, section 5.1) similarly find evidence of unconditional stability over 17 months for distributions of risk attitudes.

38. Allowing for unobserved heterogeneity, Harrison, Lau, and Yoo (2020) find evidence for temporal stability of distributions of risk preferences over 6–12 months, but only when correcting formally for sample selection and attrition. And they infer temporal instability when those corrections are not made. No prior study has corrected for selection or attrition when drawing inferences about temporal stability.

39. As any experimental economist knows, it is not easy to come up with morbidity outcomes that can be credibly and ethically delivered within the budgets we normally find ourselves working within.

40. The idea is to have one binary choice that presents a lottery with a compound risk (C) and some lottery (S) with simple risks. Then we need another binary choice that presents the actuarially-equivalent simple lottery (C′) that corresponds to C and the same lottery S. If the subject selects C (S) in the first choice and C′ (S) in the second choice then there is no violation of ROCL; if not, then there is a ROCL violation. Harrison, Martínez-Correa, and Swarthout (2015) develop a battery to test ROCL in this manner. No estimates are needed to determine the fraction of choices in such "pairs of pairs" that reflect ROCL violations.

41. We can ignore for the moment the fact that many experiments ask for choices over a number of pairs of lotteries and then select one for resolution and payment. The time taken in these choices is minimal, and what is fundamental is that the outcome be received by the subject at one point in time.

42. See Starmer (2000; p. 355ff and 344ff) for an excellent exposition of the historical context of these models.

43. This extra step is achieved directly by eliciting subjective beliefs using a binary lottery procedure that, in theory, induces risk neutrality under EUT or RDU. See Allen (1987), McKelvey and Page (1990), Hossain and Okui (2013), Harrison, Martínez-Correa, and Swarthout (2014), and Harrison, Martínez-Correa, Swarthout, and Ulm (2015).

44. As in applied economics generally, an "individual" is a single *agent*, not necessarily a single *person*. When a single utility function is assigned to a firm or a labor union or a lobby group, etc., this amounts to modeling the corporate agent as an individual.

45. In doing this, we do not mean to suggest that these statements are the most important ones. They simply state grounds for our own opinions at greater length and engagement with very large literatures than we can provide here. We also cite some main sources of the most important premises on which the arguments depend.

46. Some might suppose that when Duflo (2017) compares ideal development economists to "plumbers" she expresses a twenty-first-century echo of Keynes. This is not so, because she divides the entire labor of ideal policy assessment among different sub-sets of economists. Duflo's program implies that each individual economist might be humble, but economists as a group should rule the policy consulting ecosystem.

47. Allowing for the distortionary effects of sidepayments that are not "lump sum," as noted earlier, and applied to climate policy, tax policy, and trade policy, respectively, by Harrison and Rutherford (1999), Harrison, Jensen, Lau, and Rutherford (2002), and Harrison, Rutherford, and Tarr (2003).

48. The reader unfamiliar with Sugden's work might wonder how he considers comparative costs of opportunity set expansion without reference to standard preference orderings. The *technical* answer is that he defines a "weak dominance" relationship among preferences for opportunity sets that does not depend on consistency of preferences over the members of the sets (Sugden, 2018, chapter 5). Sugden does not do away with the concept of preference, but he can relax the definition because he does not require the standard, more restrictive, one to use for defining welfare. The *substantive* answer, details of which would require undue digression here, lies in Sugden's wider philosophy of economics, which makes markets rather than individual choices fundamental, and distinguishes opportunity sets in terms of available exchanges, both at a time and over time, in markets (Sugden, 2018, chapter 6). We think this wider philosophy has much to recommend it, and that it can be put to valuable work in many contexts. It has particular promise for policy problems in which aggregation of welfare is intractably entangled with incentive effects of regulation, as in Sugden (2018, chapter 7). We merely resist the idea that Sugden's ideas should crowd out applications of more standard approaches to welfare across the board.

49. Virtually all (incentivized) evidence for preference reversals over monetary rewards entails individuals foregoing *fractions* of pennies in foregone expected income, due to the "payoff dominance" problem: see Harrison (1992, 1994). So the prevalence of preference reversals should not be *automatically* identified with their welfare significance to the individuals. We emphasize "automatically," since we agree with Ainslie (1992, 2001) that when people lack, or fail to use, scaffolding that helps them anchor alternatives to fungible currencies of exchange, they often choose in ways that are inconsistent over time, and that could have significant welfare consequences for the individual. The clinical context which Ainslie uses as his primary source for case studies involves serious addictions that surely involve some behaviors with great welfare consequences.

50. For an example of the debate triggered by Buchak (2013), see Pettigrew (2016). Pettigrew reconstructs the domain of EUT to include utilities over actions as well as outcomes, and argues, as against Buchak, that this allows accommodation of rank-dependent preferences under the standard Savage axioms. From a purely mathematical point of view this

is unobjectionable. But here we see an illustrative instance of why economists should keep clear distance from the project of using decision theory to construct analyses of "rationality in general." Pettigrew shows no interest in the fact that his reconstruction of the domain of the axioms would disconnect individual decision theory from game theory: all of the main solution strategies for extensive-form games require that utility functions take only outcomes as arguments. No economist in her right mind would want to make this trade-off. In fact, we think there is ultimately no trade-off to be made. Game theory is core technology for social and behavioral science, whereas the project shared by Buchak and Pettigrew has no sustainable justification, even for philosophers. Philosophers who are followers of Kant will disagree. But on Kantian philosophy we applaud the attitude of Binmore (1994, 1998).

51. That is why internet phishing ploys get more sophisticated over time.

52. The only other covariate that predicted significant welfare differences was gender.

53. That is, self-interested brokers would encourage more portfolio churning rather than less.

54. What we mean by "rules" here refers to the work of Ainslie (1992, 2001). He refers to his research program, which is intended mainly for clinicians who seek to guide individuals, as "picoeconomics." This is precisely because it is about strategies by which individuals can frame their internal conflict zones as if they were markets, and thus learn personal rules for constructing stable internal "currencies" that help them exchange sooner and later rewards without undermining their own psychic investments.

55. Recall our discussion in section 3.2 of practical calculations with respect to tax policy, trade policy, and climate change policies that demonstrate how such compensation schemes can be implemented with realistic tax instruments.

56. These processes are explained in Section 3.1.

57. A caveat is in order here. Reading the best philosophy may from time to time stop an economist from recommending a policy that is literally stupid, such as institutional discouragement of gift-giving because gift-giving is bound to be inefficient.

58. In saying this, we agree with Sugden (2018) that we would like to see the end of obligatory sections in economics articles of "policy recommendations" that are not directed to any actual agency that could feasibly implement them. Even if all economics is deeply conditioned by practical concerns, many specific exercises in economics are not practical, and it does no favors to our professional reputation to pretend otherwise.

59. See Kacelnik and Bateson (1996), Bshary (2001), and Chittka (2022).

ACKNOWLEDGEMENTS

We are grateful to Jimmy Martínez-Correa, Karlijn Morsink, Jia Min Ng, and Elisabet Rutström for helpful discussions.

REFERENCES

Adler, M. D. (2012). *Well-being and fair distribution: beyond cost-benefit analysis*. New York, NY: Oxford University Press.

Adler, M. D. (2019). *Measuring social welfare: An introduction*. New York, NY: Oxford University Press.

Afriat, S. N. (1972). Efficiency estimation of production function. *International Economic Review*, *13*(3), 568–598.

Ainslie, G. (1992). *Picoeconomics*. New York, NY: Cambridge University Press.

Ainslie, G. (2001). *Breakdown of Will*. New York, NY: Cambridge University Press.

Alekseev, A., Harrison, G., Lau, M. I., & Ross, D. (2018). *Deciphering the noise: The welfare costs of noisy behavior*. CEAR Working Paper 2018-0. Center for the Economic Analysis of Risk, Robinson College of Business, Georgia State University, Atlanta, GA.

Allen, F. (1987). Discovering personal probabilities when utility functions are unknown. *Management Science*, *33*(4), 452–454.
Ambuehl, S., Bernheim, B. D., Ersoy, F., & Harris, D. (2018). *Peer advice on financial decisions: A case of the blind leading the blind?* Working Paper 25034. National Bureau of Economic Research.
Ambuehl, S., Bernheim, B. D., & Lusardi, A. (2014). *The effect of financial education on the quality of decision making*. Working Paper 20618. National Bureau of Economic Research.
Ambuehl, S., Bernheim, B. D., & Lusardi, A. (2022). Evaluating deliberative competence: A simple method with an application to financial choice. *American Economic Review*, *112*(11), 3584–3626.
Ambuehl, S. Bernheim, B. D., & Lusardi, A. (2017). *A method for evaluating the quality of financial decision making, with an application to financial education*. Working Paper 20618, National Bureau of Economic Research.
Andersen, S., Cox, J. C., Harrison, G. W., Lau, M. I., Rutström, E. E., & Sadiraj, V. (2018). Asset integration and attitudes to risk: Theory and evidence. *Review of Economics & Statistics*, *100*(5), 816–830.
Andersen, S., Fountain, J., Harrison, G. W., & Rutström, E. E. (2014). Estimating subjective probabilities. *Journal of Risk & Uncertainty*, *48*, 207–229.
Andersen, S., Harrison, G. W., Lau, M. I., & Rutström, E. E. (2008b). Lost in state space: Are preferences stable? *International Economic Review*, *49*(3), 1091–1112.
Andersen, S., Harrison, G. W., Lau, M. I., & Rutström, E. E. (2006). Elicitation using multiple price list formats. *Experimental Economics*, *9*(4), 383–405.
Andersen, S., Harrison, G. W., Lau, M. I., & Rutström, E. E. (2008a). Eliciting risk and time preferences. *Econometrica*, *76*(3), 583–618.
Andersen, S., Harrison, G. W., Lau, M. I., & Rutström, E. E. (2013). Discounting behavior and the magnitude effect: Evidence from a field experiment in Denmark. *Economica*, *80*, 670–697.
Andersen, S., Harrison, G. W., Lau, M. I., & Rutström, E. E. (2014). Discounting behavior: A reconsideration. *European Economic Review*, *71*, 15–33.
Andersen, S., Harrison, G. W., Lau, M. I., & Rutström, E. E. (2018). Multiattribute utility theory, intertemporal utility, and correlation aversion. *International Economic Review*, *59*(2), 537–555.
Applebaum, B. (2019). *The economists' hour*. Boston, MA: Little, Brown.
Armitage, P. (1985). The search for optimality in clinical trials. *International Statistical Review*, *53*(1), 15–24.
Atkinson, A. B. (2001). The strange disappearance of welfare economics. *Kyklos*, *54*(2/3), 193–206.
Atkinson, A. B. (2009). Economics as a moral science. *Economica*, *76*, 791–804.
Atkinson, A. B. (2011). The restoration of welfare economics. *American Economic Review (Papers & Proceedings)*, *101*(3), 157–161.
Baily, M. N. (1978). Some aspects of optimal unemployment insurance. *Journal of Public Economics*, *10*(3), 379–402.
Bell, D. (1982). Regret in decision making under uncertainty. *Operations Research*, *20*, 961–981.
Bell, D. (1985). Disappointment in decision making under uncertainty. *Operations Research*, *33*, 1–27.
Berman, E. (2022). *Thinking like an economist: How efficiency replaced equality in U.S. public policy*. Princeton, NJ: Princeton University Press.
Bernheim, B. D. (2009). Behavioral welfare economics. *Journal of the European Economic Association*, *7*(2–3), 267–319.
Bernheim, B. D. (2016). The good, the bad, and the ugly: A unified approach to behavioral welfare economics. *Journal of Benefit-Cost Analysis*, *7*(1), 12–68.
Bernheim, B. D., Fradkin, A., & Popov, I. (2015). The welfare economics of default options in 401(k) plans. *American Economic Review*, *105*(9), 2798–2837.
Bernheim, B. D., & Rangel, A. (2004). Addiction and cue-triggered addiction processes. *American Economic Review*, *94*, 1558–1590.
Bernheim, B. D., & Rangel, A. (2009). Beyond revealed preference: Choice-theoretic foundations for behavioral welfare economics. *Quarterly Journal of Economics*, *124*(1), 51–104.
Bernheim, B. D., & Rangel, A. (2018). Choice-theoretic foundations for behavioral welfare economics. In A. Caplin & A. Schotter (Eds.), *The foundations of positive and normative economics: A handbook* (pp. 155–192). New York, NY: Oxford University Press.

Bernheim, B. D., & Taubinksy, D. (2018). Behavioral public economics. In B. D. Bernheim, S. Della Vigna, & D. Laibson (Eds.), *Handbook of behavioral economics* (Vol. 1, pp. 381–516). New York, NY: Elsevier.

Berry, D. A., & Fristedt, B. (Eds.). (1985). *Bandit problems: Sequential allocation of experiments*. New York, NY: Springer.

Binmore, K. (1994). *Game theory and the social contract, Volume: 1: Playing fair*. Cambridge MA: MIT Press.

Binmore, K. (1998). *Game theory and the social contract, Volume 2: Just playing*. Cambridge, MA: MIT Press.

Binmore, K. (2005). *Natural justice*. New York, NY: Oxford University Press.

Binmore, K. (2009). *Rational decisions*. Princeton, NJ: Princeton University Press.

Bleichrodt, H., Pinto, J. L., & Wakker, P. P. (2001). Making descriptive use of prospect theory to improve the prescriptive use of expected utility. *Management Science*, *47*, 1498–1514.

Blundell, R., Pistaferri, L., & Preston, I. (2008). Consumption inequality and partial insurance. *American Economic Review*, *98*(5), 1887–1921.

Boadway, R., & Bruce, N. (1984). *Welfare economics*. New York, NY: Blackwell.

Bshary, R. (2001). The cleaner fish market. In R. Noë, J. van Hooff, & P. Hammerstein (Eds.), *Economics in nature* (pp. 146–172). New York, NY: Cambridge University Press.

Buchak, L. (2013). *Risk and rationality*. New York, NY: Oxford University Press.

Camerer, C., Issacharoff, S., Loewenstein, G., O'Donoghue, T., & Rabin, M. (2003). Regulation for conservatives: Behavioral economics and the case for asymmetric paternalism. *University of Pennsylvania Law Review*, *151*, 1211–1254.

Camerer, C., Loewenstein, G., & Prelec, D. (2005). Neuroeconomics: How neuroscience can inform economics. *Journal of Economic Literature*, *43*, 9–64.

Caporael, L., Griesemer, J., & Wimsatt, W. (Eds.). (2014). *Developing scaffolds in evolution, culture, and cognition*. Cambridge, MA: MIT Press.

Caria, S., Gordon, G., Kasy, M., Quinn, S., Shami, S., & Teytelboym, A. (2020). *An adaptive targeted field experiment: Job search assistance for refugees in Jordan*. Draft Working Paper. Oxford University. Retrieved from https://maxkasy.github.io/home/research/

Chambers, C., & Echenique, F. (2016). *Revealed preference theory*. New York, NY: Cambridge University Press.

Chater, N. (2018). *The mind is flat*. New Haven, CT: Yale University Press.

Cherry, T., Crocker, T., & Shogren, J. (2003). Rationality spillovers. *Journal of Environmental Economics and Management*, *45*, 63–84.

Chetty, R. (2006). A general formula for the optimal level of social insurance. *Journal of Public Economics*, *90*(10–11), 1879–1901.

Chetty, R., & Looney, A. (2006). Consumption smoothing and the welfare consequences of social insurance in developing countries. *Journal of Public Economics*, *90*, 2351–2356.

Chittka, L. (2022). *The mind of a bee*. Princeton, NJ: Princeton University Press.

Chuang, Y., & Schechter, L. (2015). Stability of experimental and survey measures of risk, time and social preferences: A review and some new results. *Journal of Development Economics*, *117*, 151–170.

Clark, A. (1998). *Being there*. Cambridge, MA: MIT Press.

Coleman, W. (2002). *Economics and its enemies: Two centuries of anti-economics*. New York, NY: Palgrave Macmillan.

Coller, M., & Williams, M. B. (1999). Eliciting individual discount rates. *Experimental Economics*, *2*(2), 107–127.

Collins, D., Morduch, J., Rutherford, S., & Ruthven, O. (2009). *Portfolios of the poor: How the world's poor live on $2 a day*. Princeton, NJ: Princeton University Press.

Cox, J. C., & Sadiraj, V. (2006). Small- and large-stakes risk aversion: Implications of concavity calibration for decision theory. *Games and Economic Behavior*, *56*, 45–60.

de Haan, T., & Linde, J. (2018). 'Good nudge lullaby': Choice architecture and default bias reinforcement. *Economic Journal*, *128*(610), 1180–1206.

Dennett, D. (1971). Intentional systems. *The Journal of Philosophy*, *68*(4), 87–106.

Dennett, D. (1987). *The intentional stance*. Cambridge, MA: MIT Press.

Dennett, D. (1991). *Consciousness explained*. Boston, MA: Little, Brown.

Dennett, D. (2017). *From bacteria to Bach and back: The evolution of minds*. New York, NY: W.W. Norton and Company.
Dowding, K., & Taylor, B. (2019). *Economic perspectives on government*. New York, NY: Palgrave Macmillan.
Duflo, E. (2017). The economist as plumber. *American Economic Review, 107*, 1–26.
Feldman, R., & Dowd, B. (1991). A new estimate of the welfare loss of excess health insurance. *American Economic Review, 81*(1), 297–301.
Feldstein, M. S. (1973). The welfare loss of excess health insurance. *Journal of Political Economy, 81*(2), 251–280.
Fishburn, P. C. (1982). Nontransitive measurable utility. *Journal of Mathematical Psychology, 26*, 31–67.
Ford, K., & Pylyshyn, Z. (Eds.). (1996). *The robot's dilemma revisited*. New York, NY: Praeger.
Friedman, M. (1953). *Essays in positive economics*. Chicago, IL: University of Chicago Press.
Gao, X. S., Harrison, G. W., & Tchernis, R. (2023). Behavioral welfare economics and risk preferences: A Bayesian approach. *Experimental Economics, 26*, 273–303
Gigerenzer, G., Todd, P., & The ABC Research Group. (1999). *Simple heuristics that make us smart*. New York, NY: Oxford University Press.
Glennerster, R. (2017). The practicalities of running randomized evaluations: Partnerships, measurement, ethics, and transparency. In A. Banerjee & E. Duflo (Eds.), *Handbook of field experiments: Volume One*. Amsterdam: North-Holland.
Gomes, F., & Michaeldes, A. (2005). Optimal life-cycle asset allocation: Understanding the empirical evidence. *Journal of Finance, 60*, 869–904.
Grüne-Yanoff, T., & Hertwig, R. (2016). Nudge *vs*. boost: How coherent are policy and theory? *Minds and Machines, 26*, 149–183.
Gul, F. (1991). A theory of disappointment aversion. *Econometrica, 59*, 667–686.
Gul, F., & Pesendorfer, W. (2008). The case for mindless economics. In A. Caplin & A. Schotter (Eds.), *The foundations of positive and normative economics: A handbook* (pp. 3–39). New York, NY: Oxford University Press.
Hadad, V., Hirshberg, D. A., Zhan, R., Wager, S., & Athey, S. (2021). Confidence intervals for policy evaluation in adaptive experiments. *Proceedings of the National Academy of Sciences, 118*(15), e2014602118. doi:10.1073/pnas.2014602118
Handel, B. R. (2013). Adverse selection and inertia in health insurance markets: When nudging hurts. *American Economic Review, 103*(7), 2643–2682.
Handel, B. R., & Kolstad, J. T. (2015). Health insurance for 'humans': Information frictions, plan choice, and consumer welfare. *American Economic Review, 105*(8), 2449–2500.
Hands, D. W. (2013). Foundations of contemporary revealed preference theory. *Erkenntnis, 78*, 1081–1108.
Hansson, B. (1988). Risk aversion as a problem of conjoint measurement. In P. Gardenfors & N.-E. Sahlin (Eds.), *Decisions, probability, and utility* (pp. 136–158). New York, NY: Cambridge University Press.
Harrison, G. W. (1992). Theory and misbehavior of first-price auctions: Reply. *American Economic Review, 82*, 1426–1443.
Harrison, G. W. (1994). Expected utility theory and the experimentalists. *Empirical Economics, 19*(2), 223–253.
Harrison, G. W. (2008). Neuroeconomics: A critical reconsideration. *Economics & Philosophy, 24*(3), 303–344.
Harrison, G. W. (2011a). Randomisation and its discontents. *Journal of African Economies, 20*(4), 626–652.
Harrison, G. W. (2011b). Experimental methods and the welfare evaluation of policy lotteries. *European Review of Agricultural Economics, 38*(3), 335–360.
Harrison, G. W. (2014). Impact evaluation and welfare evaluation. *European Journal of Development Research, 26*, 39–45.
Harrison, G. W. (2019). The behavioral welfare economics of insurance. *Geneva Risk & Insurance Review, 44*(2), 137–175.
Harrison, G. W. (2021). Experimental design and Bayesian interpretation. In H. Kincaid & D. Ross (Eds.), *Modern guide to the philosophy of economics* (pp. 66–89). Cheltenham: Elgar.

Harrison, G. W., Jensen, J., Lau, M. I., & Rutherford, T. F. (2002). Policy reform without tears. In A. Fossati & W. Weigard (Eds.), *Policy evaluation with computable general equilibrium models* (pp. 20–38). New York, NY: Routledge.

Harrison, G. W., Johnson, E., McInnes, M., & Rutström, E. E. (2005). Temporal stability of estimates of risk aversion. *Applied Financial Economics Letters, 1*, 31–35.

Harrison, G. W., Lau, M. I., Ross, D., & Swarthout, J. T. (2017). Small stakes risk aversion in experiments: A reconsideration. *Economics Letters, 160*, 24–28.

Harrison, G. W., Lau, M. I., & Yoo, H. I. (2020). Risk attitudes, sample selection and attrition in a longitudinal field experiment. *Review of Economics & Statistics, 102*(3), 552–568.

Harrison, G. W., Martínez-Correa, J., & Swarthout, J. T. (2014). Eliciting subjective probabilities with binary lotteries. *Journal of Economic Behavior and Organization, 101*, 128–140.

Harrison, G. W., Martínez-Correa, J., & Swarthout, J. T. (2015). Reduction of compound lotteries with objective probabilities: Theory and evidence. *Journal of Economic Behavior & Organization, 119*, 32–55.

Harrison, G. W., Martínez-Correa, J., Swarthout, J. T., & Ulm, E. (2015). Eliciting subjective probability distributions with binary lotteries. *Economics Letters, 127*, 68–71.

Harrison, G. W., Martínez-Correa, J., Swarthout, J. T., & Ulm, E. (2017). Scoring rules for subjective probability distributions. *Journal of Economic Behavior & Organization, 134*, 430–448.

Harrison, G. W., Morsink, K., & Schneider, M. (2022). Literacy and the quality of index insurance decisions. *Geneva Risk and Insurance Review, 47*, 66–97.

Harrison, G. W., Morsink, K., & Schneider, M. (2020). *Do no harm? The welfare consequences of behavioral interventions*. CEAR Working Paper 2020-12. Center for the Economic Analysis of Risk, Robinson College of Business, Georgia State University, Atlanta, GA.

Harrison, G. W., & Ng, J. M. (2016). Evaluating the expected welfare gain from insurance. *Journal of Risk and Insurance, 83*(1), 91–120.

Harrison, G. W., & Ng, J. M. (2018). Welfare effects of insurance contract non-performance. *Geneva Risk and Insurance Review, 43*(1), 39–76.

Harrison, G. W., & Ross, D. (2016). The psychology of human risk preferences and vulnerability to scare-mongers: Experimental economic tools for hypothesis formulation and testing. *Journal of Cognition and Culture, 16*, 383–414.

Harrison, G. W., & Ross, D. (2017). The empirical adequacy of cumulative prospect theory and its implications for normative assessment. *Journal of Economic Methodology, 24*(2), 150–165.

Harrison, G. W., & Ross, D. (2018). The methodologies of neuroeconomics. *Journal of Economic Methodology, 17*, 185–196.

Harrison, G. W., & Ross, D. (2018). Varieties of paternalism and the heterogeneity of utility structures. *Journal of Economic Methodology, 25*(1), 42–67.

Harrison, G. W., & Rutherford, T. F. (1999). Burden sharing, joint implementation, and carbon coalitions. In C. Carraro (Ed.), *International environmental agreements on climate change* (pp. 77–108). Amsterdam: Kluwer.

Harrison, G. W., Rutherford, T. F., & Tarr, D. G. (1997). Quantifying the Uruguay round. *Economic Journal, 107*, 1405–1430.

Harrison, G. W., Rutherford, T. F., & Tarr, D. G. (2003). Trade liberalization, poverty and efficient equity. *Journal of Development Economics, 71*, 97–128.

Harrison, G. W., Rutherford, T. F., & Wooton, I. (1993). An alternative welfare decomposition for customs unions. *Canadian Journal of Economics, 26*(4), 961–968.

Harrison, G. W., & Rutström, E. E. (2008). Risk aversion in the laboratory. In J. C. Cox & G. W. Harrison (Eds.), *Risk aversion in experiments* (Research in Experimental Economics Vol. 12, pp. 41–196). Bingley: Emerald.

Harrison, G. W., & Rutström, E. E. (2009). Expected utility and prospect theory: One wedding and a decent funeral. *Experimental Economics, 12*(2), 133–158.

Harrison, G. W., & Swarthout, J. T. (2023). Cumulative prospect theory in the laboratory: A reconsideration. In G. W. Harrison & D. Ross (Eds.), *Models of risk preferences: Descriptive and normative challenges* (Research in Experimental Economics, Vol. 22 pp. 107–192). Bingley: Emerald.

Hausman, D. (2011). *Preference, value, choice and welfare*. New York, NY: Cambridge University Press.

Hertwig, R., Hoffrage, U., & The ABC Research Group. (2013). *Simple heuristics in a social world*. New York, NY: Oxford University Press.

Hey, J. D. (2005). Why we should not be silent about noise. *Experimental Economics*, *8*(4), 325–345.

Hood, B. (2012). *The self illusion*. New York, NY: Oxford University Press.

Hossain, T., & Okui, R. (2013). The binarized scoring rule. *Review of Economic Studies*, *80*, 984–991.

Infante, G., Lecouteux, G., & Sugden, R. (2016). Preference purification and the inner rational agent: A critique of the conventional wisdom of behavioral welfare economics. *Journal of Economic Methodology*, *23*, 1–25.

Kacelnik, A., & Bateson, M. (1996). Risky theories? The effects of variance on foraging decisions. *American Zoologist*, *36*(4), 402–434.

Kahneman, D., Slovic, P., & Tversky, A. (Eds.). (1982). *Judgment under uncertainty: Heuritics and biases*. New York, NY: Cambridge University Press.

Kahneman, D., & Tversky, A. (1979). Prospect theory: An analysis of decision under risk. *Econometrica*, *47*, 263–291.

Karlan, D., & Appel, J. (2011). *More than good intentions: Improving the ways the world's poor borrow, save, farm, learn, and stay healthy*. New York, NY: Dutton.

Kasy, M., & Sautmann, A. (2021). Adaptive treatment assignment in experiments for policy choice. *Econometrica*, *89*(1), 113–132.

Keynes, J. M. (1936). Economic possibilities for our grand-children. Reprinted in J. M. Keynes, *Essays in persuasion* (pp. 358–373). New York, NY: Norton (1963).

Ladyman, J., & Ross, D. (2007). *Every thing must go: Metaphysics naturalised*. Oxford: Oxford University Press.

Leamer, E. E. (1978). *Specification searches: Ad hoc inference with nonexperimental data*. New York, NY: Wiley.

Leamer, E. E. (2010). Tantalus on the road to asymptopia. *Journal of Economic Perspectives*, *24*(2), 31–46.

Leamer, E. E. (2012). *The craft of economics*. Cambridge, MA: MIT Press.

Loomes, G., & Sugden, R. (1982). Regret theory: An alternative theory of rational choice under uncertainty. *Economic Journal*, *92*, 805–824.

Loomes, G., & Sugden, R. (1987). Some implications of a more general form of regret theory. *Journal of Economic Theory*, *41*(2), 270–287.

Lyons, W. (1986). *The disappearance of introspection*. Cambridge, MA: MIT Press.

Machina, M. J. (1987). Choice under uncertainty: Problems solved and unsolved. *Journal of Economic Perspectives*, *1*(1), 121–154.

Machina, M. J., & Schmeidler, D. (1992). A more robust definition of subjective probability. *Econometrica*, *60*(4), 745–780.

Machina, M. J., & Schmeidler, D. (1995). Bayes without Bernoulli: Simple conditions for probabilistically sophisticated choice. *Journal of Economic Theory*, *67*(1), 106–128.

Mäki, U. (Ed.). (2009). *The methodology of positive economics: Reflections on the Milton Friedman legacy*. New York, NY: Cambridge University Press.

Manzini, P., & Mariotti, M. (2012). Categorize then choose: Boundedly rational choice and welfare. *Journal of the European Economic Association*, *10*(5), 1141–1165.

Manzini, P., & Mariotti, M. (2014). Welfare economics and bounded rationality: The case for model-based approaches. *Journal of Economic Methodology*, *21*, 343–360.

Marglin, S. (2008). *The dismal science: How thinking like an economist undermines community*. Cambridge, MA: Harvard University Press.

Matsuda, A., Takahashi, K., & Ikegami, M. (2019). Direct and indirect impact of index-based livestock insurance in Southern Ethiopia. *Geneva Papers on Risk and Insurance: Issues and Practice*, *44*, 481–502.

McGeer, V. (2001). Psycho-practice, psycho-theory, and the contrastive case of autism: How processes of mind become second nature. *Journal of Consciousness Studies*, *8*, 109–132.

McGeer, V. (2002). Enculturating folk-psychologists. *Synthese*, *199*, 1039–1063.

McKelvey, R. D., & Page, T. (1990). Public and private information: An experimental study of information pooling. *Econometrica*, *58*(6), 1321–1339.

Nichols, S., & Stich, S. (2003). *Mindreading*. New York, NY: Oxford University Press.

Nussbaum, M. (1997). *Cultivating humanity*. New York, NY: Cambridge University Press.

Ortmann, A. (2021). On the foundations of behavioural and experimental economics. In H. Kincaid & D. Ross (Eds.), *A modern guide to philosophy of economics* (pp. 157–181). Northampton, MA: Edward Elgar.

Peto, R. (1985). Discussion of papers by J. A. Bather and P. Armitage. *International Statistical Review*, *53*(1), 31–34.

Pettigrew, R. (2016). Risk, rationality, and expected utility theory. *Canadian Journal of Philosophy*, *45*, 798–826.

Pylyshyn, Z. (Ed.). (1987). *The robot's dilemma*. Norwood, NJ: Ablex.

Rabin, M. (2000). Risk aversion and expected utility theory: A calibration theorem. *Econometrica*, *68*, 1281–1292.

Robbins, L. (1935). *An essay on the nature and significance of economic science* (2nd ed.). London: Macmillan.

Rosenberg, A. (1992). *Economics: Mathematical politics or science of diminishing returns?* Chicago, IL: University of Chicago Press.

Ross, D. (2005). *Economic theory and cognitive science: Microexplanation*. Cambridge, MA: MIT Press.

Ross, D. (2011). Hayek's speculative psychology, the neuroscience of value estimation, and the basis of normative individualism. In L. Marsh (Ed.), *Hayek in Mind: Hayek's Philosophical Psychology* (pp. 51–72). Bingley: Emerald.

Ross, D. (2012). Economic theory, anti-economics and political ideology. In U. Mäki (Ed.), *Handbook of the philosophy of science, Volume 13: Economics* (pp. 241–285). Amsterdam: Elsevier.

Ross, D. (2014). *Philosophy of economics*. London: Palgrave Macmillan.

Ross, D. (2020). Addiction is socially engineered exploitation of natural biological vulnerability. *Behavioral Brain Research*, *386*, 1–8.

Ross, D. (2023). Neo-Samuelsonian methodology, normative economics, and the quantitative intentional stance. In B. Caldwell, J. Davis, U. Mäki, & E. Sent (Eds.), *Methodology and history of economics* (pp. 90–116). New York, NY: Routledge.

Ross, D., & Stirling, W. (2021). Economics, social neuroscience, and mindshaping. In J. Harbecke & C. Herrmann-Pillath (Eds.), *Social neuroeconomics* (pp. 147–202). London: Routledge.

Ross, D., & Townshend, M. (2021). Everyday economics. In H. Kincaid & D. Ross (Eds.), *A modern guide to philosophy of economics* (pp. 344–370). Cheltenham: Edward Elgar.

Routledge, B. R., & Zin, S. E. (2010). Generalized disappointment aversion and asset prices. *Journal of Finance*, *65*(4), 1303–1332.

Rubinstein, A., & Salant, Y. (2012). Eliciting welfare preferences from behavioral datasets. *Review of Economic Studies*, *79*, 375–387.

Salant, Y., & Rubinstein, A. (2008). (A,f): Choice with frames. *Review of Economic Studies*, *75*(4), 1287–1296.

Samphantharak, K., & Townsend, R. M. (2010). *Households as corporate firms: An analysis of household finance using integrated household surveys and corporate financial accounting*. New York, NY: Cambridge University Press.

Savage, L. J. (1954). *The foundations of statistics* (2nd ed.). New York, NY: Wiley.

Savage, L. J. (1962a). Subjective probability and statistical practice. In G. A. Barnard & D. R. Cox (Eds.), *The foundations of statistical inference: A discussion* (pp. 9–35). New York, NY: Wiley.

Savage, L. J. (1962b). Discussion. In G. A. Barnard & D. R. Cox (Eds.), *The foundations of statistical inference: A discussion* (pp. 62–103). New York, NY: Wiley.

Schelling, T. (1978). Economics, or the art of self-management. *American Economic Review (Papers & Proceedings)*, *68*(2), 290–294.

Schelling, T. (1980). The intimate contest for self-command. *Public Interest*, *60*, 94–118.

Schelling, T. (1984). Self-command in practice, in policy, and in a theory of rational choice. *American Economic Review (Papers & Proceedings)*, *74*(2), 1–11.

Schmidt, U., & Zank, H. (2008). Risk aversion in cumulative prospect theory. *Management Science*, *54*, 208–216.

Schwitzgebel, E. (2011). *Perplexities of consciousness*. Cambridge, MA: MIT Press.

Simon, H. (1955). A behavioral model of rational choice. *Quarterly Journal of Economics*, *69*, 99–118.

Smith, V. L. (2007). *Rationality in economics*. New York, NY: Cambridge University Press.

Spivey, M. (2020). *Who you are*. Cambridge, MA: MIT Press.

Starmer, C. (2000). Developments in non-expected utility theory: The hunt for a descriptive theory of choice under risk. *Journal of Economic Literature*, *38*, 332–382.

Sugden, R. (2004). The opportunity criterion: Consumer sovereignty without the assumption of coherent preferences. *American Economic Review*, *94*(4), 1014–1033.

Sugden, R. (2009). Market simulation and the provision of public goods: A non-paternalistic response to anomalies in environmental evaluation. *Journal of Environmental Economics and Management*, *57*, 87–103.

Sugden, R. (2018). *The community of advantage: A behavioral economist's defence of the market*. New York, NY: Oxford University Press.

Sugden, R. (2021). A response to six comments on *the community of advantage*. *Journal of Economic Methodology*, *28*(4), 419–430.

Sunstein, C. R. (2021). Voluntary agreements. *Journal of Economic Methodology*, *28*(4), 401–408.

Sunstein, C. R., & Thaler, R. H. (2003a). Libertarian paternalism. *American Economic Review (Papers & Proceedings)*, *93*, 175–179.

Sunstein, C. R., & Thaler, R. H. (2003b). Libertarian paternalism is not an oxymoron. *University of Chicago Law Review*, *70*, 1159–1202.

Teele, D. L. (2014). Reflections on the ethics of field experiments. In D. Teele (Ed.), *Field experiments and their critics: Essays on the uses and abuses of experimentation in the social sciences* (pp. 115–140). New Haven, NJ: Yale University Press.

Tiberius, V. (2010). *The reflective life*. New York, NY: Oxford University Press.

Tiberius, V., & Plakias, A. (2010). Well-being. In J. Doris & the Moral Psychology Research Group (Eds.), *The moral psychology handbook* (pp. 402–432). New York, NY: Oxford University Press.

Townsend, R. M. (1994). Risk and insurance in village India. *Econometrica*, *62*(3), 539–591.

Tversky, A., & Kahneman, D. (1992). Advances in prospect theory: Cumulative representations of uncertainty. *Journal of Risk & Uncertainty*, *5*, 297–323.

Wakker, P. P. (2010). *Prospect theory for risk and ambiguity*. New York, NY: Cambridge University Press.

Wilcox, N. T. (2008). Stochastic models for binary discrete choice under risk: A critical primer and econometric comparison. In J. C. Cox & G. W. Harrison (Eds.), *Risk aversion in experiments* (Research in Experimental Economics, Vol. 12). Bingley: Emerald.

Wilcox, N. T. (2011). 'Stochastically more risk averse:' A contextual theory of stochastic discrete choice under risk. *Journal of Econometrics*, *162*(1), 89–104.

Williams, B. (1981). *Moral luck*. New York, NY: Cambridge University Press.

Williams, B. (2006). *Philosophy as a humanistic discipline*. Princeton, NJ: Princeton University Press.

Wilson, M. (2006). *Wandering significance*. New York, NY: Oxford University Press.

Wolpin, K. I. (2013). *The limits of inference without theory*. Cambridge, MA: MIT Press.

Yarkoni, T. (2022). The generalizability crisis. *Behavioral and Brain Sciences*, *45*, e1. https://doi.org/10.1017/S0140525X20001685

Zawidzki, T. (2013). *Mindshaping*. Cambridge, MA: MIT Press.

CHAPTER 2

UNUSUAL ESTIMATES OF PROBABILITY WEIGHTING FUNCTIONS

Nathaniel T. Wilcox

ABSTRACT

The author presents new estimates of the probability weighting functions found in rank-dependent theories of choice under risk. These estimates are unusual in two senses. First, they are free of functional form assumptions about both utility and weighting functions, and they are entirely based on binary discrete choices and not on matching or valuation tasks, though they depend on assumptions concerning the nature of probabilistic choice under risk. Second, estimated weighting functions contradict widely held priors of an inverse-s shape with fixed point well in the interior of the (0,1) interval: Instead the author usually finds populations dominated by "optimists" who uniformly overweight best outcomes in risky options. The choice pairs used here mostly do not provoke similarity-based simplifications. In a third experiment, the author shows that the presence of choice pairs that provoke similarity-based computational shortcuts does indeed flatten estimated probability weighting functions.

Keywords: Prospect theory; probability weighting; probabilistic choice; rank-dependent utility; risk; similarity

The probability weighting function of the rank-dependent family of choice theories is widely believed to follow an "inverse-s" shape on the unit square – rising

Models of Risk Preferences: Descriptive and Normative Challenges
Research in Experimental Economics, Volume 22, 69–106

ISSN: 0193-2306/doi:10.1108/S0193-230620230000022002

steeply at first but concave enough so that it crosses the 45° line from above (usually around a third or so though some report estimates near a half) and thereafter becoming convex and accelerating upward to the unit point (e.g., Prelec, 1998; Tversky & Kahneman, 1992). This belief is so widely and strongly held that many contemporary empirical scholars impose this shape a priori on their estimates of the weighting function (e.g., Nilsson et al., 2011; Scheibehenne & Pachur, 2015). Occasionally contrary evidence appears in the empirical literature (e.g., Harrison & Swarthout, this volume), but the vast majority of researchers strongly believe the inverse-s shape holds with a fixed point well inside the interior of the (0,1) interval.

This inverse-s shape explains the well-known Allais phenomena, but so does a strictly concave "optimist" shape (Quiggin, 1993). Moreover, there has long been an alternative explanation for the same phenomena based on similarity judgments, frequently associated with Rubinstein (1988) and Leland (1994) but harking back to well-known work by Tversky (1969). Some widely accepted aspects of the probability weighting function might be due to similarity-induced flattening of apparent probability weighting. If so, we might expect to estimate markedly different weighting functions when we confine decision-makers' choices to option pairs less likely to bring similarity judgments into play. I explore this and find support for it.

I perform three new risky choice experiments in which the chance device is a single roll of either a 6-sided, 4-sided or 12-sided die. In the first two experiments this confines outcome probabilities to a relatively coarse grid (sixths in the first experiment, fourths in the second), so that option pairs rarely present subjects with easy opportunities to exploit similarity-based procedures that ignore small probability differences and bypass a full judgment that weights utilities of outcomes by probability weights. The 12-sided die used for the third experiment helps to clinch this interpretation of the results. I usually find that the plurality type of decision-maker is an optimist – a person whose probability weighting function exceeds all true probabilities of the high outcome used in the experiment (in the second experiment, using the 4-sided die, they are an outright majority). This is not the received shape of the probability weighting function.

Note that the data from these three experiments are wholly discrete choices from pairs of risky options. In particular, no valuation tasks or certainty equivalent elicitations are used here. Most evidence for the inverse-s shape and its associated fourfold pattern of risk aversion comes from elicited certainty equivalents (e.g., Abdellaoui, 2000; Abdellaoui, Bleichrodt, & Paraschiv, 2007; Bruhin, Fehr-Duda, & Epper, 2010; Gonzalez & Wu, 1999; Tversky & Kahneman, 1992), and Wilcox (2017) puts the interpretation of all such evidence in doubt. Moreover, the estimates of probability weights I report here are wholly free of functional form assumptions concerning both outcome utilities and probability weights, using an approach like that of Hey et al. (2010) and Blavatskyy (2013). As mentioned earlier, many studies based on discrete choice from pairs of options impose the inverse-s shape of the weighting function a priori. When we remove studies based on certainty equivalents and do not consider studies that impose it *a priori*, there is remarkably little consistent evidence for the inverse-s shape that does not also support the optimist shape.

My estimates do depend on assumptions about the probabilistic nature of discrete choice under risk. To guard against the possibility that the results crucially depend on those assumptions, I perform the estimations with three recent but different models of probabilistic choice under risk, all of which have been shown to perform better than older models. The results are, for the most part, insensitive to the choice of one of these models or another. Optimistic decision weights appear to be the norm in my experiments that are relatively free of similarity-based opportunities for choice simplification.

1. PRELIMINARIES

In general, the notation (q_l,q_m,q_h) denotes an option's probability distribution on a vector $\langle l,m,h \rangle$ of three outcomes which I call the *context* of a choice pair. In the first experiment, each choice pair is a set $\{risky, safe\} \equiv \{(1-q_h,0,q_h),(0,1,0)\}$ of two options on a context $\langle l,m,h \rangle$. The option *safe* = (0,1,0) pays m dollars with certainty, while the option *risky* = $(1-q_h,0,q_h)$ pays h dollars with probability q_h and l dollars with probability $1-q_h$, where $h > m > l \geq$ US$40. Subjects choose between *risky* and *safe* in each pair presented to them.

The instructions to subjects in Appendix 3 show a pair where {*risky, safe*} is {(5/6,0,1/6),(0,1,0)} on the context ⟨40,50,90⟩. Table 1 shows the 100 choice pairs used in the first experiment, organized into groups of four pairs (the rows of the table) by their shared context. All *risky* lotteries are chances q_h and $1-q_h$ (in sixths, generated by a 6-sided die) of receiving high and low outcomes h and l on the context, respectively: Four values of q_h, shown on each row in Table 1 (q_h^a, q_h^b, q_h^c and q_h^d) create four *risky* lotteries on each context, and each of these is paired with *safe* (the middle outcome m of the context, paid with certainty) to create four pairs on the context. There are 25 contexts built from the nine positive money outcomes $40, $50, …, $120.

The subjects in the first experiment were 80 undergraduates at the University of Houston, recruited widely by means of a single e-mail to all undergraduates. Each subject was individually scheduled for three separate sessions on three separate days of their own choosing, almost always finishing all three sessions within a week. Only rarely did any day's session last more than an hour, and most sessions were substantially shorter than this. On each day, each subject made choices from the 100 choice pairs shown in Table 1, so that each made 300 choices in all by the end of their third day. On each day, for each subject, the 100 choice pairs were randomly ordered into two halves of 50 pairs each, separated by about 10–15minutes of other tasks (a survey and tests of arithmetic and problem-solving ability). A computer presented each choice pair, one pair at a time on each screen: Call this *separated decisions* or SED.

To conclude each subject's third day, one of their 300 chosen options was selected at random (by means of the subject drawing a ticket from a bag of 300 numbered tickets) to determine the subject's payment: Call this *random problem selection* or RPS. If the subject's selected option was *risky*, the subject picked a 6-sided die from a box of 6-sided dice (rolling them until satisfied if they wished),

Table 1. The 100 Option Pairs of the First Experiment.

	Contexts $\langle l,m,h \rangle$	Four Pairs			
		q_h^a	q_h^b	q_h^c	q_h^d
1	⟨40,50,60⟩	5/6	4/6	3/6	2/6
2	⟨40,50,70⟩	5/6	4/6	3/6	2/6
3	⟨40,50,80⟩	4/6	3/6	2/6	1/6
4	⟨40,50,90⟩	4/6	3/6	2/6	1/6
5	⟨40,60,100⟩	4/6	3/6	2/6	1/6
6	⟨40,60,110⟩	4/6	3/6	2/6	1/6
7	⟨40,60,120⟩	4/6	3/6	2/6	1/6
8	⟨50,60,90⟩	4/6	3/6	2/6	1/6
9	⟨50,70,100⟩	5/6	4/6	3/6	2/6
10	⟨50,70,110⟩	4/6	3/6	2/6	1/6
11	⟨50,70,120⟩	4/6	3/6	2/6	1/6
12	⟨60,70,90⟩	5/6	4/6	3/6	2/6
13	⟨60,80,110⟩	5/6	4/6	3/6	2/6
14	⟨60,80,120⟩	4/6	3/6	2/6	1/6
15	⟨70,80,100⟩	5/6	4/6	3/6	2/6
16	⟨70,80,110⟩	4/6	3/6	2/6	1/6
17	⟨70,80,120⟩	4/6	3/6	2/6	1/6
18	⟨70,90,110⟩	5/6	4/6	3/6	2/6
19	⟨80,90,100⟩	5/6	4/6	3/6	2/6
20	⟨80,90,110⟩	5/6	4/6	3/6	2/6
21	⟨80,90,120⟩	4/6	3/6	2/6	1/6
22	⟨80,100,120⟩	5/6	4/6	3/6	2/6
23	⟨90,100,110⟩	5/6	4/6	3/6	2/6
24	⟨90,100,120⟩	5/6	4/6	3/6	2/6
25	⟨100,110,120⟩	5/6	4/6	3/6	2/6

and that die was then rolled by the attendant to determine the payment. A detailed explanation of this protocol, as well as instructions to subjects, appears in Appendix 3.

Quiggin (1982) originally developed rank-dependent utility or RDU; later, Quiggin's rank-dependent *probability weighting function* became a part of cumulative prospect theory or CPT (Tversky & Kahneman, 1992). Under RDU (or CPT for pure gain options), the value of an option (q_l,q_m,q_h) is

$$RDU(q_l,q_m,q_h) = w(q_h)u(h) + [w(1-q_l) - w(q_h)]u(m) + [1-w(1-q_l)]u(l), \quad (1)$$

where $u(z)$ is the *utility* of outcome z and $w(q)$ is the *probability weighting function* at q. In the first experiment, the *RDU value difference* between *risky* and *safe* is simply

$$\Delta RDU = RDU(risky) - RDU(safe) = w(q_h)u(h) + [1-w(q_h)]u(l) - u(m). \quad (2)$$

I wish to estimate the utilities $u(z)$ and weights $w(q_h)$ of RDU (or CPT for pure gains) with no assumptions concerning their functional form, and using only binary choice data. To do this, I need assumptions about the nature of probabilistic discrete choice from option pairs.

2. THE PROBABILISTIC CHOICE MODELS

Beginning with Mosteller and Nogee (1951), many experiments on discrete choice under risk suggest that these choices have a strong probabilistic component. Repeated trials of choice from pairs of risky options reveal high rates of choice switching by the same subject between trials of the same pair. In some cases, the repeated trials span days (e.g., Hey, 2001; Hey & Orme, 1994; Tversky, 1969) and decision-relevant conditions might have changed between trials. Yet switching occurs even between trials separated by bare minutes, with no intervening change in wealth, background risk, or any other obviously decision-relevant variable (Ballinger & Wilcox, 1997; Camerer, 1989; Loomes & Sugden, 1998; Starmer & Sugden, 1989).

To construct observation likelihoods, assumptions about the probabilistic nature of these choices are needed. I use three different probabilistic choice models of the form

$$P \equiv Prob(risky\ chosen\ from\ \{risky, safe\}) = F\left(\lambda \frac{\Delta RDU}{D(risky, safe)}\right), \tag{3}$$

where λ is a scale (or inverse standard deviation) parameter, $D(risky, safe)$ adjusts the scale parameter, and $F: X \rightarrow [0,1]$ is an increasing function with $F(0) = 0.5$ and $F(x) = 1 - F(-x)$, where $X \subseteq \mathbb{R}$. The probabilistic models are my own "contextual utility" or CU model (Wilcox, 2011), the "decision field theory" or DFT model of Busemeyer and Townsend (1992, 1993) and the "stronger utility" or SU model of Blavatskyy (2014). Respectively, these models are:

$$P^{cu} = Prob(risky) = F\left(\lambda \frac{\Delta RDU}{u(h) - u(l)}\right),$$

contextual utility; (4)

$$P^{dft} = Prob(risky) = F\left(\lambda \frac{\Delta RDU}{[u(h) - u(l)]\sqrt{w(q_h)[1 - w(q_h)]}}\right),$$

decision field theory; and (5)

$$P^{su} = Prob(risky) = H_\lambda\left(\frac{\Delta RDU}{w(q_h)[u(h) - u(m)] + [1 - w(q_h)][u(m) - u(l)]}\right),$$

stronger utility. (6)

In the contextual utility and decision field theory models, $X = \mathbb{R}$, while in stronger utility $X = (-1,1)$. However, by way of a suitable choice of H_λ, the stronger utility model can be rewritten in a form with $F : \mathbb{R} \to [0,1]$ as well (see Appendix 1):

$$P^{su} = Prob(risky) = F\left[\lambda \ln\left(\frac{w(q_h)[u(h) - u(m)]}{[1 - w(q_h)][u(m) - u(l)]}\right)\right]. \tag{7}$$

This means that all three of these probabilistic models may be estimated using a common choice for the function F. Busemeyer and Townsend (1993) give theoretical reasons for choosing the logistic c.d.f. $\Lambda(x) = [1 + \exp(-x)]^{-1}$ for use with decision field theory (see Appendix 1) so I use it as the function F in all estimations for all three models.

Until recently (e.g., Anderson, Harrison, Lau, & Rutström, 2008), most applied econometric estimations would have been done with the simple homoscedastic latent variable model $P^h = Prob(risky) = F(\lambda \Delta RDU)$: I call this the homoscedastic model. For many reasons, much professional opinion has turned against the homoscedastic model for discrete choice under risk. Long ago Luce (1959) remarked that the ratio scale nature of probabilistic models satisfying the Choice Axiom (for instance the homoscedastic binary logit) is deeply inconsistent with interval scale theories (such as EU and RDU). Since then Loomes and Sugden (1995) noted that the homoscedastic model does not respect stochastic dominance. Still more damaging, Blavatskyy (2011), Wilcox (2011), and Apesteguia and Ballester (2018) all show that this model cannot coherently represent comparative risk aversion across agents in different choice contexts. The laboratory evidence against the homoscedastic model, for choice under risk, is now extensive (Blavatskyy, 2014; Busemeyer & Townsend, 1993; Butler, Isoni, & Loomes, 2012; Loomes & Sugden, 1998; Rieskamp, 2008; Wilcox, 2008, 2011, 2015). Previous applied econometric users of the simple homoscedastic model have put it aside in favor of the newer models (e.g., Anderson, Harrison, Lau, & Rutström, 2013). Appendix 1 presents more information on contextual utility, decision field theory and stronger utility.

There are other ways to introduce probabilistic choice into models of decision under risk. One of these is *random preferences* (Gul & Pesendorfer, 2006; Loomes & Sugden, 1995): This approach treats vectors of outcome utilities and/or probability weights as random draws from a fixed distribution of these vectors. Random preference models also exhibit context dependence (Wilcox, 2011, p. 101). There is, however, a difficult problem with considering a random preference RDU specification for the experimental data considered here: It is not possible to generalize an RDU random preference specification across more than three outcome contexts without changing estimation techniques in fundamental ways (Wilcox, 2008, pp. 252–256, 2011, pp. 101–102). The first experiment has 25 distinct outcome contexts while the second and third experiments have 10 each. Therefore, I do not consider random preferences here.

3. ESTIMATION

To discuss the estimation, it is helpful to define indices for pairs, trials (days) and subjects, as well as some important sets of indices:

$i = 1, 2, \ldots I$, indexing I distinct pairs. Here $I=100$.
Pairs i are $\{risky_i, safe_i\} \equiv \{(1-q_{hi}, 0, q_{hi}), (0,1,0)\}$ on context (l_i, m_i, h_i).
$t = 1, 2, \ldots, \tau_i$, indexing τ_i distinct trials of each pair i. Here $\tau_i = 3$ (three days).
$S = 1, 2, \ldots, S$, indexing the S distinct subjects. Here, $S=80$.
it: A double subscript indicating the tth trial of pair i.
$r_{it}^s = 1$ if subject s chose $risky_i$ in her tth trial of pair i, and 0 otherwise.
$\mathbf{r}^s$ = the observed choice vector of subject s over all pairs and trials it.

Let $u^s(z)$ and $w^s(q)$ denote utilities of outcomes z and weights associated with probabilities q, respectively, of subject s. The first experiment involves nine distinct outcomes $z \in \{\$40, \$50, \ldots, \$120\}$ across its 100 choice pairs, but because of the affine transformation invariance property of RDU and EU utilities, we can choose $u^s(40) = 0$ and $u^s(120) = 1$ for all subjects s. With this done, the unique estimable utility vector $\mathbf{u}^s$ of the seven remaining outcomes is $\langle \mathbf{u}^s = u^s(50), u^s(60), \ldots, u^s(110) \rangle$. Function-free estimations make each of those seven utilities a separate parameter to be estimated.

The first experiment involves five distinct probabilities $q_h \in \left\{\frac{1}{6}, \frac{2}{6}, \ldots, \frac{5}{6}\right\}$, so there is a vector $\mathbf{w}^s = \left\langle w^s\left(\frac{1}{6}\right), w^s\left(\frac{2}{6}\right), \ldots, w^s\left(\frac{5}{6}\right)\right\rangle$ of five weights to estimate for each subject. Function-free estimations make each of those five weights a separate parameter to be estimated. To summarize, the function-free latent index of the RDU representation, for subject s and pair i, is

$$\Delta RDU_i(\mathbf{u}^s, \mathbf{w}^s) = w^s(q_{hi})u^s(h_i) + [1 - w^s(q_{hi})]u^s(l_i) - u^s(m_i), \tag{8}$$

where

$$\mathbf{w}^s = \left\langle w^s\left(\frac{1}{6}\right), w^s\left(\frac{2}{6}\right), \ldots, w^s\left(\frac{5}{6}\right)\right\rangle, \text{ and}$$

$$\mathbf{u}^s = \langle u^s(50), u^s(60), \ldots, u^s(110) \rangle, \text{ with } u^s(40) = 0 \text{ and } u^s(120) = 1 \ \forall \text{ s}.$$

Combine Eq. 8 with Eqs. 4, 5 and 7, let $\boldsymbol{\theta}^s \equiv (\mathbf{u}^s, \mathbf{w}^s, \lambda^s)$ and choose the logistic c.d.f. as $F(x)$, and we have the following choice probability specifications:

$$P_i^{rdcu}(\boldsymbol{\theta}^s) = \Lambda\left[\lambda^s \frac{\Delta RDU_i(\mathbf{u}^s, \mathbf{w}^s)}{u^s(h_i) - u^s(l_i)}\right]; \tag{9}$$

$$P_i^{rddft}\left(\boldsymbol{\theta}^s\right)=\Lambda\left[\lambda^s\frac{\Delta RDU_i\left(\mathbf{u}^s,\mathbf{w}^s\right)}{\left[u^s\left(h_i\right)-u^s\left(l_i\right)\right]\sqrt{w^s\left(q_{hi}\right)\left[1-w^s\left(q_{hi}\right)\right]}}\right];\text{ and} \tag{10}$$

$$P_i^{rdsu}\left(\boldsymbol{\theta}^s\right)=\Lambda\left[\lambda^s\ln\left(\frac{w^s\left(q_{hi}\right)\left[u^s\left(h_i\right)-u^s\left(m_i\right)\right]}{\left[1-w^s\left(q_{hi}\right)\right]\left[u^s\left(m_i\right)-u^s\left(l_i\right)\right]}\right)\right]. \tag{11}$$

Equations 9–11 give the probability of events $r_{it}^s=1$ (subject s chose *risky* in the tth trial of pair i). Letting $P_i^{spec}\left(\boldsymbol{\theta}^s\right)$ denote any of those probabilities, the log likelihood of $\mathbf{r}^s$ is

$$\mathcal{L}^{spec}\left(\mathbf{r}^s|\boldsymbol{\theta}^s\right)=\sum\nolimits_{it}r_{it}^s\ln\left[P_i^{spec}\left(\boldsymbol{\theta}^s\right)\right]+\left(1-r_{it}^s\right)\ln\left[1-P_i^{spec}\left(\boldsymbol{\theta}^s\right)\right]. \tag{12}$$

I estimate $\boldsymbol{\theta}^s$ by a penalized maximum likelihood procedure, for each subject s; Appendix 2 contains details of this estimation.

4. SOME MONTE CARLO RESULTS

The 100 choice pairs in Table 1 were in part chosen through Monte Carlo simulations exploring estimation performance with alternative sets of choice pairs. To gain confidence in the estimations reported here – and to understand their limitations – it helps to see some Monte Carlo results. Consider a data generating process or DGP based on one of the choice probability models in Eqs. 9–11, combined with well-known parametric estimates of utility and weighting functions. For the utility function, I use the CRRA utility of money given by $u^s\left(z\,|\,\rho^s\right)=z^{1-\rho^s}/\left(1-\rho^s\right)$, normalized[1] so that $u^s(40)=0$ and $u^s(120)=1$, and begin with the parameter value $\rho^s=0.12$. (very mild concavity of utility) reported by Tversky and Kahneman (1992). For the weighting function, I use Prelec's (1998) two-parameter function, given by $w^s\left(q|\beta^s,\gamma^s\right)=\exp\left(-\beta^s\left[-\ln(q)\right]^{\gamma^s}\right)$ $\forall$ $q\in(0,1)$, $w(0)=0$ and $w(1)=1$, and begin with parameter values $\beta^s=1$ and $\gamma^s=0.65$ which, according to Prelec, match earlier estimations of weights using other weighting functions. Express the parameters of this first DGP as $(\rho,\gamma,\beta)=(0.12,0.65,1)$: These parameters are cumulative prospect theory as first conceived a quarter century ago, and I call this "Prospector I" for short. I take a more recent parametric version of cumulative prospect theory from Bruhin et al. (2010), using a second DGP $(\rho,\gamma,\beta)=(0.043,0.45,0.8)$. I call this "Prospector II" for short: It closely resembles Bruhin, Fehr-Duda, and Epper's most common subject type (that they estimated with a finite mixture model using all of their data).

For contrast, and anticipating later results, I examine two other DGPs. One of these DGPs is $(\rho,\gamma,\beta)=(3,1.5,0.4)$: I call this DGP "Optimist" since its weighting function is such that $w^s(q)>q$ for all q in the first experiment: The decision-maker overweights probabilities of highest outcomes. By itself such probability weighting would imply risk-seeking, but this DGP also has a highly concave utility function which, by itself, would imply risk aversion. The last DGP for Monte Carlo study is $(\rho,\gamma,\beta)=(1.5,3,2)$: The implied weighting function in this case is s-shaped – opposite of the inverse *s*-shape of received Cumulative Prospect Theory. This weighting function may represent a decision-maker who sometimes rounds low probabilities to zero and high probabilities to unity, so I call this DGP "Rounder."

Figs. 1–4 show results of function-free estimations of utilities (the left panels) and weights (the right panels) for 80 simulated subjects, using the contextual utility specification of Eq. 9 for the estimation. These simulated subjects all have true (DGP) choice probabilities given by the contextual utility model in Eq. 9 with $\lambda^s = 12$. In Fig. 1, the 80 simulated subjects have the "Prospector I" DGP; in Fig. 2 they have the "Prospector II" DGP; in Fig. 3 they have the "Optimist" DGP; and in Fig. 4 they have the "Rounder" DGP. On all panels, the true (DGP) utility functions or weighting functions appear as a bold black curve, while the 80 functions estimated using the function-free method appear as thinner curves of varying grays.

Figs. 1–4 show that the function-free estimates cluster around the DGP curve with little in the way of strong biases, except occasionally near the endpoints of the functions where true utilities and/or weights are close to 0 or 1 (this is expected for maximum likelihood estimates of parameters lying near a boundary of an allowed parameter space). The variability of the estimated curves (not small) is due both to the inherent variability of (simulated) observed choices that is consequent to probabilistic choice in the DGP, and to the burden of the function-free estimation.[2] Yet comparison of these four figures shows that collected function-free estimations track different DGPs: The collective impression made by the "cloud" of individual estimates matches different amounts of utility concavity and different weighting function shapes quite well.

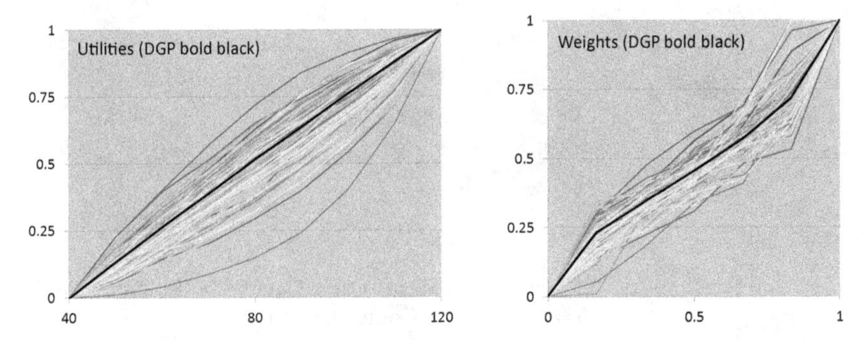

Fig. 1. 80 Function-free Estimates From Monte Carlo data with "Prospector I" DGP $(\rho, \gamma, \beta) = (0.12,0.65,1)$ and Contextual Utility.

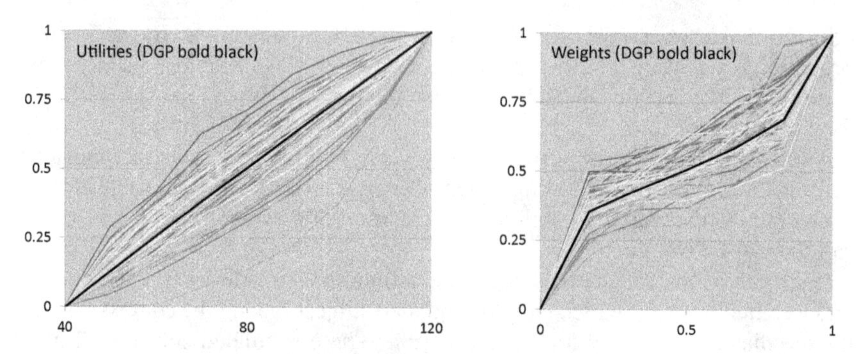

Fig. 2. 80 Function-free Estimates From Monte Carlo Data With "Prospector II" DGP $(\rho, \gamma, \beta) = (0.043, 0.45, 0.8)$ and Contextual Utility.

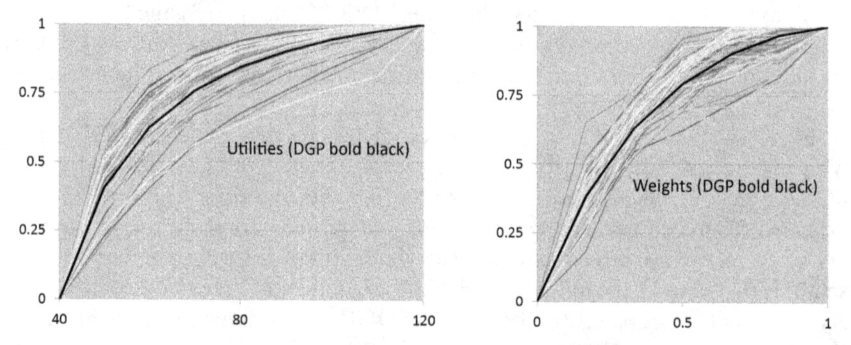

Fig. 3. 80 Function-free Estimates From Monte Carlo Data With "Optimist" DGP $(\rho, \gamma, \beta) = (3, 1.5, 0.4)$ and Contextual Utility.

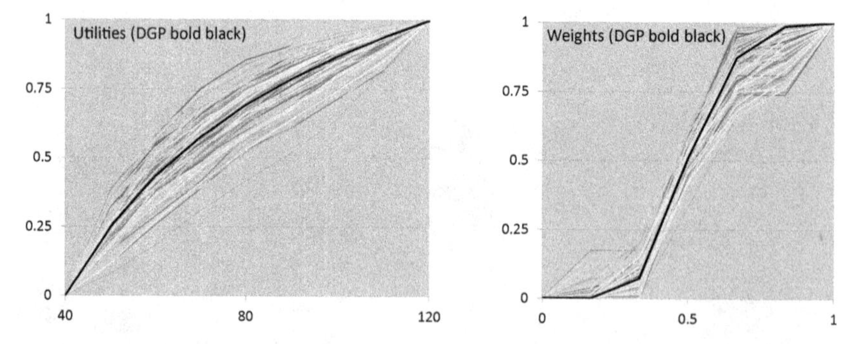

Fig. 4. 80 Function-free Estimates From Monte Carlo Data With "Rounder" DGP $(\rho, \gamma, \beta) = (1.5, 3, 2)$ and Contextual Utility.

Tables 2a–2c show distributions of five estimated weighting function shapes for 1,000 simulated subjects, using each of the four DGPs:

(1) prospector – there is a $q^* \in \left(\frac{1}{6}, \frac{5}{6}\right)$ such that $\widehat{w}^s(q) \gtrless q$ as $q \lessgtr q^*$;

(2) pessimist – $\widehat{w}^s(q) < q$ for all q;

(3) optimist – $\widehat{w}^s(q) > q$ for all q;

(4) rounder – there is a $q^* \in \left(\frac{1}{6}, \frac{5}{6}\right)$ such that $\widehat{w}^s(q) \lessgtr q$ as $q \lessgtr q^*$; and

(5) unclassified – estimated weights cross the identity line more than once.

The tables show that most estimated weighting function shapes match the shape of the DGP (usually more than 80%, but a bit less for Prospector I). These tables also bear on later results. First, Cumulative Prospect Theory DGPs (i.e., Prospector I and Prospector II) produce estimated optimist or rounder shapes less than about 8% of the time: If a sample of 80 subjects comes from a population composed solely of Prospector I and Prospector II, we expect that function-free estimation will produce about seven subjects having estimated optimist or rounder shapes.

Table 2. Monte Carlo Results: Distribution of 1,000 Function-free Estimations of Weighting Function Shapes, Using 1,000 Simulated Subjects From Four Different DGPs.

Estimated Weighting Function Shapes	DGP Utility and Weighting Function Parameters (ρ, γ, β)			
	Prospector I, as in Fig. 1 (0.12,0.65,1)	Prospector II, as in Fig. 2 (0.043,0.45,0.8)	Optimist, as in Fig. 3 (3,1.5,0.4)	Rounder, as in Fig. 4 (1.5,3,2)
2a. Contextual Utility ($\lambda^s = 12$) is in the DGP and Also Used for Estimations				
Prospector	66.7%	84.1%	8.4%	0.0%
Pessimist	10.9%	0.4%	0.0%	2.4%
Optimist	4.6%	8.1%	91.0%	0.0%
Rounder	1.8%	0.0%	0.6%	81.0%
Unclassifiable	16.0%	7.4%	0.0%	16.6%
2b. Decision Field Theory ($\lambda^s = 5$) is in the DGP and Also Used for Estimations				
Prospector	74.4%	89.8%	20.1%	0.0%
Pessimist	11.7%	2.0%	0.0%	0.0%
Optimist	3.2%	4.9%	79.1%	0.0%
Rounder	1.4%	0.1%	0.5%	88.0%
Unclassifiable	9.3%	3.2%	0.3%	12.0%
2c. Stronger Utility ($\lambda^s = 2$) is in the DGP and Also Used for Estimations				
Prospector	74.4%	89.8%	20.1%	0.0%
Pessimist	11.7%	2.0%	0.0%	0.0%
Optimist	3.2%	4.9%	79.1%	0.0%
Rounder	1.4%	0.1%	0.5%	88.0%
Unclassifiable	9.3%	3.2%	0.3%	12.0%

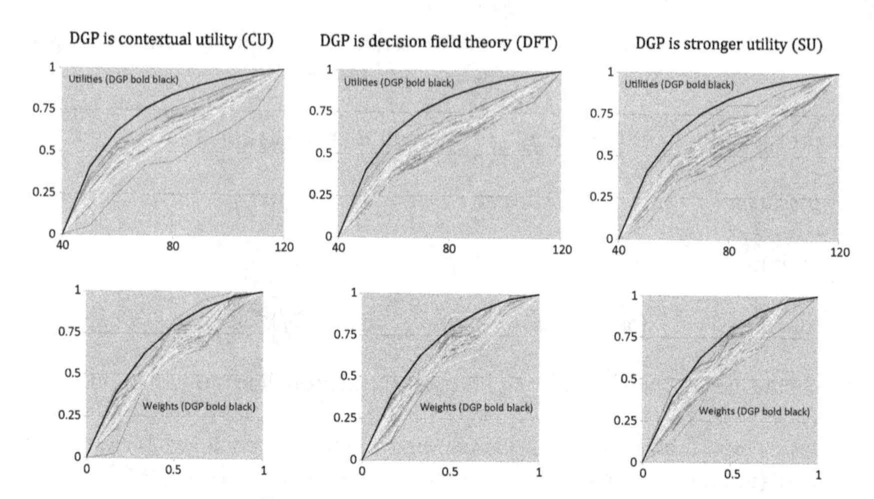

Fig. 5. 80 Function-free Estimates From Monte Carlo Data With "Optimist" DGP $(\rho, \gamma, \beta) = (3,1.5,0.4)$, Estimated With the Homoscedastic Model, When the True DGP Uses One of the Three Heteroscedastic Models: DGP is Contextual Utility (CU), DGP is Decision Field Theory (DFT) and DGP is Stronger Utility (SU).

Second, Cumulative Prospect Theory DGPs produce estimated pessimist shapes about 11% of the time: If we see 8 or so estimated pessimist shapes, these may be simply the result of sampling variability and true Cumulative Prospect Theory types in the sampled population. Finally, Prospector I DGPs produce unclassified shapes about 10–15% of the time, so we should not be surprised to estimate a small number of unclassified shapes if Prospector I DGPs (or other DGPs relatively close to identity weights) are common in the sampled population.

I noted that until recently, the simple homoscedastic latent index model $P^h = Prob(risky) = F(\lambda\Delta\,\mathrm{RDU})$ was commonly used for such estimations. Fig. 5 shows some consequences of such a homoscedastic latent index estimation when the DGP in fact features any of the three probabilistic models I use here. The DGP utility and weighting function is in all cases the Optimist DGP, that is, $(\rho, \gamma, \beta) = (3,1.5,0.4)$, which also features pronounced concavity of utility. Fig. 5 shows that for all three DGPs, this results in reliable underestimation of both utility concavity and weighting optimism: Almost all of the 80 estimates lie below the bold black DGP curves. The newer heteroscedastic probabilistic models are consequential for estimation and inferences concerning utility and weighting functions and, as mentioned earlier, there is now much evidence against the homoscedastic model.

5. RESULTS OF THE FIRST EXPERIMENT

Figs. 6–8 show most of the results of the function-free individual estimations: Fig. 6 shows contextual utility estimations; Fig. 7 shows decision field theory

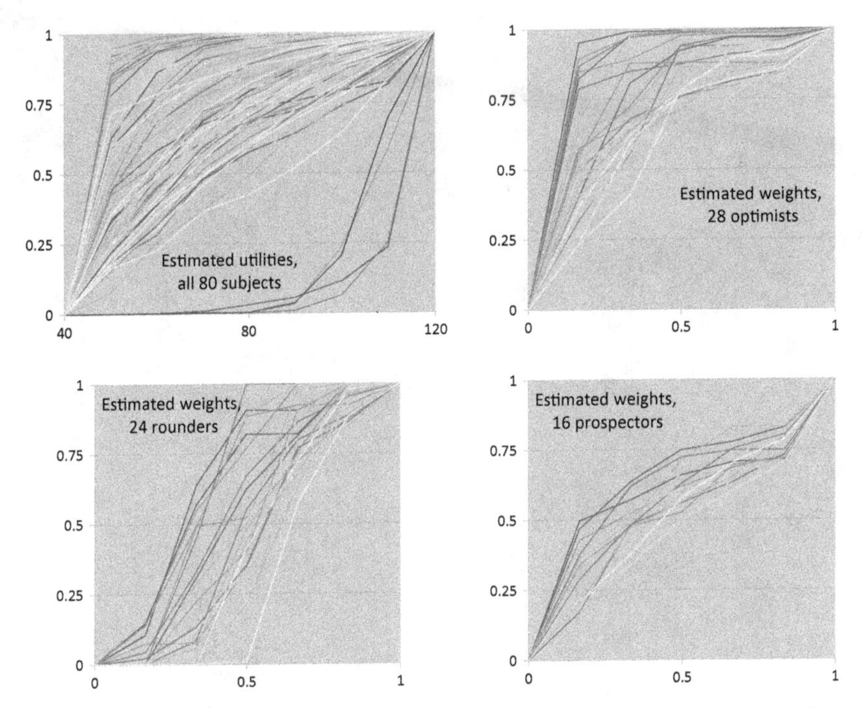

Fig. 6. 80 Function-free Individual Estimates, Estimated With the Contextual Utility Model Using Data From the First Experiment. The First Panel Shows Estimated Utility Functions Together; The Next Three Panels Show Estimated Weighting Functions of the Three Most Common Estimated Shapes (68 of the 80 subjects). The Median Estimated λ^s Is About 11.3.

estimations; and Fig. 8 shows stronger utility estimations. In each figure, the upper left panel shows 80 estimated utility functions while the remaining three panels show most (at least 68 of 80) estimated weighting functions, divided into the three most commonly estimated shapes – optimists, rounders and prospectors, generally in that order (except with decision field theory). The remaining 12 subjects (whose estimated weighting functions are not shown) break almost evenly between pessimists and unclassified,[3] certainly consistent with the sampling variability considerations of the previous section and not strong evidence that these types even exist in the sampled population. Overall, by individual-level likelihood ratio tests, about 85–95% of these estimated weighting functions significantly differ from identity weighting at the 5% level of significance, depending somewhat on the probabilistic model used.

Figs. 6 and 8, however, are clearly unusual given widely held priors concerning weighting functions: Both the contextual utility and stronger utility estimations suggest a sampled population where the plurality type of decision-maker is an optimist rather than a prospector, and where even rounders outnumber prospectors. Fig. 7 is an exception to this, but not a very convincing one: Decision field

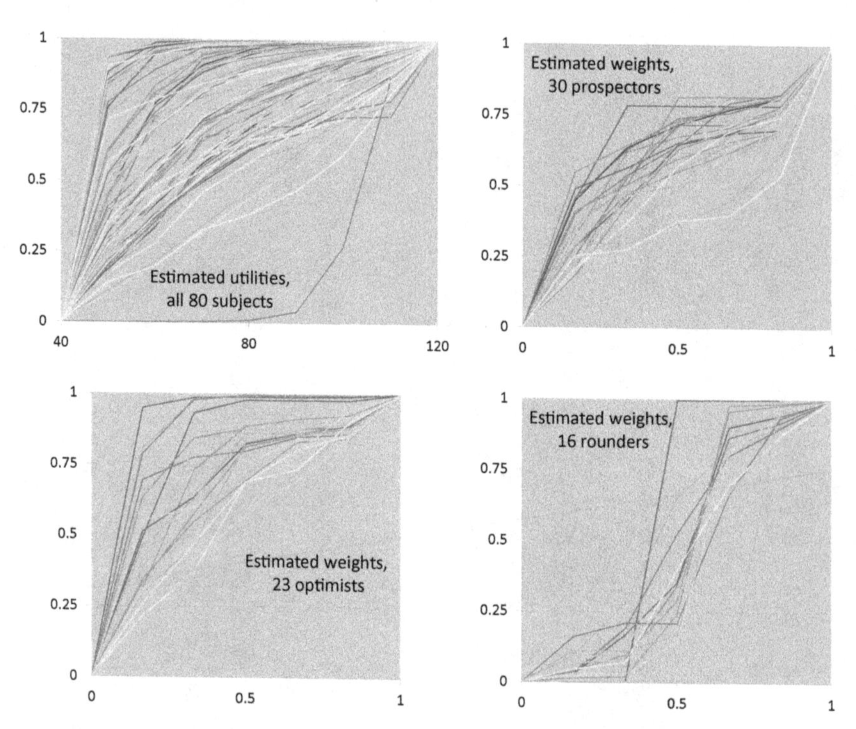

Fig. 7. 80 Function-free Individual Estimates, Estimated With the Decision Field Theory Model Using Data From the First Experiment. The First Panel Shows Estimated Utility Functions Together; The Next Three Panels Show Estimated Weighting Functions for the Most Commonly Estimated Shapes (69 of the 80 Subjects). The Median Estimated λ^s Is About 5.15.

theory estimations do produce prospectors as the plurality type, but inspection of the upper right panel (the prospector shapes) reveals that a large number of these estimated weighting functions might be optimists aside from the estimated weight at $q = 5/6$. Camerer and Ho (1994) and Wu and Gonzalez (1996) estimate that "the" weighting function crosses the identity line at some $q < 1/2$: Very few of the "prospector" shapes in the upper right panel of Fig. 7 do this. These previous estimations used the homoscedastic latent index model which, as shown in Fig. 5, tends to bias estimated weights downward – which could account for the discrepancy I point out here. The prospector shapes produced by decision field theory don't fit received Cumulative Prospect Theory priors.

6. FIRST DISCUSSION

Consider two options $safe = (1 - p_m, p_m, 0)$ and $risky = (1 - q_h, 0, q_h)$ where $p_m > q_h$ and as usual $h > m > l$. Tversky (1969), Rubinstein (1988), and Leland (1994) have all noted that if $h - m$ is large but $p_m - q_h$ is sufficiently small, so that p_m

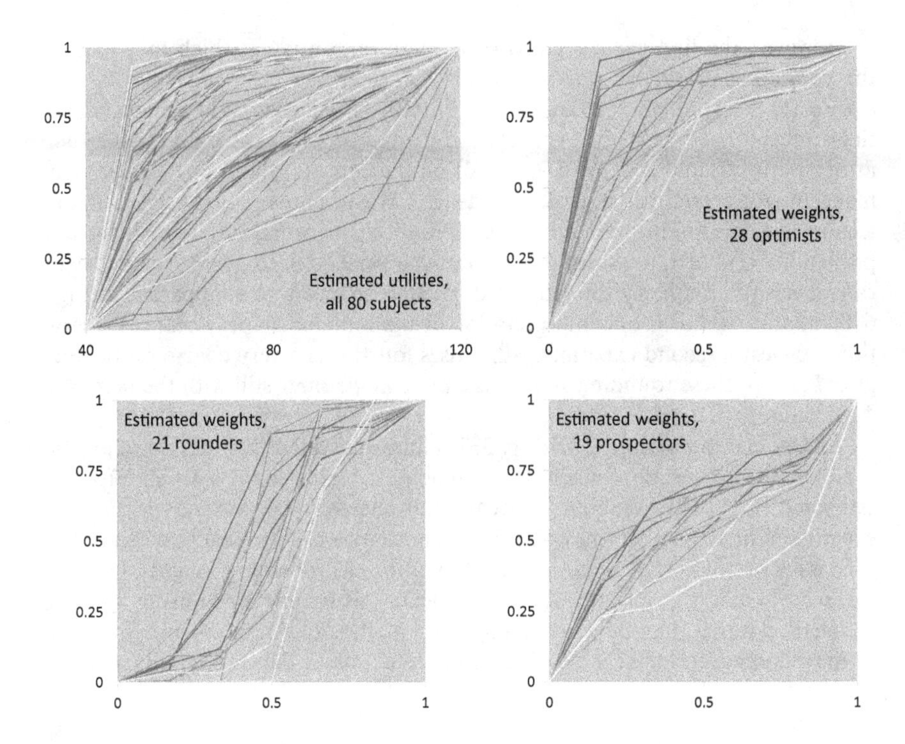

Fig. 8. 80 Function-free Individual Estimates, Estimated With the Stronger Utility Model Using Data From the First Experiment. The First Panel Shows Estimated Utility Functions Together; The Next Three Panels Show Estimated Weighting Functions for the Most Commonly Estimated Shapes (68 of the 80 Subjects). The Median Estimated λ^s Is About 2.13.

and q_h are deemed "similar" but h and m are not, a decision procedure might not bother with computing and comparing overall values of *safe* and *risky*, but instead simply ignore the similar probabilities and choose the option *risky* with the noticeably larger "prize" h. Tversky showed that such decision procedures produce intransitive choices, and both Rubinstein and Leland showed that such decision procedures account for many of the Allais phenomena. This kind of decision procedure would reveal "apparent weights" ω such that $\omega(p_m) = \omega(q_h)$. If an experiment contains many option pairs of this kind, with many paired "similar" probabilities p_m and q_h in some interval $[a,b] \subset [0,1]$, a straightforward estimation of RDU or CPT will result in an estimated probability weighting function that is too flat on $[a,b]$ – reflecting, to some extent, similarity-based computational shortcuts rather than the true difference $w(b) - w(a)$. The first experiment contains no option pairs like these, and does not often produce estimated weighting functions that are relatively flat on the range of low interior probabilities – a marker of prospector shapes.

However, the first experiment does contain option pairs which may lead to the commonly observed rounder shape. Consider the pair $safe = (0,1,0)$ and $risky = (1/6,0,5/6)$ on the context $(40,50,60)$. A decision-maker might sometimes regard *risky* as $(0,0,1)$ and choose it over *safe*. Likewise for a pair such as $safe = (0,1,0)$ and $risky = (5/6,0,1/6)$ on the context $(50,70,110)$, a decision-maker might sometimes regard *risky* as $(1,0,0)$ and choose *safe* instead. I conjecture that this kind of decision-maker produces the rounder shape. The coarse probability grid of the 6-sided die was not coarse enough to make such behavior rare, given the frequency of estimated rounder shapes that is apparent in Figs. 6–8: or, at least, this is one interpretation of the rounder shape. These considerations suggest a second experiment that uses fourths as a very coarse probability grid: Perhaps these rounding shortcuts can be made rarer still with the help of a 4-sided die.

Andreoni and Sprenger (2012, p. 3373) have suggested that "Subjects exhibit a preference for certainty when it is available ...." This could have an effect on estimated probability weighting. Because all relatively safe options in the first experiment are sure outcomes, this data is not well-suited to seeing whether this is an issue or not in the function-free estimations of probability weights. For now I observe that Cheung (2013) fails to replicate this finding when using a choice list method rather than the budget allocation method of Andreoni and Sprenger. In the second experiment, I also fail to replicate it using the choice pairs method.

7. DESIGN OF THE SECOND EXPERIMENT

In this second experiment, I mainly seek a replication of the prevalence of estimated optimism. This experiment is done with a sampled population from a different university, with different option pairs and a different random device, the 4-sided die. As suggested in the previous section, the 4-sided die is an attempt to limit the prevalence of estimated rounder shapes. The second experiment also uses option pairs going beyond the sure things versus two-outcome risks of the first experiment. Let $safe = (p_l, p_m, p_h)$ and $risky = (q_l, q_m, q_h)$ denote vectors of outcome probabilities on the context $\langle l,m,h \rangle$. In all pairs, $p_m > q_m$ while $p_l < q_l$ and $p_h < q_h$. As before, subjects choose between *safe* and *risky* in each pair presented to them. Table 3 shows the 69 option pairs used in the experiment: Some are repeated up to four times as indicated in the "trials" column, for a total of 100 choice tasks in the experiment. There are 10 distinct three outcome contexts, all created from the five positive money outcomes \$15, \$20, \$30, \$45, and \$80. There is now plenty of variation in whether the option *safe* is a sure thing $(0,1,0)$ or not, which allows a check on concerns raised by Andreoni and Sprenger (2012).

Constraining all probabilities to the set of fourths (0, 1/4, 1/2, 3/4, or 1), the option pairs (and number of trials of each pair) were selected by way of iterated Monte Carlo simulation. The iterative procedure aimed at approximately maximizing the average determinant of the function-free estimator's information matrix for the worst 10% (lowest decile of information matrix determinants) of estimated parameters in a simulated population of decision-makers whose distribution of DGPs resembled what had been previously estimated using past experimental data at Chapman University.

Table 3. The 69 Option Pairs Used in the Second Experiment.

Pair #	Trials	Context ⟨*l*,*m*,*h*⟩	*Safe* Option Outcome Probabilities			*Risky* Option Outcome Probabilities		
			p_l	p_m	p_h	q_l	q_m	q_h
1	4	⟨15,20,30⟩	0	1	0	0.75	0	0.25
2	1		0	1	0	0.25	0.5	0.25
3	3		0	1	0	0.5	0	0.5
4	1		0	1	0	0.25	0	0.75
5	1		0.25	0.75	0	0.75	0	0.25
6	1		0.25	0.75	0	0.5	0	0.5
7	4		0	0.75	0.25	0.5	0	0.5
8	1		0.5	0.5	0	0.75	0	0.25
9	1		0.25	0.5	0.25	0.5	0	0.5
10	1		0	0.5	0.5	0.25	0	0.75
11	1	⟨15,20,45⟩	0	1	0	0.75	0	0.25
12	1		0	1	0	0.5	0	0.5
13	1		0.25	0.75	0	0.75	0	0.25
14	1		0	0.75	0.25	0.5	0	0.5
15	1		0	0.75	0.25	0.25	0	0.75
16	1		0	0.5	0.5	0.25	0	0.75
17	1	⟨15,20,80⟩	0	1	0	0.75	0	0.25
18	1		0	1	0	0.5	0	0.5
19	1		0.25	0.75	0	0.5	0	0.5
20	2		0.5	0.5	0	0.75	0	0.25
21	1	⟨15,30,45⟩	0	1	0	0.5	0	0.5
22	1		0	1	0	0.25	0	0.75
23	1		0.25	0.75	0	0.75	0	0.25
24	2		0	0.75	0.25	0.5	0	0.5
25	1		0	0.75	0.25	0.25	0	0.75
26	1		0.5	0.5	0	0.75	0	0.25
27	1		0	0.5	0.5	0.25	0	0.75
28	3	⟨15,30,80⟩	0.25	0.75	0	0.75	0	0.25
29	1		0.25	0.75	0	0.5	0	0.5
30	4		0	0.75	0.25	0.25	0	0.75
31	1		0.5	0.5	0	0.75	0	0.25
32	4		0.25	0.5	0.25	0.5	0	0.5
33	1		0	0.5	0.5	0.25	0	0.75
34	1	⟨15,45,80⟩	0	1	0	0.75	0	0.25
35	1		0	1	0	0.25	0	0.75
36	1		0.25	0.75	0	0.75	0	0.25
37	1		0.25	0.75	0	0.5	0	0.5
38	2		0	0.75	0.25	0.5	0	0.5
39	1		0	0.75	0.25	0.25	0	0.75
40	1		0.5	0.5	0	0.75	0	0.25
41	1		0	0.5	0.5	0.25	0	0.75
42	2	⟨20,30,45⟩	0	1	0	0.75	0	0.25
43	1		0	1	0	0.5	0.25	0.25
44	1		0	1	0	0.25	0.5	0.25
45	4		0	1	0	0.5	0	0.5
46	1		0	1	0	0.25	0.25	0.5
47	2		0	1	0	0.25	0	0.75
48	1		0.25	0.75	0	0.75	0	0.25
49	1		0.25	0.75	0	0.5	0	0.5
50	1		0	0.75	0.25	0.5	0	0.5

(*Continued*)

Table 3. *(Continued)*

Pair #	Trials	Context $\langle l,m,h\rangle$	*Safe* Option Outcome Probabilities			*Risky* Option Outcome Probabilities		
			p_l	p_m	p_h	q_l	q_m	q_h
51	1	⟨20,30,80⟩	0.25	0.75	0	0.75	0	0.25
52	1		0.25	0.75	0	0.5	0	0.5
53	1		0.5	0.5	0	0.75	0	0.25
54	1	⟨20,45,80⟩	0	1	0	0.25	0	0.75
55	1		0.25	0.75	0	0.5	0	0.5
56	1		0	0.75	0.25	0.5	0	0.5
57	1		0	0.5	0.5	0.25	0	0.75
58	4	⟨30,45,80⟩	0	1	0	0.75	0	0.25
59	1		0	1	0	0.5	0.25	0.25
60	1		0	1	0	0.25	0.5	0.25
61	3		0	1	0	0.5	0	0.5
62	1		0	1	0	0.25	0	0.75
63	1		0.25	0.75	0	0.75	0	0.25
64	3		0.25	0.75	0	0.5	0	0.5
65	1		0	0.75	0.25	0.5	0	0.5
66	1		0	0.75	0.25	0.25	0	0.75
67	1		0.5	0.5	0	0.75	0	0.25
68	1		0.25	0.5	0.25	0.5	0	0.5
69	1		0	0.5	0.5	0.25	0	0.75

The subjects for the second experiment were 98 undergraduate students at Chapman University. Each subject participated in a single session, making choices from the choice tasks shown in Table 3. Sessions commenced with computerized instructions, including tests of understanding that returned subjects to relevant instruction sections in the event of test mistakes. Subjects had to correctly answer all questions before proceeding. The 100 choice pairs were divided into two parts (a first part of 60 pairs and a second part of 40 pairs), separated by about 10–15 minutes of other tasks (again, a survey and tests of arithmetic and problem-solving ability). At the conclusion of a session, one of each subject's 100 choice pairs was selected at random (by means of the subject rolling two 10-sided dice) and the subject was paid according to their choice in that pair. If the subject's choice in the selected pair involved chance, the subject rolled a 4-sided die (using a dice cup) to resolve payment. Sessions rarely lasted more than 70 minutes.

The second experiment involves five distinct outcomes but as before we can choose $u^s(15)=0$ and $u^s(80)=1$ for all subjects s. The unique estimable utility vector $\mathbf{u}^s$ for each subject s is the utilities of the three other outcomes $\langle \mathbf{u}^s = u^s(20), u^s(30), u^s(45)\rangle$, and function-free estimation makes those three utilities separate parameters to estimate. The experiment also involves three distinct probabilities $q \in \left\{\frac{1}{4}, \frac{2}{4}, \frac{3}{4}\right\}$, and so a vector $\mathbf{w}^s = \left\langle w^s\left(\frac{1}{4}\right), w^s\left(\frac{2}{4}\right), w^s\left(\frac{3}{4}\right)\right\rangle$ of three weights to be estimated for each subject. Function-free estimation makes those three weights separate parameters to estimate. Including the scale parameter λ^s, this makes seven total parameters for the function-free estimation. I use the same penalized maximum likelihood procedure for this estimation (see Appendix 2).

8. RESULTS OF THE SECOND EXPERIMENT

Figs. 9–11 show estimation results using the data from the second experiment. Fig. 9 shows contextual utility estimations; Fig. 10 shows decision field theory estimations; and Fig. 11 shows stronger utility estimations. In each figure, the upper left panel shows 98 estimated utility functions while the remaining three panels show most (at least 84 of the 98) estimated weighting functions, divided into the three most commonly estimated shapes – optimists, rounders and pessimists or prospectors, generally in that order (except with contextual utility). Remaining subjects (estimated weighting functions not shown) include 11 or 13 prospectors and 1 or 2 unclassified.[4] Overall, by individual-level likelihood ratio

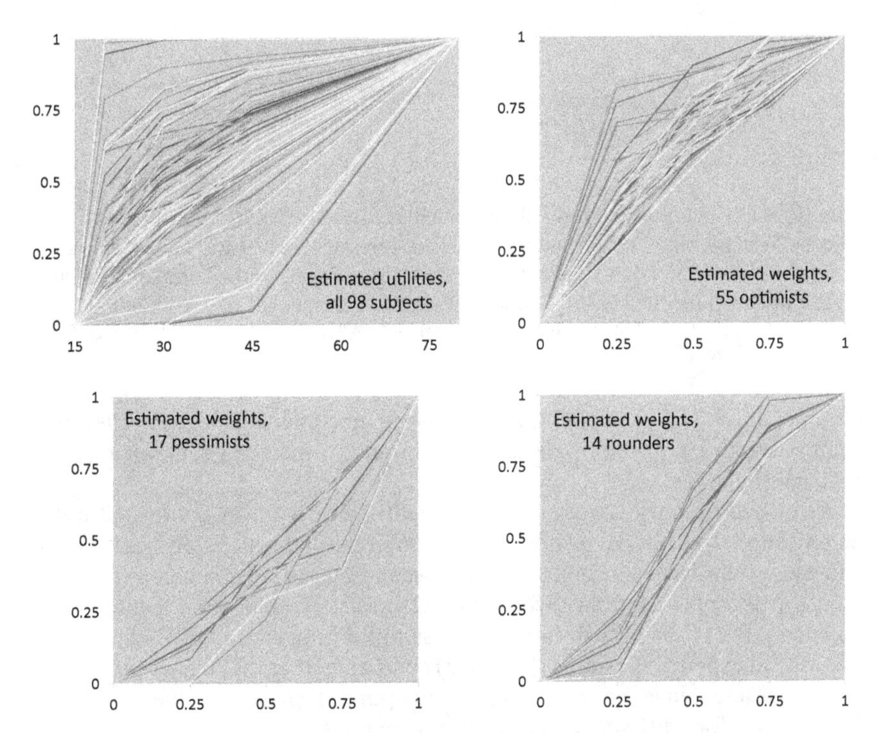

Fig. 9. 98 Function-free Individual Estimates, Estimated With the Contextual Utility Model Using Data From the Second Experiment. The First Panel Shows Estimated Utility Functions Together; The Next Three Panels Show Estimated Weighting Functions for the Most Commonly Estimated Shapes (86 of the 98 Subjects). The Median Estimated λ^s Is About 14.0.

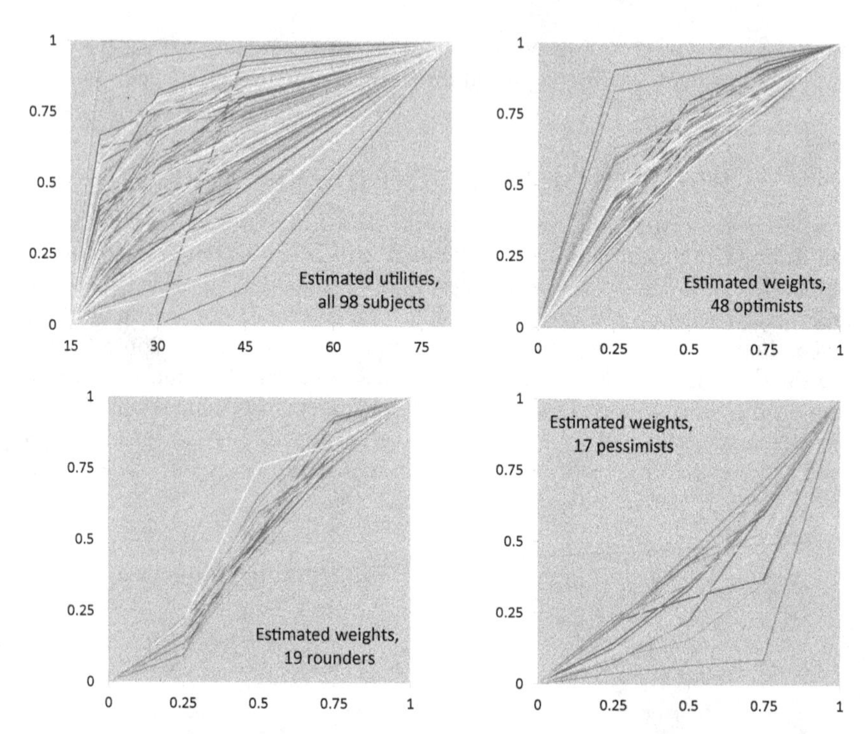

Fig. 10. 98 Function-free Individual Estimates, Estimated With the Decision Field Theory Model Using Data From the Second Experiment. The First Panel Shows Estimated Utility Functions Together; The Next Three Panels Show Estimated Weighting Functions for the Most Commonly Estimated Shapes (84 of the 98 Subjects). The Median Estimated λ^s Is About 5.65.

tests, about 65–70% of the estimated weighting functions significantly differ from identity weighting at the 5% level of significance, depending somewhat on the probabilistic model used.

Estimated optimist shapes are an outright majority under contextual utility and stronger utility (and almost half of subjects under decision field theory) and more than twice as common as the second-most-common share (rounders except with contextual utility, where it is pessimists). Keep in mind that the set of outcomes, the probability device and the sampled population are all different in this second experiment, so the (tempting) conclusion that the coarser probability grid has resulted in less rounding and more optimism (relative to the first experiment) is not formally warranted. However, optimist shapes are again the most commonly observed shape. This has been replicated with a new sample from a different population, a new die and a new outcome set.

One can modify estimations to include the possibility raised by Andreoni and Sprenger (2012, p. 3373) – that subjects "exhibit a preference for certainty when it is available." To do this, I multiply all *safe* option occurrences of $u^s(m_i)$ in Eqs.

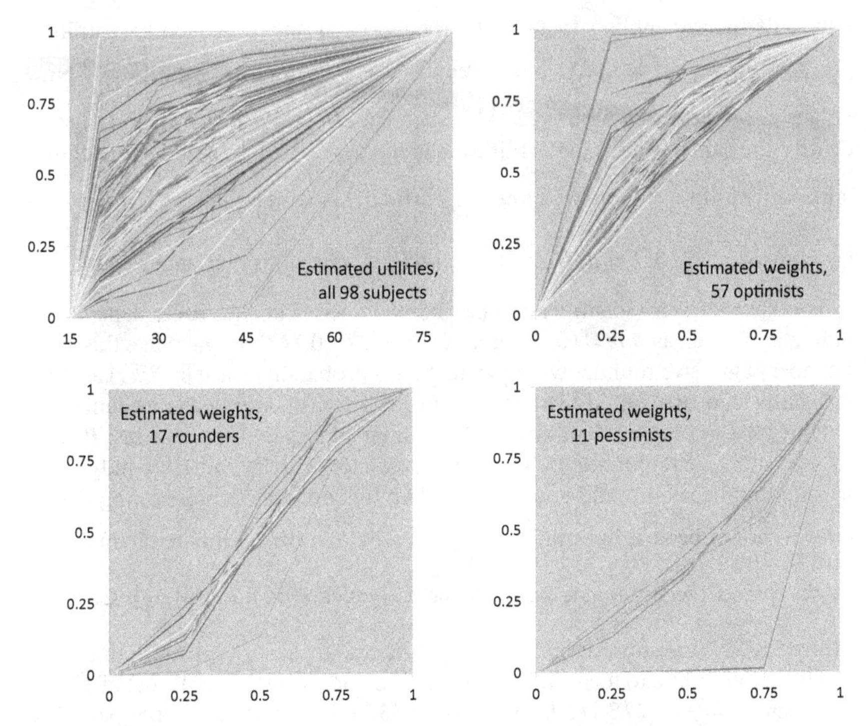

Fig. 11. 98 Function-free Individual Estimates, Estimated With the Stronger Utility Model Using Data From the Second Experiment. The First Panel Shows Estimated Utility Functions Together; The Next Three Panels Show Estimated Weighting Functions for the Most Commonly Estimated Shapes (85 of the 98 Subjects). The Median Estimated λ^s Is About 2.31.

8–10 by a factor $\left[1+\beta^s 1(p_{mi}=1)\right]$, shifting the estimated utility of the middle outcome m_i in *safe* by a multiplicative effect β^s whenever *safe* is a sure thing. Having done this and estimated these models, I find no evidence that β^s is systematically and significantly positive as suggested by the findings of Andreoni and Sprenger. Additionally, this does not change the qualitative findings in Figs. 9 and 10 much: Optimist shapes are nearly half of the estimates using either decision field theory or contextual utility as the probabilistic model.[5]

9. SECOND DISCUSSION

Optimism is again prevalent in the second experiment – even more prevalent than in the first experiment. I have suggested that the received prospector shape, characterized by relatively flat weighting functions on interior probability ranges, may frequently occur because close probabilities tend to be regarded as similar and ignored. Here is one econometric path for addressing this possibility. Begin with a design resembling that of the second experiment: It identifies utilities $\mathbf{u}^s = \langle u^s(20), u^s(30), u^s(45) \rangle$ and weights $\mathbf{w}^s = \left\langle w^s\left(\frac{1}{4}\right), w^s\left(\frac{2}{4}\right), w^s\left(\frac{3}{4}\right) \right\rangle$. Now replace the 4-sided die with a 12-sided die: We can still use the same design to identify the same weights and utilities, but suppose we wish to add some choice pairs to identify $w^s\left(\frac{1}{3}\right)$ as well and, in particular, the marginal weight between $q = 1/4$ and $q = 1/3$. Let $dw^s = w^s\left(\frac{1}{3}\right) - w^s\left(\frac{1}{4}\right)$ denoted this marginal weight.

Two routes to this identification can be imagined. The first route depends on adding pairs such as *safe* $= (0,1,0)$ and *risky* $= (2/3,0,1/3)$. In pairs like this, only the most aggressive rounder would view the 1/3 probability (of h in *risky*) as zero, and almost no one would view the 1/3 probability (of h in *risky*) as similar to certainty (of m in *safe*). I call this a "dissimilar pair" for those reasons: It does not encourage computational shortcuts based on either similarity judgments or rounding behavior. Add enough pairs like this one to the pre-existing design and we should be able to estimate $w^s\left(\frac{1}{3}\right)$ directly and then estimate the marginal weight dw^s as the difference between the estimates $\hat{w}^s\left(\frac{1}{3}\right)$ and $\hat{w}^s\left(\frac{1}{4}\right)$. Call this estimate $\widehat{dw}^s_{dis}$ (the subscript *dis* meaning "dissimilar").

The second route to identification depends on adding a different sort of choice pair such as *safe* $= (2/3,1/3,0)$ and *risky* $= (3/4,0,1/4)$. Add enough pairs like this one to the pre-existing design and we should also be able to estimate $w^s\left(\frac{1}{3}\right)$ and hence dw^s. But this is not a "dissimilar pair" as defined in the previous paragraph: I believe that many decision-makers would regard the 1/3 probability (of m in *safe*) as similar to the 1/4 probability (of h in *risky*), and would therefore ignore that probability difference and choose according to most-preferred outcome (i.e., choose *risky* since $h > m$). For that reason, I will call these "similar pairs." Although we can estimate dw^s by adding only such similar pairs, I expect that our resulting estimate – call this $\widehat{dw}^s_{sim}$ – will be much smaller than we would estimate by adding only dissimilar pairs to the pre-existing design (i.e., following the first identification strategy).

Under the hypothesis that rank-dependent weighting exists independently of similarity, the two identification strategies outlined above should result in equivalent estimates of dw^s. The final observation is that nothing prevents us from constructing a design which simultaneously follows both paths to identifying dw^s – that is, in which dw^s is overidentified, once with similar pairs and once with dissimilar pairs. The third experiment does this.

10. DESIGN OF THE THIRD EXPERIMENT

The option pairs in this third experiment begin with design considerations and choices very like those of the second experiment. As before, subjects choose between *safe* and *risky* in each pair presented to them. There are 10 distinct 3-outcome contexts, all created from the five positive money outcomes $15, $20, $30, $45, and $80. Table 4a shows 34 of the option pairs used in the experiment: Some of these are repeated up to four times as indicated in the "trials" column, for a total of 68 choice tasks. These choice tasks are the "trunk" of the design: The probabilities in this set of pairs are constrained to the set of fourths (0, 1/4, 1/2, 3/4, or 1).

The pairs in Tables 4b and 4c are the two different identification "branches" of the design: These pairs introduce options that contain the 1/3 probability of

Table 4. Option pairs used in the third experiment.

Pair #	Trials	Context $\langle l,m,h \rangle$	*Safe* Option Outcome Probabilities			*Risky* Option Outcome Probabilities		
			p_l	p_m	p_h	q_l	q_m	q_h
4a. 34 Pairs Used for Both Dissimilar and Similar Estimations (68 Total Trials)								
1	4	⟨15,20,30⟩	0	1	0	0.75	0	0.25
2	3		0	1	0	0.5	0	0.5
3	1		0	1	0	0.25	0	0.75
4	4		0	0.75	0.25	0.5	0	0.5
5	1		0.25	0.5	0.25	0.5	0	0.5
6	1		0	0.5	0.5	0.25	0	0.75
7	1	⟨15,20,45⟩	0	0.5	0.5	0.25	0	0.75
8	1	⟨15,20,80⟩	0.25	0.75	0	0.75	0	0.25
9	1		0.25	0.75	0	0.5	0	0.5
10	1	⟨15,30,45⟩	0.25	0.75	0	0.75	0	0.25
11	1		0	0.75	0.25	0.5	0	0.5
12	1		0	0.5	0.5	0.25	0	0.75
13	4	⟨15,30,80⟩	0.25	0.75	0	0.75	0	0.25
14	1		0.5	0.5	0	0.75	0	0.25
15	4		0.25	0.5	0.25	0.5	0	0.5
16	4		0	0.75	0.25	0.25	0	0.75
17	1	⟨15,45,80⟩	0.25	0.75	0	0.75	0	0.25
18	1		0.5	0.5	0	0.75	0	0.25
19	1		0	1	0	0.25	0	0.75
20	2		0	0.75	0.25	0.5	0	0.5
21	2		0	0.5	0.5	0.25	0	0.75
22	3	⟨20,30,45⟩	0	1	0	0.75	0	0.25
23	1		0	1	0	0.25	0.5	0.25
24	4		0	1	0	0.5	0	0.5
25	2		0.25	0.75	0	0.5	0	0.5
26	3		0	1	0	0.25	0	0.75
27	1		0	0.75	0.25	0.5	0	0.5
28	1	⟨20,45,80⟩	0	0.5	0.5	0.25	0	0.75
29	3	⟨30,45,80⟩	0	1	0	0.75	0	0.25
30	3		0	1	0	0.5	0	0.5
31	3		0.25	0.75	0	0.5	0	0.5
32	1		0	1	0	0.25	0	0.75
33	2		0	0.75	0.25	0.5	0	0.5
34	1		0	0.75	0.25	0.25	0	0.75

(*Continued*)

Table 4. (*Continued*)

4b. 6 "Dissimilar Pairs" Used Only for Dissimilar Estimations (16 Trials in All)								
35	3	(15,20,30)	0	1	0	0.67	0	0.33
36	4	(15,20,80)	0	1	0	0.67	0	0.33
37	1	(15,45,80)	0	1	0	0.67	0	0.33
38	3	(20,30,45)	0	1	0	0.67	0	0.33
39	1	(20,30,80)	0	1	0	0.67	0	0.33
40	4	(30,45,80)	0	1	0	0.67	0	0.33
4c. 6 "Similar Pairs" Used Only for Similar Estimations (16 Trials in All)								
41	2	(15,20,30)	0.67	0.33	0	0.75	0	0.25
42	3	(15,20,80)	0.67	0.33	0	0.75	0	0.25
43	4	(15,30,45)	0.67	0.33	0	0.75	0	0.25
44	4	(15,45,80)	0.67	0.33	0	0.75	0	0.25
45	2	(20,30,45)	0.67	0.33	0	0.75	0	0.25
46	1	(30,45,80)	0.67	0.33	0	0.75	0	0.25

a highest outcome in various options. There are six dissimilar pairs in Table 4b, and six similar pairs in Table 4c, each repeated up to four times as indicated in the "trials" column, for a total of 16 choice tasks from each of these tables. With the 68 choice tasks from Table 4a, this is a total of 100 choice tasks in the design. As with the design of the second experiment, the 68 choice tasks in Table 4a were chosen by an iterated Monte Carlo simulation procedure aimed at maximizing the efficiency of estimation for the worst decile of the sampled population. Then, the same kind of iterated Monte Carlo procedure was used to select contexts and numbers of trials for the two branches aimed at efficient estimation of dw^s in both branches.

The subjects for the third experiment were 92 undergraduate students, again at Chapman University as with the second experiment. The experimental protocol was almost identical to that of the second experiment, except that a 12-sided die was used as the random device – this being the lowest-sided die capable of producing both fourths and thirds as probabilities.

Estimation closely resembles that undertaken for data from the second experiment. The third experiment now involves four distinct probabilities $q \in \left\{\frac{1}{4}, \frac{1}{3}, \frac{2}{4}, \frac{3}{4}\right\}$, and hence a vector of four weights to estimate. As suggested by the second discussion in the previous section, we can think of the two different branches of the design as creating two possibly different vectors of weights $\mathbf{w}^s_{dis}$ and $\mathbf{w}^s_{sim}$. The *dissimilar estimation* uses only the 84 choice tasks of Tables 4a and 4b to produce an estimate $\hat{\mathbf{w}}^s_{dis}$, while the *similar estimation* uses only the 84 choice tasks of Tables 4a and 4c to produce an estimate $\hat{\mathbf{w}}^s_{sim}$. The same penalized maximum likelihood procedure was used for this estimation (see Appendix 2). With these estimates in hand, two different estimates of the marginal weight may be computed as $\widehat{dw}^s_{dis} = \hat{w}^s_{dis}\left(\frac{1}{3}\right) - \hat{w}^s_{dis}\left(\frac{1}{4}\right)$ and $\widehat{dw}^s_{sim} = \hat{w}^s_{sim}\left(\frac{1}{3}\right) - \hat{w}^s_{sim}\left(\frac{1}{4}\right)$.

11. RESULTS OF EXPERIMENT THREE

Fig. 12 shows the results of the dissimilar estimation (the left panel) and the similar estimation (the right panel) side by side, using contextual utility as the probabilistic model. Vertical lines at $q = 1/4$ and $q = 1/3$ focus attention on the change in estimated weights across this probability interval. The dissimilar estimations result in a handful of flat weighting function segments, that is, $\widehat{dw}^{s}_{dis} = 0.0001$,[6] across the interval – 11 out of 92 subjects in fact. The similar estimation shows well more than a handful of flat weighting function segments: In fact 57 of the 92 estimates result in $\widehat{dw}^{s}_{sim} = 0.0001$. This alone is strong evidence that the similar pairs quite commonly provoke the computational shortcut suggested throughout this study. Decision field theory produces the same kind of figures. Stronger utility, on other hand, only rarely produced bottom-bounded estimates.

Table 5 shows the sample mean value of $\widehat{dw}^{s}_{dis} - \widehat{dw}^{s}_{sim}$, which I will call "the similarity effect," along with related statistics. In absolute terms as well as the estimated effect size, contextual utility estimations produce the strongest similarity effect: Across the 92 subjects, the sample mean of $\widehat{dw}^{s}_{dis} - \widehat{dw}^{s}_{sim}$ is 0.0791 with a standard error[7] of 0.011 (a p-value would be gratuitous). Perspective on the size of this estimated effect is provided by identity weights (expected utility for instance) for which $dw^{s} = 1/3 - 1/4 = 0.0833$. That is, the estimated size of the similarity effect would very nearly erase identity weighting. The sample mean of the estimated similarity effect is smaller when I perform the estimation with either

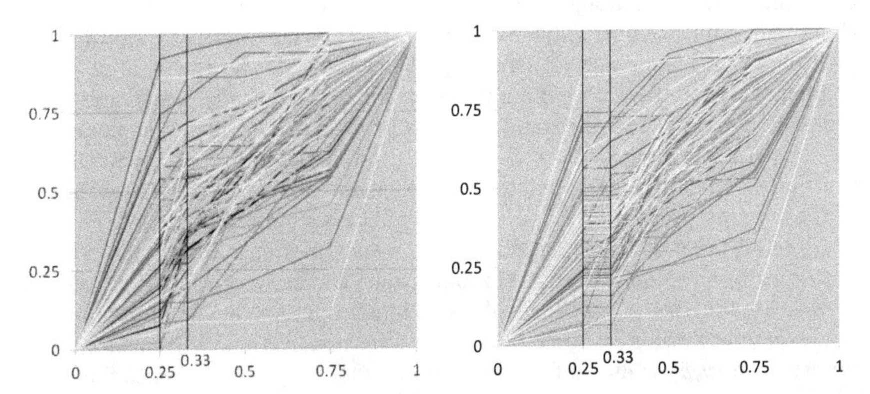

Fig. 12. 92 Function-free Individual Estimates of Weighting Functions, Estimated With the Contextual Utility Model Using Data From the Third Experiment. The Left Panel Shows Estimations Using Only the "Dissimilar Pairs" to Identify the Weight at $q = 0.33$; The Right Panel Shows Estimations Using Only the "Similar Pairs" to Identify the Weight at $q = 0.33$. Estimated Weights Using Only the Pairs in Tables 4a and 4b (the "Dissimilar Pairs"). 11 of 92 Estimated Weighting Functions Are Flat on the Interval [0.25,0.33] in This Case. Estimated Weights Using Only the Pairs in Tables 4a and 4c (the "Similar Pairs"). 57 of 92 Estimated Weighting Functions Are Flat on the Interval [0.25,0.33] in This Case.

Table 5. The Estimated Similarity Effect $\widehat{dw}^s_{dis} - \widehat{dw}^s_{sim}$ in the Third Experiment.

	Probabilistic Model Used for Estimation		
	Contextual Utility	Decision Field Theory	Stronger Utility
Sample mean	0.0791	0.0627	0.0462
Standard error	0.011	0.0104	0.0092
Standard deviation of $\widehat{dw}^s_{dis}$	0.0855	0.0868	0.0841
Effect size	0.925	0.723	0.549

Notes: The effect size is calculated as the ratio of the sample mean of $\widehat{dw}^s_{dis} - \widehat{dw}^s_{sim}$ to the standard deviation of $\widehat{dw}^s_{dis}$. An effect size of 0.5 is considered moderate while an effect size of 0.8 is considered large. (The standard deviation of $\widehat{dw}^s_{sim}$ is always smaller than that of $\widehat{dw}^s_{dis}$, so the effect sizes would be larger if that information was used too.)

decision field theory or stronger utility, but still significantly positive at any conventional significance level. This casts strong doubt on the null hypothesis that estimated probability weights are independent of similarity effects.

12. CONCLUSIONS

Optimism is the most prevalent form of rank-dependent weighting functions estimated here – not the widely believed inverse-s shape. I attribute this to several potential factors. The designs of the first and second experiments deliberately set about to minimize opportunities for reducing decision complexity by way of computational shortcuts based on similarity of probabilities and rounding of probabilities. This was done by confining probabilities to relatively coarse grids and avoiding choice pairs that juxtapose similar probabilities of high outcomes. The third experiment showed that such pairs do produce flatter probability weighting function estimates on low to moderate interior probabilities – a defining feature of the inverse-s prospector shape – in the predicted manner.

If $\underline{p}$ and $\overline{p}$ are the smallest and largest probabilities of the maximum lottery outcomes found across all lotteries in some binary choice experiment, it can always be the case that, for probabilities of a maximum outcome below $\underline{p}$, or above $\overline{p}$, that experiment will miss some bit of curvature or elevation different from that observed on $[\underline{p},\overline{p}]$ or miss a fixed point not found on $[\underline{p},\overline{p}]$. Of course that possibility is true of my three experiments. But if similarity-induced shortcuts and rounding short-circuit "normal" probability weighting of outcome utilities, pushing designed outcome probabilities ever closer to zero or one increasingly runs the risk that those probabilities get treated as zero and one, respectively. Indeed Kahneman and Tversky (1979) originally thought the probability weighting function was poorly behaved – maybe not a continuous function at all, or even a function – near its endpoints for those kinds of reasons.

Study of risk preferences requires a researcher to make several interrelated choices. Here, I chose binary discrete choice as an elicitation method. This has its virtues, not least of which is the fact that binary preference relations are the primitive of most axiomatic theories. Yet each elicitation method comes with its own econometric conundrums – for instance, where and how functional form assumptions should be deployed. Here, I chose to minimize functional assumptions concerning the utilities and weights that are the structural entities of axiomatic rank-dependent representation theorems. This has costs. Assumptions concerning probabilistic models of binary discrete choices will be needed, and I have used three such models. By and large my results are not too sensitive to a choice of one of those models or another. Another approach might minimize assumptions about probabilistic models – say exploiting new semiparametric methods for discrete choice estimation. This has its own cost: A more parametric approach to the decision-theoretic entities. This would be good and useful future work.

Finally, others choose to elicit certainty equivalents, usually employing a choice list procedure to approximate certainty equivalents (e.g., Bruhin et al., 2010; Gonzalez & Wu, 1999; Tversky & Kahneman, 1992) and then use econometric methods appropriate to certainty equivalents. Such estimations generally find the conventional inverse-s shape. However, Wilcox (2017) describes a fundamental ambiguity concerning certainty equivalent evidence having to do with different sources of the probabilistic nature of decision and judgment. Elicitation of certainty equivalents just does not free one from the necessary business of making probabilistic modeling assumptions.

Throughout this chapter I have motivated discussions in terms of "bias" in probability weighting estimation due to similarity-induced computational shortcuts or rounding behavior that short-circuit "normal" rank-dependent weighting of utilities. I argued certain kinds of experimental designs would more likely produce that kind of "bias." Of course "poor" experimental design can result in all kinds of biased estimation. From that perspective, readers may think that the chapter simply points to issues that a careful experimenter can consider to detect and avoid bad designs. But there may be no gold standard experimental design that allows estimation of that one stable probability weighting function. So now I need to come clean about that previous "bias" rhetoric. What I fear (but do not know) is that with considerations of similarity, rounding, and other things in mind, an experimenter might – by judicious selection of choice pairs – be able to demonstrate almost any rank-dependent probability weighting function shape. Asked what the probability weighting function looks like, the reply of a worldly experimenter might resemble that of the famously broad-minded corporate accountant: What do you want it to look like?

NOTES

1. This normalized version of CRRA utility is simply $u^s(z \mid \rho^s) = \left(z^{1-\rho^s} - 40^{1-\rho^s}\right) / \left(120^{1-\rho^s} - 40^{1-\rho^s}\right)$.
2. Parametric estimations produce estimates with about 80–50% of the variability of these function-free estimates (around the true DGP weighting function).
3. Six of each with contextual utility, four pessimists and seven unclassified with decision field theory, and seven pessimists and five unclassified with stronger utility.

4. 11 Prospectors and 1 unclassified with contextual utility, 11 prospectors and 2 unclassified with stronger utility, and 13 prospectors and 1 unclassified with decision field theory.
5. With estimates $\widehat{\beta}^s$ in hand for the 98 subjects, the null hypothesis $\beta^s = 0$ fails to be rejected at the 10% significance level by either a sign, signed-rank or t-test when contextual utility is the probabilistic model, and 48 of the 98 estimated weighting functions have optimist shapes. When decision field theory is the probabilistic model, estimates of β^s have a weakly significantly *negative* location ($p = 0.081$) by a signed-rank test, but not by the sign or t-test, and 51 of the 98 estimated weighting functions have optimist shapes. Application of stronger utility to this case is not straightforward since it is unclear how stochastic dominance is to be defined when there is one utility function for certain outcomes and another for uncertain outcomes.
6. As mentioned in Appendix 2, monotonicity is imposed on estimated utilities and weights in such a manner that the minimum estimated value of dw^s is constrained to be no smaller than 0.0001.
7. I treat each calculated value of $\widehat{dw}^s_{dis} - \widehat{dw}^s_{sim}$, for each subject, as an independent single observation (with one degree of freedom), and do simple statistics based on that. Any scalar quantity $y^s = f(\boldsymbol{r}^s) - g(\boldsymbol{r}^s)$, where $\boldsymbol{r}^s$ is an observation vector from subject s, can be represented as $y^s = E_s[f(\boldsymbol{r}^s) - g(\boldsymbol{r}^s)] + \varepsilon^s$, where $E_s[f(\boldsymbol{r}^s) - g(\boldsymbol{r}^s)]$ is the population mean of $f(\boldsymbol{r}^s) - g(\boldsymbol{r}^s)$ and the ε^s are independent across subjects. Therefore, where inferences about $E_s[f(\boldsymbol{r}^s) - g(\boldsymbol{r}^s)]$ are concerned, the very simplest statistics can be applied.
8. That is ($risky \vee safe$) stochastically dominates both *risky* and *safe*, but is itself stochastically dominated by every other option that stochastically dominates both *risky* and *safe*. Similarly, *risky* and *safe* both stochastically dominate ($risky \wedge safe$), and every other option stochastically dominated by both *risky* and *safe* is itself stochastically dominated by ($risky \wedge safe$).

ACKNOWLEDGMENTS

I have benefited from conversations with Pavlo Blavatskyy, Jerome Busemeyer, Chew Soo Hong, Jim Cox, Glenn Harrison, John Hey, Stefan Hoderlein, Jonathan Leland, Graham Loomes, Mark Machina, John Quiggin, Michel Regenwetter, Joerg Stoye, and an anonymous referee. I thank Stacey Joldersma for her excellent research assistance. This work was financially supported by the University of Houston and Chapman University.

REFERENCES

Abdellaoui, M. (2000). Parameter-free elicitation of utility and probability weighting functions. *Management Science*, *46*(11), 1497–1512. doi:10.1287/mnsc.46.11.1497.12080

Abdellaoui, M., Bleichrodt, H., & Paraschiv, C. (2007). Loss aversion under prospect theory: A parameter-free measurement. *Management Science*, *53*(10), 1659–1674. doi:10.1287/mnsc.1070.0711

Anderson, S., Harrison, G. W., Lau, M. I., & Rutström, E. E. (2008). Eliciting risk and time preferences. *Econometrica*, *76*(3), 583–618. doi:10.1111/j.1468-0262.2008.00848.x

Anderson, S., Harrison, G. W., Lau, M. I., & Rutström, E. E. (2013). Discounting behavior and the magnitude effect: Evidence from a field experiment in Denmark. *Economica*, *80*(320), 670–697. doi:10.1111/ecca.12028

Andreoni, J., & Sprenger, C. (2012). Risk preferences are not time preferences. *American Economic Review*, *102*(7), 3357–3376. doi:10.1257/aer.102.7.3357

Apesteguia, J., & Ballester, M. (2018). Monotone stochastic choice models: The case of risk and time preferences. *Journal of Political Economy*, *126*(1), 74–106. doi:10.1086/695504

Ballinger, T. P., & Wilcox, N. T. (1997). Decisions, error and heterogeneity. *Economic Journal, 107*(443), 1090–1105. doi:10.1111/j.1468-0297.1997.tb00009.x

Blavatskyy, P. (2013). Which decision theory? *Economics Letters, 120*(1), 40–44. doi:10.1016/j.econlet.2013.03.039

Blavatskyy, P. R. (2011). Probabilistic risk aversion with an arbitrary outcome set. *Economics Letters, 112*(1), 34–37. doi:10.1016/j.econlet.2011.03.004

Blavatskyy, P. R. (2014). Stronger utility. *Theory and Decision, 76*, 265–286. doi:10.1007/s11238-013-9366-3

Brown, A., & Healy, P. J. (2018). Separated decisions. *European Economic Review, 101*, 20–34. doi:10.1016/j.euroecorev.2017.09.014

Bruhin, A., Fehr-Duda, H., & Epper, T. (2010). Risk and rationality: Uncovering heterogeneity in probability distortion. *Econometrica, 78*(4), 1375–1412. doi:10.3982/ECTA7139

Busemeyer, J., & Townsend, J. (1992). Fundamental derivations from decision field theory. *Mathematical Social Sciences, 23*(3), 255–282. doi:10.1016/0165-4896(92)90043-5

Busemeyer, J., & Townsend, J. (1993). Decision field theory: A dynamic-cognitive approach to decision making in an uncertain environment. *Psychological Review, 100*(3), 432–459. doi:10.1037/0033-295X.100.3.432

Camerer, C. F. (1989). An experimental test of several generalized expected utility theories. *Journal of Risk and Uncertainty, 2*, 61–104. doi:10.1007/BF00055711

Camerer, C. F., & Ho, T.-H. (1994). Violations of the betweeness axiom and nonlinearity in probability. *Journal of Risk and Uncertainty, 8*, 167–196. doi:10.1007/BF01065371

Cheung, S. (2013). Risk preferences are not time preferences: On the elicitation of time preference under conditions of risk: Comment. *American Economic Review, 105*(7), 2242–2260. 10.1257/aer.20120946

Conlisk, J. (1989). Three variants on the Allais example. *American Economic Review, 79*, 392–407. Retrieved from https://www.jstor.org/stable/1806852

Cox, J. C., Sadiraj, V., & Schmidt, U. (2015). Paradoxes and mechanisms for choice under risk. *Experimental Economics, 18*, 215–250. doi:10.1007/s10683-014-9398-8

Fishburn, P. C. (1978). A probabilistic expected utility theory of risky binary choices. *International Economic Review, 19*(3), 633–646. doi:10.2307/2526329

Gonzalez, R., & Wu, G. (1999). On the shape of the probability weighting function. *Cognitive Psychology, 38*(1), 129–166. doi:10.1006/cogp.1998.0710

Gul, F., & Pesendorfer, W. (2006). Random expected utility. *Econometrica, 74*(1), 121–146. https://doi.org/10.1111/j.1468-0262.2006.00651.x

Harrison, G. W., & Swarthout, J. T. (2014). Experimental payment protocols and the bipolar behaviorist. *Theory and Decision, 77*, 423–438. doi:10.1007/s11238-014-9447-y

Hey, J. D. (2001). Does repetition improve consistency? *Experimental Economics, 4*, 5–54. doi:10.1023/A:1011486405114

Hey, J. D., Lotito, G., & Maffioletti, A. (2010). The descriptive and predictive adequacy of theories of decision making under uncertainty/ambiguity. *Journal of Risk and Uncertainty, 41*, 81–111. doi:10.1007/s11166-010-9102-0

Hey, J. D., & Orme, C. (1994). Investigating generalizations of expected utility theory using experimental data. *Econometrica, 62*(6), 1291–1329. doi:10.2307/2951750

Kahneman, D., & Tversky, A. (1979). Prospect theory: An analysis of decision under risk. *Econometrica, 47*(2), 263–291. doi:10.2307/1914185

Leland, J. W. (1994). Generalized similarity judgments: An alternative explanation for choice anomalies. *Journal of Risk and Uncertainty, 9*, 151–172. doi:10.1007/BF01064183

Loomes, G., & Sugden, R. (1995). Incorporating a stochastic element into decision theories. *European Economic Review, 39*(3–4), 641–648. doi:10.1016/0014-2921(94)00071-7

Loomes, G., & Sugden, R. (1998). Testing different stochastic specifications of risky choice. *Economica, 65*(260), 581–598. doi:10.1111/1468-0335.00147

Luce, R. D. (1959). *Individual choice behavior: A theoretical analysis*. New York, NY: Wiley. Retrieved from https://books.google.com

Mosteller, F., & Nogee, P. (1951). An experimental measurement of utility. *Journal of Political Economy, 59*(5), 371–404. doi:10.1086/257106

Nilsson, H., Rieskamp, J., & Wagenmakers, E-J. (2011). Hierarchical Bayesian parameter estimation for cumulative prospect theory. *Journal of Mathematical Psychology*, *55*(1), 84–93. doi:10.1016/j.jmp.2010.08.006

Pratt, J. W. (1964). Risk aversion in the small and in the large. *Econometrica*, *32*(1–2), 122–136. doi:10.2307/1913738

Prelec, D. (1998). The probability weighting function. *Econometrica*, *66*(3), 497–527. doi:10.2307/2998573

Quiggin, J. (1982). A theory of anticipated utility. *Journal of Economic Behavior and Organization*, *3*(4), 323–343. doi:10.1016/0167-2681(82)90008-7

Quiggin, J. (1993). *Generalized expected utility theory: The rank-dependent model*. Norwell, MA: Kluwer. Retrieved from https://books.google.com

Rieskamp, J. (2008). The probabilistic nature of preferential choice. *Journal of Experimental Psychology: Learning, Memory and Cognition*, *34*(6), 1446–1465. doi:10.1037/a0013646

Rubinstein, A. (1988). Similarity and decision making under risk (Is there a utility theory resolution to the Allais paradox?). *Journal of Economic Theory*, *46*(1), 145–153. doi:10.1016/0022-0531(88)90154-8

Scheibehenne, B., & Pachur, T. (2015). Using Bayesian hierarchical parameter estimation to assess the generalizability of cognitive models of choice. *Psychonomic Bulletin and Review*, *22*, 391–407. doi:10.3758/s13423-014-0684-4

Starmer, C., & Sugden, R. (1989). Probability and juxtaposition effects: An experimental investigation of the common ratio effect. *Journal of Risk and Uncertainty*, *2*, 159–178. doi:10.1007/BF00056135

Starmer, C., & Sugden, R. (1991). Does the random-lottery incentive system elicit true preferences? An experimental investigation. *American Economic Review*, *81*(4), 971–978. Retrieved from https://www.jstor.org/stable/2006657

Tversky, A. (1969). Intransitivity of preferences. *Psychological Review*, *76*(1), 31–48. doi:10.1037/h0026750

Tversky, A., & Kahneman, D. (1992). Advances in prospect theory: Cumulative representation of uncertainty. *Journal of Risk and Uncertainty*, *5*, 297–323. doi:10.1007/BF00122574

Wald, A. (1947). *Sequential analysis*. New York, NY: Wiley. Retrieved from https://books.google.com

Wilcox, N. T. (1993). Lottery choice: Incentives, complexity and decision time. *Economic Journal*, *103*(421), 1397–1417. doi:10.2307/2234473

Wilcox, N. T. (2008). Stochastic models for binary discrete choice under risk: A critical primer and econometric comparison. In J. C. Cox & G. W. Harrison (Eds.), *Research in experimental economics Vol. 12: Risk aversion in experiments* (pp. 197–292). Bingley: Emerald. doi:10.1016/S0193-2306(08)00004-5

Wilcox, N. T. (2011). 'Stochastically more risk averse:' A contextual theory of stochastic discrete choice under risk. *Journal of Econometrics*, *162*(1), 89–104. doi:10.1016/j.jeconom.2009.10.012

Wilcox, N. T. (2015). Error and generalization in discrete choice under risk. Retrieved from https://digitalcommons.chapman.edu/esi_working_papers/160/.

Wilcox, N. T. (2017). Random expected utility and certainty equivalents: Mimicry of probability weighting functions. *Journal of the Economic Science Association*, *3*, 161–173.

Wu, G., & Gonzalez, R. (1996). Curvature of the probability weighting function. *Management Science*, *42*(12), 1676–1690. https://doi.org/10.1287/mnsc.42.12.1676

APPENDIX 1: BACKGROUND ON THE THREE PROBABILISTIC CHOICE MODELS

The contextual utility or CU model (Wilcox, 2011) makes comparative risk aversion properties of the RDU representation and its stochastic implications consistent within and across contexts. For representations such as RDU, utility functions $u(z)$ are only unique up to a ratio of differences: Intuitively, contextual utility exploits this uniqueness to create a correspondence between functional and probabilistic definitions of comparative risk aversion. Consider the choice pairs in the first experiment: Under RDU and contextual utility, Eq. 4 can be rewritten as

$$P^{rdcu} = F\left(\lambda\left[-v(l,m,h)+w(q_h)\right]\right), \quad (A.1)$$

where

$$v(l,m,h)=\left[u(m)-u(l)\right]/\left[u(h)-u(l)\right].$$

This probability is decreasing in the ratio of differences $v(l,m,h)$. Consider two subjects Anne and Bob with identical weighting functions (this includes the case where both have EU preferences) and identical scale parameters λ, and assume that Bob is globally more risk averse than Anne in Pratt's sense (Bob's local absolute risk aversion $-u''(z)/u'(z)$ exceeds that of Anne for all z). These assumptions, Pratt's (1964) main theorem, and simple algebra shows that $v^{Bob}(l,m,h) > v^{Anne}(l,m,h)$ on all contexts. As a result (A.1) implies that Bob will have a lower probability than Anne of choosing *risky* on all contexts in the first experiment. Wilcox (2011) shows that the received homoscedastic latent index model cannot share this property, and this was my primary motivation for the contextual utility model. In the second and third experiments, the property is a somewhat weaker one appropriate to RDU when one or both options in a pair have non-zero probabilities of all three outcomes (see Wilcox, 2011, p. 97, Proposition 2), reflecting the role probability weights play in observed risk aversion.

Note that Eq. 5 is the *decision field theory* model or DFT *only* for pairs like those found in the first experiment. For those choice pairs, DFT shares CU's main property: Holding constant λ and $w(q_h)$, globally greater risk aversion (in the sense of Pratt) will imply a lower probability of choosing *risky* in all pairs on all contexts. The general formulation of $D(risky, safe)$ in DFT, which is needed for the estimations using data from the second and third experiments, depends on the underlying events that generate outcome probabilities as well as outcome utilities. Index events by $e = 1,2,\ldots,E$, let w_e be the decision weight given to event e, and let u_e^{risky} and u_e^{safe} be the utilities resulting from the choice of options *risky* and *safe*, respectively, when event e occurs. Then the general formulation of $D(risky, safe)$ in decision field theory is:

$$D(risky, safe)=\sqrt{\sum_e w_e\left(u_e^{risky}-u_e^{safe}-\Delta RDU\right)^2}\,. \quad (A.2)$$

Busemeyer and Townsend (1992, 1993) derive DFT from a computational argument: The theory is one of the early "diffusion" models of probabilistic choice. A simple intuition can be given for the model. Suppose that a decision maker's computational resources can effortlessly and quickly provide utilities of outcomes, and also suppose the decision maker wishes to choose according to relative RDU value; but suppose she does not have an algorithm for effortlessly and quickly multiplying utilities and weights together. The decision maker could proceed by *sampling* events in option pairs in proportion to their decision weights, keeping running sums of the sampled utility differences between the options, and choose when the summed differences exceed some threshold determined by the cost of sampling. In essence, the choice probability in Eq. 5 results from this kind of sequential sampling decision procedure, which can be traced back to Wald (1947). Busemeyer and Townsend also show that, as the sampling rate gets large, the function F will be the logistic c.d.f. – the reason I employ the logistic c.d.f. throughout this work.

Because decision field theory's D function is defined in terms of events, with decision weights assigned to events rather than ranked outcomes, application of decision field theory to members of the rank-dependent family is only sensible if all choice options in an experiment are comonotonic. In this case, event weights and rank-dependent weights coincide, and all three experiments are structured in this way. For example, in the first experiment, lotteries *risky* all have probabilities q_h of receiving their high outcome that are in sixths, generated by the roll of a 6-sided die. All lotteries are constructed so that $q_h = k/6$ is always the roll "1 or 2 or … k". So $w(k/6)$, the rank-dependent weight on the high outcome h in *risky*, can always be thought of as the decision weight of the event "the die roll is 1 or 2 or … k", while $1-w(k/6)$, the rank-dependent weight on the low outcome l in *risky*, can always be thought of as the decision weight of the event "the die roll is $k+1$ or $k+2$ or … 6." The events and outcome ranks are identically ordered across all option pairs in each experiment: This is *comonotonicity* (see Quiggin, 1993).

Blavatskyy's (2014) *stronger utility* or SU model is a general approach to constructing probabilistic models of risky choice that will respect first order stochastic dominance or FOSD: that is, the model always attaches a zero probability to choice of first order stochastically dominated options. In its general form, the SU model begins with a definition of two important benchmark options. Let (*risky* $\vee$ *safe*) and (*risky* $\wedge$ *safe*) denote the least upper bound and greatest lower bound, respectively, on both *risky* and *safe* in terms of FOSD.[8] Let V denote the functional representation of option value for some decision theory. Then in the general SU model, $D(risky, safe) = V(risky \vee safe) - V(risky \wedge safe)$, and

$$P^{rdbf} = Prob(risky) = H_{\lambda}\left(\frac{V(risky) - V(safe)}{V(risky \vee safe) - V(risky \wedge safe)}\right). \quad \text{(A.3)}$$

For the choice pairs in the first experiment, $(risky \vee safe) = (0, 1-q_h, q_h)$ and $(risky \wedge safe) = (1-q_h, q_h, 0)$. Applying the RDU representation to these lotteries,

$$RDU(risky \vee safe) - RDU(risky \wedge safe) = \\ w(q)u(h) + [1-w(q)]u(m) - w(q)u(m) - [1-w(q)]u(l) = \\ w(q)[u(h)-u(m)] + [1-w(q)][u(m)-u(l)], \tag{A.4}$$

which is the denominator appearing in Eq. 6 defining the SU model for these choice pairs.

Given a suitable choice of the function H_λ, equivalence of Eqs. A.3 and 7 may be established as follows. Let $R = risky$ and $S = safe$. From Eq. A.3 and the definitions $U = (R \vee S) = (0, 1-q_h, q_h)$ and $L = (R \wedge S) = (1-q_h, q_h, 0)$ for the option pairs in the first experiment, Blavatskyy's model is

$$P^{rdbf} = Prob(R) = H_\lambda\left(\frac{V(R)-V(S)}{V(U)-V(L)}\right). \tag{A.5}$$

Choose $H_\lambda(x) = \Lambda\left[\lambda \ln\left(\frac{1+x}{1-x}\right)\right]$. For $x \in (-1,1)$, this has the needed properties $H_\lambda(0) = 0.5$ and $H_\lambda(x) = 1 - H_\lambda(-x)$. With $x = \frac{V(R)-V(S)}{V(U)-V(L)}$, we have

$$\frac{1+x}{1-x} = \frac{1+\frac{V(R)-V(S)}{V(U)-V(L)}}{1-\frac{V(R)-V(S)}{V(U)-V(L)}} = \frac{V(U)-V(L)+V(R)-V(S)}{V(U)-V(L)+V(S)-V(R)} \\ = \frac{[V(U)-V(S)]+[V(R)-V(L)]}{[V(U)-V(R)]+[V(S)-V(L)]}. \tag{A.6}$$

Applying the RDU representation theorem to the four key options,

$$\begin{aligned} V(R) &= w(q_h)u(h) + [1-w(q_h)]u(l), \\ V(S) &= u(m), \\ V(U) &= w(q_h)u(h) + [1-w(q_h)]u(m), \text{ and} \\ V(L) &= w(q_h)u(m) + [1-w(q_h)]u(l). \end{aligned} \tag{A.7}$$

Substitute these into the four bracketed terms at the right end of (A.6) to get

$$\begin{aligned} [V(U)-V(S)] &= w(q_h)[u(h)-u(m)], \\ [V(R)-V(L)] &= w(q_h)[u(h)-u(m)], \\ [V(U)-V(R)] &= [1-w(q_h)][u(m)-u(l)], \text{ and} \\ [V(S)-V(L)] &= [1-w(q_h)][u(m)-u(l)]. \end{aligned} \tag{A.8}$$

Clearly $\frac{1+x}{1-x} = \frac{w(q_h)[u(h)-u(m)]}{[1-w(q_h)][u(m)-u(l)]}$, so the equivalence to Eq. 7, given RDU and a suitable choice of H_λ, has been established.

In the case of the second and third experiments, where $safe = (p_l, p_m, p_h)$ and $risky = (q_l, q_m, q_h)$, we have $(risky \vee safe) = (p_l, 1-p_l-q_h, q_h)$ and $(risky \wedge safe) = (q_l, 1-q_l-p_h, p_h)$. Algebraic steps resembling those from Eqs. A.3 to A.8 lead to the following elaborated version of Eq. A.7 that is suitable for data from the second and third experiments:

$$P^{su} = Prob(risky) = F\left[\lambda \ln\left(\frac{[w(q_h)-w(p_h)][u(h)-u(m)]}{[w(1-p_l)-w(1-q_l)][u(m)-u(l)]}\right)\right]. \quad (A.9)$$

This particular instance of Blavatskyy's (2014) stronger utility is also an instance of Fishburn's (1978) incremental expected utility advantage model of probabilistic choice, so one might usefully refer to Eq. A.9 as the Blavatskyy–Fishburn model.

APPENDIX 2: ESTIMATION NOTES

All estimations were carried out in SAS 9.2 using the non-linear programming procedure ("Proc NLP" in the SAS language) using the quasi-Newton algorithm. For function-free estimations all parameters bounded in the interval [0,1], that is, utilities and weights, were constrained to lie in [0.0001,0.9999]; additionally, monotonicity was imposed on estimated utilities and weights.

Monte Carlo simulations showed that both finite sample biases of parameter estimates and prediction log likelihoods could be noticeably improved by penalizing estimation that produced fitted probabilities very close to zero or one. By a grid search across Monte Carlo simulations, the following piecewise quadratic penalty function $p_i(\boldsymbol{\theta}^s)$ was arrived at as a good kludge for penalizing such fitted probabilities:

$p_i(\boldsymbol{\theta}^s) = 0$ if $P_i^{spec}(\boldsymbol{\theta}^s) \in [0.001, 0.999]$;

$p_i(\boldsymbol{\theta}^s) = -10 \cdot (1 - 1000 P_i^{spec}(\boldsymbol{\theta}^s))^2$ if $P_i^{spec}(\boldsymbol{\theta}^s) < 0.001$; and

$p_i(\boldsymbol{\theta}^s) = -10 \cdot (1000 P_i^{spec}(\boldsymbol{\theta}^s) - 999)^2$ if $P_i^{spec}(\boldsymbol{\theta}^s) > 0.999$.

This simply imposes a very steep but smoothly differentiable penalty on probabilities that wander within 0.001 of zero or one. The adjusted log likelihood function is

$$\mathcal{L}^{spec}(\mathbf{r}^s_{set(k)} | \boldsymbol{\theta}^s) = \sum_{it \in set(k)} \ell^{spec}(r^s_{it} | \boldsymbol{\theta}^s) + \sum_i \tau_i p_i(\boldsymbol{\theta}^s),$$

where τ_i denotes the number of trials of pair i in any experiment. This penalty was imposed on all maximum likelihood estimations.

For each subject and specification, estimations were started from a grid of starting parameter vectors to a "finalist" estimated vector from each starting vector, and the finalist with the best adjusted log likelihood was selected as the maximum likelihood estimate.

APPENDIX 3: FIRST EXPERIMENT PROTOCOL EXPLANATION AND INSTRUCTIONS TO SUBJECTS

I want to estimate utilities and weights without aggregation assumptions. Decision theories are about individuals, not aggregates, and aggregation mutilates and destroys many observable properties of decision theories (Wilcox, 2008). A large amount of choice data from each subject is needed to reliably estimate utilities and weights at the individual level. A subject will become bored, and will become careless, if she makes hundreds of decisions at one sitting. So the decisions are divided up across three days, and on each day into two parts separated by unrelated tasks providing a break from decisions.

The separation across three days, in particular, introduces a risk that some substantial event altering a subjects' wealth or background risks will occur between days, which could arguably undermine the assumption that utilities of outcomes and hence choice probabilities are stationary throughout the protocol. This is a risk I am willing to run to mitigate subject boredom with hundreds of choice tasks, and I can check whether distributions of risky choice proportions across subjects appear to be stationary across subjects' three days of decisions. No test finds any significant difference between these three daily distributions. Within-subject differences between risky choice proportions on the first and third day have zero mean by all one-sample tests. There is some evidence that decisions are less noisy on the second and third days versus the first day (see Wilcox, 2015). Econometric allowance for this (estimating a separate precision parameter for each day) has no qualitative effect on my results in Section 5.

Random problem selection or RPS is meant to result in truthful, motivated and unbiased revelation of preferences in each pair: that is, subjects should make each of their 300 choices as if it was the only choice being made, for real, and there should be no portfolio or wealth effects making choices interdependent across the tasks. Both the independence axiom of EUT and the "isolation effect" of prospect theory would imply this. To see this for EUT, notice that the independence axiom in its "unreduced compounds" form (i.e., "compound independence") implies

$$\textit{risky} \succcurlyeq \textit{safe} \text{ if and only if } \begin{array}{c} (\textit{risky} \text{ with Prob} = 1/300;\ Z \text{ with Prob} = 299/300) \\ \succcurlyeq \\ (\textit{safe} \text{ with Prob} = 1/300;\ Z \text{ with Prob} = 299/300) \end{array}$$

where Z is any other outcome or risk, including the "grand lottery" created by the subject's other 299 choices over the course of this experiment. Therefore, if subjects' preferences satisfy independence in this unreduced compounds form, random problem selection should be incentive compatible. Some evidence suggests that preferences generally satisfy the independence axiom in its unreduced compounds form (Conlisk, 1989; Kahneman & Tversky, 1979), and older direct examinations of random problem selection in binary lottery choice experiments found no systematic choice differences between tasks selected with relatively low or high probabilities (Wilcox, 1993) nor between tasks presented singly or under random problem selection (Starmer & Sugden, 1991), at least for relatively simple tasks like the pairs used here. The literature examining the RPS is moderately large; recent pessimistic evidence includes Harrison and Swarthout (2014) and Cox, Sadiraj, and Schmidt (2015) while Brown and Healy (2018) found more optimistic evidence but only when using the SED (separated decisions) feature I use in my three experiments (each option pair is presented alone on its own separate screen in random order).

The choice pairs in Table 1 are on 25 distinct contexts, all constructed from nine positive money outcomes ($40 to $120 in $10 increments). I want to estimate the utilities and weights in the function-free manner Hey and Orme (1994) pioneered for utilities, Hey, Lotito, and Maffioletti (2010) did for utilities and subjective probabilities, and Blavatskyy (2013) did for utilities and weights. Monte Carlo simulations showed that function-free identification of utilities, weights and scale parameters is greatly improved when the same events (the die rolls) are matched with many different outcomes on different contexts.

Finally, the choice of a 6-sided die for the first experiment was deliberate. Sixths are well-suited for estimation given widely held priors about the shape of weighting functions. Consider Prelec's (1998) single-parameter weighting function $w(q|\gamma)=\exp\left(-[-\ln(q)]^{\gamma}\right)$ $\forall\, q \in (0,1)$, $w(0)=0$ and $w(1)=1$: Prelec proposed $\gamma=0.65$ as a rough estimate consistent with other estimates using different weighting functions. At that value of γ, $q-w(q|0.65)$ attains its maximum very close to $q = 5/6$; and at $q = 1/6$, $q-w(q|0.65)\approx -0.065$, about 80% of the minimum value taken by $q-w(q|0.65)$ (this is about –0.081 at $q\approx 0.07$). So the differences between linear weighting (i.e., EU) and received priors concerning probability weighting are about as strong as they could be at $q = 5/6$ and $q = 1/6$.

Instructions (First Experiment Only)

You will participate in three different sessions – one session on each of three different days. On *each* of the three days, you will make *100 choices* from each of 100 pairs of monetary options. Some of the options will involve chance, in the form of a die roll. Option pairs will be presented to you as pie charts, on a computer screen: In each option pair you see, you will choose the option you would prefer to play.

At the end of your third day with us, you will have made 300 choices over your three sessions. ONE of your 300 option choices will then be randomly selected using a bag of 300 tickets with the numbers 1, 2, 3,…, 299, 300 written on them. The numbers 1 to 100 correspond to the 100 choices you will make today, in the order you make them today. Likewise, the numbers 101 to 200 (and 201 to 300) correspond to the 100 choices you will make on your second day (and then on your third day) with us, in the order you make them on those days.

At the end of your third day with us, you will reach into the bag of tickets (without looking inside), pull one out and show us the number. We will then enter that number into the computer, and it will recall that option pair and show the option you chose. That option will determine your payment for participation in this project. If the option you chose requires a die roll, we will then roll a 6-sided die to determine your payment.

Notice that since *every* option pair choice you make has a 1 in 300 chance of determining your payment for participation, you have a real reason to consider each option pair with equal care. Also, notice that *only one* of your 300 option pair choices *will* determine your payment.

Please note that you won't be able to use a calculator, or pencil and paper, to make your choices. That would take too long for 100 choices ... our lab schedule will not accommodate this.

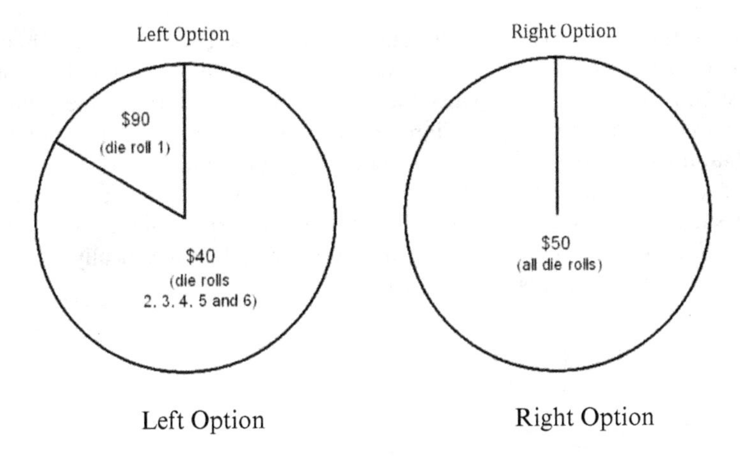

Left Option Right Option

An example of an option pair is shown above. The left option is a 1 in 6 chance of $90 and a 5 in 6 chance of $40: If you chose this option and it was selected to determine your payment, a die roll would be needed to determine the payment. The right option is a sure $50: If you chose this option and it was selected to determine your payment, no die roll would be needed.

The option pair you just saw is only one example. The money outcomes in the option pairs you see will range from $40 to $120, in $10 increments. Also, the connection between die rolls and money outcomes varies a lot over those options that involve a die roll, so remember to notice those die rolls when new option pairs appear on the screen for your consideration. Finally, note that the computer will present option pairs to you in a randomized order, and will also randomly select the left/right placement of the options in each pair. So you do not want to assume that option pairs appear in any kind of patterned sequence: They do not. The computer will remember the exact sequence, as well as what you chose, so that you can be paid properly on your last day with us.

Some questions for a break

It is difficult to maintain good attention over 100 choices. Even though the amounts of money in option pairs are not small, almost anyone will get a bit bored with making these kinds of choices after a while.

Partly for that reason, the 100 option pair choices will be broken into two halves (50 pairs in each half) on each day. Between the halves, on each day, you will answer some survey questions and respond to some questionnaire items. This will go pretty quickly on all three days (a little longer on the second day), and will give you a break each day from the option pair choices.

You'll be able to do everything at your own pace. We believe that each session will last about one hour for most people on most days, but remember that we expect you to have 90 minutes available on each day, so that you are not rushed.

If there is anything you do not understand, please ask us. We will be happiest if you understand exactly how your decisions affect you: We want you to be able to do well for yourself, whatever you believe "doing well" is. We encourage you to do what you want.

Finally, the money for this study comes from grants. This money is earmarked for payment to student participants. We have no alternative use for this money: It must be paid out to participants like you. We must of course make payments only in accordance with the procedure we have described above. But do not worry about taking that money from us: It is specifically earmarked for this and we cannot use it for anything else. We say this, only because some students worry about taking such money from professors. You should not worry about it. The money is grant money, not Dr Wilcox's money, and it is earmarked specifically for paying out to student participants like yourself.

CHAPTER 3

CUMULATIVE PROSPECT THEORY IN THE LABORATORY: A RECONSIDERATION

Glenn W. Harrison and J. Todd Swarthout

ABSTRACT

We take Cumulative Prospect Theory (CPT) seriously by rigorously estimating structural models using the full set of CPT parameters. Much of the literature only estimates a subset of CPT parameters, or more simply assumes CPT parameter values from prior studies. Our data are from laboratory experiments with undergraduate students and MBA students facing substantial real incentives and losses. We also estimate structural models from Expected Utility Theory (EUT), Dual Theory (DT), Rank-Dependent Utility (RDU), and Disappointment Aversion (DA) for comparison. Our major finding is that a majority of individuals in our sample locally asset integrate. That is, they see a loss frame for what it is, a frame, and behave as if they evaluate the net payment rather than the gross loss when one is presented to them. This finding is devastating to the direct application of CPT to these data for those subjects. Support for CPT is greater when losses are covered out of an earned endowment rather than house money, but RDU is still the best single characterization of individual and pooled choices. Defenders of the CPT model claim, correctly, that the CPT model exists "because the data says it should." In other words, the CPT model was borne from a wide range of stylized facts culled from parts of the cognitive psychology literature. If one is to take the CPT model

Models of Risk Preferences: Descriptive and Normative Challenges
Research in Experimental Economics, Volume 22, 107–192

ISSN: 0193-2306/doi:10.1108/S0193-230620230000022003

seriously and rigorously then it needs to do a much better job of explaining the data than we see here.

Keywords: Cumulative Prospect Theory; risk preferences; experimental methods; Rank-Dependent Utility; Expected Utility Theory; Dual Theory

The Cumulative Prospect Theory of Tversky and Kahneman (1992) has proven to be a highly influential model of risky choice. The theory provides three pathways to characterize the risk premium over risky lotteries, and is for many an appealing behavioral characterization of human decision-making over risk. Given the popularity of CPT, it would be reasonable to assume that the theory has been validated empirically by independent researchers in the years soon after its publication. In fact, we assumed this when we started this line of research. However, after reviewing the literature, it became clear to us that such empirical validation largely does not exist and subsequent researchers simply assume the validity, in part or in whole, of CPT. Given the paucity of laboratory evidence for CPT, we set out to conduct a new laboratory experiment evaluating CPT in its full structural form.

We appreciate that some may interpret our claim of a lack of evidence as provocative, and we do not expect our claim to be accepted at face value. We provide a thorough and critical review of the extant literature reporting laboratory evaluation and econometric estimation of CPT. We take the position that full-form CPT estimation must include all three psychological pathways introduced by Tversky and Kahneman (1992): diminishing marginal utility, probability weighting, and loss aversion. Many studies assume away one or more of these pathways and estimate only a reduced-form CPT model and thus do not provide a test of the full model. We find a litany of questionable practices in prior work, in terms of both experimental design and econometric methods. A primary conclusion of our review is that almost all laboratory evaluations of CPT in the literature fail to estimate the full structural form of the model with salient rewards. When considering only the few studies which used appropriate experimental design and econometric methods, we see only equivocal support for CPT. Because of these striking and surprising findings, new experiments are urgently needed.

We choose the laboratory[1] to undertake simple, direct tests of the hypothesis that individuals make choices over risky lotteries in the manner assumed by CPT. We go back to the "base camp" of evidence for CPT from Tversky and Kahneman (1992) and evaluate parametric, structural models for individuals making incentivized choices over risky lotteries defined over the gain frame, the loss frame, and the mixed frame. Our results are surprising.

We focus on five core models of decision-making under objective risk. One is expected utility theory and posits that the risk premium is explained solely by an aversion to variability of earnings from a prospect. The second model is Dual Theory, which assumes no aversion to variability of earnings from a prospect, but instead posits that decision-makers may be pessimistic or optimistic with respect to the probabilities of outcomes. The third model is Rank-Dependent Utility, which allows both of the latent psychological processes of EUT and DT in combination.

RDU does not rule out aversion to variability of earnings, as in DT, but just augments it with an additional latent psychological process. The fourth model is Disappointment Aversion, which assumes that individuals evaluate prospects according to an augmented version of EUT, in which they also take into account the extent to which outcomes differ from the Certainty Equivalent (CE) of the prospect. EUT, DT, RDU, and DA assume that individuals asset integrate, in the sense that they net out framed losses from some endowment. The final model is CPT, which adds to RDU an aversion to losses as a possible psychological pathway to the risk premium, and also adds the assumption that gross gains and losses matter because individuals do not locally asset integrate and evaluate net gains or losses.

We find that the vast majority of individuals in our sample appear to locally asset integrate. That is, they see the loss frame for what it is, a frame, and behave as if they evaluate the net payment rather than the gross loss when one is presented to them. This finding is devastating to the direct application of CPT to these data. We find greater support for RDU than CPT, and in many cases greater support for EUT over CPT. We find virtually no support for DT or DA. At the individual level, almost all of our subjects can be classified using EUT and RDU, with a majority being RDU.

In Section 1, we outline the experimental design we developed, in which each subject is given 100 binary lottery choices defined over the gain frame, loss frame and mixed frame. The parameter values were designed, following a neglected design of Loomes and Sugden (1998), to provide stress tests of the Independence Axiom (IA) of EUT as well as to allow for identification of a wide range of risk attitudes. In Section 2, we lay out the models to be estimated, with particular care over the specification of the CPT model. A by-product is attention to the theoretical implications for the CPT model, implications for experimental design, and a detailed statement of the manner in which mixed-frame lotteries are handled. All of these issues are "in the literature," but scattered and often neglected. In Section 3, we present results. Section 4 seeks to connect our approach and findings to the vast literature, noting the remarkably under-developed state of structural estimation for the CPT model once we apply minimal methodological requirements. We discuss limitations of our results in Section 5, and offer conclusions in Section 6, focusing on the variants that should be examined next in the rigorous evaluation of CPT.

1. EXPERIMENT

Our objective is to design a battery of tests that allows identification of all of the parameters of the EUT, DT, RDU, DA, and CPT models, that provides some "stress tests" of the EUT model, and that allows estimation of a wide range of risk preferences at the individual level. The first criterion means that we must have gain-frame lotteries, loss-frame lotteries and mixed-frame lotteries. The terminology "gain" and "loss" refer here to lotteries in which all prizes are (weakly) gains or losses, and the terminology "mixed" refers here to lotteries in which some prizes are (strictly) gains and some are (strictly) losses. The second criterion means that we need to present some *sets* of choices that generate sharp predictions under EUT, such as the classic Allais Paradox set of two choices, and the classic Common Ratio set of two choices. The third criterion means that we need to recognize that certain risk preferences could make individuals indifferent between the two lotteries in any given choice, and hence generate low-power tests of EUT, DT, or RDU. And it also means that we should try to generate stakes that are as large as possible, within obvious feasibility constraints for budgets. Following the vast literature, we focus on binary lottery choices, with a standard interface illustrated in Fig. 1.

Some of the most important batteries of tests do not satisfy all three of these, nor were they designed to do so. For instance, the justifiably influential battery developed by Hey and Orme (1994) does not have loss or mixed frames, and deliberately avoided sets of lottery pairs that had generated "knife-edge" tests of EUT. Their design mantra was to be agnostic about choice patterns, and see which models best characterized the data, rather than selecting lottery pairs designed to be hard for EUT *per se*.

Loomes and Sugden (1998) pose an important design feature for Common Ratio tests, allowing us to meet the last two criteria: variation in the "gradient" of the EUT-consistent indifference curves within a Marschak–Machina (MM) triangle. The reason for this variation is to generate some choice patterns that

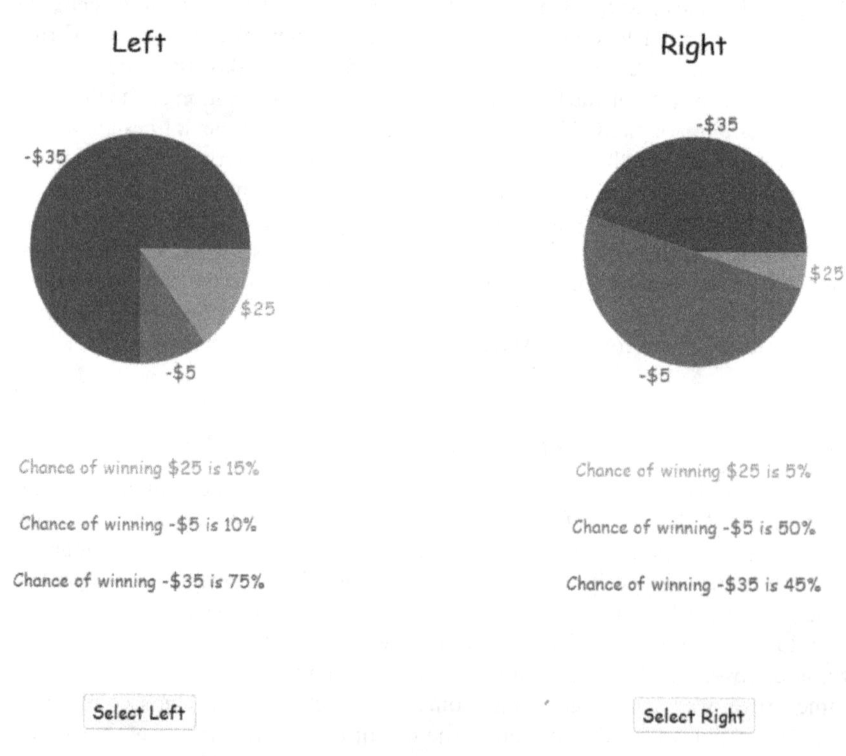

Fig. 1. Interface for Lottery Choices.

are more powerful tests of EUT for any given risk attitude. Under EUT the slope of the indifference curve within a MM triangle is a measure of risk aversion. So there always exists some risk attitude such that the subject is indifferent, as stressed by Harrison (1994), and evidence of Common Ratio violations has virtually zero power.[2] This design can be visualized instantly from Loomes and Sugden (1998, Fig. 2, p. 587). For our batteries of 100 lottery choices, explained in more detail below, the comparable MM visualizations are shown in Figs. 2 and 3.

Each panel within Figs. 2 and 3 refers to a specific context of prizes. The top left panel of Fig. 2 has prizes of $0, $5, and $25, and the panel immediately to its right has prizes of $0, $15, and $75. There are always one, two or three prizes in each lottery that have positive probability of occurring. The vertical axis in each panel shows the probability attached to the high prize of that triple, and the horizontal axis shows the probability attached to the low prize of that triple. When the probability of the highest and lowest prize is zero, then 100% weight falls on the middle prize. This specific lottery is illustrated in the bottom left corner of the very first panel, where the subject has a lottery offering $5 for certain. Any lotteries strictly in the interior of the MM triangle have positive weight on all three prizes, and any lottery on the boundary of the MM triangle has zero weight on one or two prizes.

The solid dots within each panel of Figs. 2 and 3 show specific lotteries offered to subjects, and the lines show choice pairs offered. The detailed numerical patterns are listed in Appendix A. For the top left panel of Fig. 2, we have the familiar Allais Paradox defined over real monetary outcomes. The lottery pair given by the chord in the bottom left corner has subject choose between {$0, 0; $5, 1; $25, 0} and {$0, 0.01; $5, 0.89; $25, 0.1}, and the lottery pair given by the chord in the bottom right corner has the subject choose between {$0, 0.89; $5, 0.11; $25, 0} and {$0, 0.9; $5, 0.11; $25, 0.1}. Since the slopes of these two chords are the same, and we know that indifference curves under EUT are straight lines within the MM triangle, we can easily see the choice pattern predicted by EUT: pick the first lottery in each pair or pick the second lottery in each pair. EUT is violated if the first (second) lottery is picked in the first pair, and the second (first) lottery is picked in the second pair.

The difference between the first two panels of the top row of Figs. 2 and 3 is simply the change in the prize context. The first panel shows a "low-stakes" context, and the second panel shows a "high-stakes" context.

Fig. 2 shows the 100 lottery pairs presented to 177 undergraduate students sampled from the Georgia State University population, and Fig. 3 shows the 100 lottery pairs presented to 94 MBA students sampled from the Georgia State University population. The only difference between Figs. 2 and 3 are the prizes, with the domain of *net* prizes for the undergraduates spanning $0 up to $70, and spanning $0 up to $750 for the MBA students. We deliberately had a number of prize contexts for the MBA students that were identical to the domain of prizes that the undergraduates faced, so we could ascertain the pure effect of stake size. In fact, the common lotteries themselves were identical: these 24 common choices are in the 2 panels in the bottom row of Figs. 2 and 3, and in the third panel of the penultimate row of Figs. 2 and 3.

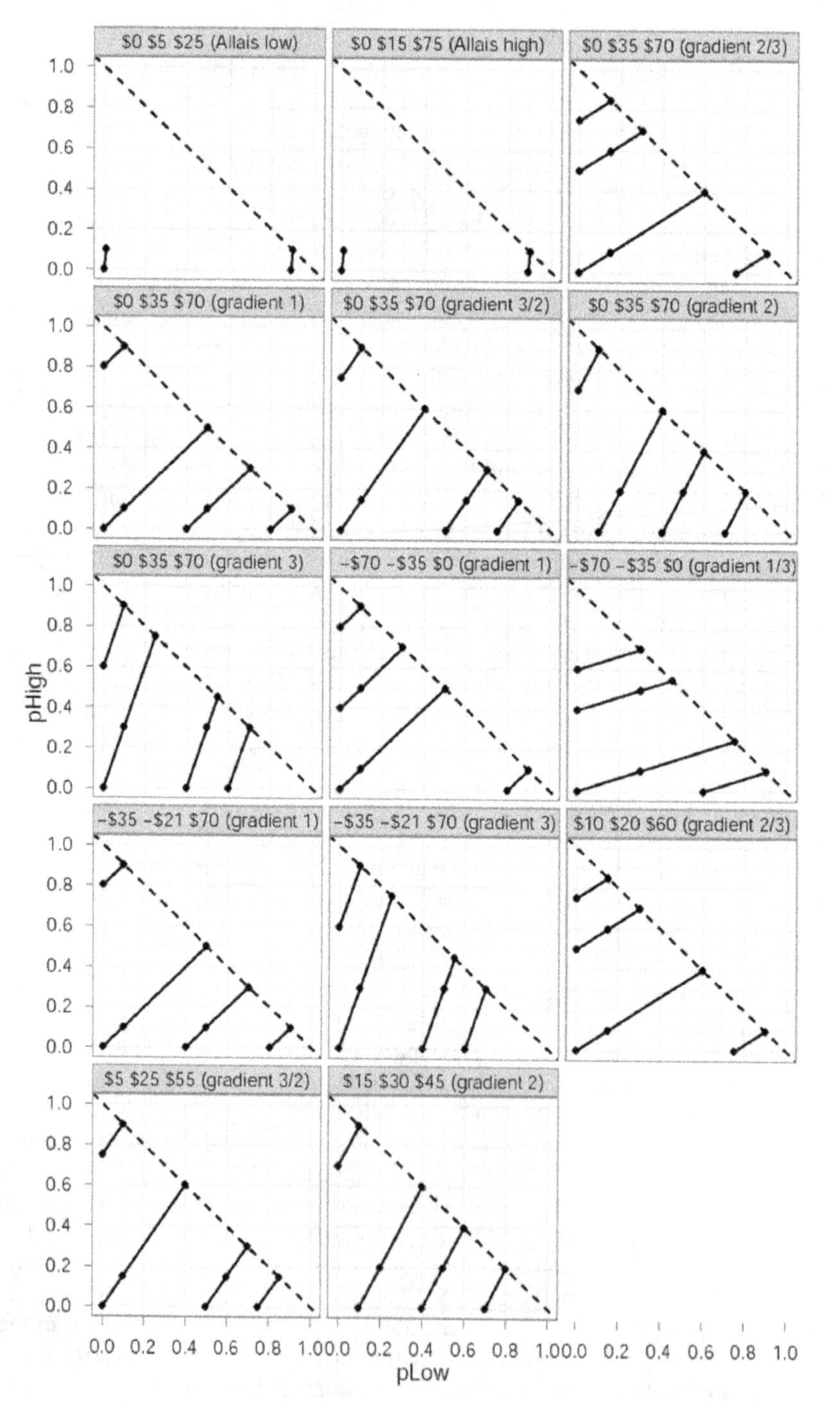

Fig. 2. Marschak–Machina Triangles for Lotteries Used With Undergraduates.

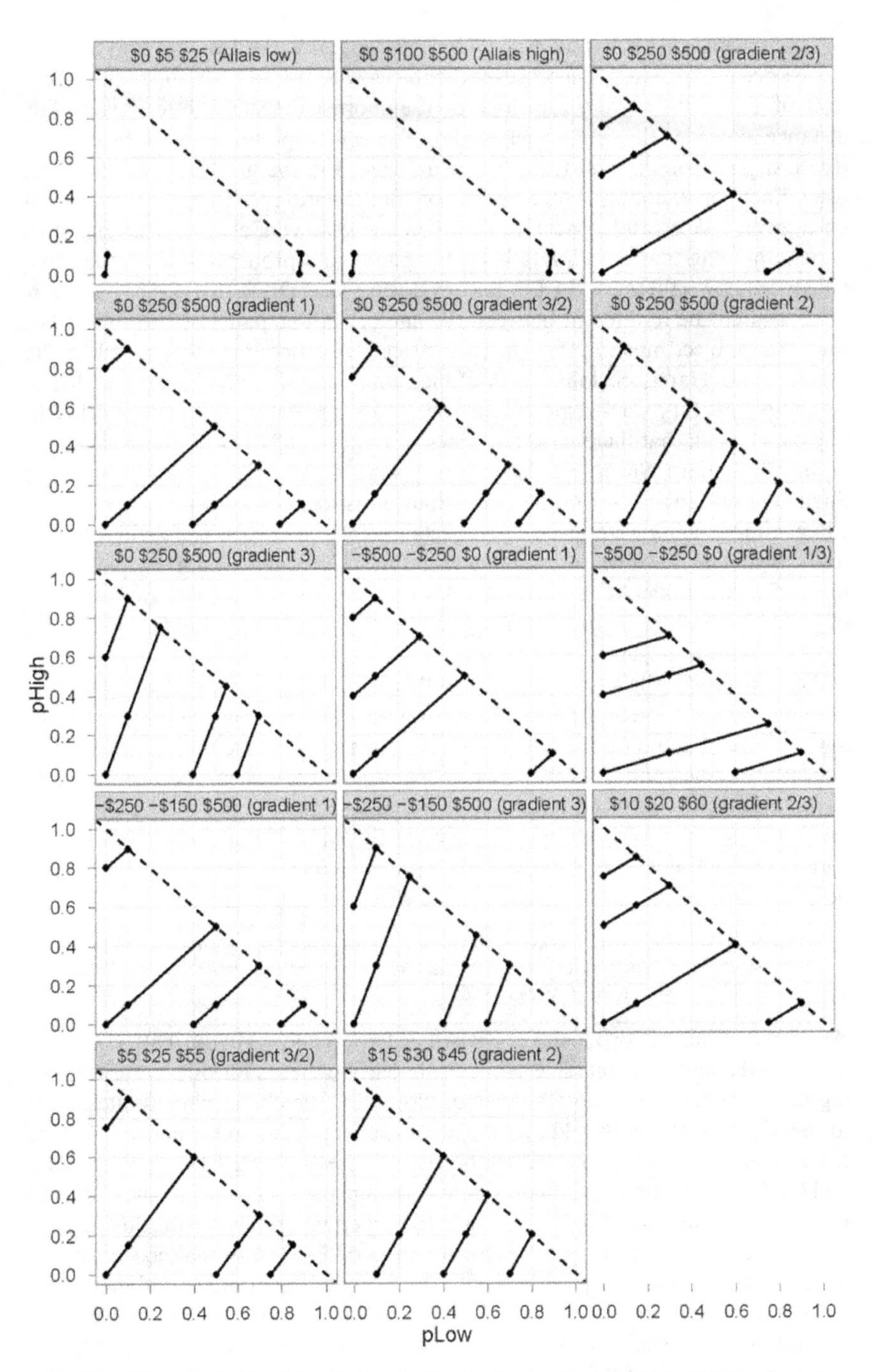

Fig. 3. Marschak–Machina Triangles for Lotteries Used With MBA Students.

Comparing panels within Fig. 2 or 3, the logic of the Loomes and Sugden (1998) design appears: to have several choices within a MM triangle that allow tests of EUT, but to vary the slope of the chord connecting lottery pairs. For instance, consider the four panels within Fig. 2 with prizes of $0, $35, and $70 (the last panel of the first row, the second row, and the first panel of the third row). Each panel contains several tests of the Common Ratio effect conditional on a given risk attitude under EUT. Then the gradients change from panel to panel, implying that one should have one panel, and probably several, that provide more powerful tests of EUT for any given risk attitude than other panels. A subject might be indifferent between the choices in one panel of these four, but then that subject must, *by design*, have strict preferences for some or all of the other panels. Harrison, Johnson, McInnes, and Rutström (2007) refer to this as a "complementary slack experimental design," since low-power tests of EUT in one panel mean that there *must* be higher-power tests of EUT in another panel.[3]

In our battery, 96 of the choice pairs were derived from the Loomes and Sugden (1998) logic. Our modest contribution is to have some prize contexts in which endowments were given to subjects and the prizes framed as losses. The result is that we have 16 lottery pairs with loss frames, and 16 lottery pairs with mixed frames. Table A1 in Appendix A lists the complete battery. Endowments of $0, $35 or $70 were provided in a given binary choice to ensure that net prizes were always non-negative.

We added two Allais Paradox pairs to this set of lottery choices. Conlisk (1989) presents a real version of the Allais Paradox, with the binary choices marked "Allais low" in Figs. 2 and 3 (the very first panel). When subjects are presented with just one lottery choice, and Conlisk compares patterns of choices on a between-subjects basis, he finds no evidence whatsoever of the Allais Paradox. For some reason, this finding does not stop many from referring to the Allais Paradox as a well-known pattern of EUT violation.[4] Starmer (1992) provided one of the first explorations of the generality of the common consequence effect, concluding (p. 829) that

> [...] if we wish to use experimental evidence as a basis for developing new theories of choice under uncertainty, we may have to accept that the behavior of individuals is rather more subtle and complex than we have previously thought.

We therefore include two instances of Allais Paradox tasks in our battery.

Fig. 4 displays the complete set of probability patterns for our battery, ignoring the prize context. The rich array of slopes for the choice chords allows one to see why this design should provide an attractive setting to estimate models of risky choice, certainly from the perspective of stress-testing EUT against RDU and CPT.[5] For the undergraduate sample, average payouts for a risk-neutral subject would be just over $39, comparable to earlier experiments with this population, but on the high side historically for tests of EUT with real consequences. We consider the effect of prize "context" by using different prizes and the lottery choices in 24 gain-frame choices. This allows us to move from having choices defined over prizes of only $0, $35, and $70, to having prizes of $0, $5, $10, $15, $20, $25, $30, $35, $45, $55, $60, and $70. This design feature will help estimation of a more precise utility function.

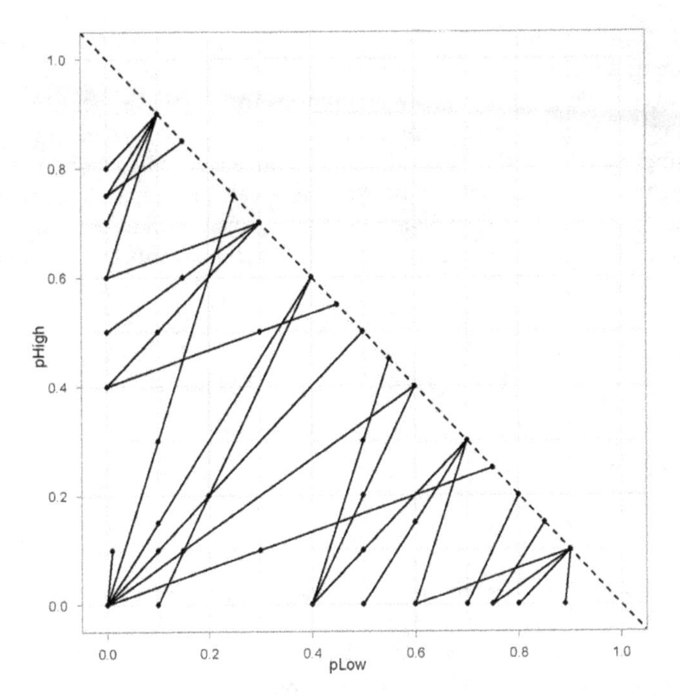

Fig. 4. Unconditional Marschak–Machina Display of All Lotteries.

The lotteries for the MBA students are qualitatively identical to those for the undergraduate sample, but many are scaled up in monetary value by a multiplicative factor of 25. In addition, subjects were offered a healthy \$40 show-up fee, to reflect the increased opportunity cost of their time compared to our convenience sample of GSU undergraduates. We scaled up 71 of the tasks, including all loss-frame and mixed-frame tasks, by 25 such that the gross prize *frame* varied from −\$500 up to +\$500 and that net prizes varied between \$0 and \$750 after the house endowment was factored in. One of the Allais Paradox tasks was scaled up by a factor of 20, so that the higher-stake prizes for this task are \$0, \$100 and \$500. The low-stakes Allais Paradox task, and 24 gain-frame tasks, were left at the original scaling to allow comparability of behavior across the samples, and to assess the effect of scaling up payoffs substantially. Table A2 in Appendix A lists the complete battery. Endowments of \$0, \$250 or \$500 were provided in a given binary choice to ensure that net prizes were always non-negative. A risk-neutral individual would expect to earn \$210.37 from these choices, before the show-up fee.

Appendix C (available on request) contains the instructions given to subjects. Subjects had no other salient task in the experiment, although they did have to answer a series of hypothetical questions about "risk tolerance" after making their choices. We also collected standard demographic information.

We opted for using the Random Lottery Incentive Method (RLIM), where one of the 100 choices was to be chosen at random for playing out and payment. We did so for two reasons, recognizing that this is not as innocent a procedure as some maintain.[6] The first reason was to ensure that we collected choices over a wide enough array of lotteries to be able to identify the three competing models. If we had opted for giving one choice to each subject, to avoid using the RLIM, this would have been infeasible. The second reason was to be able to estimate at the level of the individual, to compare those estimates to pooled estimates over all individuals. Again, this would have been infeasible if we had given each subject just one choose.[7] Total payouts from these experiments amounted to $42,258.

2. THEORETICAL MODELS

2.1 Expected Utility Theory

Assume that utility of income is defined by

$$U(x) = x^{1-r}/(1-r) \tag{1}$$

where x is the lottery prize and $r \neq 1$ is a parameter to be estimated. For $r = 1$ assume $U(x) = \ln(x)$ if needed. Thus, r is the coefficient of CRRA: $r = 0$ corresponds to risk neutrality, $r < 0$ to risk loving, and $r > 0$ to risk aversion. Let there be J possible outcomes in a lottery. Under EUT the probabilities for each outcome x_j, $p(x_j)$, are those that are induced by the experimenter, so expected utility is simply the probability weighted utility of each outcome in each lottery i:

$$EU_i = \Sigma_{j=1,J} [p(x_j) \times U(x_j)]. \tag{2}$$

The EU for each lottery pair is calculated for a candidate estimate of r, and the index

$$\nabla EU = EU_R - EU_L \tag{3}$$

is calculated, where EU_L is the "left" lottery and EU_R is the "right" lottery as presented to subjects. This latent index, based on latent preferences, is then linked to observed choices using a standard cumulative normal distribution function $\Phi(\nabla EU)$. This "probit" function takes any argument between $\pm\infty$ and transforms it into a number between 0 and 1. Thus, we have the probit link function,

$$\text{prob(choose lottery R)} = \Phi(\nabla EU) \tag{4}$$

Even though this "link function" is common in econometrics texts, it is worth noting explicitly and understanding. It forms the critical statistical link between observed binary choices, the latent structure generating the index ∇EU, and the probability of that index being observed. The index defined by (3) is linked to the observed choices by specifying that the R lottery is chosen when $\Phi(\nabla EU) > ½$, which is implied by (4).

Thus, the likelihood of the observed responses, conditional on the EUT and CRRA specifications being true, depends on the estimates of r given the above statistical specification and the observed choices. The "statistical specification" here includes assuming some functional form for the cumulative density function (CDF). The conditional log-likelihood is then

$$\ln L(r; y, \mathbf{X}) = \Sigma_i [(\ln \Phi(\nabla EU) \times \mathbf{I}(y_i = 1)) + (\ln (1 - \Phi(\nabla EU)) \times \mathbf{I}(y_i = -1))] \quad (5)$$

where $\mathbf{I}(\cdot)$ is the indicator function, $y_i = 1(-1)$ denotes the choice of the right (left) lottery in risk aversion task i, and **X** is a vector of individual characteristics reflecting age, sex, race and so on.

Harrison and Rutström (2008; Appendix F) review procedures that can be used to estimate structural models of this kind, as well as more complex non-EUT models. The goal is to illustrate how researchers can write explicit maximum likelihood (ML) routines that are specific to different structural choice models. It is a simple matter to correct for multiple responses from the same subject (clustering), as needed.

It is also a simple matter to generalize this ML analysis to allow the core parameter r to be a linear function of observable characteristics of the individual or task. We would then extend the model to be $r = r_0 + R \times \mathbf{X}$, where r_0 is a fixed parameter and R is a vector of effects associated with each characteristic in the variable vector **X**. In effect the unconditional model assumes $r = r_0$ and just estimates r_0. This extension significantly enhances the attraction of structural ML estimation, particularly for responses pooled over different subjects and treatments, since one can condition estimates on observable characteristics of the task or subject. In the present context, we can introduce variables to reflect the answers to the demographic questionnaires.

An important extension of the core model is to allow for subjects to make some *behavioral* errors. The notion of error is one that has already been encountered in the form of the statistical assumption that the probability of choosing a lottery is not 1 when the EU of that lottery exceeds the EU of the other lottery. This assumption is clear in the use of a non-degenerate link function between the latent index ∇EU and the probability of picking one or other lottery; in the case of the normal CDF, this link function is Φ(∇EU). If there were no errors from the perspective of EUT, this function would be a step function: zero for all values of $\nabla EU < 0$, anywhere between 0 and 1 for $\nabla EU = 0$, and 1 for all values of $\nabla EU > 0$.

We employ the error specification originally due to Fechner and popularized by Hey and Orme (1994). This error specification posits the latent index

$$\nabla EU = (EU_R - EU_L)/\mu \quad (3')$$

instead of (3), where μ is a structural "noise parameter" used to allow some errors from the perspective of the deterministic EUT model. This is just one of several different types of error story that could be used, and Wilcox (2008) provides a masterful review of the implications of the alternatives. As $\mu \rightarrow 0$ this specification collapses to the deterministic choice EUT model, where the choice is strictly determined by the EU of the two lotteries; but as μ gets larger and larger the choice essentially becomes random. When $\mu = 1$ this specification collapses to (3), where the probability of picking one lottery is given by the ratio of the EU of one lottery to the sum of the EU of both lotteries. Thus, μ can be viewed as a parameter that flattens out the link functions as it gets larger.

An important contribution to the characterization of behavioral errors is the "contextual error" specification proposed by Wilcox (2011). It is designed to allow robust inferences about the primitive "more stochastically risk averse than," and posits the latent index

$$\nabla EU = ((EU_R - EU_L)/\nu)/\mu \tag{3''}$$

instead of (3′), where ν is a new, normalizing term for each lottery pair L and R. The normalizing term ν is defined as the maximum utility over all prizes in this lottery pair minus the minimum utility over all prizes in this lottery pair. The value of ν varies, in principle, from lottery choice pair to lottery choice pair: hence it is said to be "contextual." For the Fechner specification, dividing by ν ensures that the *normalized* EU difference $[(EU_R - EU_L)/\nu]$ remains in the unit interval. The term ν does not need to be estimated in addition to the utility function parameters and the parameter for the behavioral error tern, since it is given by the data and the assumed values of those estimated parameters.

The specification employed here is the CRRA utility function from (1), the Fechner error specification using contextual utility from (3″), and the link function using the normal CDF from (4). The log-likelihood is then

$$\begin{aligned} \ln L(r, \mu; y, \mathbf{X}) = \Sigma_i \, [(&\ln \Phi(\nabla EU) \times \mathbf{I}(y_i = 1)) + \\ &(\ln (1 - \Phi(\nabla EU)) \times \mathbf{I}(y_i = -1))] \end{aligned} \tag{5'}$$

and the parameters to be estimated are r and μ given observed data on the binary choices y and the lottery parameters in **X**.

It is possible to consider more flexible utility functions than the CRRA specification in (1), but that is not essential for present purposes.

Once the utility function is estimated, it is a simple matter to evaluate the implications for risk aversion. Of course, the concept of risk aversion traditionally refers to "diminishing marginal utility," which is driven by the curvature of the utility function, which is in turn given by the second derivative of the utility function. Although somewhat loose, this can be viewed as characterizing individuals that are averse to mean-preserving increases in the variance of returns.

But there are also so-called "higher-order risk aversion" processes, known as prudence and temperance, that correspond to properties of the third and fourth derivative of the utility function, respectively (see Eeckhoudt & Schlesinger, 2006). Again loosely, these can be viewed as characterizing individuals that are averse to mean-preserving increases in the skewness and kurtosis of returns, respectively.

For the CRRA utility function given by (1), and widely used for our estimates, the second derivative is $-rx^{-1-r}$ and the third derivative is $-(-1-r)rx^{-2-r}$. Hence, it is a simple matter to evaluate if the individual exhibits prudence, for example.

2.2 Rank-dependent Utility

The RDU model of Quiggin (1982) extends the EUT model by allowing for decision weights on lottery outcomes. The specification of the utility function is the same parametric specification (1) considered for EUT. To calculate decision weights under RDU one replaces expected utility defined by (2) with RDU

$$RDU_i = \Sigma_{j=1,J} [w(p(M_j)] \times U(M_j)] = \Sigma_{j=1,J} [w_j \times U(M_j)] \qquad (2')$$

where

$$w_j = \omega(p_j + \cdots + p_J) - \omega(p_{j+1} + \cdots + p_J) \qquad (6a)$$

for $j = 1, \ldots, J-1$, and

$$w_j = \omega(p_j) \qquad (6b)$$

for $j = J$, with the subscript j ranking outcomes from worst to best, and $\omega(\cdot)$ is some probability weighting function.

We consider three popular probability weighting functions. The first is the simple "power" probability weighting function proposed by Quiggin (1982), with curvature parameter γ:

$$\omega(p) = p^\gamma \qquad (7)$$

So $\gamma \neq 1$ is consistent with a deviation from the conventional EUT representation. Convexity of the probability weighting function is said to reflect "pessimism" and generates, if one assumes for simplicity a linear utility function, a risk premium since $\omega(p) < p \; \forall p$ and hence the "RDU EV" weighted by $\omega(p)$ instead of p has to be less than the EV weighted by p. The rest of the ML specification for the RDU model is identical to the specification for the EUT model, but with different parameters to estimate.

The second probability weighting function is the "inverse-S" function popularized by Tversky and Kahneman (1992):

$$\omega(p) = p^\gamma/(p^\gamma + (1-p)^\gamma)^{1/\gamma} \qquad (8)$$

This function exhibits inverse-S probability weighting (optimism for small p, and pessimism for large p) for $\gamma < 1$, and S-shaped probability weighting (pessimism for small p, and optimism for large p) for $\gamma > 1$.

The third probability weighting function is a general functional form proposed by Prelec (1998) that exhibits considerable flexibility. This function is

$$\omega(p) = \exp\{-\eta(-\ln p)^{\varphi}\}, \tag{9}$$

and is defined for $0 < p \leq 1$, $\eta > 0$ and $\varphi > 0$. When $\varphi = 1$ this function collapses to the Power function $\omega(p) = p^{\eta}$. Of course, EUT assumes the identity function $\omega(p) = p$, which is the case when $\eta = \varphi = 1$. Many apply the Prelec (1998, Proposition 1, part (B)) function with constraint $0 < \varphi < 1$, which requires that the probability weighting function exhibit subproportionality (so-called "inverse-S" weighting). Contrary to received wisdom, many individuals exhibit estimated probability weighting functions that violate subproportionality, so we use the more general specification from Prelec (1998, Proposition 1, part (C)), only requiring $\varphi > 0$, and let the evidence determine if the estimated φ lies in the unit interval. This seemingly minor point often makes a major difference empirically.[8] The construction of the log-likelihood for the RDU model with Power or Inverse-S probability weighting follows the same pattern as for EUT, with the parameters r, γ, and μ to be estimated.

2.3 Dual Theory

The DT specification of Yaari (1987) is the special case of the RDU model in which the utility function is assumed to be linear. Hence diminishing marginal utility can have no influence on the risk premium, and the only thing that can explain the risk premium is "probability pessimism."

2.4 Disappointment Aversion

Gul (1991) proposed a model of decision-making under risk that allowed for a reference point for each lottery, and then posited that the decision-maker might experience "disappointment" or "elation" relative to that reference point when evaluating the lottery.

Consider a lottery A with prizes x_i and objective probabilities p_i. Assume some utility function u(x), such as the CRRA function (1) proposed earlier, with parameter r. For a given value of r, we can then easily numerically evaluate the CE of the lottery (in some special cases the CE is a closed-form expression, but in general it need not be).

Once the CE is calculated, we can define x+ to be the set of prizes greater than or equal to the CE, and x− to be the set of prizes worse than the CE. Then define the sum of probabilities for each of these components of the original lottery, for four possible outcomes:

$$p+ = \Sigma_{i=1,4}\, p_i \text{ s.t. } x_i \in x+ \tag{10}$$

$$p- = \Sigma_{i=1,4}\, p_i \text{ s.t. } x_i \in x- \tag{11}$$

We know that (p+) + (p−) = 1, by construction. Then we may construct a lottery based on A that reflects the prizes that are greater than the CE (A+) and a lottery based on A that reflects the prizes that are worse than the CE (A−) as follows:

$$A+: \Sigma_{i=1,4} (p_i/p+)\, u(x_i) \text{ s.t. } x_i \in x+ \tag{12}$$

$$A-: \Sigma_{i=1,4} (p_i/p-)\, u(x_i) \text{ s.t. } x_i \in x- \tag{13}$$

By construction, we know that A is now the lottery A+ with probability p+ and the lottery A− with probability (1 − p+) = p−. To allow different weights for disappointment and elation define a function that weights these probabilities p+ and p− as follows:

$$\psi(p+) = (p+)/[1 + (1 - (p+))\,\theta] \tag{14}$$

where $\theta \in (-1, \infty)$. The evaluation of the lottery is then just the disappointment-weighted evaluation of A+ and A−:

$$\psi(p+) \times (A+) + [1 - \psi(p+)] \times (A-) \tag{15}$$

When $\theta = 0$ we have $\psi(p+) = p+$, and (15) is just the EUT evaluation of lottery A.

When $\theta > 0$ we place greater weight on A− than we would under EUT since $\psi(p+) < p+$, and the decision-maker is said to be *disappointment averse*. When $\theta \in (-1, 0)$ we place greater weight on A+ than we would under EUT since $\psi(p+) \geq p+$, and the decision-maker is said to be *elation loving*. The upshot for structural estimation is that we have two parameters, r and θ, to estimate.[9]

2.5 Cumulative Prospect Theory

The key innovation of CPT, in comparison to RDU, is to allow sign-dependent preferences, where risk attitudes depend on whether the individual is evaluating a gain or a loss. The concept of loss aversion, or sign-dependent preferences, is one that has been formalized in different ways in the literature. It is important to review the different formalizations, and implications for experimental design and estimation.

Kahneman and Tversky (1979) introduced the notion of sign-dependent preferences, stressing the role of the reference point when evaluating lotteries. They defined loss aversion as the notion that the disutility of losses weighs more heavily than the utility of comparable gains. Here is the key paragraph (p. 279) introducing the concept:

> A salient characteristic of attitudes to changes in welfare is that losses loom larger than gains. The aggravation that one experiences in losing a sum of money appears to be greater than the pleasure associated with gaining the same amount of money [...]. Indeed, most people find symmetric bets of the form (x, .50; −x, .50) distinctly unattractive. Moreover, the aversiveness of symmetric fair bets generally increases with the size of the stake. That is, if $x > y \geq 0$, then (y, .50; −y, .50) is preferred to (x, .50; −x, .50). According to [their] equation (1), therefore,

$v(y)+v(-y)>v(x)+v(-x)$ and $v(-y)-v(-x)>v(x)-v(y)$. Setting $y=0$ yields $v(x)<-v(-x)$, and letting y approach x yields $v'(x)<v'(-x)$, provided v', the derivative of v, exists. Thus, the valuation function for losses is steeper than the value function for gains.

Note that at this stage there is no presumption that the difference between v(x) and $-v(-x)$ be a constant, λ. Indeed, that assumption is never made in Kahneman and Tversky (1979), and appears later in the literature.

But when we say that the utility decrement of a unit loss, where the absolute value of $(x-y)$ defines the unit here, is bigger than the utility increment of a unit gain, we need to be able to compare utility changes in the gain domain and the loss domain. This means that we cannot just have a utility scale that allows any order-preserving transformation: otherwise one could choose utility numbers such that the statement was true or false. This just means that we have to be more restrictive than allowing positive affine transformations, and restrict ourselves to defining utility on a ratio scale rather than an interval scale. This result is not easy to identify in the literature. Chateauneuf and Wakker (1999; Theorem 2.3, p. 142) present axiomatizations for CPT under objective risk that appear to allow value functions to be unique up to an *interval scale*, which is the same as allowing arbitrary *positive affine transformations*. But this is due to them imposing a "tradeoff consistency" assumption that effectively restricts the analysis to prospects that are either all defined over the gain domain or all defined over the loss domain. Thus, one rules out so-called "mixed prospects," which are the general case and central to the robust empirical identification of utility loss aversion. The general version of this theorem, again applying solely for "loss prospects" and "gain prospects," is provided by Wakker and Tversky (1993, Theorem 4.3, p. 155), where the value function is again unique up to an *interval scale*. The general case, in fact referred to as "the truly mixed case" in the statement of the theorem, is provided by Wakker and Tversky (1993, Theorem 6.3, p. 159), and there the value function is only unique up to a *ratio scale*. In this case, the value functions are unique up to transformations by a positive constant.

Note also the final discussion in the quote from Kahneman and Tversky (1979) about defining loss aversion in terms of the derivatives of the utility function around a zero reference point, which is $y = 0$ in the quote. This suggestion anticipates later proposals for defining loss aversion from Köbberling and Wakker (2005) and others.

Tversky and Kahneman (1992, p. 309) popularized the functional forms we often see for loss aversion, using a CRRA specification of utility:

$$U(m) = m^{1-\alpha}/(1-\alpha) \text{ when } m \geq 0 \tag{16a}$$

$$U(m) = -\lambda[(-m)^{1-\beta}/(1-\beta)] \text{ when } m < 0, \tag{16b}$$

where we redefine the notation for utility $U(\cdot)$ from (1), and where λ is the loss aversion parameter. Here, we have the assumption that the degree of loss aversion for small unit changes is the same as the degree of loss aversion for large unit changes: the same λ applies locally to gains and losses of the same monetary magnitude around 0 as it does globally to any size gain or loss of the same magnitude. This is not a criticism, just a restrictive parametric turn in the specification compared to Kahneman and Tversky (1979).

Another way to write this, following Wakker (2010, p. 239) is as follows:

> The phenomenon can be modeled by a regular *basic utility function* u and a *loss aversion parameter* $\lambda > 0$, with $u(0) = 0$, and the utility function U of the form $U(\alpha) = u(\alpha)$ for $\alpha \geq 0$ [and] $U(\alpha) = \lambda u(\alpha)$ for $\alpha < 0$. The idea behind this definition is that u captures the intrinsic value of outcomes and satisfies usual regularity conditions such as being smooth and differentiable at $\alpha = 0$, and λ is a factor separate from u. To distinguish U from u, we sometimes call U the *overall utility*. The unqualified term utility will continue to refer to U. We use the following scaling conventions for u and λ, which are plausible if u is differentiable at 0 and is approximately linear on the small interval [-1, 1]. [...].
>
> $u(1) = 1, u(-1) = -1, U(1) = 1$, so that $\lambda = -U(-1)$
>
> This scaling convention was implicitly adopted by Tversky and Kahneman (1992), who chose $u(\alpha) = \alpha^{\theta}$ for gains and $u(\alpha) = \alpha^{\theta'}$ for $\alpha < 0$, with a θ' that possibly differs from θ. These scaling choices amount to the convention of $u(1) = 1$ and $u(-1) = -1$, [...].

To anticipate, and remove a technical side issue, the analytical problems for loss aversion come when the coefficients θ and θ' differ. Using the definition proposed by Köbberling and Wakker (2005), loss aversion is infinite if $\theta > \theta'$ and zero if $\theta < \theta'$. So, we shall assume they are the same, which is one of the assumptions Köbberling and Wakker (2005, §7) and Wakker (2010, §9.6) propose themselves.[10] Extending the notation from Wakker (2010, p. 239) to be explicit, and using the specification (16a) and (16b) from Tversky and Kahneman (1992, p. 309) with $\alpha = \beta$, we have

$$U(m) = u(m) = m^{1-\alpha}/(1 - \alpha) \text{ for } m \geq 0 \tag{17a}$$

$$U(m) = -\lambda\, u(-m) = -\lambda[(-m)^{1-\alpha}/(1 - \alpha)] \text{ for } m < 0\,. \tag{17b}$$

Does this discussion have any implications for what choice tasks can be used to identify loss aversion? If one has choice data *solely in the gain domain* it is possible to estimate the basic utility function, as defined above. Then one can look at choices defined *solely in the loss domain*, and estimate the λ that best explains them, in effect "holding basic utility constant" based on the choices in the gain domain. This is one solution to the identification problem of picking a λ and a basic utility function at the same time, critically assuming $\alpha = \beta$. Note that one could use choices from the gain domain and choices from the mixed domain just as well, *or* choices from the loss domain and choices from a mixed domain, but one needs to have *some* choices from the gain or loss domain. In our design, we have no problems of this kind, since we have gain-frame, loss-frame *and* mixed-frame lotteries.

Must one have mixed-frame lotteries in order to estimate the loss aversion parameter λ? It is apparent that λ does not affect preferences over two gain-frame lotteries, or for that matter between two loss-frame lotteries. In the former case, λ literally plays no role, and in the latter case it scales the total utility of all lotteries equally, so cannot change their *ranking*. Hence, variations in λ do not affect observed binary choices.[11]

Apart from the critical role of the same intrinsic utility function, one must also *avoid* applying the "contextual utility" normalization of Wilcox (2011) that was appropriate for EUT and RDU, and affected (3″). This is why it is important to be clear about the scaling restrictions on intrinsic utility clarified earlier, that intrinsic utility be unique up to a *ratio* scale (and not the weaker interval scale).[12]

There is a clear statement of the "exchange rate assumptions" needed to define loss aversion in Abdellaoui, Bleichrodt, and Paraschiv (2007, p. 1662), as well as a tabulation of the range of definitions that have been proposed in the literature. For instance, Fishburn and Kochenberger (1979) and Pennings and Smidts (2003) defined loss aversion as $U'(-x)/U'(x)$, Tversky and Kahneman (1992) as $-U(-1)/U(1)$, Bleichrodt, Pinto, and Wakker (2001) as $-U(-x)/U(x)$, and Schmidt and Traub (2002, p. 235) as $U(x) - U(y) \leq U(-y) - U(-x) \; \forall \, x > y \geq 0$. One can make the exchange rate assumptions formally *de minimus* by defining an index of loss aversion solely in terms of the directional derivatives at the reference point, $U' \rightarrow (0)/U' \leftarrow (0)$, as proposed by Köbberling and Wakker (2005) and Booij and van de Kuilen (2009). But this has the very unfortunate effect, as honestly emphasized by Wakker (2010, p. 247), that *global* properties of loss aversion are being driven by very, very *local* properties of estimated utility functionals,[13] and that puts a great strain on empirics and functional form assumptions.

For comparability with the "base camp" of the mountain of estimations of CPT, we follow Tversky and Kahneman (1992) and define utility loss aversion as $\lambda \equiv -U(-1)/U(1)$. Hence the empirical strategy is to evaluate estimates of α and β, and then infer λ by evaluating the implied utility function at ± 1.[14] Estimates of all three parameters are then used, along with estimated decision weights, to evaluate each lottery using (16a) and (16b).

What if the probability weighting functions for the gain domain differ from the probability weighting functions for the loss domain? There is nothing *a priori* in CPT to rule this out, and good reasons to want to de-couple the extent of probability weighting in the gain and loss frames. Even if the basic utility functions for gains and losses are linear, and conventional loss aversion is absent ($\lambda = 1$), differences in the *decision weights* for gains and losses could induce the same behavior as if there were utility loss aversion. This is called "probabilistic loss aversion" by Schmidt and Zank (2008, p. 213). Imagine that there is no probability weighting on the gain domain, so the decision weights are the objective probabilities, but that there is some probability weighting on the loss domain. Then one could easily have losses weighted more than gains, from the implied decision weights.

To see the point intuitively, assume a power probability weighting function, so statements about concave or convex probability weighting apply for all objective probabilities. Then one simply needs to have the probability weighting function for losses be convex (overweighting) and the probability weighting function for gains be linear for there to be probabilistic loss aversion.[15] In this case we have probability neutrality for gains and probability pessimism for losses, implying, *ceteris paribus*, risk neutrality over gains and risk aversion over losses. These assumptions are stronger than needed, but illustrate the importance for estimates of the "utility loss aversion" parameter λ of allowing flexible degrees of probability weighting in the gain and loss domains.[16]

We allow flexibility in the probability weighting for losses and gains with the power probability weighting function by using

$$\omega(p) = p^{\gamma^+} \text{ for } m \geq 0 \tag{18a}$$

$$\omega(p) = p^{\gamma^-} \text{ for } m < 0 \tag{18b}$$

and where the p in question is the objective probability associated with that specific m. For the inverse-S function we use

$$\omega(p) = p^{\gamma^+} / (p^{\gamma^+} + (1-p)^{\gamma^+})^{1/\gamma^+} \text{ for } m \geq 0 \tag{19a}$$

$$\omega(p) = p^{\gamma^-} / (p^{\gamma^-} + (1-p)^{\gamma^-})^{1/\gamma^-} \text{ for } m < 0\,. \tag{19b}$$

For the Prelec function we use

$$\omega(p) = \exp\{-\eta^+ (-\ln p)^{\varphi^+}\} \tag{20a}$$

$$\omega(p) = \exp\{-\eta^- (-\ln p)^{\varphi^-}\}. \tag{20b}$$

The construction of the log-likelihood for the CPT model follows the same pattern as for EUT and RDU, with the parameters α, β, λ, γ^+, and γ^- (or η^+, φ^+, η^-, and φ^-) as well as a Fechner error term μ, to be estimated. One difference is that the "contextual utility" normalization is inappropriate on theoretical grounds, as noted earlier. A second difference is that loss-frame lotteries have their decision weights based on a rank-ordering from worst prize to best, rather than the rank-ordering from best to worst used for gain-frame lotteries (and all lotteries under RDU). Appendix B explains this difference.

A final difference with CPT is that *mixed*-frame lotteries are "parsed" into a gain-frame version and a loss-frame version, which are then separately evaluated. The evaluation of the overall mixed-frame lottery is then the *sum* of these two components, as explained in detail in §2 of Appendix B. This assumption is known in the literature as "gain–loss separability," and has been questioned in some hypothetical surveys by Wu and Markle (2008) and Birnbaum and Bahra (2007).[17] The batteries developed to test gain-loss separability should, at some point, be evaluated with salient rewards and rigorous econometric methods.[18]

3. ESTIMATES

We first estimate each of the alternative models with data pooled across all subjects, to allow a characterization of representative individual behavior. We initially assume homogeneous preferences to keep things simple, illustrate results and explain how we classify behavior as being best characterized by one model. We then allow for heterogeneous preferences by estimating for each individual.

The bottom line of our analysis is a comparison of the performance of the five models, shown in Fig. 5 for the sample of 177 undergraduates and in Fig. 6 for the sample of 95 MBA students with higher stakes. We conclude that RDU is the best characterization overall, followed by EUT. There is virtually no support for DT, DA or CPT.

The simple reason for the poor performance of CPT is that our subjects locally asset integrate over the frames presented to them. As stressed earlier, this is a key difference between CPT and the other models.[19] We expect DT and EUT to underperform RDU, since they are each nested in RDU. Finally, the poor showing for DA is consistent with extensive evidence from the early experimental work on EUT rejecting the Betweenness Axiom (BWA)[20] that it uses as an alternative to the IA, see Camerer and Ho (1994, p. 191) and Starmer (2000, p. 358).

3.1 Estimates for the Representative Agent

Although individual-level estimates are our focus, it is useful to consider the estimates for each model when it is assumed to characterize every subject. Table 1 presents maximum likelihood estimates for each model.[21] EUT shows moderate risk aversion, at a level generally consistent with many years of evidence from laboratory experiments. We can also see the EUT estimate as a "descriptive" way to flag that there is a risk premium for the representative agent, even if the other models decompose and calculate it differently.

With DT and the Prelec probability weighting function, allowing $\eta > 0$ and $\varphi > 0$, we have evidence of probability pessimism for almost all the range of

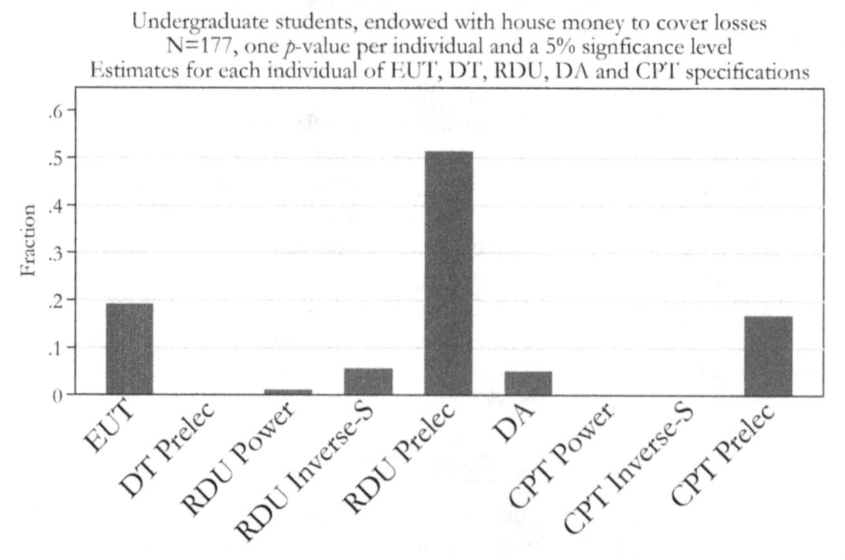

Fig. 5. Classifying Undergraduate Subjects as EUT, DT, RDU, DA or CPT.

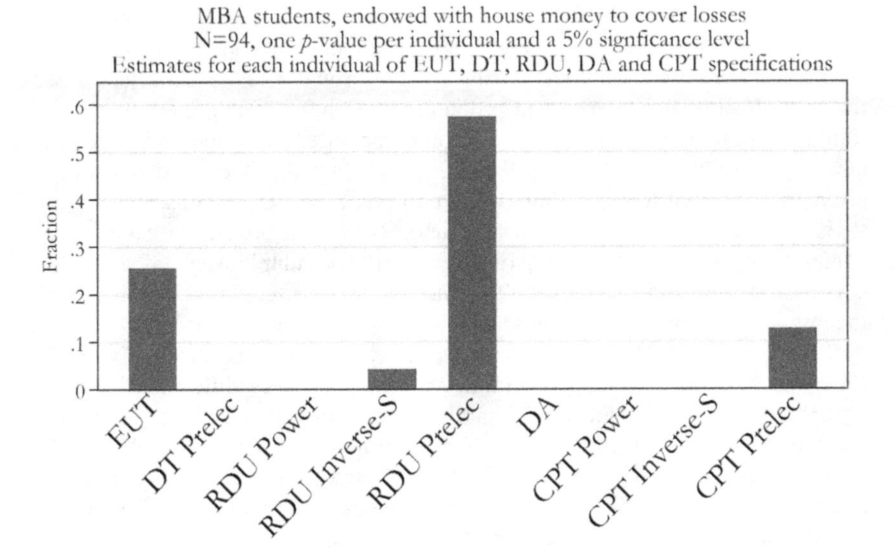

Fig. 6. Classifying MBA Subjects as EUT, DT, RDU, DA or CPT.

Table 1. Estimates for EUT, DT, RDU, DA, and CPT Models With Pooled Data.

Parameter	Point Estimate	Standard Error	*p*-Value	95% Confidence Interval	
A. Expected Utility					
r	0.45	0.028	<0.001	0.39	0.50
B. Dual Theory					
η	1.20	0.041	<0.001	1.12	1.28
φ	0.55	0.026	<0.001	0.50	0.61
C. Rank Dependent Utility					
r	0.70	0.019	<0.001	0.66	0.74
η	0.51	0.025	<0.001	0.46	0.56
φ	0.91	0.010	<0.001	0.84	0.99
D. Disappointment Aversion					
r	0.68	0.018	<0.001	0.65	0.71
θ	0.54	0.035	<0.001	0.47	0.60
E. Cumulative Prospect Theory					
α	0.21	0.021	<0.001	0.17	0.25
β	0.06	0.054	0.29	−0.05	0.16
λ	1.34	0.103	<0.001 (H_0: $\lambda = 1$)	1.14	1.54
η^+	1.04	0.052	<0.001	0.94	1.14
φ^+	0.44	0.035	<0.001	0.37	0.51
η^-	0.75	0.057	<0.001	0.63	0.86
φ^-	0.97	0.039	<0.001	0.90	1.05

$N = 177$ undergraduates with house money to cover losses. DT, RDU, and CPT estimates with the Prelec probability weighting function.

probabilities, as shown in Fig. 7. The left panel of Fig. 7 shows the estimated probability weighting function, and the right panel shows the implied decision weights for the ranked outcomes, using an equi-probable reference lottery to see the pure effect of rank-dependent probability weighting. The top (second) [bottom] line in the right panel shows a two-outcome lottery in which both outcomes have a probability of ½ (⅓) [¼]. We see in each case that the worst outcome is given greater decision weight than the best outcome, but the best outcome is given slightly more weight than the intermediate outcomes for lotteries with 3 or 4 outcomes. This probability weighting function has the popular "inverse-S" shape, but is predominately convex. Hence, DT generates a risk premium, consistent with the implication from the EUT model.

Turning to the RDU model, we focus here just on the specification with the Prelec probability weighting function. We now get a very different pattern of probability weighting than the DT model, as demonstrated by Fig. 8 and comparison to Fig. 7. This probability weighting function is concave, implying risk-loving behavior *ceteris paribus* the effect of the curvature of the utility function. Since we know from the EUT and DT estimates that there is a risk premium overall, we can expect that there must be a more concave utility function than EUT in order for the net effect of probability optimism and diminishing marginal utility to generate a modest risk premium. This is exactly what we find, in Table 1, with the CRRA coefficient estimate of 0.70 compared to the EUT estimate of 0.45. For both DT and RDU, we can easily reject the hypothesis that there is no probability weighting (i.e., that $\eta = \varphi = 1$) (Fig. 8).

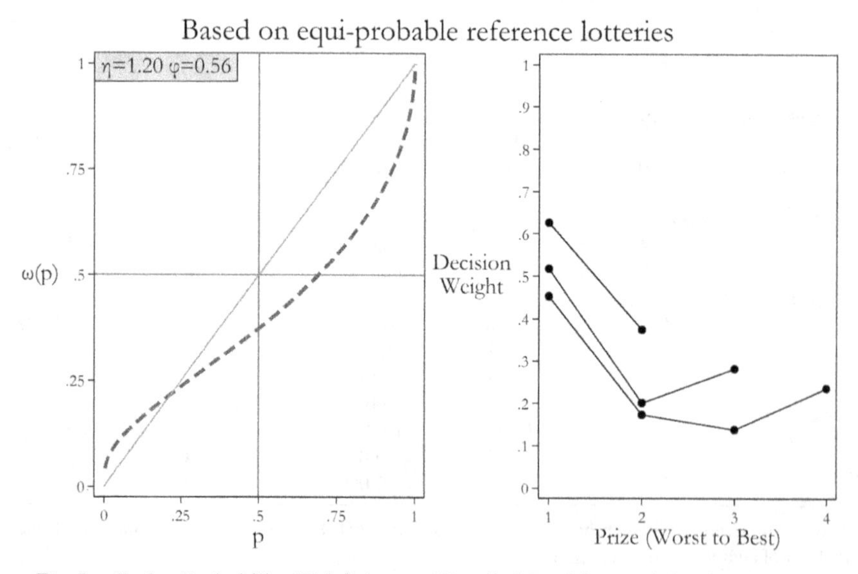

Fig. 7. Prelec Probability Weighting and Implied Decision Weights for the Dual Theory Model.

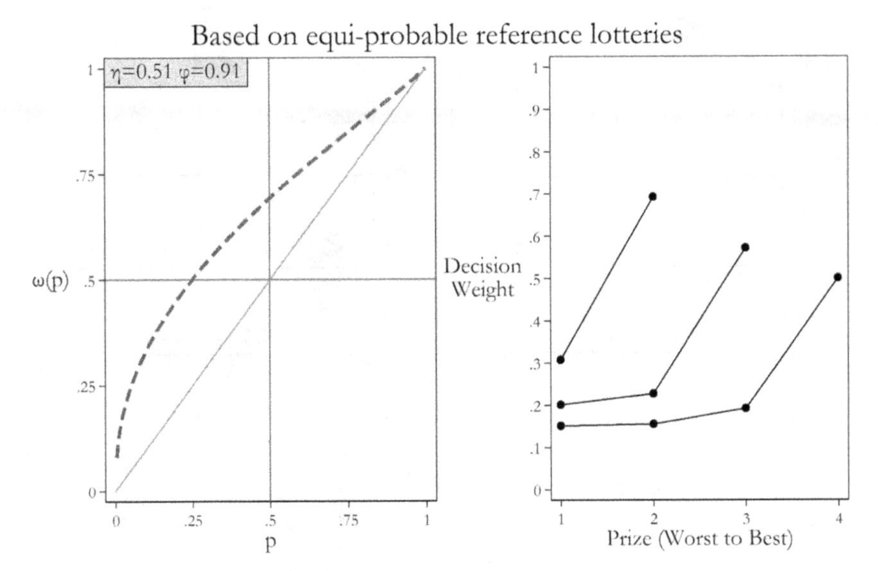

Fig. 8. Prelec Probability Weighting and Implied Decision Weights for the Rank-dependent Model.

The DA model estimates in Table 1 imply statistically significant concave utility ($r = 0.70 > 0$) and DA ($\theta = 0.51 > 0$). This model has to do as well as EUT, since EUT is nested when $\theta = 0$. It might be expected to do as well as RDU, since if there are only two prizes then the DA model literally collapses to RDU (Abdellaoui & Bleichrodt, 2007); on other hand, we have up to four prizes per lottery in these data, and in those cases RDU and DA are not the same.

Finally, we consider the CPT model with the Prelec probability weighting function. Table 1 presents the estimates, and Figs. 9 and 10 visualize their implications. We find concave utility in the gain frame ($\alpha > 0$), linear utility in the loss frame ($\beta \approx 0$), and mild evidence for utility loss aversion ($\lambda > 1$). The top left panel of Fig. 9 shows the estimated "intrinsic" utility functions, and the top right panel then shows the "full" utility functions. These full utility functions are the same in the gain frame as the intrinsic utility function, but the full utility function in the loss frame also incorporates the effect of utility loss aversion, and is shown in the solid line.

The CPT estimates for probability weighting imply the pattern shown in Fig. 10: classic "inverse-S" probability weighting for gains, and concave utility weighting for losses. The implication of concave probability weighting for losses is to put greater (lower) weight on the worst (best) outcomes, so that we would have probabilistic loss aversion if there had been no probability weighting for gains.

The "hit rates" of successful predictions for EUT, DT, RDU, DA, and CPT are 71%, 70%, 73%, 72%, and 76%, respectively, for the undergraduates using house money to cover any losses.[22] The log-likelihoods are −10818, −10952, −10456, −10722, and −10936. So by both metrics, RDU dominates EUT which in turn dominates CPT. Of course, neither EUT nor RDU is nested within CPT.[23]

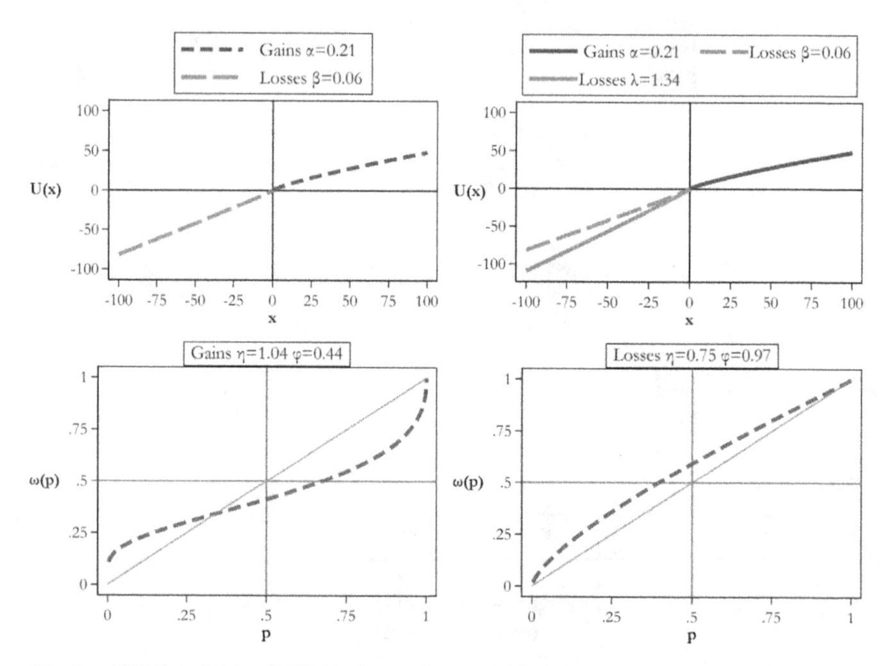

Fig. 9. CPT Model for GSU Undergraduates With House Money to Cover Losses, I.

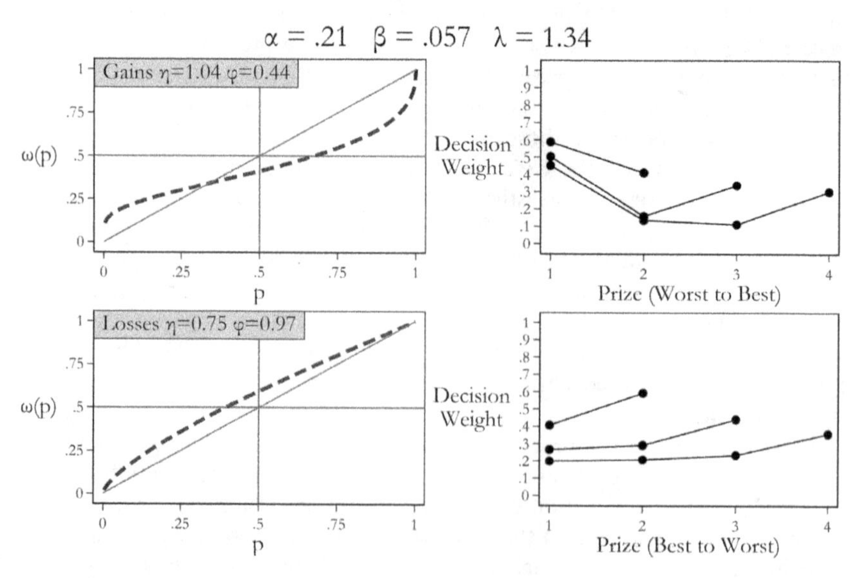

Fig. 10. CPT Model for GSU Undergraduates With House Money to Cover Losses, II.

For the non-nested model comparisons, we use tests that compare models by looking at the likelihoods for the same observation, and defining a statistic on those observation-specific comparisons, rather than the sum of likelihoods. The two most popular tests are the Vuoung (1989) test and the Clarke (2003, 2007) test, described in Harrison and Rutström (2009). Using them, we are able to test the null hypothesis that the two models are equally close to the true specification, and that one cannot discriminate between them. Each test allows us to say which model is "favored," but also provides some statistical confidence in the rejection of the null in the direction of the favored model. Using these tests, we can draw a strong conclusion for the *representative agent* comparisons: the CPT model is favored over each of the EUT, DT, RDU, and DA models in terms of both tests, each test allows one to reject the null hypothesis of non-discrimination with p-values below 0.01, and the distribution of data underlying the test statistics is non-Gaussian so the Clarke test should be used.[24] As it happens both tests lead to the same conclusion: CPT wins.

Both tests generate the same conclusions, which flows primarily from the huge sample size with all of the pooled choices. There is some evidence that the ratio of log-likelihoods is non-Gaussian, and leptokurtic, when sample sizes are less than 500: the asymptotic convergence to a Gaussian distribution of the ratio of log-likelihoods is slow for smaller sample sizes, and the distribution tends to resemble a double exponential (Clarke & Signorino, 2010, p. 377). In that case, the Clarke test is much more reliable. We will see below that this point is of some importance when evaluating individual subjects, since the sample size is 100 there and we do see differences between the conclusions from the two tests.

A final way to evaluate the risk preferences of the *representative agent* is by means of a mixture model, following Harrison and Rutström (2009). Focusing only on the mixture between the EUT and CPT models, and the RDU and CPT models, the first result is that the RDU model characterizes 66% of the choices: indeed, even the EUT model characterized 68% of the choices in a comparable mixture model. The second result is that we have a very concave utility function for the RDU choices, but an optimistic probability weighting function, more or less offsetting each other. In fact, if we estimate an EUT and CPT model, we find that the utility function is concave, *suggesting* that the net effect of the offsetting processes in the RDU model is to be risk averse.

The third result from the estimates under the mixture specification is that we have a concave utility function for gains under CPT, but a linear utility function for losses. Utility loss aversion is significant. We also find very little probability weighting in either gain or loss frames, as shown below. This differs from some prior estimates in which we get very little utility loss aversion, but significant probabilistic loss aversion, at least at the pooled level.

3.2 Hypothesis Tests to Discriminate Between Models

When typing individuals as EUT, DT or RDU we have the benefit of a direct hypothesis test that $\omega(p) = p$ for EUT and $r = 0$ for DT. Similarly, when typing individuals as EUT or DA, we can similarly directly test the hypothesis that $\theta = 0$. But when we have CPT we have to either estimate a mixture model for each subject or apply some non-nested hypothesis tests. The former can be challenging numerically for samples of just 100 observations, and the latter can be reliably undertaken if we have log-likelihoods for each observation and for each model being preferred.[25] Hence, we first consider how the nested hypotheses tests allow us to discriminate between the EUT, DT, RDU, and DA models, and then consider the extension to discriminating between these models and CPT.

Fig. 11 displays the models selected using the nested hypothesis tests with respect to EUT. The left panel displays the distribution of p-values on these tests, with one p-value for each subject. We select the winning model for each subject based on log-likelihoods, and then check if the null hypothesis of EUT can be rejected at the 1%, 5% or 10% significance level. Unless the alternative to EUT exhibits statistically significant rejection of EUT, we retain the EUT classification.[26] We find a relatively low fraction, just over 25%, of EUT-consistent subjects for samples from this population. There are virtually no subjects classified as DT, and very few classified as DA. The modal risk preference type is RDU, with the Prelec probability weighting function dominating.

Now consider extending this model discrimination exercise to include CPT. Start with a subject for whom RDU is favored over CPT, such as subject #2 (in turn, EUT was rejected for this subject in the comparison with RDU). In Fig. 12, we show the "jagged" distribution of the log-likelihood ratios that form the basis of the Vuoung test of the non-nested model. We also show a fitted Normal distribution to this empirical distribution, since the Vuoung test requires that this distribution be Normal, as it is asymptotically.[27] It is apparent that the empirical distribution is more peaked than the normal, consistent

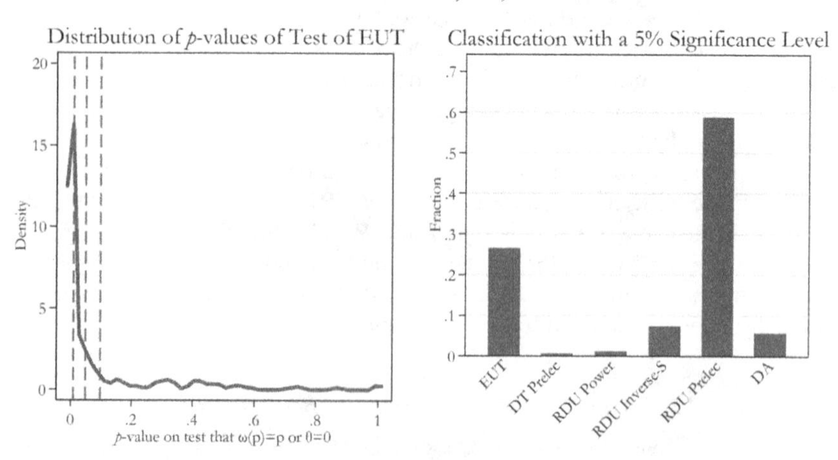

Fig. 11. Classifying Subjects as EUT, DT, RDU or DA Using Hypothesis Test that $\omega(p) = p$ or $\theta = 0$ and a Significance Level of 5% to Reject EUT.

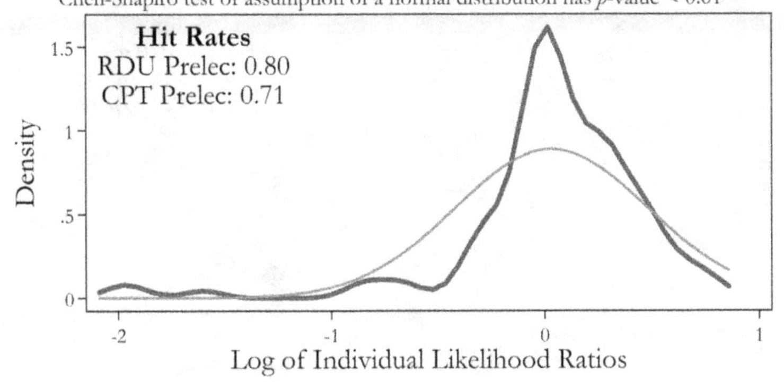

Fig. 12. Distribution of Log-likelihood Ratios for Non-nested Tests of RDU Prelec and CPT Prelec Models for Subject #2 Making 100 Choices.

with the tendency in samples below 500 for this distribution to be leptokurtic. In fact, in the last subtitle line we show the p-value from the Chen and Shapiro (1995) test of Normalcy, as implemented by Brzezinski (2012); this test has been shown to be more robust than the popular Shapiro–Wilk test. This p-value is less than 0.01, implying that we can reject the hypothesis that the log-likelihood ratios are distributed Normally, and hence we must use the Clarke test rather than the Vuoung test.[28]

Doing so, we find that the Clarke test favors the RDU model over the CPT model, and that the p-value on the null hypothesis of non-discrimination between the RDU and CPT models is below 0.01. Hence, at the 5% significance level we can reject that null, and infer that the RDU model is favored over the CPT model for this subject. The hit rates of the fitted models are also consistent with this conclusion: the CPT hit rate is only 71% compared to the RDU hit rate of 80%. In this instance, we see the importance of determining if the conditions for the Vuoung test are met: the p-value on non-discrimination for that test is only 0.49, and we would not have concluded that the RDU model was superior to the CPT model.

An example in which CPT wins is subject #7, shown in Fig. 13. In this instance, both non-nested hypothesis tests favor the CPT model over RDU, as well as CPT have a superior hit rate. Again, the Chen–Shapiro test rejects the assumption required for the Vuoung test, although in this instance that is moot.

There are many instances in which EUT dominates CPT, and Fig. 14 illustrates the case of subject #8. In this instance, the Clarke test favors EUT, and indeed the hit rate for EUT is greater than the hit rate for CPT. However, the p-value on the Clarke test being unable to statistically discriminate between EUT

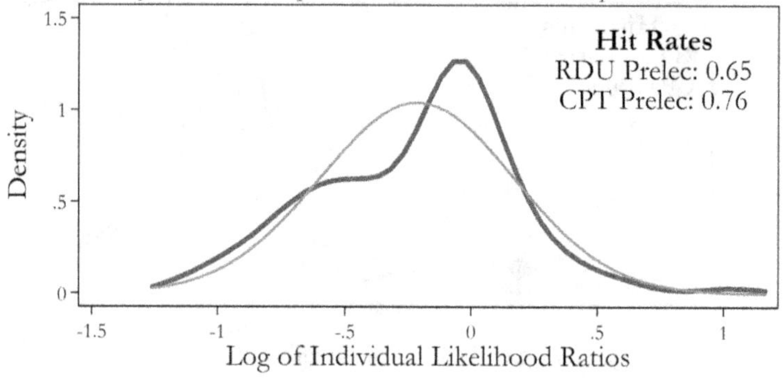

Fig. 13. Distribution of Log-likelihood Ratios for Non-nested Tests of RDU Prelec and CPT Prelec Models for Subject #7 Making 100 Choices.

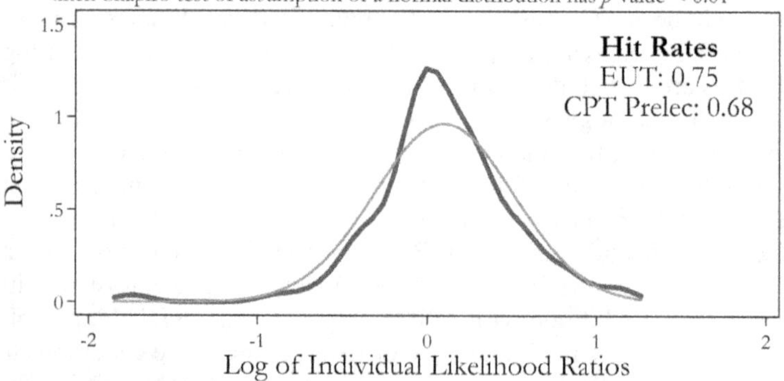

Fig. 14. Distribution of Log-likelihood Ratios for Non-nested Tests of EUT and CPT Prelec Models for Subject #8 Making 100 Choices.

and CPT is 0.09, so in this instance the subject is classified as EUT since CPT is not favored in a statistically significant manner.

A similar example arises for subject #3, shown in Fig. 15, where the CPT model is favored over the EUT, but not in a statistically significant manner. Again, we therefore classify this subject as an EUT decision-maker, in the absence of statistically significant evidence to the contrary.

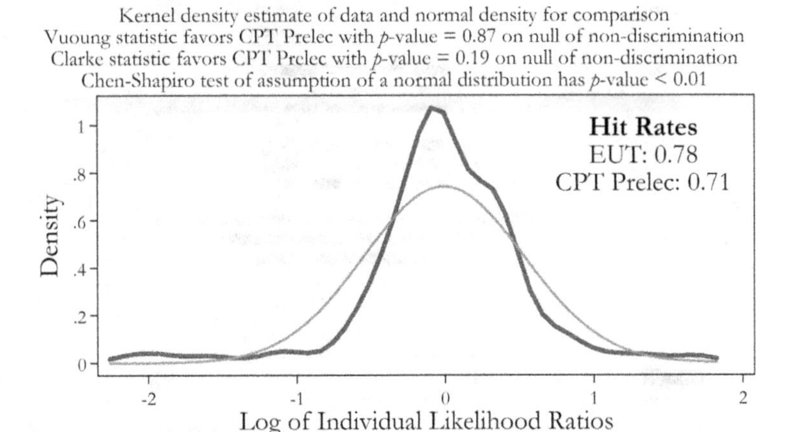

Fig. 15. Distribution of Log-likelihood Ratios for Non-nested Tests of EUT and CPT Prelec Models for Subject #3 Making 100 Choices.

Turning from individual instances, we can characterize the general trend of these hypothesis tests. Fig. 16 shows the fraction of cases in black for which the "base model" named on the far left is favored by the non-nested hypothesis test indicated by the Chen–Shapiro test of Normalcy of the log-likelihood ratios. The fraction of cases in light blue or grey show where the CPT model is favored compared to the base model. Of course, each subject is classified as one or other of these two base models, but these unconditional results illustrate the pattern more clearly than just focusing on shares for the preferred base model for each subject.

In general, we see that the CPT model fares better when compared to the EUT model rather than the RDU model, as one might expect from the added flexibility of the RDU model. But these shares, again, do not tell us whether the favored model was favored *in a statistically significant manner*. For that we need to look to the p-values on the null hypothesis of non-discrimination, as illustrated for the specific examples considered earlier. Fig. 17 shows these for the cases in which the non-nested hypothesis test favored the CPT model (i.e., the sub-sample from Fig. 16 shown in light blue or grey). These are the cases we care about to understand why the CPT model, although favored, was not favored in a statistically significant manner. Fig. 17 shows the *average* p-values in this case, although one could equally look at the median or interquartile range. We show one of the nine complete distributions of p-values later, to verify this point. Fig. 17 suggests that it does not matter which non-nested hypothesis test, Vuoung or Clarke, is used when comparing RDU and CPT models: in both cases the average of p-values is well above 10%. Hence, for the subjects classified as RDU from the nested hypothesis test, which is around 60% of the sample (see Figs. 5 and 6), it is very unlikely that the non-nested hypothesis test

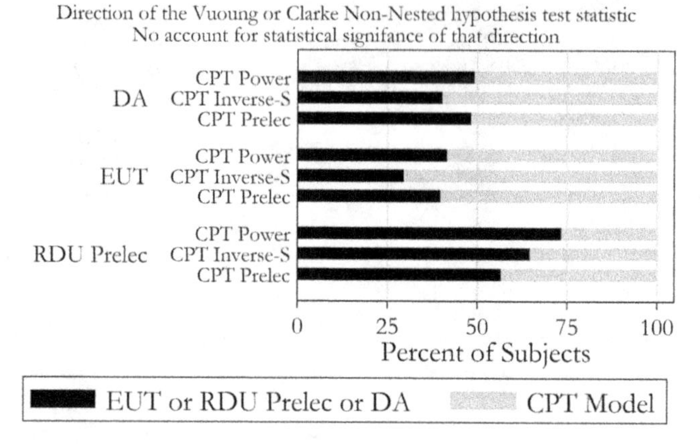

Fig. 16. Share of Subjects Favoring One of the CPT Models.

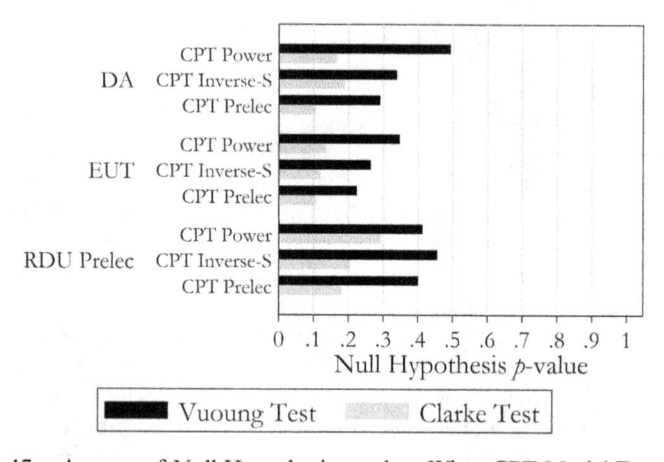

Fig. 17. Average of Null Hypothesis *p*-values When CPT Model Favored.

would *positively and statistically significantly* favor the CPT model (and recall that this is the average for the cases in which the CPT model was favored).

However, Fig. 17 does suggest that it matters whether the Vuoung or Clarke test is used when comparing EUT and CPT models, or DA and CPT models. The Vuoung test has average *p*-values that are between 0.10 and 0.19, suggesting that there could be a decent fraction below 1%, 5% or 10%. But the Clarke test has very high *p*-values, virtually ensuring that the CPT model would *not be positively and statistically significantly* favored over the EUT or DA model. The final piece in this story, then, is to see how often the Vuoung test is used when the CPT model is favored. Fig. 18 makes it clear, if one considers the tiny values on

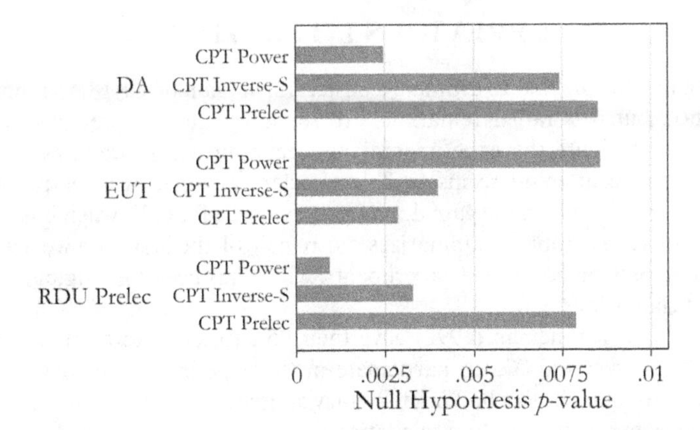

Fig. 18. Average of Null Hypothesis p-values for Test of Normal Distribution of Vuoung Statistic When CPT Model Favored.

the bottom axis, that the Clarke test is almost always used. This figure shows the average p-values of the Chen–Shapiro test of Normalcy of the ratio of log-likelihoods: rejecting that hypothesis implies that we must use the Clarke test instead of the Vuoung test, as noted above for the four individual examples.

Finally, Fig. 19 shows a complete distribution of p-values for the Clarke non-nested hypothesis comparing RDU Prelec and CPT Prelec, in contrast to the average shown in Fig. 17 in the light blue or grey bars. The kernel density approximation does "bleed" below 0 and above 1 slightly,[29] but the point is clear: the vast bulk of the p-values are greater than the 1%, 5%, and 10% levels shown in the vertical dashed lines.

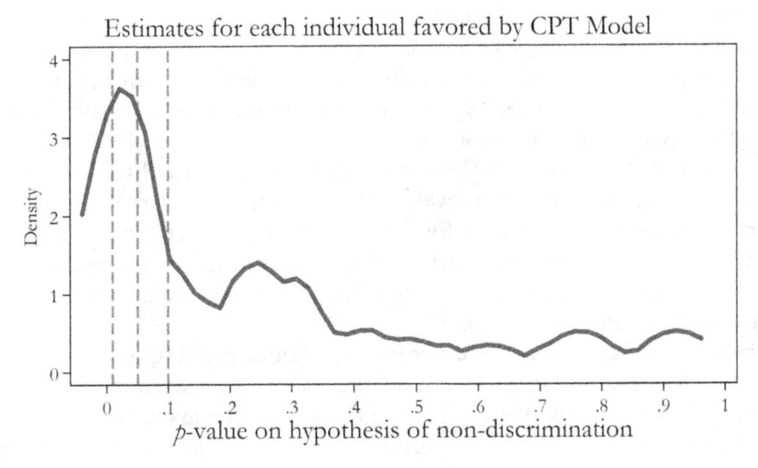

Fig. 19. Distribution of p-values of Clarke Test of Hypothesis of Non-discrimination for RDU Prelec and CPT Prelec Models.

4. PREVIOUS LITERATURE

Surely we are not the first to estimate a structural version of CPT? As it happens, we are not, but it is rather remarkable to see how light the previous evidence is when one weights the experimental and econometric procedures carefully. Moreover, a recent trend seems to be to declare any evidence for probability weighting, even if only in the gain domain, as evidence for CPT when it is literally evidence for RDU. Table 2 summarizes our review of the literature we are aware of, focusing only on controlled experiments, which has been the original basis of empirical claims for CPT.

Tversky and Kahneman (1992) gave their 25 subjects a total of 64 choices. Their subjects received $25 to participate in the experiment, but rewards were not salient, so their choices had no monetary consequences. The majority of data from their experiments used an elicitation procedure that we would now call a multiple price list, in the spirit of Holt and Laury (2002). Subjects were told the expected value of the risky lottery, and seven certain amounts were presented in a logarithmic scale, with values spanning the extreme payouts of the risky lottery. The subject made seven binary choices between the given risky lottery and the series of certain amounts. To generate more refined choices, the subject was given a second series of seven CE for the same risky lottery, zeroing in on the interval selected in the first stage. This variant is called an *iterative* multiple price list by Andersen, Harrison, Lau, and Rutström (2006). Furthermore, "switching" was ruled out, with the computer program enforcing a single switch between the risky lottery and the certain values. This variant is called a *sequential* multiple price list by Andersen et al. (2006). All risky prospects used two prizes, and there were 56 prospects evaluated in this manner. One half of these prospects were in the gain frame, and one half were in the loss frame, with the latter being a "reflection" of the former in terms of the values employed.

A further eight tasks involved mixed-frame gambles. In these choices, the subject was asked to Fill-In-the-Blank (FIB) by entering a value $x that would make the risky lottery ($a, ½; $b, ½) equivalent to ($c, ½; $x, ½), for given values of a, b and c. The probabilities for the initial 56 gain-frame and loss-frame choices were 0.01, 0.05, 0.1, 0.25, 0.5, 0.75, 0.9, 0.95, and 0.99, whereas the sole probability for the eight mixed-frame choices was ½.[30]

Tversky and Kahneman (1992) estimate a structural model of CPT using non-linear least squares, and at the level of the individual. Remarkably, they then report the *median* point estimate, for each structural parameter, over the 25 estimated values. So over all 25 subjects, and using our notation, the median value for α was 0.88, the median value of λ was 2.22, the median value of γ^+ was 0.61, and the median value of γ^- was 0.69.[31]

These parameter estimates are remarkable in three respects, given the prominence they have received in the literature. First, whenever one sees point estimates estimated for individuals, one can be certain that there are many "wild" estimates from an *a priori* perspective,[32] so reporting the median value alone might be quite unrepresentative of the average value, and provides no information whatsoever on the variability across subjects. Second, there is no mention at all of standard

Table 2. The Existing Literature Claiming to Estimate CPT.

Study	Rewards	Frames	Comments
Tversky and Kahneman (1992)	Non-salient	Gain, Loss	"Median" estimates reported.
Camerer and Ho (1994)	Real	Gain	
Wu and Gonzalez (1996)	Hypothetical	Gain	
Gonzalez and Wu (1999)	Real	Gain	
Fennema and van Assen (1998)	Hypothetical	Gain, Loss, Mixed	
Abdellaoui (2000)	Real Hypothetical	Gain Loss	
Schmidt and Traub (2002)	Hypothetical	Gain, Loss	
Harbaugh, Krause, and Vesterlund (2002)	Real	Gain, Loss	Assumes no utility loss aversion. Claim to be unable to jointly estimate probability weighting and the value function
Pennings and Smidts (2003)	Hypothetical	Gain, Loss[a]	
Etchart-Vincent (2004)	Hypothetical	Loss	
Mason, Shogren, Settle, and List (2005)	Real	Loss	
Schunk and Betsch (2006)	Real Hypothetical	Gain Loss	
Stott (2006)	"Slightly Real" [c]	Gain	Does not mention loss aversion
Fehr-Duda, Gennaro, and Schubert (2006)	Real	Gain, Loss	Assumes no utility loss aversion
Abdellaoui, Bleichrodt, and L'Haridon (2008)	Real Hypothetical	Gain Loss, Mixed	
Rieskamp (2008)	"Slightly Real"[b]	Gain, Loss, Mixed	Constrained to show loss aversion
Booij and van de Kuilen (2009)	Hypothetical	Gain, Loss	
Booij, van Praag, and van de Kuilen (2010)	Hypothetical	Gain, Loss, Mixed	
Bruhin, Fehr-Duda, and Epper (2010)	Real	Gain, Loss	Assumes no utility loss aversion
Pachur, Hanoch, and Gummerum (2010)	Hypothetical	Gain, Loss, Mixed	
von Gaudecker, van Soest, and Wengström (2011)	Real	Gain, Mixed	Assumes no probability weighting
Nilsson, Rieskamp, and Wagenmakers (2011)	"Slightly Real"[b]	Gain, Loss, Mixed	
Glöckner and Pachur (2012)	Real	Gain, Loss, Mixed	"Median" estimates reported, apparently with no standard errors
Zeisberger, Vrecko, and Langer (2012)	Real[d]	Gain, Loss, Mixed	Becker, DeGroot, and Marschak (1964) method used to elicit certainty equivalents
Abdelloui, L'Haridon, and Paraschiv (2013)	Real	Gain	

(*Continued*)

Table 2. (Continued)

Study	Rewards	Frames	Comments
Scholten and Read (2014)	Non-salient	Gain, Loss	Assumes no utility loss aversion
Vieider et al. (2015)	Real	Gain, Loss, Mixed	Single mixed frame prospect
Balcombe and Fraser (2015)		Gain	Does not mention loss aversion
Bouchouicha and Vieider (2017)	Hypothetical Real[e]	Gain, Loss Gain	Assumes no utility loss aversion
Pachur, Schulte-Mecklenbeck, Murphy, and Hertwig (2018)	Real[f]	Gain, Loss, Mixed	
Murphy and ten Brincke (2018)	Real	Gain, Loss, Mixed	
L'Haridon and Vieider (2019)	Real	Gain, Loss, Mixed	Single mixed frame prospect
Vieider, Martinsson, Nam, and Truong (2019)	Real	Gain, Loss, Mixed	Single mixed frame prospect

[a]Subject elicitations were all in the gain frame, but the authors' assumed (p. 1254) some positive reference point in their analysis and treated gains below that as "losses" for the purposes of analysis.
[b]Subjects made binary choices over lotteries with outcomes between +€100 and −€100, one of 180 choices was selected for payment and realization, and then 5% of the outcome added or subtracted from an endowment of €15.
[c]Lottery prizes up to £40,000 were included in binary lottery choices. Each subject was given a fixed £3, and one of the 90 choices selected, re-scaled so that the maximum prize would be £5, and then played out.
[d]One subject in 10 was selected for payment, but the losses in that case were substantial (up to €60) out of an endowment that had been earned in a previous task in that session.
[e]Two participants out of 47 total were selected randomly to for payment.
[f]Realized monetary outcomes were scaled down to 10% of the amounts displayed on screen to subjects during the choices.

errors, so we have no way of knowing, for example, if the oft-repeated value of λ is statistically significantly different from 1. Third, the median value of any given parameter is not linked in any manner to the median value of any other parameter: these are *not the values of some representative, median subject*, which is often how they are implicitly portrayed.[33] The subject who actually generated the median value of λ, for instance, might have had any value for α, β, γ^+, and γ^-.

These shortcomings of the Tversky and Kahneman (1992) study have not, to our knowledge, led anyone to replicate their experiments with salient rewards and report complete sets of parameter estimates with standard errors. The fault is not that of Tversky and Kahneman (1992), who otherwise employed quite modern methods, but the subsequent CPT literature. Anybody casually using these estimates as statistically representative should simply stop doing so and instead demand a more rigorous treatment of CPT estimates.

Camerer and Ho (1994) is a remarkable study, with many insights. It was also one of the first to propose and estimate a structural model of CPT using maximum likelihood (§6.1). The data employed were choice patterns from a wide range of studies, but the analysis was explicitly restricted to the gain frame (p. 188).

Hence it could be said to be the first structural estimation of the RDU model, but not of a CPT model including losses.

Wu and Gonzalez (1996) focus entirely on the probability weighting function. They stress the point that they estimate the probability weighting function without having to make assumptions about utility functions, and view the need to make those assumptions as a methodological flaw. The reason it is said to be a flaw is that inferences about the probability weighting function could be confounded by mis-specifications of the true utility function (p. 1678). They propose a simple method for eliciting probability weights based on a series of choices with only two common outcomes, $200 or $240. Hence one could normalize utilities of these outcomes to 0 and 1, and avoid making any further assumptions about the utility function. Unfortunately, this procedure was implemented in a non-salient, hypothetical choice task, and only for the gain frame (§4). When Wu and Gonzalez (1996) undertake maximum likelihood estimation, via a non-linear least squares method, they assume a power utility function and also restrict themselves to gain-frame choices (§5). One could adapt the Wu and Gonzalez (1996) method for eliciting a probability weighting function for the gain frame to eliciting functions for the gain *and* loss frame, but they did not do so. Gonzalez and Wu (1999) estimate (non-parametric) probability weighting functions *and* utility functions for 10 subjects based on elicited CE for two-outcome lotteries solely in the gain frame. They at least employed salient rewards for their small number of subjects.

Harbaugh, Krause, and Vesterlund (2002) paid for one of the 24 lotteries studied. Each lottery had two outcomes, with zero payment possible in every lottery. In half the lotteries the second payment was positive, and the other half of lotteries had a negative second payment; thus, there were no mixed-frame lotteries. Each decision was between one of the lotteries and a certain amount, which was usually the expected value of the lottery. Decisions were presented to subjects on separate plastic cards, with each lottery presented as a pie chart with a "spinner" in the middle of the circle. Extra care was given to the method of task presentation, since subjects were as young as five years old. They do not undertake structural estimation of the CPT model, claiming (p. 83) that, "Given our data it is not possible to simultaneously estimate both the probability weighting function and the value function." They do not consider utility loss aversion at all.

Mason, Shogren, Settle, and List (2005) evaluate behavior over risky lotteries defined solely in a loss frame. They do not consider gain-frame choices or mixed-frame choices, but they do employ salient, real rewards.

Stott (2006) examines a wide range of parametric functional forms for CPT, but only considers data from hypothetical tasks defined over the gain frame.[34]

Fehr-Duda, Gennaro, and Schubert (2006) paid subjects for one of 50 binary choices over lotteries with two outcomes. Half of the battery of losses were for gains, half were for losses, and there were no mixed-frame choices. For each lottery, an ordered MPL with 20 certain amounts was used to elicit a CE. The certain amounts spanned the two outcomes of the lottery, so each subject faced 50 MPLs each with 20 rows. The utility loss aversion parameter λ was not estimated, because of the absence of mixed-frame lotteries (p. 295).

Fennema and van Assen (1998), Abdellaoui (2000), Etchart-Vincent (2004), Schunk and Betsch (2006), Abdellaoui, Bleichrodt, and L'Haridon (2008), and Booij and van de Kuilen (2009) are widely cited as having used the "tradeoff method" to estimate the utility function for losses. Fennema and van Assen (1998), Etchart-Vincent (2004), and Booij and van de Kuilen (2009) used hypothetical survey questions, with no real consequences. Abdellaoui (2000, p. 1502) and Schunk and Betsch (2006, p. 389) used real incentives for the gain frame, but hypothetical survey questions for the loss frame; neither asked any questions in the mixed frame. Abdellaoui et al. (2008) also asked real questions in the gain frame, but only hypothetical survey questions in the loss and mixed frames. Brooks and Zank (2005) used real losses, and focused on testing certain implications for choice patterns from utility loss aversion, not estimating the full CPT structure. In a similar vein, Brooks, Peters, and Zank (2014) used real losses from a house endowment, and generated choice predictions based on assumed parametric values for a standard CPT specification. No CPT model was estimated from the 105 binary choices each subject made over gain, mixed and loss frames.

Rieskamp (2008) uses "slightly real" rewards and all three frames. Subjects made binary choices over lotteries with outcomes between +€100 and −€100, one of 180 choices was selected for payment and realization, and then 5% of the outcome added or subtracted from an endowment of €15. So the rewards were salient, but not substantial. Nonetheless, this is a great advance from virtually all other studies. The structural estimates employed both α and β in power utility functions, with no discussion of the implications for identifying utility loss aversion. As it happened, the estimates of these two parameters were virtually identical, as in Tversky and Kahneman (1992). The utility loss aversion parameter was constrained to be greater than 1, ruling out utility loss seeking. And the parameters for the Inverse-S probability weighting functions were constrained to be less than 1 for both gains and losses. Pooled over all subjects, the estimates (p. 1455) were $\alpha = \beta = 0.91$, $\lambda = 1$, $\gamma^+ = 0.69$, and $\gamma^- = 0.71$. It is an open question what these estimates would be if λ had not "hit" the imposed lower boundary value.

Booij, van Praag, and van de Kuilen (2010) estimate parametric models of CPT, but use hypothetical survey questions.

Bruhin, Fehr-Duda, and Epper (2010) estimated parametric models of CPT that assumed that the utility loss aversion parameter λ was 1, noting wryly that "our specification of the value function seems to lack a prominent feature of prospect theory, loss aversion …" (p. 1382). They did this because their design only included lotteries in the gain frame and the loss frame, and none in the mixed frame. Estimation of utility loss aversion is, in general, logically impossible without mixed-frame choices. They did provide real incentives for decisions, and employed an endowment of house money just as we did.

Pachur, Hanoch, and Gummerum (2010) studied inmates in a UK prison, as well as UK non-prisoners. Choices were hypothetical, as the inmates received no compensation of any kind, and the non-prisoners received only a fixed £3 pound participation payment that was non-salient.

Nilsson, Rieskamp, and Wagenmakers (2011) utilized the same "slightly real" data of Rieskamp (2008) and applied a Bayesian hierarchical model to estimate structural CPT parameters. They indirectly recognized the identification problem with power utility specifications when $\alpha \neq \beta$. They initially simulated data using the popular point estimates from Tversky and Kahneman (1992), to test the ability of their model to recover them. They found that their model underestimated λ and that α was estimated to be much lower than β, rather than $\alpha \approx \beta$. They concluded (p. 89) as follows:

> It is likely that these results are caused by a peculiarity of CPT, that is, its ability to account for loss aversion in multiple ways. The most obvious way for CPT to account for loss aversion is by parameter λ (after all, the purpose of λ is to measure loss aversion). A second way, however, is to decrease the marginal utility at a faster pace for gains than for losses. This occurs when α is smaller than β. Based on this reasoning, we hypothesized that the parameter estimation routines compensate for the underestimation of λ by assigning lower values to α than to β; in this way, CPT accounts for the existing loss aversion indirectly in a manner that we had not anticipated.

Of course, this is just the *theoretical* identification issue that requires an "exchange rate assumption," as noted earlier and discussed in Köbberling and Wakker (2005, §7) and Wakker (2010, §9.6). In any event, they optionally estimate all models with $\alpha = \beta$, and avoid this identification problem. Using the Inverse-S probability weighting function they reported Bayesian posterior modes (standard deviations) over the pooled sample of $\alpha = \beta = 0.91$ (0.16), $\lambda = 1.02$ (0.26), $\gamma^+ = 0.68$ (0.11) and $\gamma^- = 0.89$ (0.19). Unlike Rieskamp (2008), they did not constrain λ to be greater than 1.

These estimates are the Bayesian counterparts of random coefficients: hence each parameter is a distribution, which can be summarized in several ways. Reporting the mode is a more robust alternative to the mean, given the symmetric nature of their visual display of estimates, and the standard deviation provides information on the estimated variability across the 30 subjects, each making 180 binary choices. They find no evidence for utility loss aversion. Fig. 20 shows the two probability weighting functions estimated, and implied decision weights. There is *very* slight evidence of probabilistic loss aversion for small probabilities, since there is slight risk loving over gains and extremely slight risk aversion for losses. For large probabilities this evidence suggests probabilistic loss seeking, albeit modest.[35]

Glöckner and Pachur (2012) undertook incentivized experiments, presenting subjects with 138 binary choices over two-outcome lotteries spanning the gain, loss and mixed frames. A house endowment of €22 was used to cover potential losses of up to €9.90 from the one lottery choice that was selected to play out.[36] Structural CPT estimates were generated, and one of their metrics for selecting parameters reflected likelihoods, rather than the unweighted hit rate. However, it appears that their estimation procedures do not generate standard errors, as illustrated by the tests of the hypothesis of stability of choices over two sessions.[37] Median estimates of parameters across individuals are reported (Table 4, p. 27), following the unfortunate procedure of Tversky and Kahneman (1992), so one cannot say what any individual or representative agent's parameters were. EUT is compared (p. 29), but only with respect to the unweighted hit rate; there is no comparison to RDU, although a long list of *ad hoc* heuristics (Table 2, p. 26) are compared in terms of unweighted hit rates.

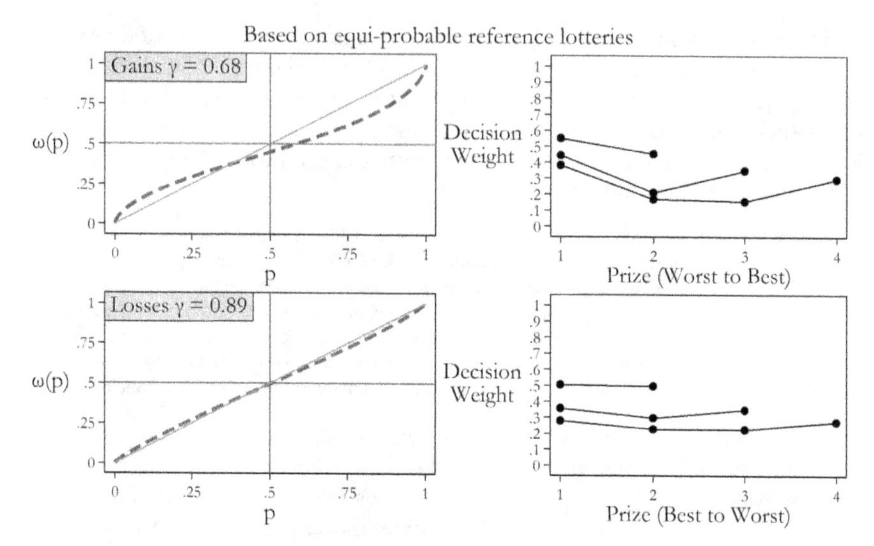

Fig. 20. Probability Weighting and Decision Weights From Mode of Bayesian Posterior Distributions Estimated by Nilsson, Rieskamp, and Wagenmakers (2011).

von Gaudecker, van Soest, and Wengström (2011) estimated parametric models of CPT that assumed a complete absence of probability weighting, on both gain and loss frames. They note clearly (p. 675) that their specification entails

> [...] departures from the original prospect theory specification. [...] it does not involve nonlinear probability weighting because our goal is to estimate individual-level parameters, and the dimension of the estimation problem is large already. Adding a parameter that is highly colinear with utility curvature in our experimental setup would result in an infeasibly large number of parameters, given the structure of our data. Furthermore, typical probability weighting functionals develop the highest impact at extreme probabilities, which are absent from our experiment.

Unfortunately, these justifications are tenuous. The fact that the goal is individual-level estimation does not, by itself, have any theoretical implications for why one can pick and choose aspects of the CPT model. Indeed, adding one or two parameters for probability weighting, assuming one of the popular one parameter specifications and the possibility of constraining probability weighting to be the same in the gain and loss frames, does add to the dimensionality of the estimation problem. But numerical convenience is hardly an acceptable rationale for mis-specification of the CPT model. Colinearity with utility curvature is actually a theoretical point of some importance, and to be expected, and not an econometric nuisance. Indeed, it extends to colinearity with the utility loss aversion parameter, unless one assumes away *a priori* the possibility of probabilistic loss aversion. If one parameter plays a significant role in explaining the risk premium for an individual, then assuming it away surely biases conclusions about the strength and even sign of other psychological pathways. The final point, about not having sufficient variability in probabilities to estimate probability weighting functions, is even less clear. Their initial lottery choices varied the probability of the high prize from 0.25 to 0.5, 0.75, and 1; then their second stage choice interpolated the probability weights between one of these gaps (0 to 0.25, 0.25 to 0.5, 0.5 to 0.75, or 0.75 to 1) in grids of roughly 10% points. Even from the first stage choices, if one assumes the popular Power or Inverse-S function then one only needs one interior probability to allow estimation. In fact, they always have the three interior probabilities of the first stage, and typically have refinements within one of those intervals. In sum, these arguments sound as though they were constructed "after the fact" of extensive numerical and econometric experimentation, and in the face of *a priori* unreliable numerical results.

von Gaudecker et al. (2011) employed a design in which all payments were to be sent to participants three months after their choices were made. This was to allow the design to vary the time of resolution of risk (now or in the future), without confounding that treatment with the timing of payment and discount rates. Their payoff configurations (Table 1, p. 669) include gain-frame lotteries, mixed-frame lotteries and no loss-frame lotteries. Four of the seven payoff configurations have all risk resolved at the time of choice, although by means of a computer realization (raising issues of credibility).

Zeisberger, Vrecko, and Langer (2012) estimate a structural CPT model from experimental data from 89 students, who earned €60 in an experiment a month prior, with payment only for the two sessions. One in 10 students were paid, based on their choices for one random task out of 30. They elicited CE for lotteries in the gain, mixed and loss frames, using the Becker, De Groot, and Marschak (1964) procedure. They estimated a "full" model for each subject in which all CPT parameters are jointly estimated using maximum likelihood methods. For some reason standard errors needed to be generated by bootstrapping (e.g., Table 5, p. 375), and no hypothesis tests of parameters are presented. Median estimates are presented (Table 4, p. 373), but at least interquartile ranges are also presented. The median pooled estimate of loss aversion is $\lambda = 1.37$. No estimates for a representative agent are presented. Individual point estimates are presented (Table 5, p. 375ff.), and exhibit some "wild" estimates. This may be due to the small number of choices for each subject, although if the CE is reliably elicited it embeds more information than a binary choice. No comparison between CPT and other models is presented.

Abdelloui, L'Haridon, and Paraschiv (2013) estimated parametric models of an RDU model defined over gains, but referred to this as a CPT model even if there were no losses at all in the stimuli. They did use real incentives, and told 65 couples that "they could be selected to play out one of their choices for real ..."; it is not clear if one of the 65 would be selected for salient rewards, or this means that there was some probability that each couple could be selected. In any event, this is not a CPT model since losses played no part.

Bouchouicha and Vieider (2017) report the results of two experiments. One experiment employs only gain-frame lotteries with weakly-salient rewards: two of the 47 participants were randomly selected to play a choice for monetary reward. The other experiment uses hypothetical rewards over loss-frame lotteries. No mixed-frame lotteries were presented in either experiment, and thus loss aversion was not estimated.

Pachur, Schulte-Mecklenbeck, Murphy, and Hertwig (2018) conduct an experiment[38] with a total of 91 pairs of lotteries: 25 loss frame, 35 gain frame and 31 mixed frame. Incentives included a fixed amount of €10 and salient reward that averaged €1.26 (with a range of −€9.1 and €9.8). Each of the 90 participants attended two sessions, with the same lotteries presented in different order in each session. They estimated CPT with a hierarchical Bayesian procedure at the individual level and separately for each session, with power utility curvature assumed to be the same over gains and losses (i.e., $\alpha = \beta$, in our notation). Of particular note, they do not find evidence of loss aversion: the first session mean loss aversion estimate is $\lambda = 0.905$ (95% credible interval $0.816 \leftrightarrow 0.996$) and the second session estimate is $\lambda = 0.985$ ($0.891 \leftrightarrow 1.085$).

Murphy and ten Brincke (2018) estimate parametric structural models of CPT at the individual level, using mixed estimation methods to condition individual estimates based on pooled estimates. They assume that $\alpha = \beta$ in order to avoid making any "exchange rate assumption," but of course that is an assumption nonetheless. Although they used the flexible Prelec (1998) probability weighting function (9), they assumed the same probability weighting function for gains and losses, another restrictive assumption; their rationale (fn. 4) was "... parsimony and as a first pass, given the relatively low number of binary observations compared to the number of model parameters." They report (§6.1) values for λ of 1.11 and 1.18 in two sessions, one later than the other, but do not say if these estimates were statistically significantly different from 1. Fig. 21 displays estimated distributions, "given by medians of estimates" (fn. 9) for the pooled sample.[39] There appears to be no statistical significant loss aversion, with $\lambda \approx 1$, and virtually no probability weighting on average, with $\eta \approx \varphi \approx 1$. Fig. 22 shows the implied utility functions and probability weighting functions, using the means of the distributions in Fig. 21.

L'Haridon and Vieider (2019) conduct an experiment with 2,939 participants from 30 countries and estimate a CPT model with country-level fixed effects. Although the primary estimates use a constrained CPT model assuming linear utility, the appendix reports the results of estimating an unconstrained CPT model. The global loss aversion parameter estimate from this unconstrained version of CPT is λ=1.63, with notable variation across countries: a low of $\lambda =$ 1.11 in Germany, a high of $\lambda = 2.81$ in Nigeria, and $\lambda = 1.31$ in the USA.[40] Of note, this experiment relied upon a single mixed frame prospect to identify loss aversion.

In summary, Table 2 shows that very few studies estimate an unconstrained version of CPT with real, salient incentives for gain, loss and mixed frames. Those that meet these methodological criteria are shaded. Of the 33 studies reviewed, only nine meet these methodological requirements. And of these nine, none report average loss aversion parameter estimates close the $\lambda = 2.25$ value that is often casually bandied about in the literature.[41] In fact, all of these studies report loss aversion estimates less than 2, and roughly half of them report loss aversion values near 1, which implies no loss aversion.[42] Clearly, the evidence in support of loss aversion, and thus CPT, is not monolithic as commonly claimed.

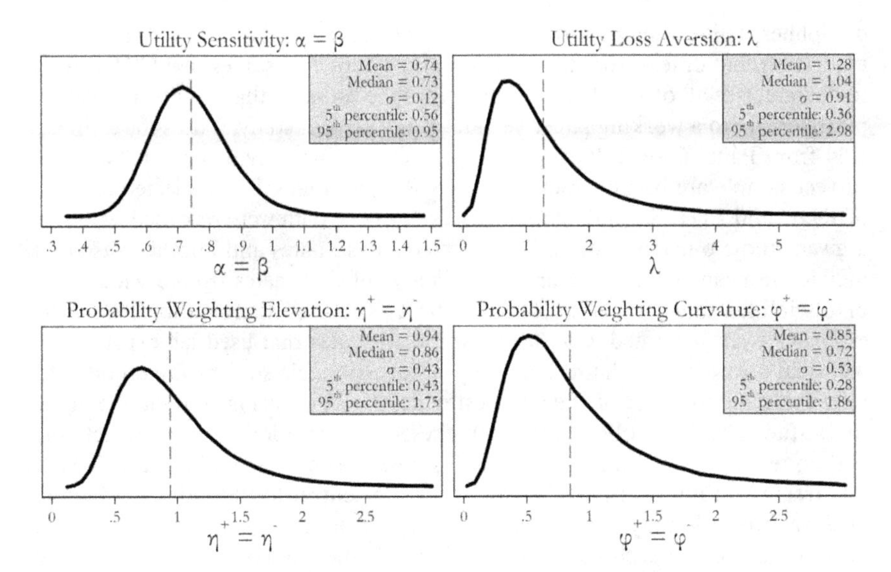

Fig. 21. CPT Model Estimates From Murphy and ten Brincke (2018).

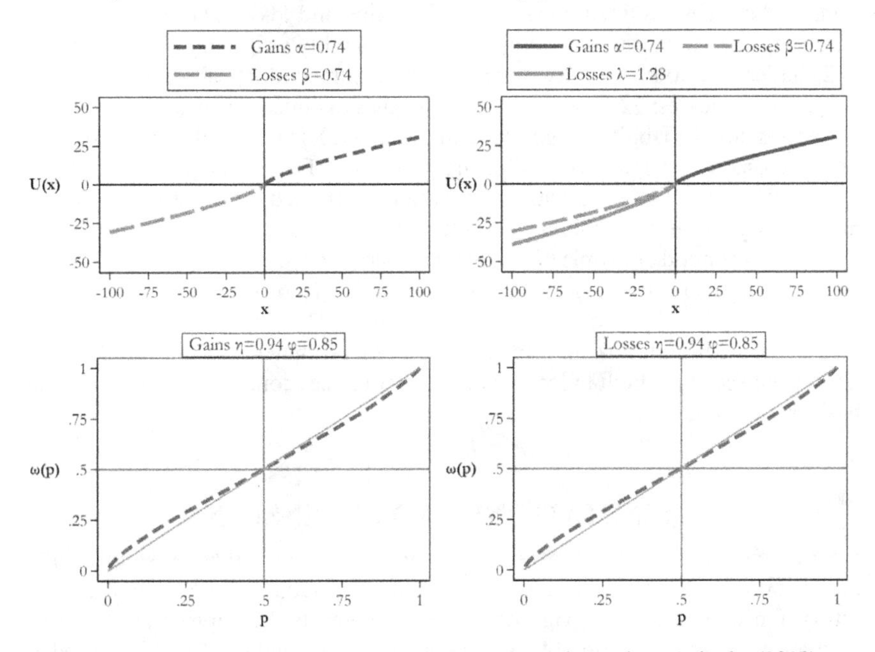

Fig. 22. CPT Model Estimates Means From Murphy and ten Brincke (2018).

Finally, a meta-analysis of loss aversion estimates by Brown, Imai, Vieider, and Camerer (2023) reports a mean estimate of λ with a 95% probability of being between 1.81 and 2.11 based on 607 estimates from 150 studies across many disciplines. This estimate must be taken with a grain of salt. First, it is answering a question that differs from the question asked here. It assumes that CPT is used to characterize all of the data, and examines the estimate that results. For example, referring to a working paper version of the present study, it uses the estimate 1.34 from Panel C of Table 1. But Fig. 5 shows that only around 18% of the subject sample are best characterized by CPT, and that CPT is rejected in favor of RDU and EUT. Second, in many cases the same data were recorded twice for a given study: one based on individual median estimates and another based on individual mean estimates. Third, it explicitly culls estimates from a wide range of disciplines, and adopts a casual "come as you are" stance toward how the estimates were generated. Consider just the estimates that used lab experiments with real rewards, and that did not rely on questionable statistical methods[43] to infer the standard error of the point estimate of λ. This brings the sample down to 46 studies and 146 observations. Of these, 2 observations in 1 study actually had no real rewards; 4 observations in 2 studies did not use real rewards for the loss-frame and mixed-frame choices, which are central to the estimate of λ; 32 observations in 1 study assumed linear utility for both gains and losses, and had only one mixed-frame choice; 1 observation in 1 study had only one mixed-frame choice when allowing different utility curvatures for gains and losses; 25 observations in 9 studies assumed linear utility for gains and losses and no probability weighting; 1 observation in 1 study had no probability weighting; 6 observations in 2 studies had no probability weighting and assumed identical utility curvature for gains and losses; 22 observations in 9 studies assumed linear utility for gains and losses, no probability weighting, and estimated λ from less than a handful of observations for each subject, following Tom, Fox, Trepel, and Poldrack (2007) from neuroscience; 18 observations in 2 studies assumed point estimates for the utility functions and probability weighting functions, and then estimated λ with a profile likelihood maximization; and 1 observation in 1 study that had no λ estimate that could be found. In the end, there are 17 of the original 46 studies (29 less), and 34 of the original 146 observations (112 less). In principle there is no issue with undertaking a meta-analysis of estimates, but one would want appropriate controls built in for varying quality of the economic and econometric basis of the estimates.

5. LIMITATIONS AND EXTENSIONS

We are well aware of limitations of our results, and we view them as simply shifting the burden of proof back on to those that claim support for CPT in the laboratory. On other hand, we vigorously defend them as the appropriate place to start a rigorous examination of the general empirical validity of the CPT model, claims about the importance of loss aversion in general, and the psychological pathway for loss aversion. The reason for our vigor should be apparent from the appalling state of the literature reviewed in §4 and Table 2.[44] We consider limitations from the perspective of theory, experimental procedure and econometrics, recognizing that these are not independent domains.

5.1 Theoretical Issues

5.1.1 The Reference Point

The first theoretical point is the vexing question of the specification of the "right" reference point. Kahneman and Tversky (1979) were explicitly agnostic on this issue, Tversky and Kahneman (1992) were silent, and the issue has been dormant until the recent development of "endogenous reference point" models by Kőszegi and Rabin (2006, 2007) and Schmidt, Starmer, and Sugden (2008). Obviously any theoretical specification of the reference point that differs from the framed reference point in our experiments will make a difference to the effect of frames, since that reference point acts to define what choices fall into which frame.[45] These theoretical specifications are, however, surprisingly vague as to how they are to be operationalized, and their rigorous evaluation remains open pending those specifications. Of course, the CE in DA models provides one, early endogenous reference point specification.

5.1.2 Asset Integration

A second theoretical point is global asset integration, by which we mean the assumed manner in which earnings within the laboratory are combining with extra-lab income or wealth. In one sense the issue of global asset integration, which raises the calibration critique of estimates of risk aversion from small stakes, is one reason one might want to rigorously model loss aversion. Rabin (2000, p. 1288) used loss aversion as the primary throw-away explanation of why one actually observes subjects picking safer lotteries over riskier lotteries, even when they perfectly integrate "wealth" with income from experimental lotteries:

> What *does* explain risk aversion over modest stakes? While this paper provides a "proof by calibration" that expected-utility theory does not help explain some risk attitudes, there are of course more direct tests showing that alternative models better capture risk attitudes. [...] Many of these models seem to provide a more plausible account of modest-scale risk attitudes ... [...] indeed, what is empirically the most firmly established feature of risk, loss aversion, is a departure from expected-utility theory that provides a direct explanation for modest-scale risk aversion.

We disagree with many, in fact all, of the assertions here, but the point is that non-EUT specifications are viewed as one way of accounting for calibration puzzles.[46] Moreover, the historical evidence for CPT has been accumulated with utility functions defined solely over experimental income.

5.1.3 Rank-dependent Probability Weighting

One of the main innovations of CPT over the Original Prospect Theory (OPT) of Kahneman and Tversky (1979) was the use of rank-dependent probability weighting in order to remove the possibility of violations of first-order stochastic dominance. Of course, Kahneman and Tversky (1979) had addressed this concern in their "editing process," assumed to occur prior to the "evaluation process" that most economists focus on. There is clear evidence that subjects tend to avoid such blatant violations: see Carbone and Hey (1995), Hey (2001), and Loomes and Sugden (1998). If one has a sufficiently strong prior that a theory ought not to allow such violations, then the rank-dependent model of RDU and CPT is one popular option; Blavatsky (2012) reviews other options.

From an empirical perspective, what is the implication of estimating a model of OPT? If subjects do indeed avoid violations of first-order stochastic dominance, then choices implied by that behavior should, to some extent, condition the maximum likelihood estimates of an OPT model so as not to predict them. On other hand, some violations might be consistent with a maximum likelihood OPT model if they sufficiently improve the aggregate log-likelihood with respect to other choice patterns (e.g., violations that have little economic significance to the decision-maker). Moreover, structural models of decision-making under risk allow for behavioral errors of one form or another, and they are designed to accommodate unexplained violations of this kind.[47]

Fig. 23 displays the results of estimating our structural model, but assuming OPT instead of CPT. Here, we use the data from undergraduates who had house money to cover losses, so Fig. 9 provides the CPT counterpart. One immediate result is that the aggregate log-likelihood of the OPT model is superior to the aggregate log-likelihood of the CPT model. However, since OPT and CPT are not nested with each other, comparisons of *aggregate* log-likelihoods are not appropriate.[48] It turns out that the non-nested Vuoung test supports CPT over OPT, but the assumptions for the validity of that test are strikingly violated, so one must use the Clarke variant, and it strongly supports OPT over CPT. The significance of this result is that it is, to our knowledge, the first head-to-head comparison of OPT and CPT in a full, structural model where violations of first-order stochastic dominance are viewed along with all other behavior patterns. In other words, assuming CPT because of the *possibility* of these violations implicitly places a dogmatic prior on avoiding those violations. Our OPT estimates simply weigh their significance along with other deviations from trial parameter values, and decides on a maximum likelihood basis whether they should be "allowed" or not. Recall that the likelihood of an observed binary choice is the probability of that choice, given the trial parameter values. So, when we refer to "weighing" of violations, we are referring to the chance of the model making the right probabilistic prediction for the full set of observations.

The specific parameter estimates in Fig. 23 differ from those for the CPT model by having a much lower estimate of the β parameter, in fact implying *concave* utility in the loss frame. The implied loss aversion parameter λ is 1.96, much higher than with CPT. Probability weighting in the gain frame is similar for OPT and CPT, but virtually absent in the loss frame for OPT.

5.2 Experimental Procedures

5.2.1 Earned Endowments

If someone had undertaken a prior task, with some real task, and with real earnings rather than some artefactual earnings from "house money," would they exhibit greater loss aversion?

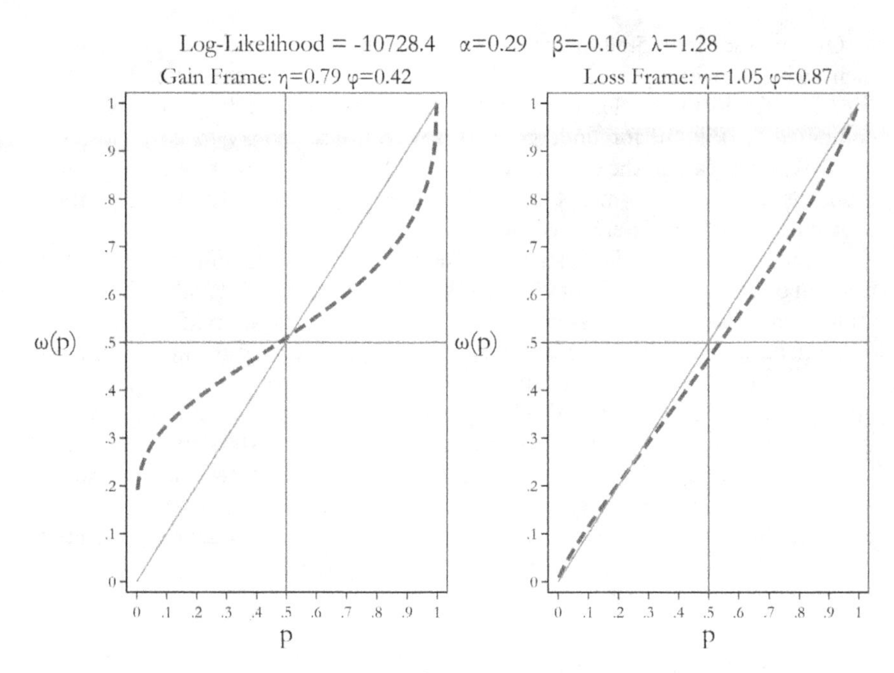

Fig. 23. Original Prospect Theory for Undergraduates With House Money to Cover Losses.

This is an easy extension to make to our design. Following Laury, McInnes, and Swarthout (2009), we modified our procedures to provide subjects with a quiz of 15 questions in which they could earn $80 or $40 depending on their knowledge of current events, American history and geography. We also explained that any earnings or losses from later choice tasks would be added to or subtracted from the earnings from the quiz. We therefore generated an endowment that applied equally to all three frames: the "house money" of our main experiments only applied to the mixed frame and loss frame. It would be artificial, and disingenuous, to generate an "earned endowment" that can only be retained if someone was running the risk of losing it. Indeed, the cash earnings were paid out immediately and left in sight, on top of the desk during the lottery choice task. Appendix D (available on request) contains the introductory text to the experiment that explained the connection between the quiz that generated an earned endowment and the later choice tasks. It also contains the quiz itself, which was designed to be relatively easy to score 8 or more correct answers, and hence $80. The main instructions in Appendix C were modified to explain that any gains or losses would be added or subtracted from the quiz earnings, but were otherwise the same as those in the main experiments.

The choice tasks were those given to undergraduates, involving maximal losses of $70, so nobody would lose their entire endowment if they had earned $80. All net earnings were on top of the show-up fee. We had prepared an alternative set of choice questions with maximal losses of $40 in the event that someone failed to earn $80 from the quiz, but that did not happen.

Over two sessions, 58 undergraduate GSU subjects participated in the experiment, which obviously was not cheap to run because of the earned endowment. Fig. 24 displays the pooled estimates for this samples of undergraduates, to be compared to Fig. 10 for undergraduates with house money to cover losses.[49] There is an increase in the estimate of β from 0.06 to 0.23 as we move from house money to earned endowments, and λ increases from 1.34 to 1.76. The form of probability weighting over gains and losses is virtually identical.

At the level of individual estimation, however, this treatment did increase the fraction of subjects classified as CPT, at the expense of those classified EUT and RDU. Fig. 25 shows the classifications, to be contrasted with Fig. 5.

Somebody wanting to defend CPT might argue that our earned endowment task was facile, and that it amounted in effect to just another "house money" treatment in the minds of subjects. Alternative procedures for generating earned endowments, with time to integrate them into extra-lab wealth, have been proposed (e.g., Bosch-Domènech & Silvestre, 2010; Cárdenas, De Roux, Jaramillo, & Martinez, 2014) and could be evaluated. Clearly, however, at some point the burden has to rest on advocates of CPT to propose an operationally meaningful way to endow subjects and then evaluate behavior in a more rigorous econometric manner.

5.2.2 Alternative Elicitation Methods

Would there be any effect from using alternative elicitation methods than binary choices? One popular alternative is to elicit a CE of some lottery, allowing one

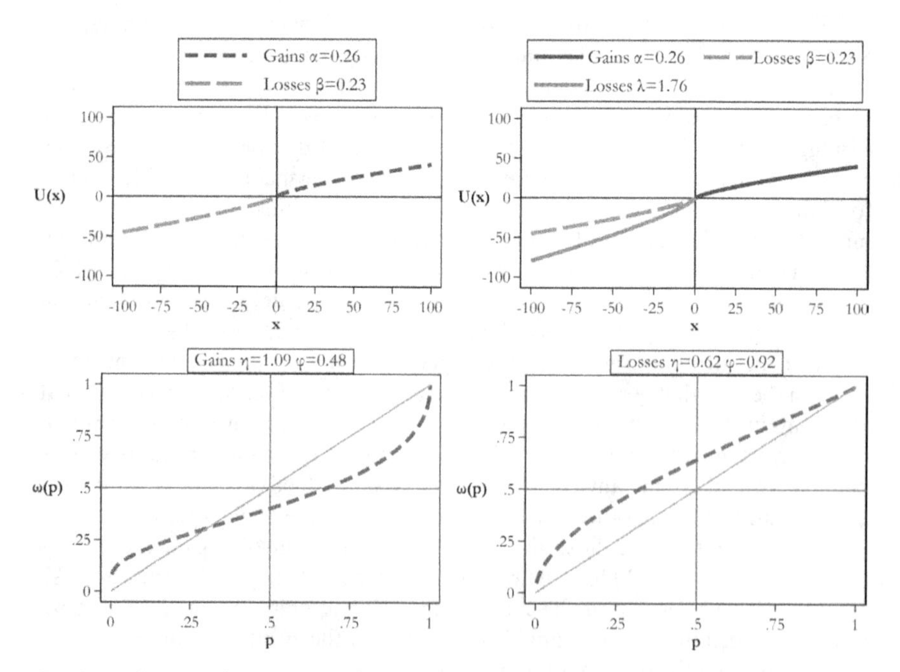

Fig. 24. CPT Model Estimates for GSU Undergraduates with Earned Endowments to Cover Losses.

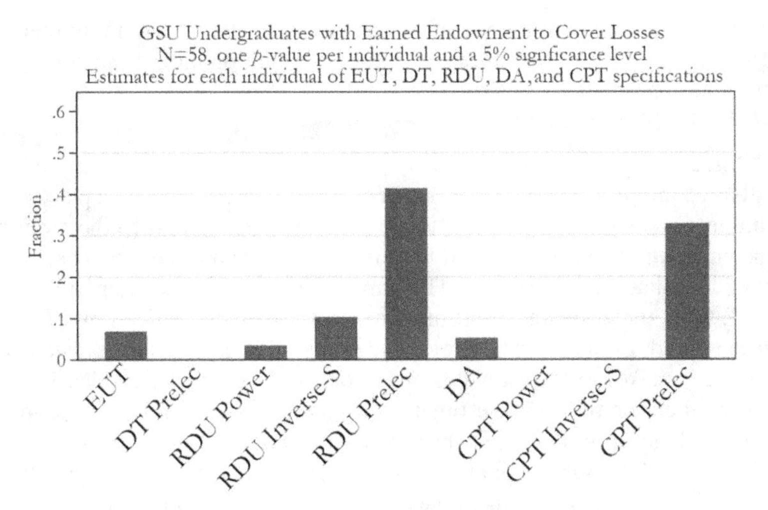

Fig. 25. Classifying Subjects as EUT, DT, RDU, DA or CPT with Earned Endowments.

to directly infer the risk premium conditional on believing that the CE has been reliably elicited. The use of the open-ended, "fill in the blank," Becker et al. (1964) elicitation method for CE is controversial: many experimenters believe that it performs poorly in practice, for various reasons. One can devise iterative multiple price lists, in the sense of Tversky and Kahneman (1992) and Andersen et al. (2006), that can "drill down" in a series of ordered, binary choice tasks to effectively elicit a tight interval for the CE. The incentive-compatibility of these methods are more likely to be understood by subjects than the open-ended methods.

5.3 Econometric Issues

We characterize heterogenous preferences by estimating at the level of the individual, with a design that allows that because there are 100 binary choices for each individual. Another way to account for unobserved individual heterogeneity is to estimate structural models using random coefficients that reflect the latent population distribution of the parameters across subjects. Econometric methods for the estimation of non-linear systems, of the kind we encounter with the EUT, DT, RDU, DA, and CPT structural models, have been developed by Andersen, Harrison, Hole, Lau, and Rutström (2012). Although we see these as valuable techniques to characterize heterogeneity, we do not expect them to fundamentally alter our conclusions about the ability of CPT to explain the broad pattern of observed behavior.

Finally, there is a perennial issue in econometrics of parametric specifications versus non-parametric specifications. In fact, there are three issues here: the use of parametric assumptions about the utility and probability weighting functions, the use of non-parametric predictions of theories (typically about choice patterns), and the use of parametric assumptions about the stochastic error processes. In each case, we are open to the use of non-parametrics, but caution that there is a tradeoff in power when one does so, of course conditional on us having "good" or "flexible" parametric specifications.

5.3.1 "Second Best" Econometrics

In public economics, the theory of the second best tells us that if you place a constraint on a system whose outcome is subject to optimization, then the properties of the unconstrained system might be very different, and there is no easy way to be confident that they are similar. The same point applies to econometric models of CPT. Over the years an astonishing array of restricted versions of CPT have been estimated, as our literature review identified. Here, we quickly review what difference it makes to the estimates of the original-recipe CPT model. For simplicity, we focus on the pooled estimates with undergraduates using house money for losses. Hence, Fig. 10 is the benchmark set of parameter estimates: $\alpha = 0.21$, $\beta = 0.006$, $\lambda = 1.34$, substantial inverse-S probability weighting in the gain frame, and globally concave weighting in the loss frame. The 95% confidence interval for λ is between 1.14 and 1.54.

The first special case is where the coefficients for the intrinsic utility functions are set equal to each other: $\alpha = \beta$. The only rationale for this assumption is that Tversky and Kahneman (1992) found that these were similar; there is no theoretical rationale.[50] Of course, while their econometric methods were reasonable, these "representative estimates" were a Frankenstein composed of the median α from one subject and the median β from another subject; it is embarrassing to see such estimates viewed as representative. In any event, Fig. 26 shows what happens with

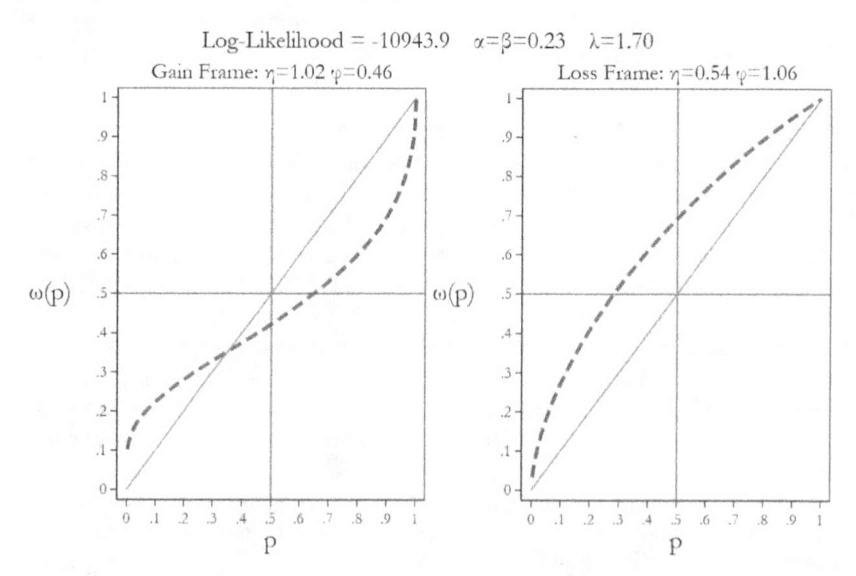

Fig. 26. CPT Estimates When α is Assumed to Equal β: GSU Undergraduates With House Money to Cover Losses.

the same data used to estimate the unrestricted CPT model. The joint parameter for utility functions is estimated to be 0.23, close to the unrestricted estimate for α, but λ is now inferred to be much higher, at 1.70. The pattern of probability weighting is similar to the unrestricted version. So these data suggest that this restriction leads to an over-estimate of utility loss aversion for the sample from a specific population.

The second special case is when utility functions are assumed to be linear: $\alpha = \beta = 1$. The usual rationale is an appeal to Rabin (2000), which as noted earlier refers to the claim from Hansson (1988) and Rabin (2000) that utility functions under EUT had been close to linear for the "small stakes" seen in the lab, or else *a priori* implausible risk aversion is implied for large stakes. As noted earlier, Harrison, Lau, Ross, and Swarthout (2017) demonstrated that the empirical premiss, when properly posed to match the theoretical premiss, does not apply to samples from the population studied here.[51] Moreover, it is strange to see an argument against the ability of EUT to explain large stakes risk aversion used to justify assuming linear utility functions in CPT, when it was utility loss aversion that Rabin (2000) conjectured as the explanation for large stakes risk aversion. Nonetheless, the estimates that result from this restriction are shown in Fig. 27. Of course, λ collapses by definition to 1 in this case. And while the qualitative pattern of probability weighting in the gain frame formally remains inverse-S, it has a much more significant convex region for a wide range of probabilities.[52]

The third special case is to assume sign-independent probability weighting, so that the same probability weighting function applies in the gain frame and in the loss frame: $\eta^+ = \eta^-$ and $\varphi^+ = \varphi^-$. Again, the only rationale we have seen for this derives from the Frankenstein "representative agent" estimates for γ^+ and γ^- in

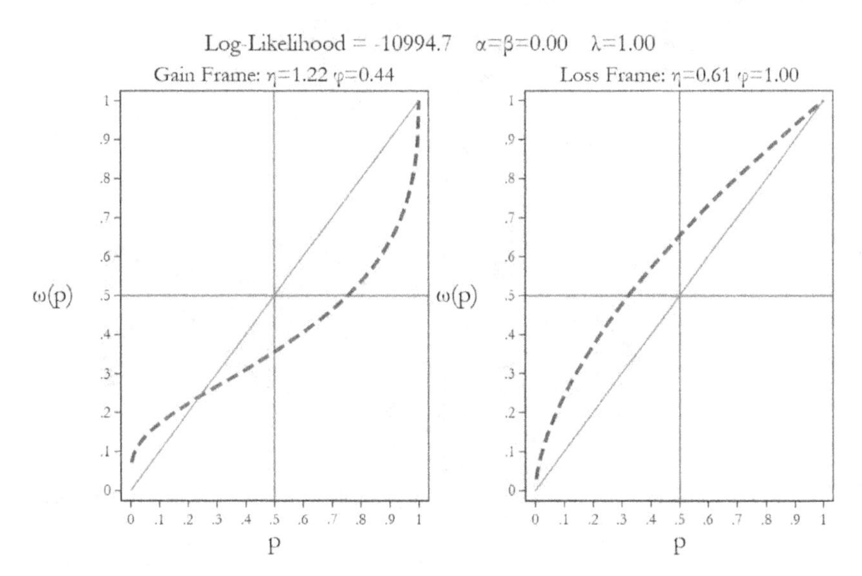

Fig. 27. CPT Estimates With Linear Utility Functions: GSU Undergraduates With House Money to Cover Losses.

Tversky and Kahmeman (1992) being close to each other, despite γ^+ being the median estimate from one subject and γ^- being the median estimate for another subject. The effect is shown in Fig. 28. The concavity of the gain-frame utility function is reduced, the loss-frame utility function becomes distinctly concave, the loss aversion parameter λ drops to 0.99, and probability weighting for the two frames becomes slightly inverse-S.

The fourth special case is to assume away probability weighting altogether, as critically reviewed earlier in reference to von Gaudecker et al. (2011). Fig. 29 displays the results of making this assumption. The concavity of the gain-frame utility function is higher, the slightly convex loss-frame utility function becomes slightly concave, and loss aversion stays about the same, at $\lambda = 1.34$. Although there is no significant change in loss aversion, the aggregate log-likelihood is much worse than the full specification, and in this case these comparisons are nested: these restrictions can be rejected with a p-value below 0.0001.

The fifth special case is to assume away the need for mixed-frame lotteries altogether, as critically reviewed in reference to Bruhin et al. (2010). Here, we infer an estimate of λ whenever we have estimates of α and β, since we can infer $\lambda \equiv -U(-1)/U(1)$ directly. Employing the CRRA functional form for utility in (16a) and (16b), this means that we infer λ as $[m^{1-\beta}/(1-\beta)]/[m^{1-\alpha}/(1-\alpha)]$ where $m = 1$. From a mathematical point of view, it is feasible to infer a point estimate and standard error for λ if one has point estimates and standard errors (and a covariance between these standard errors) for α and β. The problem is that λ plays no role theoretically to affect any choice in the battery, which now consists of only gain-frame and loss-frame tasks. Hence one cannot reliably infer the correct value of λ, since it had no role in affecting the log-likelihoods of observed

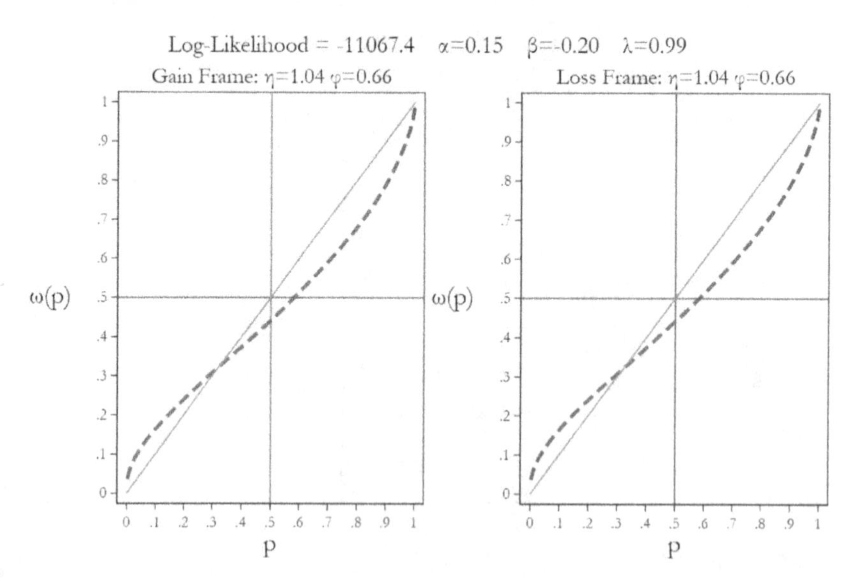

Fig. 28. CPT Estimates With Sign-independent Probability Weighting: Undergraduates With House Money.

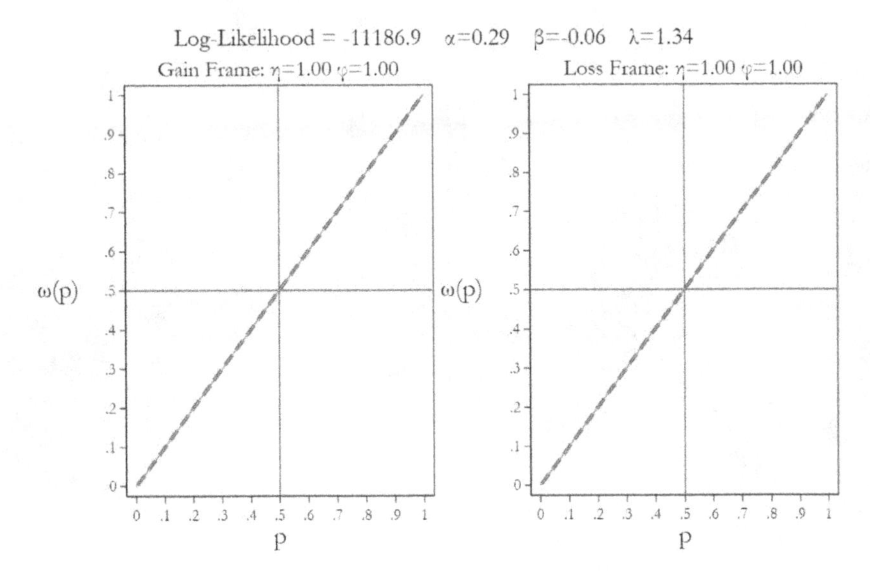

Fig. 29. CPT Estimates With No Probability Weighting: GSU Undergraduates With House Money to Cover losses.

choices. Intuitively, if there is some true β and some true $\lambda \neq 1$ that the decision-maker has, and we have no mixed-frame lotteries, the *estimated* CPT values of β can be viewed as incorrectly picking up the *joint* effect of the *true* values of β and λ. Fig. 30 illustrates this case with our data. The utility function for gains is slightly more concave, the utility function for losses is significantly more convex, the estimate $\lambda = 2.0$ of loss aversion is much higher than the true value, and the extent of probability weighting is qualitatively similar to the unrestricted model in Fig. 10.

The final special case is a slight variant on the last one, where we consider only *one* mixed-frame lottery in the battery, following Vieider et al. (2015), Vieider, Martinsson, Nam, and Truong (2019), and L'Haridon and Vieider (2019). In our battery, there were 16 mixed-frame lotteries, so the simplest way to evaluate the effect of this case is to consider each mixed-frame lottery one at a time. The results are generally very close to the case in which there are no mixed-frame lotteries, as one would expect from only adding one more choice to the battery. Fig. 31 displays the effects of these variants, shown in the last 16 lines in the form of point estimates and 95% confidence intervals. Although there is some arbitrariness in estimates of λ from selecting one particular mixed-frame lottery, the effects are always relatively close to the case of having no mixed-frame lotteries at all.

Fig. 31 also serves as a summary of the effects of these special cases on estimates of the loss aversion parameter λ. In general, we see various deviations from the estimate of λ from the unrestricted model, in all but one case statistically significant deviations. Given the propensity of the literature to rationalize restrictions of this kind, we caution that these are for one large sample from a specific population, and depend on the specific battery used here. Further, these

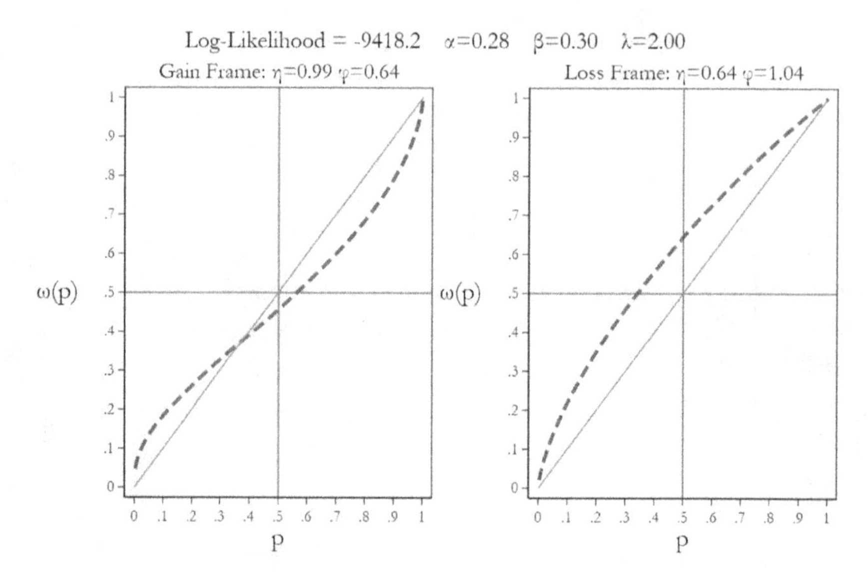

Fig. 30. CPT Estimates With No Mixed-frame Lotteries: GSU Undergraduates With House Money to Cover Losses.

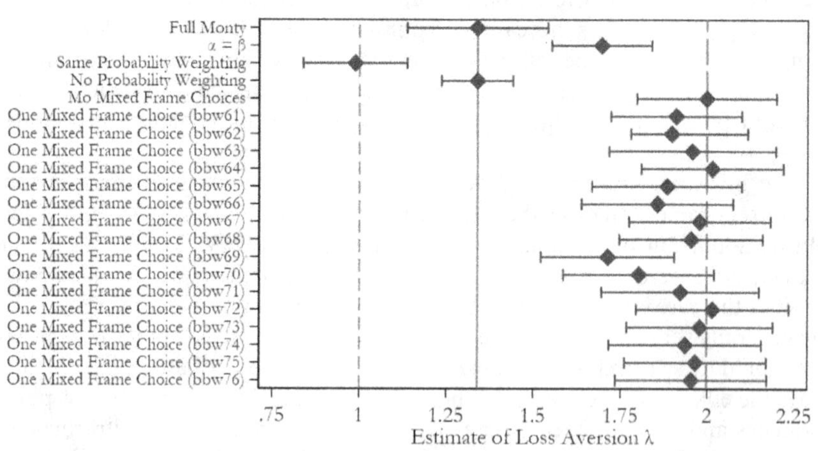

Fig. 31. Second Best Estimates of the CPT Model for Undergraduates With House Money for Losses.

are pooled estimates of a representative individual, assuming away the considerable individual heterogeneity stressed throughout. The most important implication of that heterogeneity is that if one looked at pooled estimates of CPT in

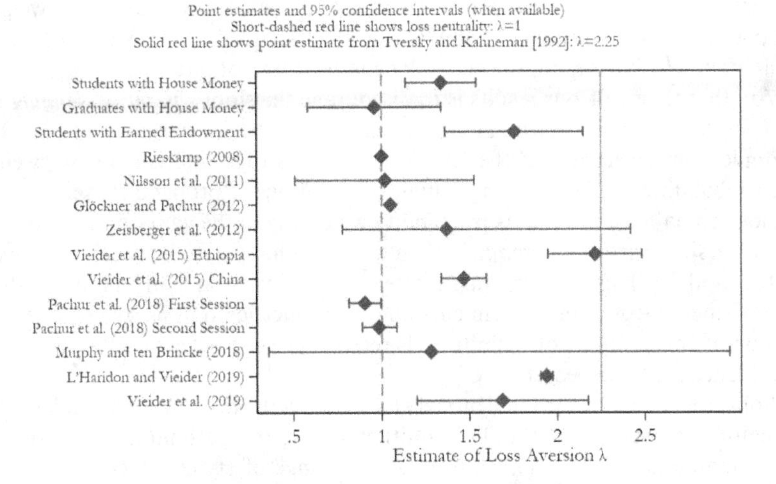

Fig. 32. Estimates of the CPT Model From Methodologically Acceptable Studies.

isolation, one might conclude that the data support a standard CPT specification, albeit without the coveted point estimates from Tversky and Kahneman (1992). However, that inference would be a mistake, since we demonstrated earlier in Fig. 5 that a very small fraction of our individual subjects were best characterized as consistent with CPT. The correct inference from Fig. 31 is quite clear: one should not take seriously estimates of CPT models that impose these restrictions.

For comparison purposes, Fig. 32 summarizes the estimates of λ found in the studies from Table 2 that meet our minimal methodological criteria. Several of these involves designs that we regard as "second-best" as identified in Fig. 31: for example, Vieider et al. (2015), L'Haridon and Vieider (2019), and Vieider et al. (2019) all use the same design that had just one mixed-frame lottery, and our estimates from Fig. 30 suggest systematic bias from that limitation. If we review the estimates in Fig. 32 that do not use special cases flagged in Fig. 31, we see lower estimates of loss aversion than claimed from Tversky and Kahnemen (1992), and many that show no statistically significant evidence for utility loss aversion. Again, we caution that these are all estimates from pooled data for representative agents that assume the validity of the CPT model, and this assumption is sharply rejected on the basis of our estimates at the level of the individual.

6. CONCLUSIONS

CPT does not obviously dominate alternative specifications of decision-making under risk. In all treatments, RDU explains the behavior of more subjects, although with earned endowments the superiority of RDU is not as great as with the use of house money. The reason for this poor performance of CPT, where "poor" is in relation to the hyperbole found in the behavioral literature, is that subjects locally asset integrate over frames, and then apply probability weighting consistent with an RDU model. Of course, extended versions of CPT might explain these behavior, but the core CPT model does not fare well.

Another theme of our results is to discourage the sloppy habit of *defining* the CPT model in terms of the qualitative properties of specific parameter values. For example, some behave as if the CPT *model* claims that "individuals overweight low probabilities and underweight high probabilities," "probability weighting in the loss domain is the same as probability weighting in the gain domain," or that "loss aversion drives risk premia," when these just happen to be specific *instances* of the model.[53] This is a semantic matter, but an important one. None of these claims emerge from our experiments and econometric analysis. A more serious version of this problem of definitions is referring to estimates of an RDU model as evidence for "prospect theory."

Some defenders of the CPT model claim, correctly, that the CPT model exists "because the data says it should." In other words, the CPT model was born, in Kahneman and Tversky (1979), from a wide range of stylized facts culled from parts of the cognitive psychology literature. If one is to take the CPT model seriously and rigorously then it needs to do a much better job of explaining the data than we see here.

Our own constructive suggestion is to extend the econometric modeling of CPT to Bayesian Hierarchical Models (BHM), as illustrated by Gao, Harrison, and Tchernis (2022) for EUT and RDU models. The idea of a BHM is that the pooled responses over all subjects can provide informative priors for the estimation of models of individual responses, rather than evaluating the behavior of each subject "as an island of data" with uninformative priors. Quite apart from the descriptive value of obtaining reliable estimates of risk preferences at the level of the individual, such estimates are essential for accurate *normative* evaluations of choices under risk, as illustrated by Harrison and Ng (2016) for choices over the humble full-indemnity insurance contract. The BHM approach is ideal for CPT, since it is a model that needs a lot of data to estimate, and those data *must* span gain, loss and mixed frames. And CPT adds considerable sources of non-linearity to responses. This is not at all just a matter of adding parameters, although that happens as well: CPT models offer several routes to the same presumed behavior patterns, as our discussion of "utility loss aversion" and "probabilistic loss aversion" illustrates. A BHM can also recognize, with an extra hierarchy, that the pooled responses might be better viewed as coming from a mixture of EUT, RDU or CPT data-generating processes, following Harrison and Rutström (2009). Since EUT and RDU are not nested in CPT, this would allow a more flexible generate of informative priors for individual-level estimation.

NOTES

1. We appreciate that there is a substantial literature claiming that CPT, and specifically loss aversion, is well-documented in the field. We are staunch advocates of the value of field experiments, as in Harrison and List (2004), but only as a complement to what we can more efficiently learn from the laboratory. For instance, Ray, Shum, and Camerer (2015,

p. 376) note that loss aversion "… was originally discovered in laboratory choices among monetary risks […], but has since become evident in allocations, behavior, and institutional rules in many markets." Given the paucity of evidence for CPT in the controlled setting of the laboratory when we demand the use of real incentives, experimental designs that allow the conceptual identification of loss aversion, and explicit structural estimation, we are skeptical about claims from the field, where there are always acknowledged confounds to clean inference. We define the laboratory in the conventional manner, including artefactual field experiments, following the definitions in Harrison and List (2004). The latter field experiments are often referred to as "lab-in-the field" experiments.

2. EUT does not, then, predict 50:50 choices, as some casually claim. It does say that the expected utility differences will not explain behavior, and that then allows all sorts of psychological factors to explain behavior. In effect, EUT has *no* prediction in this instance, and that is not the same as predicting an even split.

3. The experimental setting in which they proposed this terminology is when one conducts Common Ratio tests for the usual gradients and also conducts Preference Reversal tests for the usual lottery patterns. The former tests generate indifference or low power for modest and widely observed levels of risk aversion, and the latter tests generate indifference or low power for risk neutral subjects. If one can identify, to some statistical tolerance, whether a subject is risk neutral or not, conducting both types of tests allows one to know *a priori* that *one* of the tests should be a more powerful test of EUT. Of course, no single test can be a powerful test of EUT for all subjects, if one allows a mix of risk averse and risk neutral subjects. The basic idea was clearly stated in Loomes and Sugden (1998, p. 589, especially fn. 3).

4. This result is acknowledged by some, but not welcome. For instance, Cubitt, Starmer, and Sugden (1989, p. 130) comment that these results are "… sometimes quoted as evidence that violations of EUT are less frequent in single choice than in random lottery designs. Conlisk investigated the Common Consequence effect using a single choice design. In each of the two relevant tasks, almost all subjects (26 out of 27 in one case, 24 out of 26 in the other) chose the riskier option. Clearly, this distribution of responses between riskier and safer choices is far too asymmetric for the experiment to be a satisfactory test for systematic deviations from EUT." The logic of the final sentence is hard to ascertain. Moreover, the evidence for the Common Consequence effect in *incentivized* "random lottery designs" is decidedly mixed: Burke, Carter, Gominiak, and Ohl (1996) and Fan (2002) find no evidence of an EUT violation, whereas Starmer and Sugden (1991) do.

5. We use all 40 of the Loomes and Sugden (1998) choice patterns, given by triangles I through V of their design. Triangle VI was used for their £20 sample, and triangle V for their £30 sample. These provide us with 40 gain-frame choice pairs. We then use the choices from their triangles II and V for 16 loss-frame lottery pairs, and 16 mixed-frame lottery pairs. Triangle II shows considerable evidence of their subjects picking the "safe" lottery, so this will test if loss frames induce risk-seeking: there is somewhere for the choices to go, compared to the gain frame expectations. Triangle V has a mix of safe and risky choices, just slightly dominated by risky choices, so it provides a non-extreme baseline to see the effect of loss frames. Triangle V is also likely to be more statistically informative than taking triangles III or IV on top of triangle II, due to the change in gradient.

6. See Cox, Sadiraj, and Schmidt (2015) and Harrison and Swarthout (2014) for detailed arguments and evidence, as well as extensive literature discussion.

7. The use of the RLIM is problematic, for well-known theoretical reasons (Holt, 1986; Karni & Safra, 1987). Its use entails a certain "bipolar hypothesis" about the independence axiom when estimating RDU or CPT models: that the axiom works as it should when subjects evaluate the compound lottery over 100 simple lotteries that is implied by payment protocol, but that it magically blows up when subjects evaluate each simple lottery in the choice pair. One has to be simultaneously depressed and optimistically manic about the independence axiom to maintain these two positions. Moreover, Harrison and Swarthout (2014) find evidence that it *does* make a difference behaviorally when estimating RDU models, but not, as one would expect, when estimating EUT models. One logical response

to this problem is just to assume two independence axioms: one axiom that applies to the evaluation of a given prospect, and that is assumed to be violated by DT, DA, RDU, and CPT, and another axiom that applies to the evaluation of the experimental payment protocol. One can then assume failure of the former axiom, when estimating non-EUT models, but validity of the latter axiom. Brown and Healy (2018) report results that show that ordered prospects, akin to those in a multiple price list (Andersen, Harrison, Lau, & Rutström, 2006; Holt & Laury, 2002), generate different choice patterns on a between-subjects basis when *presented* to subjects in that order compared to when they are *presented* to subjects in a random order. The choice pattern in the latter case is the same as when just one prospect is presented to subjects, suggesting that the random presentation is eliciting preferences reliably even if RLIM is used to reward subjects. Harrison and Swarthout (2014), in contrast, presented *non-ordered* prospects in a random order when applying RLIM, rather than *ordered* prospects in a random order. And their inferences concerned the inferred risk preferences under EUT or RDU, not just an evaluation of choice pattern differences for one, single prospect. Brown and Healy (2018) cannot evaluate models of EUT or RDU in the two payment treatments, since they only looked at the same prospect in the treatment in which just one prospect was presented to subjects.

8. One often finds applications of the one-parameter Prelec (1998) function, on the grounds that it is "flexible" and only uses one parameter. The additional flexibility over the Inverse-S probability weighting function is real, but minimal compared to the full two-parameter function. The need to allow for a wider range of probability weighting functions than the Inverse-S is also stressed by Wilcox (2023).

9. We add some modest constraints on r so that the CE evaluations do not become degenerate.

10. The same issue with identification arises if one employs more flexible functional forms than the power utility function or CRRA functions in general. For example, the two-parameter Expo-Power utility function popularized by Holt and Laury (2002) collapses to CRRA for certain parameter values, so it also runs into the same theoretical issues. It is curious to see how the literature on CPT tries to "kill off" power utility *per se*, rather than accept the restriction that is implied for identification. For example, Schmidt and Zank (2008, p. 214) note that "The preceding analysis shows that strong risk aversion and CPT exclude power utility. More generally, the [loss aversion ratio] is not well defined for power utility under CPT unless the two powers are equal." These are two different statements. The first says that one can never use power utility, and the second says that power utility is valid under a simple restriction on the powers in the gain and loss frame. Later, they note (p. 214) that Köbberling and Wakker (2005, §7) "... showed that power utility is problematic for the index of loss aversion. They suggested an alternative parametric form ...." Again, the word "problematic" just means that one should not try to estimate *separate* powers in the gain and loss frame, not that one has to discard power utility, CRRA utility, or its natural generalizations such as Expo-Power.

11. Bruhin, Fehr-Duda, and Epper (2010, p. 1382) claim that one cannot identify λ in the all-or-nothing sense by just comparing preferences over lotteries in the loss domain (one of their "lotteries" is a certainty-equivalent, but that is not essential to the argument). This is correct, and noted above: preference over two loss-frame lotteries are not affected by the value of λ. So, we agree with their conclusion that "... when there are no mixed lotteries available, estimating such a parameter is neither feasible nor meaningful" if we qualify the claim to refer to estimating the correct λ value. One can estimate a CPT model and obtain *an estimate* of λ but, as we demonstrate in §5.C, one cannot do so and obtain the *correct* estimate.

12. It is apparent that one should not apply contextual utility, due to Wilcox (2011), to CPT. Does it follow, however, that normalization of any kind should be used for CPT? There is a strong case to be made that one should consider *some* normalization, even if it is not contextual utility. The logic that leads one to apply a (contextual utility) normalization for EUT and RDU equally applies, for example, to the various lottery pairs in the gain frame under CPT. Hence, one should be wary of the effect of giving CPT a "get out

of jail card for free" when it comes to using a normalization, solely on *a priori* grounds. From a practical perspective, perhaps the poor empirical performance of CPT is due to the lack of a normalization, potentially implying fragile inferences about the primitive "more stochastically risk averse than." The appropriate stochastic normalization for CPT remains an open research question for those who seek to apply CPT.

13. In other words, the utility loss aversion for a loss of one penny is the same proportionally as the utility loss aversion of one million dollars.

14. It is common to assume that u(x) is weakly increasing in x, and that $u(0) = 0$, hence that U(0)=0. This implies that $\lambda > 0$, so that the utility values for losses are all negative. If we do not impose the arbitrary normalization $u(0) = 0$, then weak monotonicity only implies that $\lambda \geq -1$, since we then have $U(x) \geq U(-x)$ if we have the same "intrinsic" utility function u(x). Values of λ that are negative have the same interpretation in this case as values of λ that are positive. The general, non-parametric definition of loss aversion proposed by Schmidt and Traub (2002, p. 235), that $U(x) - U(y) \leq U(-y) - U(-x)\ \forall\ x > y \geq 0$, evaluates identically whether λ is positive or negative, providing monotonicity holds. We set $u(0) = [u(\tau) + u(-\tau)]/2$ for $\tau \to 0$, and the exact, small value of τ makes no difference to results; we use $\tau = \$0.50$. This assigns a value to u(0) that depends on the specific utility function and parameters being estimated, and ensures that we have monotonicity at 0 if $\lambda<0$. For comparability with other studies, we always report $|\lambda|$.

15. Note that the effect on risk aversion of overweighting and underweighting for losses is the opposite of the effect for gains. As noted by Neilson and Stowe (2002, p. 34) CPT "weights extreme outcomes first," the *best* outcome under gains and the *worst* outcome under losses. Appendix B discusses this point in more detail. We generally avoid the expressions "optimism" and "pessimism" in CPT, since it can lead to confusion in general. Wakker (2010, p. 289) offers an excellent definition of these terms, which generalizes from RDU to CPT: optimism (pessimism) is when an improvement in the rank is associated with a higher (lower) decision weight. Of course, to add potential semantic confusion, this definition further assumes the use of what Wakker (2010, §7.6) calls gain-ranks rather than loss-ranks. The former is now the default, but the latter was used in early studies on RDU, such as the classic by Chew, Karni, and Safra (1987), since it is more natural when referring to CDFs in statistics.

16. There can be a probabilistic loss aversion or loss seeking effect even if the probability weighting functions for gains and losses are the same. The point is rather that if sign-dependence is the key insight of CPT then one should not *a priori* hardwire one of the determinants of (probabilistic) loss aversion with that constraint.

17. In fact, Birnbaum and Bahra (2007) let 3% of their sample play out one choice for payment. We do not regard this as effectively salient, but appreciate that a theorist might.

18. One implication of violations in gain–loss separability is the possibility that the probability weighting functions for mixed frame lotteries might differ from the probability weighting functions for gain or loss frame lotteries, as posited by Wu and Markle (2008) and Pachur and Kellen (2013). Since one can generate the effect of "losses looming larger than gains" through the pathway of *probabilistic* loss aversion, this implication would likely cause serious identification problems for *utility* loss aversion (viz., the beloved λ) without experimental designs that address that problem.

19. There is good reason to be verbose on this point, since a number of studies referenced in Section 5 estimate an RDU model but casually refer to it as CPT. By this they presumably mean that the RDU model contains the same probability weighting as CPT, but that is only on the gain frame. RDU and CPT are otherwise very different models.

20. The difference is easy to explain, and important to understand for the positive evidence in favor of RDU. The usual IA states that preferences over lotteries A and B are not changed if we consider some lottery consisting of a p chance of A and a $(1 - p)$ chance of C and some lottery consisting of a p chance of B and a $(1 - p)$ chance of C, for any C and all p. In words, preferences over two lotteries are not affected by adding a common consequence C with the same probability weight. The BWA simply restricts C to be some mixture of A or B. The important consequence of this change from the IA to the BWA is that indifference

curves within the Marschak–Machina probability simplex are *still linear* but do *not have to be parallel*, as required under EUT. The BWA axiom also underlies the Chew–Dekel class of risk preferences, which play a critical role in Epstein–Zinn preferences in finance.

21. Table E1 in Appendix E (available on request) shows comparable estimates for the MBA sample.

22. Unless otherwise stated, we only report results for the most flexible probability weighting specification for DT, RDU and CPT: the Prelec function.

23. If one uses the "information criteria" AIC and BIC, which allow comparisons of non-nested models using *ad hoc* punishment terms for additional parameters, the same ranking applies.

24. The only exception was a p-value between the RDU and CPT models of 0.04.

25. When sample sizes are large enough, the mixture model is preferred for reasons spelled out in Harrison and Rutström (2009, §5).

26. We also check the DA and RDU models using non-nested hypothesis tests, and they do not change the rankings based solely on the aggregate log-likelihoods.

27. In fact, the requirement is that the distribution be a *unit* Normal, and the fitted Normal shown here, and implicitly used in the statistical tests of Normalcy, is not constrained to have zero mean or standard deviation of 1, but that only makes our tests conservative with respect to rejecting Normalcy.

28. One can adjust the Clarke and Voung test statistics to "punish" models with relatively more parameters (e.g., Clarke & Signorino, 2010, p. 376), but the correction factors are the same *ad hoc* ones noted earlier for the AIC and BIC "information criteria," and again have no convincing methodological foundation. These corrections would only strengthen a conclusion *not* to adopt the CPT model, so they would not increase the share of individuals classified as CPT decision-makers.

29. This is entirely due to the kernel density being a local approximation around 0 and 1. One could alternatively display a histogram, to ensure values in the unit interval, but then one loses information on the interior shape of the distribution.

30. Wakker (2010, p. 175) sharply admonishes anyone that only uses one probability to elicit risk attitudes. Of course, Tversky and Kahneman (1992) used several probabilities in the gain frame and in the loss frame, so it is surprising that they did not do likewise in the mixed frame. No obvious "all-or-nothing" identification problems arise from their choice set design overall, but identification of probabilistic loss aversion is surely improved, in the broader sense, if one allows various probabilities in mixed frame lotteries.

31. They also estimated β and apparently obtained *exactly* the same median value as α, which is quite remarkable from a numerical perspective.

32. This issue is the focus of the use of "hierarchical" methods by Nilsson, Rieskamp, and Wagenmakers (2011) and Murphy and ten Brincke (2018), which are in principle well-suited to handling this particular problem, which is not unique to CPT.

33. Tversky and Kahneman (1992, p. 312) do note that the "parameters estimated from the median data were essentially the same." It is not clear how to interpret this sentence. It may mean that the median CE for the initial 56 choices, and the median values of $x for the final eight choices, were combined to form a synthetic "median subject," and then estimates obtained from those data. The expression "median data" does not lead one to suspect that it was any one actual subject. Nor is there any reference to standard errors for these estimates.

34. Stott (2006, p. 113) notes that one choice was incentivized by scaling prizes down from nominal amounts up to £40,000 to actual payment amounts up to £5. Average salient payments were just £2.13. We view this as effectively hypothetical.

35. They also report (Table 2, p. 91) ML estimates for each of the 30 subjects, and comment about the relative imprecision of these estimates compared to those obtained from the pooled Bayesian hierarchical methods. We agree with this likely outcome from individual-level estimates, as noted earlier, even when there are 180 binary choices per subject. Earlier they anticipated this finding, noting (p. 87) that they "... illustrate how single-subject ML, one of the most popular estimation methods for CPT (e.g., Harless & Camerer, 1994;

Harrison & Rutström, 2009; Stott, 2006), can produce extreme, implausible point estimates for parameters estimated with high uncertainty." The first two studies referenced here did not in fact estimate at the level of the individual, as claimed, and Stott (2006) used hypothetical choice data.

36. An unfortunate, but popular, use of a "lab currency" allowed them to state outcomes ranging between −€1000 and +€1200. These amounts were scaled down by 100 if chosen for payment. This procedure is unattractive, since it only affects behavior if subjects exhibit money illusion and are unable to infer the true payoff in the natural currency. If subjects exhibit money illusion then there is a loss of control over stimuli, by definition, since one does not know how the illusion manifests itself (e.g., non-linearly). We prefer to deal with the budgetary consequences of presenting monetary amounts in the natural currency.

37. They consider correlations of parameter estimates for each subject between the two sessions (p. 28), rather than a direct test of the hypothesis that the estimate *distributions* are the same.

38. In fact, they report two experiments, but we discuss only their first experiment. Their second experiment involved a manipulation of participants' attention to gains and losses to test for variation of the loss aversion parameter estimate, and thus did not provide unbiased estimates of all CPT parameters.

39. Their Fig. 4 is generated by considering the distribution for each parameter separately, since no information is provided about the full multivariate distribution spanning all parameters. It is unlikely that this would affect qualitative statements about the statistical (in)significance of utility loss aversion.

40. While their appendix reports results of a full CPT model with country fixed effects, it does not report global estimates. We thank Ferdinand Vieider for providing us with these estimates.

41. To be clear, Tversky and Kahneman (1992) report a *median* loss aversion estimate of 2.25 and we are not criticizing this result. Rather, we are criticizing the subsequent literature that treated this initial singular empirical observation as a behavioral constant.

42. We review this summary conclusion below in §5.C and in Fig. 32.

43. The reported Inter-Quartile Range of a distribution of point estimates of λ for a given study is used in some cases to approximate the Standard Deviation of the distribution of point estimates, and then for some reason used as a measure of the (mean) Standard Error of the (mean or median) point estimate of λ. In other cases, the reported Standard Deviation is apparently used directly. To state the obvious, the Standard Deviation of the distribution of point estimates of a parameter has no relation whatsoever to the Standard Error of any of the individual estimates, or even any statistic of the distribution of Standard Errors of the point estimates. One could impute the Standard Error from reported estimates of other studies, but then one would need to treat the imputation as an estimate, and not data, by using familiar "multiple imputation" methods.

44. We also see this literature review as a challenge to methodologists to explain how such a false consensus could have emerged and been sustained for so long. Harrison and Ross (2017) begin that methodological explanation.

45. Without developing a theory of "the" reference point, Harrison and Rutström (2008, pp. 95–98) evaluate a wide range of parametrically assumed reference points, and construct a "profile likelihood" for each of them. The reference point with the best profile likelihood was not $0, as assumed here, but some positive amount possibly reflecting some "homegrown reference point" that the subject brought to the lab based on expected earnings. What is relevant here is not their method of finding the empirically best-performing reference point, which was a-theoretical, but that the structural parameter estimates for utility loss aversion were much more in accord with *a priori* beliefs when that alternative reference point was assumed.

46. These calibration puzzles were independently developed by Hansson (1988) and Rabin (2000), and rest on an empirical premiss that subjects exhibit risk aversion over a wide enough range of wealth and lotteries defined over small stakes. Building on an ingenious design independently due to Cox and Sadiraj (2006, 2008, p. 33) and Wilcox (2013)

and Harrison, Lau, Ross, and Swarthout (2017) show that this premiss is strikingly false for subjects drawn from the same population as the experiments reported here. Andersen et al. (2018) show that it is *not* false for other populations of interest, such as adult Danes, at least for the finite range of lab wealth considered in their experiments.

47. These behavioral errors are distinct from the standard errors of the structural model parameters, which can also accommodate unexplained violations by getting larger than they would otherwise be.

48. As explained earlier, and in greater detail in Harrison and Rutström (2009), all of the non-nested tests are based on statistics derived from a *vector of observation-wise* comparisons of log-likelihoods.

49. Table E in Appendix E (available on request) lists the full set of estimates for all major models.

50. Parsimony with respect to the number of parameters is not a theoretical rationale. Nor, as it happens, do we view it as well-motivated econometrically, but that is a separate debate.

51. On other hand, Andersen et al. (2018) found evidence consistent with the empirical premiss for the adult Danish population.

52. One often sees linear utility functions assumed when no probability weighting is also assumed, with λ as the sole parameter. This requires a deviation from the implied definition of λ through various "exchange rate assumptions." We were unable to solve such a "myopic loss aversion" model with only the λ parameter and the μ behavioral noise parameter. We doubt that anyone has actually estimated this model with data spanning gain, mixed and loss frames.

53. These claims are familiar from the literature, but one can document one for completeness. Wakker (2010, p. 234) makes the astonishing empirical claim that "I think that more than half of the risk aversion empirically observed has nothing to do with utility curvature or with probability weighting. Instead, it is generated by loss aversion …."

54. This expression leads to what Wakker (2010, §7.6) usefully calls the "gain-rank." The "loss-rank" would be based on the answer to the question, "what is the probability of getting Y or *less*?" Loss-ranks were popular with some of the earlier studies in RDU.

55. The prominent exception is the probability weighting function suggested by Kahneman and Tversky (1979), which had interior discontinuities at p=0 and p=1.

56. Wakker (2010, pp. 255, 261) discusses the implications of the decisions weights for mixed frame lotteries summing to more than 1. There are none.

ACKNOWLEDGEMENTS

We are grateful to *Bloomberg Wealth* for funding, and to Morten Lau, Elisabet Rutström, and Nathaniel Wilcox for valuable discussions.

REFERENCES

Abdellaoui, M. (2000). Parameter-free elicitation of utilities and probability weighting functions. *Management Science*, *46*, 1497–1512.

Abdellaoui, M., & Bleichrodt, H. (2007). Eliciting Gul's theory of disappointment aversion by the tradeoff method. *Journal of Economic Psychology*, *28*, 631–645.

Abdellaoui, M., Bleichrodt, H., & L'Haridon, O. (2008). A tractable method to measure utility and loss aversion under prospect theory. *Journal of Risk & Uncertainty*, *36*, 245–266.

Abdellaoui, M., Bleichrodt, H., & Paraschiv, C. (2007). Loss aversion under prospect theory: A parameter-free approach. *Management Science*, *53*(10), 1659–1674.

Abdellaoui, M., L'Haridon, O., & Paraschiv, C. (2013). Individual vs. couple behavior: An experimental investigation of risk preferences. *Theory and Decision*, *75*(2), 175–191.

Andersen, S., Cox, J., Harrison, G. W., Lau, M. I., Rutström, E. E., & Sadiraj, V. (2018). Asset integration and attitudes to risk: Theory and evidence. *Review of Economics & Statistics*, *100*(5), 816–830.

Andersen, S., Harrison, G. W., Hole, A. R., Lau, M. I., & Rutström, E. E. (2012). Non-linear mixed logit. *Theory and Decision*, *73*, 77–96.

Andersen, S., Harrison, G. W., Lau, M. I., & Rutström, E. E. (2006). Elicitation using multiple price lists. *Experimental Economics*, *9*(4), 383–405.

Balcombe, K., & Fraser, I. (2015). Parametric preference functionals under risk in the gain domain: A bayesian analysis. *Journal of Risk & Uncertainty*, *50*, 161–187.

Becker, G. M., DeGroot, M. H., & Marschak, J. (1964). Measuring utility by a single-response sequential method. *Behavioral Science*, *9*, 226–232.

Birnbaum, M. H., & Bahra, J. P. (2007). Gain-loss separability and coalescing in risky decision making. *Management Science*, *53*(6), 1016–1028.

Blavatsky, P. R. (2012). Probabilistic choice and stochastic dominance. *Economic Theory*, *50*, 59–83.

Bleichrodt, H., Pinto, J. L., & Wakker, P. P. (2001). Making descriptive use of prospect theory to improve the prescriptive use of expected utility. *Management Science*, *47*, 1498–1514.

Booij, A. S., & van de Kuilen, G. (2009). A parameter-free analysis of the utility of money for the general population under prospect theory. *Journal of Economic Psychology*, *30*, 651–666.

Booij, A. S., van Praag, B. M. S., & van de Kuilen, G. (2010). A parametric analysis of prospect theory's functionals for the general population. *Theory and Decision*, *68*, 115–148.

Bosch-Domènech, A., & Silvestre, J. (2010). Averting risk in the face of large losses: Bernoulli vs. Tversky and Kahnman. *Economics Letters*, *107*, 180–182.

Bouchouicha, R., & Vieider, F. M. (2017). Accommodating stake effects under prospect theory. *Journal of Risk & Uncertainty*, *55*(1), 1–28.

Brooks, P., Peters, S., & Zank, H. (2014). Risk behavior for gain, loss, and mixed prospects. *Theory and Decision*, *77*, 153–182.

Brooks, P., & Zank, H. (2005). Loss averse behavior. *Journal of Risk & Uncertainty*, *31*(3), 301–325.

Brown, A. L., & Healy, P. J. (2018). Separated decisions. *European Economic Review*, *101*, 20–34.

Brown, A. L., Imai, T., Vieider, F. M., & Camerer, C. F. (2023). Meta-analysis of empirical estimates of loss aversion. *Journal of Economic Literature* (forthcoming). Retrieved from https://osf.io/preprints/metaarxiv/hnefr/

Bruhin, A., Fehr-Duda, H., & Epper, T. (2010). Risk and rationality: Uncovering heterogeneity in probability distortion. *Econometrica*, *78*(4), 1375–1412.

Brzezinski, M. (2012). The Chen–Shapiro test for normality. *The Stata Journal*, *12*(3), 368–374.

Burke, M. S., Carter, J. R., Gominiak, R. D., & Ohl, D. F. (1996). An experimental note on the Allais paradox and monetary incentives. *Empirical Economics*, *21*(4), 617–632.

Camerer, C., & Ho, T. H. (1994). Violations of the betweenness axiom and nonlinearity in probability. *Journal of Risk & Uncertainty*, *8*, 167–196.

Carbone, E., & Hey, J. (1995). A comparison of the estimates of EU and non-EU preference functionals using data from pairwise choice and complete ranking experiments. *Geneva Papers on Risk and Insurance Theory*, *20*, 111–133.

Cárdenas, J. C., De Roux, N., Jaramillo, C. R., & Martinez, L. R. (2014). Is it my money or not? An experiment on risk aversion and the house-money effect. *Experimental Economics*, *17*, 47–60.

Chateauneuf, A., & Wakker, P. (1999). An axiomatization of cumulative prospect theory for decisions under risk. *Journal of Risk and Uncertainty*, *18*(2), 137–145.

Chen, L., & Shapiro, S. S. (1995). An alternative test for normality based on normalized spacings. *Journal of Statistical Computation and Simulation*, *53*, 269–288.

Chew, S. H., Karni, E., & Safra, Z. (1987). Risk aversion in the theory of expected utility with rank dependent probabilities. *Journal of Economic Theory*, *42*(2), 370–381.

Clarke, K. A. (2003). Nonparametric model discrimination in international relations. *Journal of Conflict Resolution*, *47*(1), 72–93.

Clarke, K. A. (2007). A simple distribution-free test for non-nested model selection. *Political Analysis*, *15*(3), 347–363.

Clarke, K. A., & Signorino, C. S. (2010). Discriminating methods: Tests for non-nested discrete choice models. *Political Studies*, *58*, 368–388.

Conlisk, J. (1989). Three variants on the allais example. *American Economic Review*, *79*(3), 392–407.

Cox, J. C., & Sadiraj, V. (2006). Small- and large-stakes risk aversion: Implications of concavity calibration for decision theory. *Games and Economic Behavior*, *56*, 45–60.
Cox, J. C., & Sadiraj, V. (2008). Risky decisions in the large and in the small: Theory and experiment. In J. Cox & G. W. Harrison (Eds.), *Risk aversion in experiments* (Research in Experimental Economics, Vol. 12, pp. 9–40). Bingley: Emerald Group Publishing Limited.
Cox, J. C., Sadiraj, V., & Schmidt, U. (2015). Paradoxes and mechanisms for choice under risk. *Experimental Economics*, *18*(2), 215–250.
Cubitt, R. P., Starmer, C., & Sugden, R. (1998). On the validity of the random lottery incentive system. *Experimental Economics*, *1*(2), 115–131.
Eeckhoudt, L., & Schlesinger, H. (2006). Putting risk in its proper place. *American Economic Review*, *96*, 280–289.
Etchart-Vincent, N. (2004). Is probability weighting sensitive to the magnitude of consequences? An experimental investigation on losses. *Journal of Risk & Uncertainty*, *28*, 217–235.
Fan, C.-P. (2002, November). Allais paradox in the small. *Journal of Economic Behavior & Organization*, *49*(3), 411–421.
Fehr-Duda, H., Gennaro, M., & Schubert, R. (2006). Gender, financial risk, and probability weights. *Theory and Decision*, *60*, 283–313.
Fennema, H., & van Assen, M. (1998). Measuring the utility of losses by means of the trade-off method. *Journal of Risk & Uncertainty*, *17*, 277–295.
Fishburn, P. C., & Kochenberger, G. A. (1979). Two-piece von Neumann-Morgenstern utility functions. *Decision Sciences*, *10*, 503–518.
Gao, X. S., Harrison, G. W., & Tchernis, R. (2023). Behavioral welfare economics and risk preferences: A Bayesian approach. *Experimental Economics*, *26*, 273–303.
Glöckner, A., & Pachur, T. (2012). Cognitive models of risky choice: Parameter stability and predictive accuracy of prospect theory. *Cognition*, *123*(1), 21–32.
Gonzalez, R., & Wu, G. (1999). On the shape of the probability weighting function. *Cognitive Psychology*, *38*, 129–166.
Gul, F. (1991). A theory of disappointment aversion. *Econometrica*, *59*, 667–686.
Hansson, B. (1988). Risk aversion as a problem of conjoint measurement. In P. Gardenfors & N.-E. Sahlin (Eds.), *Decisions, probability, and utility* (pp. 136–158). New York, NY: Cambridge University Press.
Harbaugh, W. T., Krause, K., & Vesterlund, L. (2002). Risk attitudes of children and adults: Choices over small and large probability gains and losses. *Experimental Economics*, *5*, 53–84.
Harless, D. W., & Camerer, C.F. (1994). The predictive utility of generalized expected utility theories. *Econometrica*, *62*(6), 1251–1289.
Harrison, G. W. (1994). Expected utility theory and the experimentalists. *Empirical Economics*, *19*(2), 223–253.
Harrison, G. W., Johnson, E., McInnes, M. M., & Rutström, E. E. (2007). Measurement with experimental controls. In M. Boumans (Ed.), *Measurement in economics: A handbook* (pp. 79–104). San Diego, CA: Elsevier.
Harrison, G. W., Lau, M., Ross, D., & Swarthout, J. T. (2017). Small-stakes risk aversion in the laboratory: A reconsideration. *Economics Letters*, *160*, 24–28.
Harrison, G. W., & List, J. A. (2004). Field experiments. *Journal of Economic Literature*, *42*(4), 1013–1059.
Harrison, G. W., & Ng, J. M. (2016). Evaluating the expected welfare gain of insurance. *Journal of Risk & Insurance*, *83*(1), 91–120.
Harrison, G. W., & Ross, D. (2017). The empirical adequacy of cumulative prospect theory and its implications for normative assessment. *Journal of Economic Methodology*, *24*(2), 150–165.
Harrison, G. W., & Rutström, E. E. (2008). Risk aversion in the laboratory. In J. C. Cox & G. W. Harrison (Eds.), *Risk aversion in experiments* (Research in experimental economics, Vol. 12, pp. 41–196). Bingley: Emerald Group Publishing Limited.
Harrison, G. W., & Rutström, E. E. (2009). Expected utility and prospect theory: One wedding and a decent funeral. *Experimental Economics*, *12*(2), 133–158.
Harrison, G. W., & Swarthout, J. T. (2014). Experimental payment protocols and the bipolar behaviorist. *Theory and Decision*, *77*(3), 423–438.
Hey, J. (2001). Does repetition improve consistency? *Experimental Economics*, *4*, 5–54.

Hey, J. D., & Orme, C. (1994). Investigating generalizations of expected utility theory using experimental data. *Econometrica, 62*(6), 1291–1326.
Holt, C. A. (1986). Preference reversals and the independence axiom. *American Economic Review, 76*, 508–514.
Holt, C. A., & Laury, S. K. (2002). Risk aversion and incentive effects. *American Economic Review, 92*(5), 1644–1655.
Kahneman, D., & Tversky, A. (1979). Prospect theory: An analysis of decision under risk. *Econometrica, 47*, 263–291.
Karni, E., & Safra, Z. (1987). Preference reversals and the observability of preferences by experimental methods. *Econometrica, 55*, 675–685.
Köbberling, V., & Wakker, P. P. (2005). An index of loss aversion. *Journal of Economic Theory, 122*, 119–131.
Kőszegi, B., & Rabin, M. (2006). A model of reference-dependent preferences. *Quarterly Journal of Economics, 121*(4), 1133–1165.
Kőszegi, B., & Rabin, M. (2007). Reference-dependent risk attitudes. *American Economic Review, 97*(4), 1047–1073.
L'Haridon, O., & Vieider, F. (2019). All over the map: A worldwide comparison of risk preferences. *Quantitative Economics, 10*, 185–215.
Laury, S. K., McInnes, M. M., & Swarthout, J. T. (2009). Insurance decisions for low-probability losses. *Journal of Risk and Uncertainty, 39*, 17–44.
Loomes, G., & Sugden, R. (1998). Testing different stochastic specifications of risky choice. *Economica, 65*, 581–598.
Mason, C. F., Shogren, J. F., Settle, C., & List, J. A. (2005). Investigating risky choices over losses using experimental data. *Journal of Risk and Uncertainty, 31*(2), 187–215.
Murphy, R. O., & ten Brincke, R. H. W. (2018). Hierarchical maximum likelihood parameter estimation for cumulative prospect theory: Improving the reliability of individual risk parameter estimates. *Management Science, 64*(1), 308–326.
Neilson, W., & Stowe, J. (2002). A further examination of cumulative prospect theory paramaterizations. *Journal of Risk and Uncertainty, 24*(1), 31–46.
Nilsson, H., Rieskamp, J., & Wagenmakers, E.-J. (2011). Hierarchical Bayesian parameter estimation for cumulative prospect theory. *Journal of Mathematical Psychology, 55*, 84–93.
Pachur, T., Hanoch, Y., & Gummerum, M. (2010). Prospects behind bars: Analyzing decisions under risk in a prison population. *Psychonomic Bulletin and Review, 17*, 630–636.
Pachur, T., & Kellen, D. (2013). Modeling gain-loss asymmetries in risk choice: The critical role of probability weighting. In M. Knauff, M. Pauen, N. Sebanz, & I. Wachsmith (Eds.), *Proceedings of the annual conference of the cognitive science society, 35*, 3205–3210.
Pachur, T., Schulte-Mecklenbeck, M, Murphy, R. O., & Hertwig, R. (2018). Prospect theory reflects selective allocation of attention. *Journal of Experimental Psychology: General, 147*(2), 147–169.
Pennings, J. M. E., & Smidts, A. (2003). The shape of utility functions and organizational behavior. *Management Science, 24*, 1251–1263.
Prelec, D. (1998). The probability weighting function. *Econometrica, 66*, 497–527.
Quiggin, J. (1982). A theory of anticipated utility. *Journal of Economic Behavior & Organization, 3*(4), 323–343.
Rabin, M. (2000). Risk aversion and expected utility theory: A calibration theorem. *Econometrica, 68*, 1281–1292.
Ray, D., Shum, M., & Camerer, C. F. (2015). Loss aversion in post-sale purchases of consumer products and their substitutes. *American Economic Review (Papers & Proceedings), 105*(5), 376–380.
Rieskamp, J. (2008). The probabilistic nature of preferential choice. *Journal of Experimental Psychology: Learning, Memory and Cognition, 34*(6), 1446–1465.
Schmidt, U., Starmer, C., & Sugden, R. (2008). Third-generation prospect theory. *Journal of Risk & Uncertainty, 36*(3), 203–223.
Schmidt, U., & Traub, S. (2002). An experimental test of loss aversion. *Journal of Risk & Uncertainty, 25*, 233–249.
Schmidt, U., & Zank, H. (2008). Risk aversion in cumulative prospect theory. *Management Science, 54*, 208–216.

Scholten, M., & Read, D. (2014). Prospect theory and the 'forgotten' fourfold pattern of risk preferences. *Journal of Risk & Uncertainty*, *48*(1), 67–83.

Schunk, D., & Betsch, C. (2006). Explaining heterogeneity in utility functions by individual differences in decision modes. *Journal of Economic Psychology*, *27*, 386–401.

Starmer, C. (1992). Testing new theories of choice under uncertainty using the common consequence effect. *Review of Economic Studies*, *59*, 813–830.

Starmer, C. (2000). Developments in non-expected utility theory: The hunt for a descriptive theory of choice under risk. *Journal of Economic Literature*, *38*, 332–382.

Starmer, C., & Sugden, R. (1989). Violations of the independence axiom in common ratio problems: An experimental test of some competing hypotheses. *Annals of Operational Research*, *19*, 79–102.

Starmer, C., & Sugden, R. (1991). Does the random-lottery incentive system elicit true preferences? An experimental investigation. *American Economic Review*, *81*, 971–978.

Stott, H. P. (2006). Cumulative prospect theory's functional menagerie. *Journal of Risk and Uncertainty*, *32*, 101–130.

Tom, S., Fox, C. R., Trepel, C., & Poldrack, R. A. (2007). The neural basis of loss aversion in decision-making under risk, *Science*, *315*(5811), 515–518.

Tversky, A., & Kahneman, D. (1992). Advances in prospect theory: Cumulative representations of uncertainty. *Journal of Risk & Uncertainty*, *5*, 297–323.

Vieider, F. M., Chmura, T., Fisher, T., Kusakawa, T., Martinsson, P., Thompson, F. M., & Sunday, A. (2015). Within-versus between-country differences in risk attitudes: Implications for cultural comparisons. *Theory and Decision*, *78*, 209–218.

Vieider, F. M., Martinsson, P., Nam, P. K., & Truong, N. (2019). Risk preferences and development revisited. *Theory and Decision*, *86*, 1–21.

von Gaudecker, H.-M., van Soest, A., & Wengström, E. (2011). Heterogeneity in risky choice behavior in a broad population. *American Economic Review*, *101*, 664–694.

Vuong, Q. H. (1989). Likelihood ratio tests for model selection and non-nested hypotheses. *Econometrica*, *57*(2), 307–333.

Wakker, P. P. (2010). *Prospect theory: For risk and ambiguity*. New York, NY: Cambridge University Press.

Wakker, P. P., & Tversky, A. (1993). An axiomatization of cumulative prospect theory. *Journal of Risk and Uncertainty*, *7*(7), 147–176.

Wilcox, N. T. (2008). Stochastic models for binary discrete choice under risk: A critical primer and econometric comparison. In J. Cox & G. W. Harrison (Eds.), *Risk aversion in experiments* (Research in Experimental Economics, Vol. 12, pp. 197–292). Bingley: Emerald Group Publishing Limited.

Wilcox, N. T. (2011). 'Stochastically more risk averse:' A contextual theory of stochastic discrete choice under risk. *Journal of Econometrics*, *162*(1), 89–104.

Wilcox, N. T. (2013). Is the premise of risk calibration theorems plausible? *CEAR Workshop on Decision Making Under Risk and Uncertainty*, University College, Durham.

Wilcox, N. T. (2023). Unusual estimates of probability weighting functions. In G. W. Harrison & D. Ross (Eds.), *Models of risk preferences: Descriptive and normative challenges*. (Research in Experimental Economics Vol. 23, pp. 69–106). Bingley: Emerald Group Publishing Limited.

Wu, G., & Gonzalez, R. (1996). Curvature of the probability weighting function. *Management Science*, *42*, 1676–1690.

Wu, G., & Markle, A. B. (2008). An empirical test of gain-loss separability in prospect theory. *Management Science*, *54*(7), 1322–1335.

Yaari, M. E. (1987). The dual theory of choice under risk. *Econometrica*, *55*(1), 95–115.

Zeisberger, S., Vrecko, D., & Langer, T. (2012). Measuring the time stability of prospect theory preferences. *Theory and Decision*, *72*, 359–386.

APPENDIX A: PARAMETERS OF EXPERIMENTS

Table A1. Battery of 100 lottery tasks in choices made by undergraduate subjects

Task	EV left	EV right	EV ratio	Left $ 1	Left p 1	Left $ 2	Left p 2	Left $ 3	Left p 3	Right $ 1	Right p 1	Right $ 2	Right p 2	Right $ 3	Right p 3	Notes
1	$5.00	$6.95	–28%	$0	0	$5	1	$0	0	$0	0.01	$5	0.89	$25	0.1	Allais – lower stakes
2	$0.55	$2.50	–78%	$0	0.89	$5	0.11	$0	0	$0	0.9	$5	0	$25	0.1	Allais – lower stakes
3	$15.00	$20.85	–28%	$0	0	$15	1	$0	0	$0	0.01	$15	0.89	$75	0.1	Allais – higher stakes
4	$1.65	$7.50	–78%	$0	0.89	$15	0.11	$0	0	$0	0.9	$15	0	$75	0.1	Allais – higher stakes
5	$59.50	$61.25	–3%	$0	0.15	$35	0	$70	0.85	$0	0	$35	0.25	$70	0.75	LS1: Loomes and Sugden
6	$49.00	$50.75	–3%	$0	0.3	$35	0	$70	0.7	$0	0.15	$35	0.25	$70	0.6	LS2: Loomes and Sugden
7	$49.00	$52.50	–7%	$0	0.3	$35	0	$70	0.7	$0	0	$35	0.5	$70	0.5	LS3: Loomes and Sugden
8	$50.75	$52.50	–3%	$0	0.15	$35	0.25	$70	0.6	$0	0	$35	0.5	$70	0.5	LS4: Loomes and Sugden
9	$33.25	$35.00	–5%	$0	0.15	$35	0.75	$70	0.1	$0	0	$35	1	$70	0	LS5: Loomes and Sugden
10	$28.00	$35.00	–20%	$0	0.6	$35	0	$70	0.4	$0	0	$35	1	$70	0	LS6: Loomes and Sugden
11	$28.00	$33.25	–16%	$0	0.6	$35	0	$70	0.4	$0	0.15	$35	0.75	$70	0.1	LS7: Loomes and Sugden
12	$7.00	$8.75	–20%	$0	0.9	$35	0	$70	0.1	$0	0.75	$35	0.25	$70	0	LS8: Loomes and Sugden
13	$63.00	$63.00	0%	$0	0.1	$35	0	$70	0.9	$0	0	$35	0.2	$70	0.8	LS9: Loomes and Sugden

(*Continued*)

Table A1. (Continued)

Task	EV left	EV right	EV ratio	Left $ 1	Left p 1	Left $ 2	Left p 2	Left $ 3	Left p 3	Right $ 1	Right p 1	Right $ 2	Right p 2	Right $ 3	Right p 3	Notes
14	$35.00	$35.00	0%	$0	0.5	$35	0	$70	0.5	$0	0.1	$35	0.8	$70	0.1	LS10: Loomes and Sugden
15	$35.00	$35.00	0%	$0	0.5	$35	0	$70	0.5	$0	0	$35	1	$70	0	LS11: Loomes and Sugden
16	$35.00	$35.00	0%	$0	0.1	$35	0.8	$70	0.1	$0	0	$35	1	$70	0	LS12: Loomes and Sugden
17	$21.00	$21.00	0%	$0	0.7	$35	0	$70	0.3	$0	0.5	$35	0.4	$70	0.1	LS13: Loomes and Sugden
18	$21.00	$21.00	0%	$0	0.7	$35	0	$70	0.3	$0	0.4	$35	0.6	$70	0	LS14: Loomes and Sugden
19	$21.00	$21.00	0%	$0	0.5	$35	0.4	$70	0.1	$0	0.4	$35	0.6	$70	0	LS15: Loomes and Sugden
20	$7.00	$7.00	0%	$0	0.9	$35	0	$70	0.1	$0	0.8	$35	0.2	$70	0	LS16: Loomes and Sugden
21	$63.00	$61.25	3%	$0	0.1	$35	0	$70	0.9	$0	0	$35	0.25	$70	0.75	LS17: Loomes and Sugden
22	$42.00	$36.75	14%	$0	0.4	$35	0	$70	0.6	$0	0.1	$35	0.75	$70	0.15	LS18: Loomes and Sugden
23	$42.00	$35.00	20%	$0	0.4	$35	0	$70	0.6	$0	0	$35	1	$70	0	LS19: Loomes and Sugden
24	$36.75	$35.00	5%	$0	0.1	$35	0.75	$70	0.15	$0	0	$35	1	$70	0	LS20: Loomes and Sugden
25	$21.00	$19.25	9%	$0	0.7	$35	0	$70	0.3	$0	0.6	$35	0.25	$70	0.15	LS21: Loomes and Sugden
26	$21.00	$17.50	20%	$0	0.7	$35	0	$70	0.3	$0	0.5	$35	0.5	$70	0	LS22: Loomes and Sugden
27	$19.25	$17.50	10%	$0	0.6	$35	0.25	$70	0.15	$0	0.5	$35	0.5	$70	0	LS23: Loomes and Sugden

28	$10.50	$8.75	20%	$0	0.85	$35	0	$70	0.15	$0	0.75	$35	0.25	$70	0	LS24: Loomes and Sugden
29	$63.00	$59.50	6%	$0	0.1	$35	0	$70	0.9	$0	0	$35	0.3	$70	0.7	LS25: Loomes and Sugden
30	$42.00	$35.00	20%	$0	0.4	$35	0	$70	0.6	$0	0.2	$35	0.6	$70	0.2	LS26: Loomes and Sugden
31	$42.00	$31.50	33%	$0	0.4	$35	0	$70	0.6	$0	0.1	$35	0.9	$70	0	LS27: Loomes and Sugden
32	$35.00	$31.50	11%	$0	0.2	$35	0.6	$70	0.2	$0	0.1	$35	0.9	$70	0	LS28: Loomes and Sugden
33	$28.00	$24.50	14%	$0	0.6	$35	0	$70	0.4	$0	0.5	$35	0.3	$70	0.2	LS29: Loomes and Sugden
34	$28.00	$21.00	33%	$0	0.6	$35	0	$70	0.4	$0	0.4	$35	0.6	$70	0	LS30: Loomes and Sugden
35	$24.50	$21.00	17%	$0	0.5	$35	0.3	$70	0.2	$0	0.4	$35	0.6	$70	0	LS31: Loomes and Sugden
36	$14.00	$10.50	33%	$0	0.8	$35	0	$70	0.2	$0	0.7	$35	0.3	$70	0	LS32: Loomes and Sugden
37	$63.00	$56.00	13%	$0	0.1	$35	0	$70	0.9	$0	0	$35	0.4	$70	0.6	LS33: Loomes and Sugden
38	$52.50	$42.00	25%	$0	0.25	$35	0	$70	0.75	$0	0.1	$35	0.6	$70	0.3	LS34: Loomes and Sugden
39	$52.50	$35.00	50%	$0	0.25	$35	0	$70	0.75	$0	0	$35	1	$70	0	LS35: Loomes and Sugden
40	$42.00	$35.00	20%	$0	0.1	$35	0.6	$70	0.3	$0	0	$35	1	$70	0	LS36: Loomes and Sugden
41	$28.00	$21.00	33%	$0	0.5	$35	0.2	$70	0.3	$0	0.4	$35	0.6	$70	0	LS37: Loomes and Sugden
42	$31.50	$21.00	50%	$0	0.55	$35	0	$70	0.45	$0	0.4	$35	0.6	$70	0	LS38: Loomes and Sugden
43	$31.50	$28.00	13%	$0	0.55	$35	0	$70	0.45	$0	0.5	$35	0.2	$70	0.3	LS39: Loomes and Sugden
44	$21.00	$14.00	50%	$0	0.7	$35	0	$70	0.3	$0	0.6	$35	0.4	$70	0	LS40: Loomes and Sugden

(*Continued*)

Table A1. (Continued)

Task	EV left	EV right	EV ratio	Left $ 1	Left p 1	Left $ 2	Left p 2	Left $ 3	Left p 3	Right $1	Right p 1	Right $ 2	Right p 2	Right $ 3	Right p 3	Notes
45	($63.00)	($63.00)	0%	$0	0.1	($35)	0	($70)	0.9	$0	0	($35)	0.2	($70)	0.8	LS9: Loomes and Sugden
46	($35.00)	($35.00)	0%	$0	0.5	($35)	0	($70)	0.5	$0	0.1	($35)	0.8	($70)	0.1	LS10: Loomes and Sugden
47	($35.00)	($35.00)	0%	$0	0.5	($35)	0	($70)	0.5	$0	0	($35)	1	($70)	0	LS11: Loomes and Sugden
48	($35.00)	($35.00)	0%	$0	0.1	($35)	0.8	($70)	0.1	$0	0	($35)	1	($70)	0	LS12: Loomes and Sugden
49	($21.00)	($21.00)	0%	$0	0.7	($35)	0	($70)	0.3	$0	0.5	($35)	0.4	($70)	0.1	LS13: Loomes and Sugden
50	($21.00)	($21.00)	0%	$0	0.7	($35)	0	($70)	0.3	$0	0.4	($35)	0.6	($70)	0	LS14: Loomes and Sugden
51	($21.00)	($21.00)	0%	$0	0.5	($35)	0.4	($70)	0.1	$0	0.4	($35)	0.6	($70)	0	LS15: Loomes and Sugden
52	($7.00)	($7.00)	0%	$0	0.9	($35)	0	($70)	0.1	$0	0.8	($35)	0.2	($70)	0	LS16: Loomes and Sugden
53	($63.00)	($56.00)	13%	$0	0.1	($35)	0	($70)	0.9	$0	0	($35)	0.4	($70)	0.6	LS33: Loomes and Sugden
54	($52.50)	($42.00)	25%	$0	0.25	($35)	0	($70)	0.75	$0	0.1	($35)	0.6	($70)	0.3	LS34: Loomes and Sugden
55	($52.50)	($35.00)	50%	$0	0.25	($35)	0	($70)	0.75	$0	0	($35)	1	($70)	0	LS35: Loomes and Sugden
56	($42.00)	($35.00)	20%	$0	0.1	($35)	0.6	($70)	0.3	$0	0	($35)	1	($70)	0	LS36: Loomes and Sugden
57	($28.00)	($21.00)	33%	$0	0.5	($35)	0.2	($70)	0.3	$0	0.4	($35)	0.6	($70)	0	LS37: Loomes and Sugden
58	($31.50)	($21.00)	50%	$0	0.55	($35)	0	($70)	0.45	$0	0.4	($35)	0.6	($70)	0	LS38: Loomes and Sugden
59	($31.50)	($28.00)	13%	$0	0.55	($35)	0	($70)	0.45	$0	0.5	($35)	0.2	($70)	0.3	LS39: Loomes and Sugden

60	($21.00)	($14.00)	50%	$0	0.7	($35)	0	($70)	0.3	$0	0.6	($35)	0.4	($70)	0	LS40: Loomes and Sugden
61	$59.50	$51.80	15%	($35)	0.1	($21)	0	$70	0.9	($35)	0	($21)	0.2	$70	0.8	LS9: Loomes and Sugden
62	$17.50	($13.30)	−232%	($35)	0.5	($21)	0	$70	0.5	($35)	0.1	($21)	0.8	$70	0.1	LS10: Loomes and Sugden
63	$17.50	($21.00)	−183%	($35)	0.5	($21)	0	$70	0.5	($35)	0	($21)	1	$70	0	LS11: Loomes and Sugden
64	($13.30)	($21.00)	−37%	($35)	0.1	($21)	0.8	$70	0.1	($35)	0	($21)	1	$70	0	LS12: Loomes and Sugden
65	($3.50)	($18.90)	−81%	($35)	0.7	($21)	0	$70	0.3	($35)	0.5	($21)	0.4	$70	0.1	LS13: Loomes and Sugden
66	($3.50)	($26.60)	−87%	($35)	0.7	($21)	0	$70	0.3	($35)	0.4	($21)	0.6	$70	0	LS14: Loomes and Sugden
67	($18.90)	($26.60)	−29%	($35)	0.5	($21)	0.4	$70	0.1	($35)	0.4	($21)	0.6	$70	0	LS15: Loomes and Sugden
68	($24.50)	($32.20)	−24%	($35)	0.9	($21)	0	$70	0.1	($35)	0.8	($21)	0.2	$70	0	LS16: Loomes and Sugden
69	$59.50	$33.60	77%	($35)	0.1	($21)	0	$70	0.9	($35)	0	($21)	0.4	$70	0.6	LS33: Loomes and Sugden
70	$43.75	$4.90	793%	($35)	0.25	($21)	0	$70	0.75	($35)	0.1	($21)	0.6	$70	0.3	LS34: Loomes and Sugden
71	$43.75	($21.00)	−308%	($35)	0.25	($21)	0	$70	0.75	($35)	0	($21)	1	$70	0	LS35: Loomes and Sugden
72	$4.90	($21.00)	−123%	($35)	0.1	($21)	0.6	$70	0.3	($35)	0	($21)	1	$70	0	LS36: Loomes and Sugden
73	($0.70)	($26.60)	−97%	($35)	0.5	($21)	0.2	$70	0.3	($35)	0.4	($21)	0.6	$70	0	LS37: Loomes and Sugden
74	$12.25	($26.60)	−146%	($35)	0.55	($21)	0	$70	0.45	($35)	0.4	($21)	0.6	$70	0	LS38: Loomes and Sugden
75	$12.25	($0.70)	−1850%	($35)	0.55	($21)	0	$70	0.45	($35)	0.5	($21)	0.2	$70	0.3	LS39: Loomes and Sugden

(*Continued*)

Table A1. (Continued)

Task	EV left	EV right	EV ratio	Left $ 1	Left p 1	Left $ 2	Left p 2	Left $ 3	Left p 3	Right $ 1	Right p 1	Right $ 2	Right p 2	Right $ 3	Right p 3	Notes
76	($3.50)	($29.40)	−88%	($35)	0.7	($21)	0	$70	0.3	($35)	0.6	($21)	0.4	$70	0	LS40: Loomes and Sugden
77	$52.50	$50.00	5%	$10	0.15	$20	0	$60	0.85	$10	0	$20	0.25	$60	0.75	LS1: Loomes and Sugden
78	$45.00	$42.50	6%	$10	0.3	$20	0	$60	0.7	$10	0.15	$20	0.25	$60	0.6	LS2: Loomes and Sugden
79	$45.00	$40.00	13%	$10	0.3	$20	0	$60	0.7	$10	0	$20	0.5	$60	0.5	LS3: Loomes and Sugden
80	$42.50	$40.00	6%	$10	0.15	$20	0.25	$60	0.6	$10	0	$20	0.5	$60	0.5	LS4: Loomes and Sugden
81	$22.50	$20.00	13%	$10	0.15	$20	0.75	$60	0.1	$10	0	$20	1	$60	0	LS5: Loomes and Sugden
82	$30.00	$20.00	50%	$10	0.6	$20	0	$60	0.4	$10	0	$20	1	$60	0	LS6: Loomes and Sugden
83	$30.00	$22.50	33%	$10	0.6	$20	0	$60	0.4	$10	0.15	$20	0.75	$60	0.1	LS7: Loomes and Sugden
84	$15.00	$12.50	20%	$10	0.9	$20	0	$60	0.1	$10	0.75	$20	0.25	$60	0	LS8: Loomes and Sugden
85	$50.00	$47.50	5%	$5	0.1	$25	0	$55	0.9	$5	0	$25	0.25	$55	0.75	LS17: Loomes and Sugden
86	$35.00	$27.50	27%	$5	0.4	$25	0	$55	0.6	$5	0.1	$25	0.75	$55	0.15	LS18: Loomes and Sugden
87	$35.00	$25.00	40%	$5	0.4	$25	0	$55	0.6	$5	0	$25	1	$55	0	LS19: Loomes and Sugden
88	$27.50	$25.00	10%	$5	0.1	$25	0.75	$55	0.15	$5	0	$25	1	$55	0	LS20: Loomes and Sugden
89	$20.00	$17.50	14%	$5	0.7	$25	0	$55	0.3	$5	0.6	$25	0.25	$55	0.15	LS21: Loomes and Sugden

90	$20.00	$15.00	33%	$5	0.7	$25	0	$55	0.3	$5	0.5	$25	0.5	$55	0	LS22: Loomes and Sugden
91	$17.50	$15.00	17%	$5	0.6	$25	0.25	$55	0.15	$5	0.5	$25	0.5	$55	0	LS23: Loomes and Sugden
92	$12.50	$10.00	25%	$5	0.85	$25	0	$55	0.15	$5	0.75	$25	0.25	$55	0	LS24: Loomes and Sugden
93	$42.00	$40.50	4%	$15	0.1	$30	0	$45	0.9	$15	0	$30	0.3	$45	0.7	LS25: Loomes and Sugden
94	$33.00	$30.00	10%	$15	0.4	$30	0	$45	0.6	$15	0.2	$30	0.6	$45	0.2	LS26: Loomes and Sugden
95	$33.00	$28.50	16%	$15	0.4	$30	0	$45	0.6	$15	0.1	$30	0.9	$45	0	LS27: Loomes and Sugden
96	$30.00	$28.50	5%	$15	0.2	$30	0.6	$45	0.2	$15	0.1	$30	0.9	$45	0	LS28: Loomes and Sugden
97	$27.00	$25.50	6%	$15	0.6	$30	0	$45	0.4	$15	0.5	$30	0.3	$45	0.2	LS29: Loomes and Sugden
98	$27.00	$24.00	13%	$15	0.6	$30	0	$45	0.4	$15	0.4	$30	0.6	$45	0	LS30: Loomes and Sugden
99	$25.50	$24.00	6%	$15	0.5	$30	0.3	$45	0.2	$15	0.4	$30	0.6	$45	0	LS31: Loomes and Sugden
100	$21.00	$19.50	8%	$15	0.8	$30	0	$45	0.2	$15	0.7	$30	0.3	$45	0	LS32: Loomes and Sugden

Table A2. Battery of 100 Lottery Tasks in Choices Made by MBA Students.

Task	EV left	EV Right	EV Ratio	Left $ 1	Left p 1	Left $ 2	Left p 2	Left $ 3	Left p 3	Right $ 1	Right p 1	Right $ 2	Right p 2	Right $ 3	Right p 3	Notes
1	$5.00	$6.95	–0.2806	$0	0	$5	1	$0	0	$0	0.01	$5	0.89	$25	0.1	Allais - lower stakes
2	$0.55	$2.50	–0.78	$0	0.89	$5	0.11	$0	0	$0	0.9	$5	0	$25	0.1	Allais - lower stakes
3	$100.00	$139.00	–0.2806	$0	0	$100	1	$0	0	$0	0.01	$100	0.89	$500	0.1	Allais - higher stakes
4	$11.00	$50.00	–0.78	$0	0.89	$100	0.11	$0	0	$0	0.9	$100	0	$500	0.1	Allais - higher stakes
5	$425.00	$437.50	–0.029	$0	0.15	$250	0	$500	0.85	$0	0	$250	0.25	$500	0.75	LS1: Loomes and Sugden
6	$350.00	$362.50	–0.034	$0	0.3	$250	0	$500	0.7	$0	0.15	$250	0.25	$500	0.6	LS2: Loomes and Sugden
7	$350.00	$375.00	–0.067	$0	0.3	$250	0	$500	0.7	$0	0	$250	0.5	$500	0.5	LS3: Loomes and Sugden
8	$362.50	$375.00	–0.033	$0	0.15	$250	0.25	$500	0.6	$0	0	$250	0.5	$500	0.5	LS4: Loomes and Sugden
9	$237.50	$250.00	–0.05	$0	0.15	$250	0.75	$500	0.1	$0	0	$250	1	$500	0	LS5: Loomes and Sugden
10	$200.00	$250.00	–0.2	$0	0.6	$250	0	$500	0.4	$0	0	$250	1	$500	0	LS6: Loomes and Sugden
11	$200.00	$237.50	–0.1579	$0	0.6	$250	0	$500	0.4	$0	0.15	$250	0.75	$500	0.1	LS7: Loomes and Sugden
12	$50.00	$62.50	–0.2	$0	0.9	$250	0	$500	0.1	$0	0.75	$250	0.25	$500	0	LS8: Loomes and Sugden
13	$450.00	$450.00	0	$0	0.1	$250	0	$500	0.9	$0	0	$250	0.2	$500	0.8	LS9: Loomes and Sugden
14	$250.00	$250.00	0	$0	0.5	$250	0	$500	0.5	$0	0.1	$250	0.8	$500	0.1	LS10: Loomes and Sugden

15	$250.00	$250.00	0	$0	0.5	$250	0	$500	0.5	$0	0	$250	1	$500	0	LS11: Loomes and Sugden
16	$250.00	$250.00	0	$0	0.1	$250	0.8	$500	0.1	$0	0	$250	1	$500	0	LS12: Loomes and Sugden
17	$150.00	$150.00	0	$0	0.7	$250	0	$500	0.3	$0	0.5	$250	0.4	$500	0.1	LS13: Loomes and Sugden
18	$150.00	$150.00	0	$0	0.7	$250	0	$500	0.3	$0	0.4	$250	0.6	$500	0	LS14: Loomes and Sugden
19	$150.00	$150.00	0	$0	0.5	$250	0.4	$500	0.1	$0	0.4	$250	0.6	$500	0	LS15: Loomes and Sugden
20	$50.00	$50.00	0	$0	0.9	$250	0	$500	0.1	$0	0.8	$250	0.2	$500	0	LS16: Loomes and Sugden
21	$450.00	$437.50	0.0286	$0	0.1	$250	0	$500	0.9	$0	0	$250	0.25	$500	0.75	LS17: Loomes and Sugden
22	$300.00	$262.50	0.14286	$0	0.4	$250	0	$500	0.6	$0	0.1	$250	0.75	$500	0.15	LS18: Loomes and Sugden
23	$300.00	$250.00	0.2	$0	0.4	$250	0	$500	0.6	$0	0	$250	1	$500	0	LS19: Loomes and Sugden
24	$262.50	$250.00	0.05	$0	0.1	$250	0.75	$500	0.15	$0	0	$250	1	$500	0	LS20: Loomes and Sugden
25	$150.00	$137.50	0.0909	$0	0.7	$250	0	$500	0.3	$0	0.6	$250	0.25	$500	0.15	LS21: Loomes and Sugden
26	$150.00	$125.00	0.2	$0	0.7	$250	0	$500	0.3	$0	0.5	$250	0.5	$500	0	LS22: Loomes and Sugden
27	$137.50	$125.00	0.1	$0	0.6	$250	0.25	$500	0.15	$0	0.5	$250	0.5	$500	0	LS23: Loomes and Sugden
28	$75.00	$62.50	0.2	$0	0.85	$250	0	$500	0.15	$0	0.75	$250	0.25	$500	0	LS24: Loomes and Sugden
29	$450.00	$425.00	0.0588	$0	0.1	$250	0	$500	0.9	$0	0	$250	0.3	$500	0.7	LS25: Loomes and Sugden
30	$300.00	$250.00	0.2	$0	0.4	$250	0	$500	0.6	$0	0.2	$250	0.6	$500	0.2	LS26: Loomes and Sugden

(Continued)

Table A2. (Continued)

Task	EV left	EV Right	EV Ratio	Left $ 1	Left p 1	Left $ 2	Left p 2	Left $ 3	Left p 3	Right $ 1	Right p 1	Right $ 2	Right p 2	Right $ 3	Right p 3	Notes
31	$300.00	$225.00	0.33333	$0	0.4	$250	0	$500	0.6	$0	0.1	$250	0.9	$500	0	LS27: Loomes and Sugden
32	$250.00	$225.00	0.11111	$0	0.2	$250	0.6	$500	0.2	$0	0.1	$250	0.9	$500	0	LS28: Loomes and Sugden
33	$200.00	$175.00	0.14286	$0	0.6	$250	0	$500	0.4	$0	0.5	$250	0.3	$500	0.2	LS29: Loomes and Sugden
34	$200.00	$150.00	0.33333	$0	0.6	$250	0	$500	0.4	$0	0.4	$250	0.6	$500	0	LS30: Loomes and Sugden
35	$175.00	$150.00	0.16667	$0	0.5	$250	0.3	$500	0.2	$0	0.4	$250	0.6	$500	0	LS31: Loomes and Sugden
36	$100.00	$75.00	0.33333	$0	0.8	$250	0	$500	0.2	$0	0.7	$250	0.3	$500	0	LS32: Loomes and Sugden
37	$450.00	$400.00	0.125	$0	0.1	$250	0	$500	0.9	$0	0	$250	0.4	$500	0.6	LS33: Loomes and Sugden
38	$375.00	$300.00	0.25	$0	0.25	$250	0	$500	0.75	$0	0.1	$250	0.6	$500	0.3	LS34: Loomes and Sugden
39	$375.00	$250.00	0.5	$0	0.25	$250	0	$500	0.75	$0	0	$250	1	$500	0	LS35: Loomes and Sugden
40	$300.00	$250.00	0.2	$0	0.1	$250	0.6	$500	0.3	$0	0	$250	1	$500	0	LS36: Loomes and Sugden
41	$200.00	$150.00	0.33333	$0	0.5	$250	0.2	$500	0.3	$0	0.4	$250	0.6	$500	0	LS37: Loomes and Sugden
42	$225.00	$150.00	0.5	$0	0.55	$250	0	$500	0.45	$0	0.4	$250	0.6	$500	0	LS38: Loomes and Sugden
43	$225.00	$200.00	0.125	$0	0.55	$250	0	$500	0.45	$0	0.5	$250	0.2	$500	0.3	LS39: Loomes and Sugden
44	$150.00	$100.00	0.5	$0	0.7	$250	0	$500	0.3	$0	0.6	$250	0.4	$500	0	LS40: Loomes and Sugden
45	($450.00)	($450.00)	0	$0	0.1	($250)	0	($500)	0.9	$0	0	($250)	0.2	($500)	0.8	LS9: Loomes and Sugden

46	($250.00)	($250.00)	0	$0	0.5	($250)	0	($500)	0.5	$0	0.1	($250)	0.8	($500)	0.1	LS10: Loomes and Sugden
47	($250.00)	($250.00)	0	$0	0.5	($250)	0	($500)	0.5	$0	0	($250)	1	($500)	0	LS11: Loomes and Sugden
48	($250.00)	($250.00)	0	$0	0.1	($250)	0.8	($500)	0.1	$0	0	($250)	1	($500)	0	LS12: Loomes and Sugden
49	($150.00)	($150.00)	0	$0	0.7	($250)	0	($500)	0.3	$0	0.5	($250)	0.4	($500)	0.1	LS13: Loomes and Sugden
50	($150.00)	($150.00)	0	$0	0.7	($250)	0	($500)	0.3	$0	0.4	($250)	0.6	($500)	0	LS14: Loomes and Sugden
51	($150.00)	($150.00)	0	$0	0.5	($250)	0.4	($500)	0.1	$0	0.4	($250)	0.6	($500)	0	LS15: Loomes and Sugden
52	($50.00)	($50.00)	0	$0	0.9	($250)	0	($500)	0.1	$0	0.8	($250)	0.2	($500)	0	LS16: Loomes and Sugden
53	($450.00)	($400.00)	0.125	$0	0.1	($250)	0	($500)	0.9	$0	0	($250)	0.4	($500)	0.6	LS33: Loomes and Sugden
54	($375.00)	($300.00)	0.25	$0	0.25	($250)	0	($500)	0.75	$0	0.1	($250)	0.6	($500)	0.3	LS34: Loomes and Sugden
55	($375.00)	($250.00)	0.5	$0	0.25	($250)	0	($500)	0.75	$0	0	($250)	1	($500)	0	LS35: Loomes and Sugden
56	($300.00)	($250.00)	0.2	$0	0.1	($250)	0.6	($500)	0.3	$0	0	($250)	1	($500)	0	LS36: Loomes and Sugden
57	($200.00)	($150.00)	0.33333	$0	0.5	($250)	0.2	($500)	0.3	$0	0.4	($250)	0.6	($500)	0	LS37: Loomes and Sugden
58	($225.00)	($150.00)	0.5	$0	0.55	($250)	0	($500)	0.45	$0	0.4	($250)	0.6	($500)	0	LS38: Loomes and Sugden
59	($225.00)	($200.00)	0.125	$0	0.55	($250)	0	($500)	0.45	$0	0.5	($250)	0.2	($500)	0.3	LS39: Loomes and Sugden
60	($150.00)	($100.00)	0.5	$0	0.7	($250)	0	($500)	0.3	$0	0.6	($250)	0.4	($500)	0	LS40: Loomes and Sugden
61	$425.00	$370.00	0.14865	($250)	0.1	($150)	0	$500	0.9	($250)	0	($150)	0.2	$500	0.8	LS9: Loomes and Sugden

(Continued)

Table A2. (Continued)

Task	EV left	EV Right	EV Ratio	Left $ 1	Left p 1	Left $ 2	Left p 2	Left $ 3	Left p 3	Right $ 1	Right p 1	Right $ 2	Right p 2	Right $ 3	Right p 3	Notes
62	$125.00	($95.00)	−2.3158	($250)	0.5	($150)	0	$500	0.5	($250)	0.1	($150)	0.8	$500	0.1	LS10: Loomes and Sugden
63	$125.00	($150.00)	−1.8333	($250)	0.5	($150)	0	$500	0.5	($250)	0	($150)	1	$500	0	LS11: Loomes and Sugden
64	($95.00)	($150.00)	−0.3667	($250)	0.1	($150)	0.8	$500	0.1	($250)	0	($150)	1	$500	0	LS12: Loomes and Sugden
65	($25.00)	($135.00)	−0.8148	($250)	0.7	($150)	0	$500	0.3	($250)	0.5	($150)	0.4	$500	0.1	LS13: Loomes and Sugden
66	($25.00)	($190.00)	−0.8684	($250)	0.7	($150)	0	$500	0.3	($250)	0.4	($150)	0.6	$500	0	LS14: Loomes and Sugden
67	($135.00)	($190.00)	−0.2895	($250)	0.5	($150)	0.4	$500	0.1	($250)	0.4	($150)	0.6	$500	0	LS15: Loomes and Sugden
68	($175.00)	($230.00)	−0.2391	($250)	0.9	($150)	0	$500	0.1	($250)	0.8	($150)	0.2	$500	0	LS16: Loomes and Sugden
69	$425.00	$240.00	0.77083	($250)	0.1	($150)	0	$500	0.9	($250)	0	($150)	0.4	$500	0.6	LS33: Loomes and Sugden
70	$312.50	$35.00	7.92857	($250)	0.25	($150)	0	$500	0.75	($250)	0.1	($150)	0.6	$500	0.3	LS34: Loomes and Sugden
71	$312.50	($150.00)	−3.0833	($250)	0.25	($150)	0	$500	0.75	($250)	0	($150)	1	$500	0	LS35: Loomes and Sugden
72	$35.00	($150.00)	−1.2333	($250)	0.1	($150)	0.6	$500	0.3	($250)	0	($150)	1	$500	0	LS36: Loomes and Sugden
73	($5.00)	($190.00)	−0.9737	($250)	0.5	($150)	0.2	$500	0.3	($250)	0.4	($150)	0.6	$500	0	LS37: Loomes and Sugden
74	$87.50	($190.00)	−1.4605	($250)	0.55	($150)	0	$500	0.45	($250)	0.4	($150)	0.6	$500	0	LS38: Loomes and Sugden
75	$87.50	($5.00)	−18.5	($250)	0.55	($150)	0	$500	0.45	($250)	0.5	($150)	0.2	$500	0.3	LS39: Loomes and Sugden
76	($25.00)	($210.00)	−0.881	($250)	0.7	($150)	0	$500	0.3	($250)	0.6	($150)	0.4	$500	0	LS40: Loomes and Sugden

77	$52.50	$50.00	0.05	$10	0.15	$20	0	$60	0.85	$10	0	$20	0.25	$60	0.75	LS1: Loomes and Sugden
78	$45.00	$42.50	0.0588	$10	0.3	$20	0	$60	0.7	$10	0.15	$20	0.25	$60	0.6	LS2: Loomes and Sugden
79	$45.00	$40.00	0.125	$10	0.3	$20	0	$60	0.7	$10	0	$20	0.5	$60	0.5	LS3: Loomes and Sugden
80	$42.50	$40.00	0.0625	$10	0.15	$20	0.25	$60	0.6	$10	0	$20	0.5	$60	0.5	LS4: Loomes and Sugden
81	$22.50	$20.00	0.125	$10	0.15	$20	0.75	$60	0.1	$10	0	$20	1	$60	0	LS5: Loomes and Sugden
82	$30.00	$20.00	0.5	$10	0.6	$20	0	$60	0.4	$10	0	$20	1	$60	0	LS6: Loomes and Sugden
83	$30.00	$22.50	0.33333	$10	0.6	$20	0	$60	0.4	$10	0.15	$20	0.75	$60	0.1	LS7: Loomes and Sugden
84	$15.00	$12.50	0.2	$10	0.9	$20	0	$60	0.1	$10	0.75	$20	0.25	$60	0	LS8: Loomes and Sugden
85	$50.00	$47.50	0.0526	$5	0.1	$25	0	$55	0.9	$5	0	$25	0.25	$55	0.75	LS17: Loomes and Sugden
86	$35.00	$27.50	0.27273	$5	0.4	$25	0	$55	0.6	$5	0.1	$25	0.75	$55	0.15	LS18: Loomes and Sugden
87	$35.00	$25.00	0.4	$5	0.4	$25	0	$55	0.6	$5	0	$25	1	$55	0	LS19: Loomes and Sugden
88	$27.50	$25.00	0.1	$5	0.1	$25	0.75	$55	0.15	$5	0	$25	1	$55	0	LS20: Loomes and Sugden
89	$20.00	$17.50	0.14286	$5	0.7	$25	0	$55	0.3	$5	0.6	$25	0.25	$55	0.15	LS21: Loomes and Sugden
90	$20.00	$15.00	0.33333	$5	0.7	$25	0	$55	0.3	$5	0.5	$25	0.5	$55	0	LS22: Loomes and Sugden
91	$17.50	$15.00	0.16667	$5	0.6	$25	0.25	$55	0.15	$5	0.5	$25	0.5	$55	0	LS23: Loomes and Sugden
92	$12.50	$10.00	0.25	$5	0.85	$25	0	$55	0.15	$5	0.75	$25	0.25	$55	0	LS24: Loomes and Sugden

(Continued)

Table A2. (Continued)

Task	EV left	EV Right	EV Ratio	Left $ 1	Left p 1	Left $ 2	Left p 2	Left $ 3	Left p 3	Right $ 1	Right p 1	Right $ 2	Right p 2	Right $ 3	Right p 3	Notes
93	$42.00	$40.50	0.037	$15	0.1	$30	0	$45	0.9	$15	0	$30	0.3	$45	0.7	LS25: Loomes and Sugden
94	$33.00	$30.00	0.1	$15	0.4	$30	0	$45	0.6	$15	0.2	$30	0.6	$45	0.2	LS26: Loomes and Sugden
95	$33.00	$28.50	0.15789	$15	0.4	$30	0	$45	0.6	$15	0.1	$30	0.9	$45	0	LS27: Loomes and Sugden
96	$30.00	$28.50	0.0526	$15	0.2	$30	0.6	$45	0.2	$15	0.1	$30	0.9	$45	0	LS28: Loomes and Sugden
97	$27.00	$25.50	0.0588	$15	0.6	$30	0	$45	0.4	$15	0.5	$30	0.3	$45	0.2	LS29: Loomes and Sugden
98	$27.00	$24.00	0.125	$15	0.6	$30	0	$45	0.4	$15	0.4	$30	0.6	$45	0	LS30: Loomes and Sugden
99	$25.50	$24.00	0.0625	$15	0.5	$30	0.3	$45	0.2	$15	0.4	$30	0.6	$45	0	LS31: Loomes and Sugden
100	$21.00	$19.50	0.0769	$15	0.8	$30	0	$45	0.2	$15	0.7	$30	0.3	$45	0	LS32: Loomes and Sugden

APPENDIX B: NUMERICAL EXAMPLES OF DECISION WEIGHTS

To understand the mechanics of evaluating lotteries using RDU and CPT it is useful to see worked numerical examples. Although this is purely a pedagogic exercise, in our experience many users of RDU and CPT are not familiar with these mechanics, and they are critical to the correct application of these models. Even the best pedagogic source available, Wakker (2010), leaves many worked examples as exercises, and many of the examples are correctly contrived to make a special pedagogic point. The most general source, actually, is an online computer program on Peter Wakker's home page that calculates values for CPT using the Inverse-S probability weighting function and up to four outcomes:

http://people.few.eur.nl/wakker/miscella/calculate.cpt.kobb/index.htm

We use this program to generate some examples to illustrate the logic of decision weights under CPT.

The building block for understanding the construction of decision weights under CPT, for the general case of a mixed-frame lottery, is the construction of decision weights for gains under RDU. We provide one detailed example there, and then examine the CPT extension.

B.1 Rank-dependent Decision Weights

Assume a simple power probability weighting function $\omega(p) = p^{\gamma}$ and let $\gamma = 1.25$. To see the pure effect of probability weighting, assume $U(x) = x$ for $x \geq 0$. Start with a two-prize lottery, then consider three prizes and four prizes to see the general logic.

In the two-prize case, let y be the smaller prize and Y be the larger prize, so $Y > y \geq 0$. Again, to see the pure effect of probability weighting, assume objective probabilities $p(y) = p(Y) = ½$. The first step is to get the decision weight of the largest prize. This uses the answer to the question, "what is the probability of getting at *least* Y?"[54] This is obviously ½, so we then calculate the decision weight using the probability weighting function as $\omega(½) = (½)^{\gamma} = 0.42$. To keep notation for probability weights and decision weights similar but distinct, denote the *decision* weight for Y as w(Y). Then we have $w(Y) = 0.42$.

The second step for the two-prize case is to give the other, smaller prize y the residual weight. This uses the answer to the question, "what is the probability of getting at *least* y?" Since one always gets at least y, the answer is obviously 1. Since $\omega(1) = 1$ for any of the popular probability weighting functions,[55] we can attribute the decision weight $\omega(1) - \omega(½) = 1 - 0.42 = 0.58$ to the prize y. Another way to see the same thing is to directly calculate the decision weight for the smallest prize to ensure that the decision weights sum to 1, so that the decision weight w(y) is calculated as $1 - w(Y) = 1 - 0.42 = 0.58$. The two-prize case actually makes it harder to see the rank-dependent logic than when we examine the three-prize or four-prize case, and can be seen in retrospect as a special case.

With these two decision weights in place, the RDU evaluation of the lottery is $0.42 \times U(Y) + 0.58 \times U(y)$, or $0.42Y + 0.58y$ given our simplifying assumption of a linear utility function. Inspection of this RDU evaluation, and viewing the decision weights as if they were probabilities, shows why the RDU evaluation has to be less than the Expected Value (EV) of the lottery using the true probabilities, since that is $0.5Y + 0.5y$. The RDU evaluation puts more weight on the worst prize, and greater weight on the better prize, so it has to have a CE that is less than the EV (this last step is helped by the fact that $U(x) = x$, of course). Hence probability weighting in this case generates a CE that is less than the EV, and hence a risk premium.

However, the two-prize case collapses the essential logic of the RDU model. Consider a three-prize case in which we use the same probability weighting functions and utility functions, but have three prizes, y, Y and **Y**, where $\mathbf{Y} > Y > y$, and $p(y) = p(Y) = p(\mathbf{Y}) = ⅓$.

The decision weight for **Y** is evaluated first, and uses the answer to the question, "what is the probability of getting at least **Y**?" The answer is ⅓, so the decision weight for **Y** is then directly evaluated as $w(\mathbf{Y}) = \omega(⅓) = (⅓)^{\gamma} = 0.25$.

The decision weight for Y is evaluated next, and uses the answer to the more interesting question, "what is the probability of getting at *least* Y?" This is $p(Y) + p(\mathbf{Y}) = ⅓ + ⅓ = ⅔$, so the probability weight is $\omega(⅔) = (⅔)^{\gamma} = 0.60$. But the only part of this probability weight that is to be attributed solely to Y is the part that is not already attributed to **Y**, hence the decision weight for Y is $\omega(⅔) - \omega(⅓) = \omega(Y) - \omega(\mathbf{Y}) = 0.60 - 0.25 = 0.35$. This intermediate step shows the rank-dependent logic in the clearest fashion. One could equally talk about *cumulative* probability weights, rather than just probability weights, but the logic is simple enough when one thinks of the question being asked "psychologically" and the partial attribution to Y that flows from it. In the two-prize case this partial attribution is skipped over.

The decision weight for y is again evaluated residually, as in the two-prize case. We can either see this by evaluating $\omega(1) - \omega(⅔) = 1 - 0.60 = 0.40$, or by evaluating $1 - w(Y) - w(\mathbf{Y}) = 1 - 0.35 - 0.25 = 0.40$.

The general logic may now be stated in words as follows:

1. Rank the prizes from best to worst.
2. Use the probability weighting function to calculate the probability of getting at least the prize in question.
3. Then assign the decision weight for the best prize directly as the weighted probability of that prize.
4. For each of the intermediate prizes in declining order, assign the decision weight using the weighted cumulative probability for that prize less the decision weights for better prizes (or, equivalently, the weighted cumulative probability for the immediately better prize).
5. For the worst prize the decision weight is the residual decision weight to ensure that the decision weights sum to 1.

The key is to view the decision weights as the *incremental* decision weight attributable to that prize.

Table B1 collects these steps for each of the examples, and adds a four-prize example. From a programming perspective, these calculations are tedious but not difficult as long as one can assume that prizes are rank-ordered as they are evaluated. Our computer code in *Stata* allows for up to four prizes, which spans most applications in laboratory or field settings, and is of course applicable for lotteries with any number of prizes up to four. The logic can be easily extended to more prizes.

Fig. B1 illustrates these calculations using the power probability weighting function. The dashed line in the left panel displays the probability weighting function $\omega(p) = p^{\gamma} = p^{1.25}$, with the vertical axis showing underweighting of the objective probabilities displayed on the bottom axis. The implications for decision weights are then shown in the right panel, for the two-prize, three-prize, and four-prize cases. In the right panel the bottom axis shows prizes ranked from worst to best, so one immediately identifies the "probability pessimism" at work with this probability weighting function. Values of $\gamma < 1$ generate overweighting of the objective probabilities and "probability optimism," as one might expect.

Fig. B2 shows the effects of using the "inverse-S" probability weighting function $\omega(p) = p^{\gamma}/ (p^{\gamma} + (1 - p)^{\gamma})^{1/\gamma}$ for $\gamma = 0.65$. This function exhibits inverse-S probability weighting (optimism for small p, and pessimism for large p) for $\gamma < 1$, and S-shaped probability weighting (pessimism for small p, and optimism for large p) for $\gamma > 1$. Although one observes a wide range of values of γ in careful applied work, for many CPT advocates the qualitative assumption that $\gamma < 1$ is often regarded as a critical component of CPT.

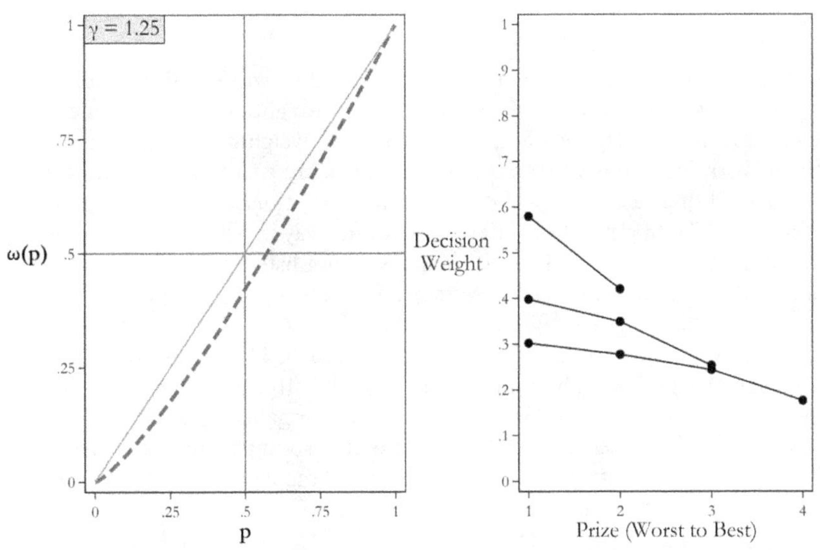

Fig. B1. Power Probability Weighting and Implied Decision Weights for Gains.

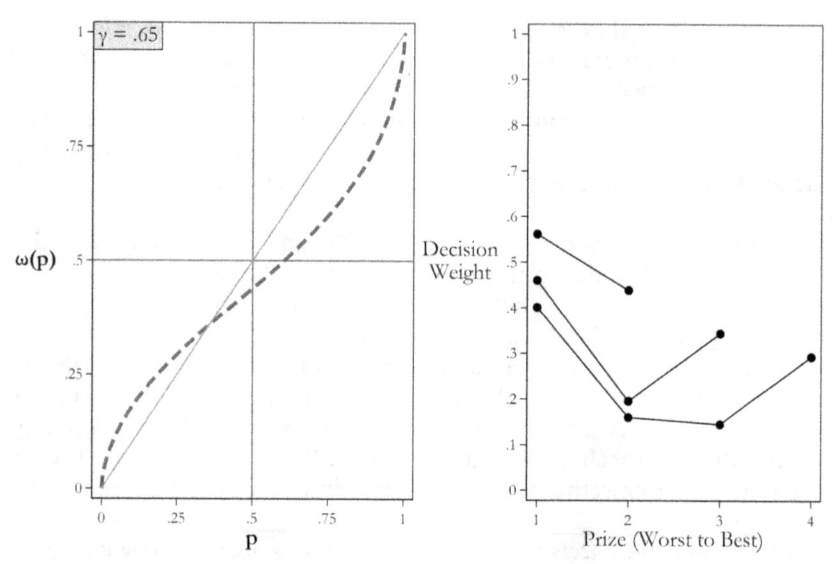

Fig. B2. Inverse-S Probability Weighting and Implied Decision Weights for Gains.

B.2 Cumulative Prospect Theory Decision Weights

The calculation of decision weights for CPT builds on this RDU logic. Indeed, for lotteries that are in the gain frame, there is nothing to add. But for lotteries that are in the loss frame or mixed frame, one has to be careful in applying these procedures.

B.2.1 Loss-frame Decision Weights

Consider a lottery that pays −100, −50, −25 and 0 with equal probability ¼ and EV of −43.75. Assume a Power probability weighting function, since this specification allows us to look at the effects of underweighting and overweighting without worrying about whether the probabilities are small or large. Start with the overweighting case, in which γ^- is 0.5. The tabulations are shown in panel A of Table B2. The first point of difference with the way in which decision weights were calculated for gains in Table B1 is that we have listed the probabilities from Worst to Best, rather than Best to Worst. In fact, that is the only point of difference, apart from using the weighting function with $\gamma^- = 0.5$. This is an application of the notion of loss-ranks, stressed by Wakker (2010, §7.6) in an explication of the history of RDU thought, and then in Wakker (2010, §9.1) when introducing the sign-dependence of CPT. Gain-ranks are used for gains under CPT, and loss-ranks are used for losses under CPT. This point is so important that it is worth being verbose and restate the RDU logic using the language of gain-ranks, so that the parallel with loss-ranks becomes evidence.

Table B1. Tabulations of RDU Examples.

Prize	Probability	Cumulative Probability	Weighted Cumulative Probability	Decision Weight
		A. Two prizes		
Y	0.5	0.5	$0.42 = 0.5^{1.25}$	0.42
y < Y	0.5	1	$1 = 1^{1.25}$	$0.58 = 1 - 0.42$
		B. Three Prizes		
Y	0.33	0.33	$0.25 = 0.33^{1.25}$	0.25
Y < **Y**	0.33	0.67	$0.60 = 0.67^{1.25}$	$0.35 = 0.60 - 0.25$
y < Y < **Y**	0.33	1	$1 = 1^{1.25}$	$0.40 = 1 - 0.60$ $= 1 - 0.35 - 0.25$
		C. Four Prizes		
Best	0.25	0.25	$0.18 = 0.25^{1.25}$	0.18
2nd Best	0.25	0.5	$0.42 = 0.50^{1.25}$	$0.24 = 0.42 - 0.18$
3rd Best	0.25	0.75	$0.70 = 0.75^{1.25}$	$0.28 = 0.70 - 0.42$ $= 1 - 0.24 - 0.18$
Worst	0.25	1	$1^{1.25}$	$0.30 = 1 - 0.70$ $= 1 - 0.28 - 0.24$ $- 0.18$

For gains, in panel C of Table B1, we rank the *best* prize as #1, the second best prize as #2, the third best prize as #3, and the *worst* prize as #4. The probability whose outcome has *gain*-rank 1 is assigned a decision weight that is equal to the weighted probability for that outcome (0.18). Then the probability whose outcome has *gain*-rank 2 is assigned a decision weight equal to the weighted cumulative probability of getting that outcome (0.42) minus the weighted cumulative probability of getting the outcome with *gain*-rank 1 (0.18, so the decision weight is $0.24 = 0.42 - 0.18$). And so on for the remaining outcomes.

Now turn to panel A of Table B2, with losses. We rank the *worst* prize as #1, the second worst prize as #2, the third worst prize as #3, and the *best* prize as #4. The probability whose outcome has *loss*-rank 1 is assigned a decision weight that is equal to the weighted probability for that outcome (0.50). Then the probability whose outcome has *loss*-rank 2 is assigned a decision weight equal to the weighted

Table B2. Tabulations of CPT Loss-frame Examples.

Prize	Probability	Cumulative probability	Weighted cumulative probability	Decision weight
		A. Overweighting		
Worst	0.25	0.25	$0.50 = 0.25^{0.5}$	0.5
2nd Worst	0.25	0.5	$0.71 = 0.50^{0.5}$	$0.21 = 0.71 - 0.50$
3rd Worst	0.25	0.75	$0.87 = 0.75^{0.5}$	$0.16 = 0.87 - 0.71$
Best	0.25	1	$1^{0.5}$	$0.13 = 1 - 0.87$
		B. Underweighting		
Worst	0.25	0.25	$0.18 = 0.25^{1.25}$	0.18
2nd Worst	0.25	0.5	$0.42 = 0.50^{1.25}$	$0.24 = 0.42 - 0.18$
3rd Worst	0.25	0.75	$0.70 = 0.75^{1.25}$	$0.28 = 0.70 - 0.42$
Best	0.25	1	$1^{1.25}$	$0.30 = 1 - 0.70$

cumulative probability of getting that outcome (0.71) minus the weighted cumulative probability of getting the outcome with loss-rank 1 (0.50, so the decision weight is 0.21 = 0.71 − 0.50). And so on for the remaining outcomes.

To drive home the parallel nature of the calculations, once the shift from gain-ranks to loss-ranks has been made, in panel B of Table B2 we consider an underweighting Power probability weighting with $\gamma^{-} = 1.25$, exactly the same function that was used in panel C of Table B1. Apart from the listing of probabilities from worst outcome to best outcome, the calculations are identical!

Putting aside the mechanics of calculating these decision weights, focus on the effect of overweighting and underweighting on the final decision weights, recalling of course that the underlying objective probabilities were each ¼. In the overweighting case the decisions weights put greater weight on the worst outcomes compared to the best outcomes, so if the utility function was linear, it is apparent that the CE would be lower than the EV by construction, implying a positive risk premium and, *ceteris paribus*, risk aversion. In the underweighting case the decisions weights put greater weight on the best outcomes compared to the worst outcomes, so if the utility function was linear the CE would be higher than the EV, implying a negative risk premium and, *ceteris paribus*, risk seeking. So we end up with the reverse effect of overweighting and underweighting in terms of risk aversion compared to the gain frame.

B.2.2 Mixed-frame Decision Weights

The logic here is to initially parse the mixed-frame lottery into a gain lottery and a loss lottery, evaluate each of those two parsed lotteries while ensuring that each has residual weight on the "zero outcome," and then add the parsed evaluations. The "zero outcome" here is in quotation marks because it refers to the assumed reference point, which need not be zero in any currency units, although it often is. In our analysis the "zero outcome" is in fact the endowment given to subjects, and hence it embodies the assumption that subjects fail to locally asset integrate the endowment with the framed prizes. The logic of the example below is general, but one needs to keep this distinction in mind when generalizing CPT to other reference points.

We employ the following notation, found in many CPT studies. Rank order the n outcomes so that

$$x_1 \geq \cdots \geq x_k \geq 0 \geq x_{k+1} \geq \cdots \geq x_n$$

so that the kth and k + 1th outcomes mark the dividing line between gains and losses. Then define the mixed-frame lottery as

$$P: (x_1, p_1; \ldots; x_k, p_k; 0, p_0; x_{k+1}, p_{k+1}; \ldots; x_n, p_n)$$

Note that it is quite possible that $p_0 = 0$ in the specification of P. The mixed-frame lottery is then parsed into a gain-frame component and a loss-frame component. The gain-frame component is defined as

$$P+: (x_1, p_1; \ldots; x_k, p_k; 0, p_0 + p_{k+1} + \ldots + p_n),$$

where the "zero outcome" is assigned all of the probability mass for *losses*, as well as any probability mass originally assigned to p_0. The loss-frame component is defined as

$$P-: (0, p_1 + \cdots + p_k + p_0; x_{k+1}, p_{k+1}; \ldots; x_n, p_n),$$

where the "zero outcome" is assigned all of the probability mass for *gains*, as well as any probability mass originally assigned to p_0. One then evaluates the cumulative prospective utility of P+ and P−, which we can denote CPU(P+) and CPU(P−), and then these are literally added together to get the cumulative prospective utility of the mixed-frame lottery P:

$$CPU(P) = CPU(P+) + CPU(P-)$$

Thus if we know how to evaluate the RDU decision weights for P+ using gain-ranks, and the decision weights for loss-frame prospects such as P− using loss-ranks, we can generate the decision weights for all types of lotteries using CPT.[56]

To take a textbook example, consider Exercise 9.34 from Wakker (2010, p. 257). In this case $u(x) = x^{\alpha}$ for $x \geq 0$ and $u(x) = x^{\beta}$ for $x < 0$, with $\alpha = \beta = 0.5$, $\omega(p^+) = (p^+)^2$ for gains, $\omega(p^-) = p^-$ for losses, and $\lambda = 2$. Let the mixed-frame gamble be

$$P: (9, 0.1; 4, 0.4; -4, 0.4, -9, 0.1)$$

so the parsed gain-frame component is

$$P+: (9, 0.1; 4, 0.5; 0, 0.5)$$

and the parsed loss-frame component is

$$P-: (0, 0.5; -4, 0.4, -9, 0.1)\,.$$

Tables B3 and B4 show the detailed application of this parsing process.

To take a full-blooded example, consider the default lottery on the web page referred to earlier. This specification uses the Inverse-S probability weighting function, with parameters $\gamma^+ = 0.61$ and $\gamma^- = 0.69$ in terms of our notation. There are two negative prizes, and two positive prizes in the lottery, and equal probability ¼ for each outcome. Table B5 spells out the calculations in the manner in which we have been presenting them, ending up with exactly the same answers apart from trivial rounding errors. We explicitly list the "fake 0 reference point" that is added to P+ and P−, although these are arithmetically irrelevant. The symbol ✂ means that the numerical value in that cell is cut out, since it is not needed to identify the final decision weights.

Table B3. Initial Tabulation of CPT Example.

x	p	u(x)	$-\lambda u(-x)$	x+ or x−	'p	ω ('p)	w(x)
			I. Evaluation of P+				
−9	0.1		$-6 = -2\times\sqrt{9}$	0	1	1	0.19
−4	0.4		$-4 = -2\times\sqrt{4}$	0	0.9	0.81	0.56
4	0.4	$2 = \sqrt{4}$		4	0.5	0.25	0.24
9	0.1	$3 = \sqrt{9}$		9	0.1	0.01	0.01
			II. Evaluation of P-				
−9	0.1		$-6 = -2\times\sqrt{9}$	−9	0.1	0.1	0.1
−4	0.4		$-4 = -2\times\sqrt{4}$	−4	0.5	0.5	0.4
4	0.4	$2 = \sqrt{4}$		0	0.9	0.9	0.4
9	0.1	$3 = \sqrt{9}$		0	1	1	0.1

Table B4. Final Tabulation of CPT Example.

x	P	U(x) = u(x)	U(x) = $-\lambda \times u(-x)$	w(x) if $x \geq 0$	w(x) if $x < 0$	CPU(x) = w(x)×U(x)	EU(x) = p × u(x)
−9	0.1		−6		0.1	−0.6	−0.3
−4	0.4		−4		0.4	−1.6	−0.8
4	0.4	2		0.24		0.48	0.8
9	0.1	3		0.01		0.03	0.3
Sum						−1.69	0

Table B5. Tabulations of CPT Mixed-frame Examples From Wakker Home Page.

Prize	Probability	Cumulative Probability	Weighted Cumulative Probability	Decision Weight
		A. Gain Frame		
Best (200)	0.25	0.25	0.29	0.29
2nd Best (50)	0.25	0.5	0.42	0.13 = 0.42 − 0.29
3rd Best (Fake 0)	0.25	0.75	✂	✂
Worst (Fake 0)	0.25	1	✂	✂
		B. Loss Frame		
Worst (−200)	0.25	0.25	0.29	0.29
2nd Worst (−50)	0.25	0.5	0.45	0.16 = 0.45 − 0.29
3rd Worst (Fake 0)	0.25	0.75	✂	✂
Best (Fake 0)	0.25	1	✂	✂

CHAPTER 4

TEMPORAL STABILITY OF CUMULATIVE PROSPECT THEORY

Morten I. Lau, Hong Il Yoo and Hongming Zhao

ABSTRACT

We evaluate the hypothesis of temporal stability in risk preferences using two recent data sets from longitudinal lab experiments. Both experiments included a combination of decision tasks that allows one to identify a full set of structural parameters characterizing risk preferences under Cumulative Prospect Theory (CPT), including loss aversion. We consider temporal stability in those structural parameters at both population and individual levels. The population-level stability pertains to whether the distribution of risk preferences across individuals in the subject population remains stable over time. The individual-level stability pertains to within-individual correlation in risk preferences over time. We embed the CPT structure in a random coefficient model that allows us to evaluate temporal stability at both levels in a coherent manner, without having to switch between different sets of models to draw inferences at a specific level.

Keywords: Cumulative Prospect Theory; risk preferences; temporal stability; laboratory experiment; random coefficient; maximum simulated likelihood

1. INTRODUCTION

Temporal stability of risk preferences is a common assumption in evaluations of economic behavior, yet there is very little empirical information on the stability

Models of Risk Preferences: Descriptive and Normative Challenges
Research in Experimental Economics, Volume 22, 193–226

ISSN: 0193-2306/doi:10.1108/S0193-230620230000022004

of risk attitudes over time. Chuang and Schechter (2015) identify 19 empirical studies on this topic, but the list shrinks to nine studies after excluding experiments with hypothetical decision tasks, and further down to four studies once one focuses on studies that quantified risk attitudes structurally in relation to decision theories.[1] Temporal stability has direct implications for the validity of studies that utilize the earlier estimates of risk attitudes as input into further theorizing and empirical investigations. A prominent example is the large body of studies in finance that apply CPT to explain market anomalies (e.g., Barberis, Mukherjee, & Wang, 2016; Kaustia, 2010), based on the point estimates reported by Tversky and Kahneman (1992) in their seminal study. Admittedly, it is often claimed that subsequent studies using data from lab experiments have repeatedly found similar point estimates. Harrison and Swarthout (2023), however, conduct a critical review of the existing empirical findings on CPT and refute such claims.

We test the assumption of temporal stability in risk preferences, by analyzing data from two existing longitudinal laboratory experiments used by Murphy and ten Brincke (2018) (MTB) and Glöckner and Pachur (2012) (GP). Our main focus is on structural econometric models of CPT that characterize risk preferences in terms of utility curvature, loss aversion and probability weighting. We also consider a more parsimonious model based on Expected Utility Theory (EUT), which equates risk preferences with utility curvature. Most studies evaluate temporal stability *either* at the population level *or* at the individual level, as they use standard models for interval data or discrete choice data that preclude drawing inferences at both levels simultaneously. In contrast, we adopt a random coefficient approach based on Harrison, Lau, and Yoo (2020) to specify a coherent structural model, which allows us to evaluate temporal stability at both the population level and the individual level. In a nutshell, we assume that individual-level structural parameters follow a population distribution that varies over time, and allow for correlation between the population distributions at different time periods. The full set of correlation coefficients measure within-individual correlation in structural parameters within and between the two waves of the longitudinal experiment. We evaluate temporal stability at the population level by testing for stability in the population distribution, and at the individual level by examining the correlation coefficients between the two waves of the longitudinal experiment.

As noted at the outset, Chuang and Schechter (2015) identified four studies that used data from experiments with real monetary rewards to test for temporal stability of risk preferences. Harrison, Johnson, McInnes, and Rutström (2005) and Andersen, Harrison, Lau, and Rutström (2008) evaluate stability in the population mean of risk preferences under EUT, while Wölbert and Riedl (2013) focuses on within-individual correlation in risk preferences under Rank Dependent Utility (RDU). Our study is closely related to the remaining study by Harrison et al. (2020), which considers both EUT and RDU. This study also considers temporal stability at both the population and the individual level. They find mixed results under either decision theory: the population distribution of risk preferences remains stable over the one-year time period in their experiment, and there is positive, albeit imperfect, within-individual correlation in risk attitudes over time.[2]

We are also aware of three studies that evaluated temporal stability of risk preferences under CPT, though none of them appears in the review by Chuang and Schechter (2015) presumably because they have been published outside the economics literature. Glöckner and Pachur (2012) and Zeisberger, Vrecko, and Langer (2012) evaluate temporal stability at the individual level, by estimating one set of structural parameters for each individual subject, and comparing the point estimates over one-week and one-month time intervals, respectively.[3] They do not, however, consider temporal stability at the population level. Murphy and ten Brincke (2018) similarly evaluate temporal stability at the individual level, although they briefly comment on the point estimates for a restrictive population distribution that assumes away within-individual correlation in risk attitudes over time.[4]

We draw several conclusions from our statistical analysis. First, *we find temporal instability at the population level under CPT*. The entire population distribution of risk preferences may be said to be stable when the population joint distribution of all parameters in the CPT model is stable, and we reject this hypothesis for both data sets. Moreover, for the MTB data set, we also find temporal instability in the population marginal distribution of all but one parameters.[5] By contrast, for the GP data set, we cannot reject temporal stability in any population marginal distribution. The latter results suggest that temporal stability in the population marginal distributions of the parameters does not necessarily lead to temporal stability in the population joint distribution of those parameters in a statistical sense.

Second, when we focus on the within-individual correlation coefficients of risk preferences, *we draw mixed conclusions on temporal stability at the individual level.* We find strong positive between-wave correlations for all the estimated parameters in the CPT model for the MTB data, but much weaker and insignificant correlation coefficients for the GP data. The range of results on temporal stability reflect the strengths of our empirical specifications that allow us to define and test temporal stability in several ways.

Third, *we find temporal stability at both the individual level and the population level under EUT*. We cannot reject the hypothesis that the estimated population distributions of risk preferences are temporally stable for each data set, and we also find significant positive correlation between the estimated random coefficients for both data sets. Hence, our inferences on temporal stability depend on the underlying specification of risk preferences; we find temporal stability of risk preferences in the single-parameter EUT framework, but temporal instability at the population level in the multi-parameter CPT framework.

2. DATA

We use binary choice data from two existing longitudinal studies that allow one to estimate the full set of parameters in CPT models and test for temporal parameter stability. We focus only on longitudinal experiments with incentivized decision tasks, and more specifically on the experiments by Glöckner and Pachur (2012) and Murphy and ten Brincke (2018). Both studies adopted binary choice methods to elicit individual risk preferences, where each option in the decision tasks was a lottery with two monetary outcomes.[6]

The experimental designs in GP and MTB are similar in many respects and the experiments were conducted with student samples at two different German universities. Risk attitudes were evaluated from data in which subjects made a series of binary lottery choices. There were 138 (91) risk aversion tasks in the GP (MTB) experiment, and they asked each subject to respond to all decision tasks. The GP experiment was conducted at the University of Bonn with a sample of 66 subjects and repeated one week after the first experiment with a sub-sample of 64 subjects. The MTB experiment was conducted at the Max Planck Institute for Human Development in Berlin with a sample of 142 subjects and repeated two weeks after the initial experiment with the same sample.[7] Prizes in the decision tasks varied between –€10 and €12 in the GP experiment and between –€10 and €10 in the MTB experiment, and in both experiments one decision task was randomly selected for payment at the end of the session. The subjects were paid a fixed fee for their participation, €22 in the GP experiment and €10 in the MTB experiment, which was sufficient to cover any possible losses from the decision tasks.

Both MTB and GP used decision tasks with a combination of pairwise choices in the gain frame, loss frame, and mixed frame. MTB used the same set of 91 decision tasks in both waves of the experiment, with 35 decisions in the gain frame, 25 decisions in the loss frame, and the remaining 31 decisions in the mixed frame. GP used two sets of 138 decision tasks, one set in the first wave and another set in the second wave, where 38 of the decision tasks were identical across the two waves. Responses to pairwise lottery choices in the gain frame can be used to identify utility curvature and probability weighting over gains, along with the scale of a stochastic error term for gains; responses to choices in the loss frame can be used to identify utility curvature and probability weighting over losses, and the scale of a stochastic error term for losses; and responses to mixed frame lotteries can be used to identify the loss aversion parameter and the scale of a stochastic error term for mixed outcomes.

3. STRUCTURAL ESTIMATION OF RISK PREFERENCES

We first write out a structural model to estimate risk attitudes assuming EUT to illustrate our maximum simulated likelihood estimation method, and then discuss the extension to the CPT model that accounts for probability weighting and loss aversion. The CPT model allows for different utility and probability weighting functions over gains and losses in both waves. The CPT model also allows for the full set of pairwise correlation coefficients for all specified random coefficients within and across the two waves of the longitudinal experiment.

3.1 Baseline EUT Specification

Consider the estimation of risk preferences in the simplest possible model of decision-making under risk, EUT. In the two experiments that we consider here, each decision task presented a choice between two lotteries, and each lottery had two potential outcomes where some are framed as positive and some as negative. EUT assumes full integration of endowments and prizes in the decision tasks, which implies that all outcomes are treated as positive.[8] Let M_{ij} be the jth outcome of lottery i, where i = A,B and j = 1,2. Assume that the utility of an outcome is given by the hyperbolic absolute risk aversion (HARA) specification:

$$U(M_{ij}) = (M_{ij} + \kappa)^r/r - \kappa^r/r \text{ for } M_{ij} \geq 0 \text{ and } r \neq 0, \tag{1}$$

where r is the HARA coefficient, and κ is a small positive constant that we set to 0.0001. Then, under EUT, $r = 1$ denotes risk neutral behavior, $r < 1$ denotes risk aversion, and $r > 1$ denotes risk seeking behavior. Of course, when κ is close to 0 as in our case, this function is almost identical to the usual constant relative risk aversion (CRRA) utility function.[9] The reason for using the HARA specification instead of the canonical CRRA specification will become evident in our discussion of CPT in the following subsection.

EUT predicts that the observed choice is the lottery with the higher expected utility (EU). Probabilities for each outcome, $p(M_{ij})$, are induced by the experimenter, so the EU of lottery i is

$$EU_i = p(M_{i1}) \times U(M_{i1}) + p(M_{i2}) \times U(M_{i2}), \tag{2}$$

where $p(M_{i2}) = 1 - p(M_{i1})$. Let y denote a binary indicator of whether the observed choice is lottery B ($y = 1$) or lottery A ($y = 0$). Using the indicator function $\mathbf{I}(.)$, the observed choice under EUT can be written as $y = \mathbf{I}[(EU_B - EU_A) > 0]$.

To allow observed choices to deviate from deterministic theoretical predictions, the EUT model is combined with a stochastic behavioral error term. Specifically, assume that the choice depends not only on the EU difference, but also on a random error term ε such that $y = \mathbf{I}[(EU_B - EU_A) + \varepsilon > 0]$. Assume further that ε is normally distributed with the standard deviation of μ, $\varepsilon \sim N(0, \mu^2)$. The choice probability of lottery B is then $\Phi(\nabla EU/\mu)$ where $\Phi(.)$ is the standard normal cumulative density function (CDF), and ∇EU is the expected utility difference

$$\nabla EU = (EU_B - EU_A). \tag{3}$$

It follows that the likelihood function for each choice observation takes the form

$$P(r, \mu) = \Phi(\nabla EU/\mu)^y \times (1 - \Phi(\nabla EU/\mu))^{(1-y)}. \tag{4}$$

As the noise parameter μ approaches 0, this stochastic EUT specification collapses to the deterministic EUT model; conversely, as μ gets arbitrarily large, it converges to an uninformative model which predicts a 50:50 chance regardless of the underlying EU difference. This is one of several types of behavioral error stories that could be used (Wilcox, 2008).

To clarify our econometric methods, more notation is needed than one would typically see in the context of non-linear models for panel data. We subscript the choice-level likelihood function in Eq. (4) as $P_{ntw}(r_{nw}, \mu)$ henceforth, to emphasize that it describes subject n's choice in decision task t of panel wave w.[10] The utility curvature parameter r_{nw} is indexed by subject n and wave w for two reasons. First, to capture unobserved preference heterogeneity across individuals, we model the utility curvature parameter as an individual-specific random coefficient drawn from a population distribution of risk preferences. Second, to test temporal stability, we allow the underlying population distribution, as well as the utility curvature parameter drawn from it, to vary freely across waves. We use $f(r_{n1}, r_{n2}; \theta)$ to denote the joint density function for the random utility curvature parameters, where θ is a set of parameters that characterize their joint distribution.

It is possible to estimate the set of parameters θ directly and draw inferences about the population distribution of risk preferences, once the joint density $f(r_{n1}, r_{n2}; \theta)$ is fully specified. Assume that r_{n1} and r_{n2} are jointly normal so that $\theta = (\bar{r}_1, \bar{r}_2, \sigma_{r1}, \sigma_{r2,} \sigma_{r1r2})$, where $\bar{r}_w$ and σ_{rw} are the population mean and standard deviation of the utility curvature parameter r_{nw}, and σ_{r1r2} is the covariance between r_{n1} and $r_{n2.}$ Conditional on a particular pair of values drawn for r_{n1} and r_{n2}, the likelihood of observing a series of choices made by subject n in both waves can be specified as

$$CL_n(r_{n1}, r_{n2}, \mu) = \Pi_t P_{nt1}(r_{n1}, \mu) \times \Pi_t P_{nt2}(r_{n2}, \mu)\,. \tag{5}$$

Since r_{n1} and r_{n2} are modeled as random coefficients, the "unconditional" (Train, 2019, p. 146) or actual likelihood of subject n's choices is then obtained by taking the expected value of $CL_n(r_{n1}, r_{n2}, \mu)$ over the joint density $f(r_{n1}, r_{n2}; \theta)$

$$\begin{aligned} &L_n(\bar{r}_1, \bar{r}_2, \sigma_{r1}, \sigma_{r2,} \sigma_{r1r2}, \mu) = L_n(\theta, \mu) \\ &= \int\int CL_n(r_{n1}, r_{n2}, \mu) f(r_{n1}, r_{n2}; \theta) dr_{n1} dr_{n2}. \end{aligned} \tag{6}$$

The unconditional likelihood function $L_n(\theta, \mu)$ does not have a closed-form expression, but can be approximated using simulation methods (Train, 2019, pp. 144–145). We compute maximum simulated likelihood (MSL) estimates of risk preference parameters θ and the behavioral noise parameter μ by maximizing a simulated analogue to the sample log-likelihood function $\Sigma_n \ln(L_n(\theta, \mu))$.

Our modeling framework offers several ways to define and analyze temporal stability of risk attitudes. One can test if the entire population distribution of risk preferences is stable, which can be expressed as a joint hypothesis H_0: $\bar{r}_1 = \bar{r}_2$ and $\sigma_{r1} = \sigma_{r2}$. Alternatively, one can test the temporal stability of the average person's risk attitude (H_0: $\bar{r}_1 = \bar{r}_2$), or test the temporal stability of unobserved preference heterogeneity (H_0: $\sigma_{r1} = \sigma_{r2}$). The analysis can focus on temporal stability at the individual level as well. By normalizing the scale of covariance σ_{r1r2}, one can derive a coefficient $\rho_{r1r2} = \sigma_{r1r2}/(\sigma_{r1} \times \sigma_{r2})$ that directly measures the within-individual correlation of the utility curvature parameters over time. The two random coefficients, r_{n1} and r_{n2}, are uncorrelated if $\rho_{r1r2} = 0$ and perfectly correlated if $\rho_{r1r2} = \pm 1$.

3.2 Extension to CPT

Our econometric specification extends naturally to CPT with sign-dependent preferences. Of course, one has to specify the sign-dependent utility and probability weighting functions and estimate the additional parameters, but the logic behind our econometric model and statistical tests for temporal stability remains the same.

Suppose that the subject perceives framed gains and losses as actual gains and losses, instead of integrating their endowment into the framed outcomes. Then, under CPT, the subject's evaluation of lottery i is represented by a preference functional

$$\begin{aligned} CPT_i &= \omega^+(p_{i1}) \times U(M_{i1}) + (1 - \omega^+(p_{i1})) \times U(M_{i2}) \text{ if } M_{i1} > M_{i2} > 0 \\ &= \omega^-(p_{i2}) \times U(M_{i2}) + (1 - \omega^-(p_{i2})) \times U(M_{i1}) \text{ if } 0 > M_{i1} > M_{i2} \\ &= \omega^+(p_{i1}) \times U(M_{i1}) + \omega^-(p_{i2}) \times U(M_{i2}) \text{ if } M_{i1} > 0 > M_{i2}, \end{aligned} \tag{7}$$

where U(M) is a utility function defined over outcome M, and $w^+(p)$ and $w^-(p)$ are probability weighting functions associated with positive and negative outcomes, respectively.

We parameterize utility using the HARA function

$$\begin{aligned} U(M) &= (M + \kappa)^{\alpha+}/\alpha^+ - \kappa^{\alpha+}/\alpha^+ \text{ for } M > 0 \\ &= 0 \text{ for } M = 0 \\ &= \lambda[-(-M + \kappa)^{\alpha-}/\alpha^- + \kappa^{\alpha-}/\alpha^-] \text{ for } M < 0, \end{aligned} \tag{8}$$

where α^+ and α^- are utility curvature parameters, λ is the loss aversion parameter, and κ is a small positive constant that we set to 0.0001. The HARA function is concave over gains when $\alpha^+ < 1$ and convex over losses when $\alpha^- < 1$, and vice versa when α^+ and α^- are greater than 1. We prefer this HARA function to the CRRA function, since continuity of the CRRA function at $M = 0$ requires that α^+ and α^- are positive. Hence, the CRRA function restricts the extent of risk aversion over gains and the extent of risk seeking over losses. The HARA function, on the other hand, is continuous at $M = 0$ for any non-zero combinations of α^+ and α^-. The loss aversion parameter λ is positive to maintain monotonicity in the loss domain, and the subject is often said to be loss averse when $\lambda > 1$ and gain seeking when $\lambda < 1$.

For non-linear probability weighting, we use Prelec's (1998) two-parameter functional form to specify separate probability weighting functions for gains and losses

$$\omega^+(p) = \exp\{^-\eta^+(-\ln p)^{\varphi+}\} \tag{9}$$

$$\omega^-(p) = \exp\{-\eta^-(-\ln p)^{\varphi-}\} \tag{10}$$

which are defined for $0 < p < 1$ and the latent parameters η^+, φ^+, η^-, and φ^- take positive values. This flexible functional form nests various types of S shaped ($\varphi^+ > 1$ or $\varphi^- > 1$), inverse-S shaped ($\varphi^+ < 1$ or $\varphi^- < 1$), and power functions ($\varphi^+ = 1$ or $\varphi^- = 1$) as special cases.[11] Given the sign dependence of decision weights in Eq. (7), p refers to the objective probability of the best outcome in $\omega^+(p)$ and the worst outcome in $\omega^-(p)$. This means that overweighting and underweighting of p have opposite behavioral implications under $\omega^+(p)$ and $\omega^-(p)$. For example, when $\omega^+(p) > p$, probability weighting enhances risk seeking since the subject behaves as though the best outcome is weighted more than the objective probability of that outcome; and when $\omega^-(p) > p$, probability weighting enhances risk aversion since a higher weight is placed on the worst outcome relative to the objective probability.

As with EUT, we assume that the choice depends not only on the latent CPT difference between the two lotteries, but also on a random error term ε such that $y = \mathbf{I}[(CPT_B - CPT_A) + \varepsilon > 0]$. Assume further that ε is normally distributed with a mean of zero and a standard deviation of μ^f that varies with whether {A, B} is a pair of lotteries in the gain frame ($\mu^f = \mu^+$), the loss frame ($\mu^f = \mu^-$) or the mixed frame ($\mu^f = \mu^\pm$); we note that in the two experiments we analyze, each lottery was paired with another lottery in the same frame. Then the likelihood function for each choice observation takes the form of

$$P(\theta^+, \mu^+) = \Phi(\nabla CPT/\mu^+)^y \times \Phi(-\nabla CPT/\mu^+)^{(1-y)} \text{ in gain frame} \quad (11)$$

$$P(\theta^-, \lambda, \mu^-) = \Phi(\nabla CPT/\mu^-)^y \times \Phi(-\nabla CPT/\mu^-)^{(1-y)} \text{ in loss frame} \quad (12)$$

$$P(\theta^+, \theta^-, \lambda, \mu^\pm) = \Phi(\nabla CPT/\mu^\pm)^y \times \Phi(-\nabla CPT/\mu^\pm)^{(1-y)} \text{ in mixed frame} \quad (13)$$

where $\Phi(.)$ is the standard normal CDF, $\nabla CPT = (CPT_B - CPT_A)$ is a structural utility difference between the two lotteries evaluated using Eqs. (7) through (10), and $\theta^+ = \{\alpha^+, \varphi^+, \eta^+\}$ and $\theta^- = \{\alpha^-, \varphi^-, \eta^-\}$ collect sign-dependent structural parameters.

While seemingly repetitive, the likelihood functions in (11), (12), and (13) highlight the key logic behind the structural estimation of CPT using combined data on three distinct types of lottery pairs. Data on pairwise lottery choices in the gain frame allow one to identify the curvature parameters describing the utility function and the probability weighting function over gains. Data in the loss frame allow one to identify the corresponding curvature parameters for losses, but not the loss aversion parameter λ: The index $\nabla CPT/\mu^-$ in Eq. (12) is proportional to λ as well as the inverted noise parameter $1/\mu^-$, which means that one cannot disentangle λ from the composite parameter λ/μ^- without further information. Data in the mixed frame provide the extra information that is needed: The index $\nabla CPT/\mu^\pm$ in Eq. (13) is proportional to $1/\mu^\pm$ but not to λ because the lotteries in question involve a mix of positive and negative outcomes, and λ is thus distinguished from $1/\mu^\pm$ in the mixed frame.

We model utility curvature α^+ and α^- as normally distributed random coefficients α_{nw}^+ and α_{nw}^- that vary across individuals n and waves w. To impose the sign restrictions required for monotonicity, we model φ^+, φ^-, and λ as log-normally distributed random coefficients φ_{nw}^+, φ_{nw}^- and λ_{nw} that also vary across individuals n and waves w. We estimate a separate pair of population means of η_{nw}^+ and η_{nw}^- in each wave, but do not treat these two parameters as random coefficients. One can also estimate the two-parameter Prelec specification and treat all four parameters as random coefficients. However, under this specification, one cannot easily define temporal stability of the probability weighting function. For example, one cannot identify the average or median person. While it is straightforward to identify the mean and median of each parameter separately, a person with a mean or median value of η does not necessarily have a mean or median value of φ.

Allowing for the full set of correlations amongst the random coefficients means that the CPT specification involves 62 more parameters to estimate than the EUT specification. The variance-covariance matrix for the random coefficients α_{n1}^+, α_{n2}^+, α_{n1}^-, α_{n2}^-, λ_{n1}, λ_{n2}, φ_{n1}^+, φ_{n2}^+, φ_{n1}^- and φ_{n2}^- is a 10-by-10 matrix, with 45 distinct covariance parameters and 10 identified variance parameters. We also need to estimate the population means of those 10 random coefficients as well as the degenerate coefficients η_{nw}^+ and η_{nw}^-. In comparison, the EUT specification involves 1 covariance parameter, 2 identified variance parameters and 2 population means. The likelihood function can be set up in broadly the same manner as the EUT case nevertheless. We can use equations (11), (12), and (13) to specify a conditional likelihood function corresponding to Eq. (5), and integrate the conditional likelihood function over the joint density of the 10 random coefficients to derive a counterpart to Eq. (6).

4. RESULTS

We are interested in testing several hypotheses. First, is the population distribution of risk attitudes under CPT temporally stable over the time periods considered in the two experiments? Second, are risk attitudes under CPT temporally stable at the individual level? Third, are risk preferences under EUT temporally stable in those two senses?

We use maximum simulated likelihood to estimate the full statistical model that captures unobserved preference heterogeneity.[12] By modeling the joint likelihood of observing all responses by each subject and adjusting standard errors for clustering at the subject level, our statistical approach addresses the panel dimension of the data at both modeling and inferential stages. Panel-robust Wald statistics are used to test all hypotheses. We transform several estimates into alternative forms that are easier to interpret. All tables below report correlation coefficients instead of covariance parameters. In case of the log-normal random coefficients λ, φ^+, and φ^- in the CPT model, all results are reported for λ, φ^+, and φ^- instead of $\ln(\lambda)$, $\ln(\varphi^+)$ and $\ln(\varphi^-)$. Similarly, we report population means of the degenerate coefficients η^+ and η^- rather than those of $\ln(\eta^+)$ and $\ln(\eta^-)$.[13]

4.1 Temporal Stability of Risk Attitudes Under CPT

We draw mixed conclusions on temporal stability of inferred risk attitudes under CPT that depend on which aspect of temporal stability that one is interested in. Under CPT, risk preferences are characterized by the α^+ and α^- parameters as well as the loss aversion parameter, λ, and the probability weighting parameters, φ^+, φ^-, η^+, and η^-. The entire population distribution of risk preferences may be said to be stable when the joint distribution of the seven parameters in the CPT model is stable. More formally, this joint hypothesis requires stability in the estimated population means of the α^+, α^-, λ, φ^+, φ^-, η^+, and η^- parameters; the estimated population standard deviations of these parameters; and the estimated correlation coefficients between them. We reject this type of temporal stability in both the MTB and GP experiment; the associated $\chi^2(22)$ test statistics have p-values < 0.001.[14]

Tables 1 and 2 report the estimated coefficients for the MTB and GP data, respectively. Looking first at the MTB data in Table 1, the estimated *population mean* of utility curvature over gains, α^+, is equal to 0.601 in wave 1, and equal to 0.645 in wave 2; the estimated difference in the two mean population coefficients is equal to 0.043, which is not significantly different from 0 with a p-value of 0.108. However, we find that the estimated *population standard deviation* of utility curvature over gains is temporally unstable; the estimated standard deviation of the α^+ parameter, σ_α^+, increases from 0.266 in wave 1 to 0.326 in wave 2, and the estimated difference between the two coefficients is significantly different (p-value $= 0.001$). Turning to utility curvature over losses, α^-, we find that the estimated population mean coefficient is equal to 0.820 in wave 1 and equal to 0.742 in wave 2. The estimated difference is equal to -0.078, which is significantly different from 0 at the 5% significance level (p-value $= 0.048$). We also find some instability in the estimated population standard deviation of utility curvature over losses; the estimated standard deviation of the α^- parameter, σ_α^-, increases from 0.191 in wave 1 to 0.260 in wave 2, and the estimated difference between the two coefficients is significantly different from 0 at the 10% significance level (p-value of 0.081). A joint test of the two estimated population mean coefficients of utility curvature for gains and losses, α^+ and α^-, the population standard deviations, σ_α^+ and σ_α^-, and the correlation coefficient, $\rho_{\alpha^+\alpha^-}$, between the two waves allows us to evaluate whether the joint population distribution of α^+ and α^- is temporally stable. The $\chi^2(5)$ test statistic has a p-value < 0.001, so we reject the hypothesis of temporal stability.

The upper panel in Fig. 1 shows the estimated population distributions of utility curvature over gains and losses across the two waves for the MTB data. The population distribution of utility curvature for gains shifts to the right in wave 2 compared to wave 1, but the apparent decrease in risk aversion is not statistically significant, as noted above.[15] We also observe that the population distribution of utility curvature for losses shifts to the left in wave 2 compared to wave 1, and the increase in risk seeking is statistically significant. Finally, the estimated population standard deviation of utility curvature increases from wave 1 to wave 2 for both gains and losses, and the results thus suggest that unobserved heterogeneity in estimated utility curvature increases over time for both gains and losses.

Table 1. Estimates of CPT Parameters: Murphy and ten Brincke (2018) Data.

Variable	Estimate	SE	*p*-value	95% Confidence Interval	
A. Estimated population means in wave 1 and wave 2					
α_1^+	0.601	0.028	<0.001	0.546	0.656
α_2^+	0.645	0.031	<0.001	0.584	0.705
α_1^-	0.820	0.040	<0.001	0.742	0.898
α_2^-	0.742	0.037	<0.001	0.670	0.814
λ_1	1.103	0.075	<0.001	0.957	1.250
λ_2	1.290	0.079	<0.001	1.136	1.445
φ_1^+	0.633	0.040	<0.001	0.555	0.711
φ_2^+	0.689	0.038	<0.001	0.616	0.763
φ_1^-	0.706	0.039	<0.001	0.629	0.783
φ_2^-	0.787	0.047	<0.001	0.695	0.878
η_1^+	0.788	0.034	<0.001	0.721	0.855
η_2^+	0.800	0.036	<0.001	0.729	0.871
η_1^-	0.778	0.037	<0.001	0.704	0.851
η_2^-	0.688	0.042	<0.001	0.605	0.771
B. Tests for temporal stability of population means					
$\alpha_2^+ - \alpha_1^+$	0.043	0.027	0.108	−0.010	0.006
$\alpha_2^- - \alpha_1^-$	−0.078	0.039	0.048	−0.155	−0.001
$\lambda_2 - \lambda_1$	0.187	0.059	0.001	0.072	0.302
$\varphi_2^+ - \varphi_1^+$	0.057	0.045	0.206	−0.031	0.145
$\varphi_2^- - \varphi_1^-$	0.081	0.055	0.139	−0.026	0.188
$\eta_2^+ - \eta_1^+$	0.012	0.027	0.651	−0.041	0.066
$\eta_2^- - \eta_1^-$	−0.089	0.035	0.010	−0.158	−0.021
C. Estimated population standard deviations in wave 1 and wave 2					
$\sigma_{\alpha 1}^+$	0.266	0.022	<0.001	0.223	0.308
$\sigma_{\alpha 2}^+$	0.326	0.017	<0.001	0.293	0.358
$\sigma_{\alpha 1}^-$	0.191	0.030	<0.001	0.132	0.250
$\sigma_{\alpha 2}^-$	0.260	0.033	<0.001	0.195	0.325
$\sigma_{\lambda 1}$	0.569	0.096	<0.001	0.381	0.756
$\sigma_{\lambda 2}$	0.715	0.080	<0.001	0.559	0.871
$\sigma_{\varphi 1}^+$	0.435	0.078	<0.001	0.282	0.588
$\sigma_{\varphi 2}^+$	0.621	0.086	<0.001	0.452	0.790
$\sigma_{\varphi 1}^-$	0.237	0.066	<0.001	0.107	0.367
$\sigma_{\varphi 2}^-$	0.531	0.083	<0.001	0.368	0.695
D. Tests for temporal stability of population standard deviations					
$\sigma_{\alpha 2}^+ - \sigma_{\alpha 1}^+$	0.060	0.018	0.001	0.025	0.096
$\sigma_{\alpha 2}^- - \sigma_{\alpha 1}^-$	0.069	0.040	0.081	−0.009	0.147
$\sigma_{\lambda 2} - \sigma_{\lambda 1}$	0.146	0.101	0.147	−0.052	0.344
$\sigma_{\varphi 2}^+ - \sigma_{\varphi 1}^+$	0.186	0.106	0.079	−0.022	0.394
$\sigma_{\varphi 2}^- - \sigma_{\varphi 1}^-$	0.294	0.097	0.002	0.105	0.484
E. Estimated correlation coefficients					
$\rho_{\alpha 1^+ \alpha 2^+}$	0.901	0.036	<0.001	0.830	0.971
$\rho_{\alpha 1^- \alpha 2^-}$	0.738	0.099	<0.001	0.543	0.933
$\rho_{\lambda 1 \lambda 2}$	0.826	0.043	<0.001	0.742	0.910
$\rho_{\varphi 1^+ \varphi 2^+}$	0.824	0.051	<0.001	0.725	0.923
$\rho_{\varphi 1^- \varphi 2^-}$	0.688	0.121	<0.001	0.450	0.925
$\rho_{\alpha 1^+ \alpha 1^-}$	0.545	0.153	<0.001	0.245	0.844

(Continued)

Table 1. (Continued)

Variable	Estimate	SE	p-value	95% Confidence Interval	
$\rho_{\alpha2^+\alpha2^-}$	0.211	0.129	0.102	−0.042	0.464
$\rho_{\varphi1^+\varphi1^-}$	0.762	0.124	<0.001	0.519	1.006
$\rho_{\varphi2^+\varphi2^-}$	0.752	0.075	<0.001	0.605	0.898
$\rho_{\alpha1^+\alpha2^-}$	0.060	0.128	0.638	−0.190	0.311
$\rho_{\alpha2^+\alpha1^-}$	0.574	0.134	<0.001	0.311	0.836
$\rho_{\varphi1^+\varphi2^-}$	0.594	0.087	<0.001	0.423	0.765
$\rho_{\varphi2^+\varphi1^-}$	0.626	0.104	<0.001	0.423	0.829
$\rho_{\alpha1^+\varphi1^+}$	0.017	0.101	0.868	−0.181	0.214
$\rho_{\alpha1^+\varphi2^+}$	−0.171	0.077	0.026	−0.321	−0.021
$\rho_{\alpha1^+\varphi1^-}$	−0.168	0.165	0.311	−0.491	0.156
$\rho_{\alpha1^+\varphi2^-}$	−0.248	0.144	0.084	−0.530	0.033
$\rho_{\alpha1^-\varphi1^+}$	−0.496	0.136	<0.001	−0.763	−0.229
$\rho_{\alpha1^-\varphi2^+}$	−0.563	0.062	<0.001	−0.684	−0.441
$\rho_{\alpha1^-\varphi1^-}$	−0.526	0.149	<0.001	−0.817	−0.235
$\rho_{\alpha1^-\varphi2^-}$	−0.417	0.152	0.006	−0.715	−0.119
$\rho_{\alpha2^+\varphi1^+}$	−0.141	0.078	0.071	−0.294	0.012
$\rho_{\alpha2^+\varphi2^+}$	−0.240	0.055	<0.001	−0.348	−0.133
$\rho_{\alpha2^+\varphi1^-}$	−0.193	0.159	0.224	−0.505	0.118
$\rho_{\alpha2^+\varphi2^-}$	−0.245	0.103	0.018	−0.448	−0.042
$\rho_{\alpha2^-\varphi1^+}$	−0.350	0.149	0.019	−0.643	−0.058
$\rho_{\alpha2^-\varphi2^+}$	−0.481	0.116	<0.001	−0.709	−0.253
$\rho_{\alpha2^-\varphi1^-}$	−0.221	0.183	0.228	−0.579	0.138
$\rho_{\alpha2^-\varphi2^-}$	−0.295	0.144	0.041	−0.578	−0.012
$\rho_{\lambda1\,\alpha1^+}$	−0.690	0.066	<0.001	−0.819	−0.562
$\rho_{\lambda1\,\alpha2^+}$	−0.587	0.064	<0.001	−0.712	−0.463
$\rho_{\lambda1\,\alpha1^-}$	−0.625	0.100	<0.001	−0.821	−0.428
$\rho_{\lambda1\,\alpha2^-}$	−0.236	0.142	0.097	−0.515	0.043
$\rho_{\lambda1\,\varphi1^+}$	0.128	0.163	0.430	−0.191	0.447
$\rho_{\lambda1\,\varphi2^+}$	0.221	0.125	0.077	−0.024	0.466
$\rho_{\lambda1\,\varphi1^-}$	0.570	0.179	0.001	0.219	0.922
$\rho_{\lambda1\,\varphi2^-}$	0.398	0.228	0.081	−0.049	0.844
$\rho_{\lambda2\,\alpha1^+}$	−0.496	0.069	<0.001	−0.631	−0.360
$\rho_{\lambda2\,\alpha2^+}$	−0.490	0.076	<0.001	−0.638	−0.341
$\rho_{\lambda2\,\alpha1^-}$	−0.456	0.091	<0.001	−0.635	−0.278
$\rho_{\lambda2\,\alpha2^-}$	−0.235	0.107	0.029	−0.446	−0.025
$\rho_{\lambda2\,\varphi1^+}$	0.067	0.133	0.615	−0.194	0.328
$\rho_{\lambda2\,\varphi2^+}$	0.045	0.122	0.712	−0.194	0.284
$\rho_{\lambda2\,\varphi1^-}$	0.462	0.122	<0.001	0.223	0.700
$\rho_{\lambda2\,\varphi2^-}$	0.251	0.268	0.350	−0.274	0.775

Log-simulated likelihood = −13,579.355 for 25,844 observations on 142 subjects in waves 1 and 2 using 100 Halton draws.

We next consider temporal stability in utility curvature at the individual level for the MTB data. The estimated correlation coefficient between utility curvature for gains in wave 1 and 2, $\rho_{\alpha1^+\alpha2^+}$, is equal to 0.901, which is significantly different from 0 (p-value < 0.001). We also find a strong positive correlation in utility curvature for losses across the two waves; the estimated correlation coefficient, $\rho_{\alpha1^-\alpha2^-}$, is equal to 0.707, which also is significantly different from 0 (p-value < 0.001). The significant positive correlation coefficients suggest that utility curvature for both

Table 2. Estimates of CPT Parameters: Glöckner and Pachur (2012) Data.

Variable	Estimate	SE	*p*-value	95% Confidence Interval	
A. Estimated population means in wave 1 and wave 2					
α_1^+	0.652	0.034	<0.001	0.586	0.719
α_2^+	0.689	0.035	<0.001	0.620	0.758
α_1^-	0.698	0.035	<0.001	0.629	0.766
α_2^-	0.793	0.084	<0.001	0.627	0.959
λ_1	1.338	0.131	<0.001	1.080	1.595
λ_2	1.240	0.106	<0.001	1.032	1.449
φ_1^+	0.736	0.034	<0.001	0.670	0.802
φ_2^+	0.802	0.063	<0.001	0.679	0.926
φ_1^-	1.240	1.102	<0.001	1.040	1.440
φ_2^-	1.241	0.296	<0.001	0.662	1.821
η_1^+	1.054	0.040	<0.001	0.975	1.133
η_2^+	1.112	0.052	<0.001	1.011	1.214
η_1^-	0.622	0.044	<0.001	0.535	0.710
η_2^-	0.713	0.043	<0.001	0.628	0.798
B. Tests for temporal stability of population means					
$\alpha_2^+ - \alpha_1^+$	0.037	0.043	0.391	−0.047	0.121
$\alpha_2^- - \alpha_1^-$	0.095	0.085	0.259	−0.070	0.261
$\lambda_2 - \lambda_1$	−0.098	0.126	0.438	−0.344	0.149
$\varphi_2^+ - \varphi_1^+$	0.067	0.073	0.359	−0.076	0.209
$\varphi_2^- - \varphi_1^-$	0.001	0.288	0.997	−0.563	0.565
$\eta_2^+ - \eta_1^+$	0.059	0.064	0.362	−0.067	0.185
$\eta_2^- - \eta_1^-$	0.091	0.063	0.148	−0.032	0.213
C. Estimated population standard deviations in wave 1 and wave 2					
$\sigma_{\alpha 1}^+$	0.175	0.028	<0.001	0.120	0.231
$\sigma_{\alpha 2}^+$	0.218	0.021	<0.001	0.176	0.260
$\sigma_{\alpha 1}^-$	0.207	0.050	<0.001	0.109	0.306
$\sigma_{\alpha 2}^-$	0.208	0.086	0.016	0.039	0.377
$\sigma_{\lambda 1}$	0.620	0.205	0.002	0.219	1.020
$\sigma_{\lambda 2}$	0.431	0.190	0.023	0.058	0.803
$\sigma_{\varphi 1}^+$	0.286	0.034	<0.001	0.218	0.353
$\sigma_{\varphi 2}^+$	0.730	0.385	0.058	−0.025	1.484
$\sigma_{\varphi 1}^-$	0.772	0.167	0.000	0.445	1.099
$\sigma_{\varphi 2}^-$	0.988	0.561	0.078	−0.111	2.088
D. Tests for temporal stability of population standard deviations					
$\sigma_{\alpha 2}^+ - \sigma_{\alpha 1}^+$	0.042	0.033	0.194	−0.022	0.106
$\sigma_{\alpha 2}^- - \sigma_{\alpha 1}^-$	0.001	0.080	0.994	−0.157	0.158
$\sigma_{\lambda 2} - \sigma_{\lambda 1}$	−0.189	0.380	0.619	−0.934	0.556
$\sigma_{\varphi 2}^+ - \sigma_{\varphi 1}^+$	0.444	0.385	0.248	−0.310	1.198
$\sigma_{\varphi 2}^- - \sigma_{\varphi 1}^-$	0.216	0.560	0.699	−0.882	1.314
E. Estimated correlation coefficients					
$\rho_{\alpha 1^+ \alpha 2^+}$	0.307	0.192	0.110	−0.070	0.684
$\rho_{\alpha 1^- \alpha 2^-}$	−0.251	1.043	0.810	−2.294	1.792
$\rho_{\lambda 1 \lambda 2}$	−0.361	0.392	0.357	−1.130	0.408
$\rho_{\varphi 1^+ \varphi 2^+}$	0.029	0.131	0.828	−0.229	0.286
$\rho_{\varphi 1^- \varphi 2^-}$	−0.220	0.494	0.656	−1.188	0.748
$\rho_{\alpha 1^+ \alpha 1^-}$	0.674	0.116	<0.001	0.447	0.902

(Continued)

Table 2. (Continued)

Variable	Estimate	SE	*p*-value	95% Confidence Interval	
$\rho_{\alpha2^+ \alpha2^-}$	0.630	1.481	0.670	−2.272	3.533
$\rho_{\varphi1^+ \varphi1^-}$	0.809	0.086	0.000	0.641	0.977
$\rho_{\varphi2^+ \varphi2^-}$	0.684	0.287	0.017	0.123	1.246
$\rho_{\alpha1^+ \alpha2^-}$	0.012	0.521	0.981	−1.010	1.034
$\rho_{\alpha2^+ \alpha1^-}$	0.042	0.207	0.841	−0.364	0.447
$\rho_{\varphi1^+ \varphi2^-}$	−0.261	0.259	0.314	−0.770	0.247
$\rho_{\varphi2^+ \varphi1^-}$	0.103	0.191	0.589	−0.271	0.477
$\rho_{\alpha1^+ \varphi1^+}$	0.323	0.114	0.005	0.100	0.547
$\rho_{\alpha1^+ \varphi2^+}$	0.084	0.030	0.005	0.026	0.143
$\rho_{\alpha1^+ \varphi1^-}$	0.015	0.159	0.924	−0.297	0.327
$\rho_{\alpha1^+ \varphi2^-}$	−0.032	0.120	0.791	−0.267	0.203
$\rho_{\alpha1^- \varphi1^+}$	0.399	0.176	0.024	0.053	0.745
$\rho_{\alpha1^- \varphi2^+}$	−0.124	0.074	0.093	−0.268	0.021
$\rho_{\alpha1^- \varphi1^-}$	0.029	0.207	0.888	−0.376	0.435
$\rho_{\alpha1^- \varphi2^-}$	−0.282	0.219	0.199	−0.712	0.148
$\rho_{\alpha2^+ \varphi1^+}$	0.064	0.205	0.754	−0.337	0.465
$\rho_{\alpha2^+ \varphi2^+}$	0.225	0.077	0.004	0.074	0.377
$\rho_{\alpha2^+ \varphi1^-}$	0.220	0.391	0.573	−0.546	0.986
$\rho_{\alpha2^+ \varphi2^-}$	−0.266	0.196	0.176	−0.651	0.119
$\rho_{\alpha2^- \varphi1^+}$	0.216	0.524	0.680	−0.810	1.242
$\rho_{\alpha2^- \varphi2^+}$	0.383	0.493	0.438	−0.584	1.350
$\rho_{\alpha2^- \varphi1^-}$	0.504	0.551	0.360	−0.576	1.585
$\rho_{\alpha2^- \varphi2^-}$	0.005	1.609	0.998	−3.149	3.158
$\rho_{\lambda1\, \alpha1^+}$	−0.476	0.115	<0.001	−0.702	−0.250
$\rho_{\lambda1\, \alpha2^+}$	−0.093	0.237	0.695	−0.557	0.371
$\rho_{\lambda1\, \alpha1^-}$	−0.912	0.035	<0.001	−0.982	−0.843
$\rho_{\lambda1\, \alpha2^-}$	0.205	1.371	0.881	−2.481	2.892
$\rho_{\lambda1\, \varphi1^+}$	−0.414	0.181	0.022	−0.769	−0.059
$\rho_{\lambda1\, \varphi2^+}$	0.181	0.062	0.003	0.060	0.302
$\rho_{\lambda1\, \varphi1^-}$	−0.108	0.239	0.652	−0.576	0.360
$\rho_{\lambda1\, \varphi2^-}$	0.439	0.253	0.083	−0.058	0.935
$\rho_{\lambda2\, \alpha1^+}$	0.153	0.247	0.535	−0.330	0.637
$\rho_{\lambda2\, \alpha2^+}$	0.054	0.866	0.950	−1.642	1.751
$\rho_{\lambda2\, \alpha1^-}$	0.375	0.227	0.099	−0.070	0.819
$\rho_{\lambda2\, \alpha2^-}$	−0.135	0.882	0.879	−1.864	1.594
$\rho_{\lambda2\, \varphi1^+}$	0.097	0.235	0.678	−0.363	0.557
$\rho_{\lambda2\, \varphi2^+}$	−0.370	0.153	0.016	−0.670	−0.069
$\rho_{\lambda2\, \varphi1^-}$	0.156	0.387	0.687	−0.602	0.914
$\rho_{\lambda2\, \varphi2^-}$	−0.351	0.578	0.543	−1.483	0.781

Log-simulated likelihood = −8,732.306 for 17,940 observations on 66 subjects in wave 1 and 64 subjects in wave 2 using 100 Halton draws.

gains and losses are temporally stable at the individual level, in the sense that someone with an above-average α^+ (α^-) parameter in wave 1 also tends to have an above-average α^+ (α^-) parameter in wave 2, and we reject the hypothesis that the population distributions for α^+ and α^- are independent over time.

Fig. 2 displays the estimated population distributions of the loss aversion parameter for each wave. The estimated distributions in the upper panel refer to the MTB data, and we observe that the estimated population mean of the λ

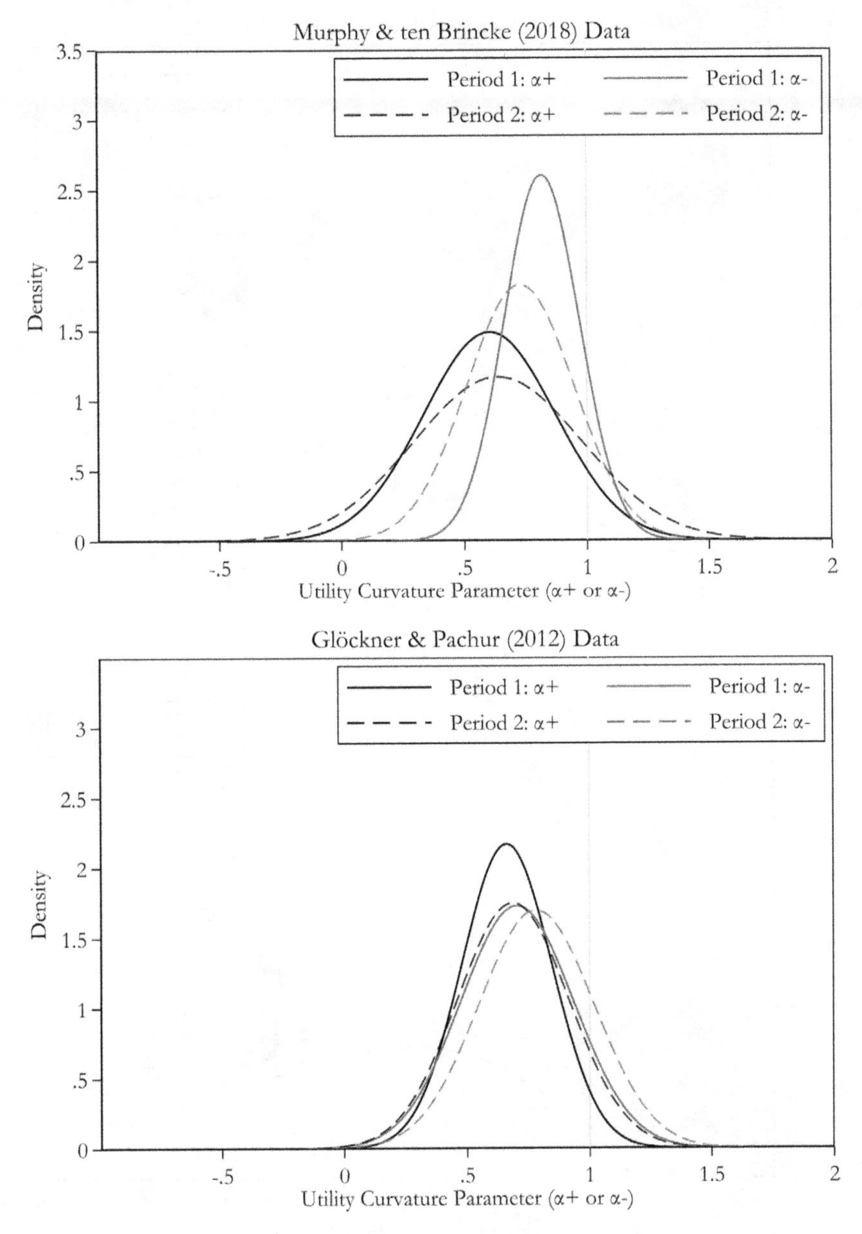

Fig. 1. Population Distributions of Utility Curvature for Gains and Losses.

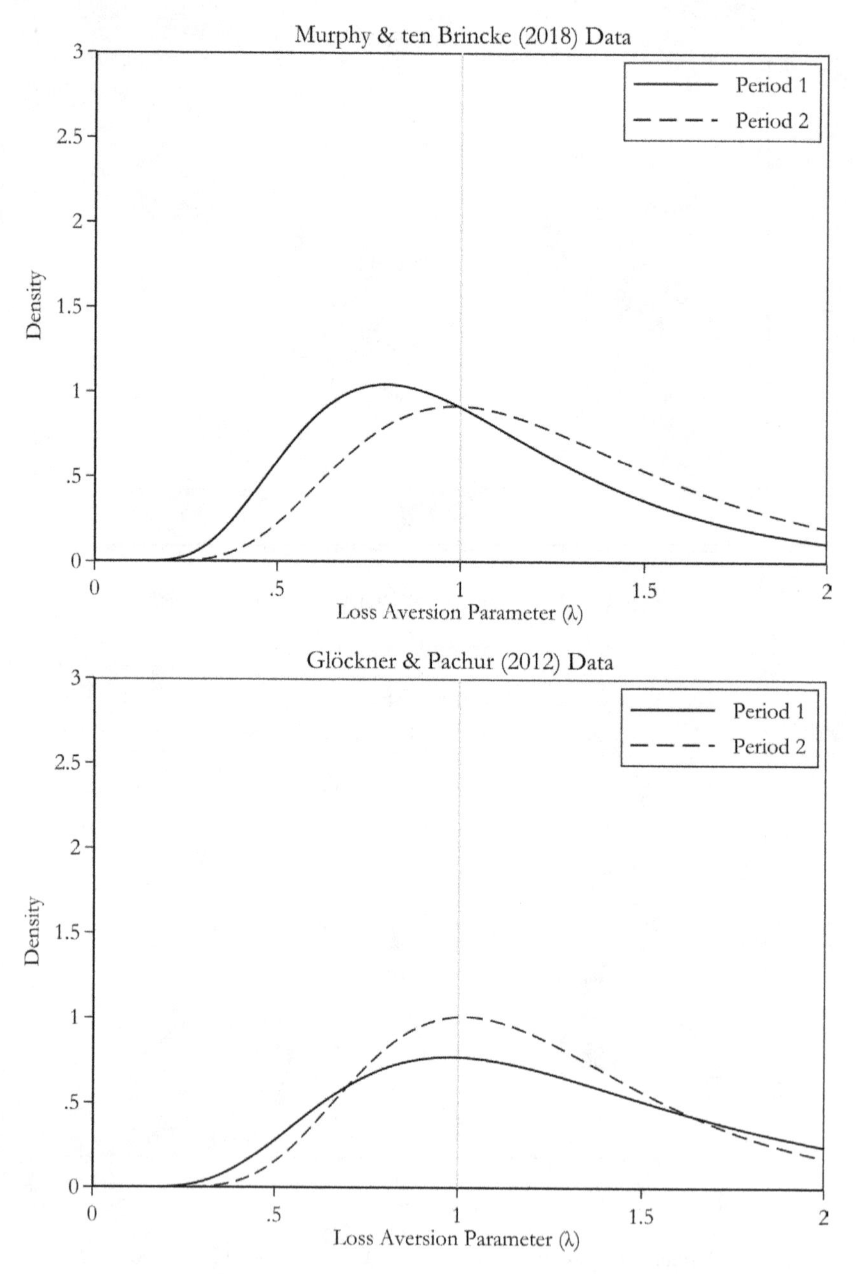

Fig. 2. Population Distributions of Loss Aversion.

parameter increases over time: it is equal to 1.103 in wave 1 and 1.290 in wave 2, and the estimated between-wave difference in the population mean is statistically significant (p-value of 0.001). We also observe that the population distribution in wave 2 has a higher standard deviation than the distribution in wave 1; the estimated standard deviation is 0.569 in wave 1 and 0.715 in wave 2, and we cannot reject the null hypothesis that the estimated difference in the two coefficients is equal to 0 (p-value of 0.147). Overall, we find *temporal instability* with respect to the population distribution of the λ parameter: the $\chi^2(2)$ test statistic has a p-value $= 0.006$, so we reject the hypothesis of temporal stability. The estimated correlation coefficient between the population distributions of the λ parameter over time, $\rho_{\lambda 1 \lambda 2}$, is equal to 0.826, and we reject the hypothesis that the two population distributions of the loss aversion parameter are independent.

The estimated population distributions of the probability weighting parameter φ^+ and φ^- are displayed in Fig. 3. Again, the distributions in the upper panel refer to the MTB data, and we draw different conclusions regarding temporal stability in the estimated population distributions of the φ^+ and φ^- parameters. We cannot reject the hypothesis that the population distribution of the φ^+ parameter is temporally stable (the $\chi^2(2)$ test statistic has a p-value of 0.211), however, we reject this hypothesis with respect to the population distribution of φ^- parameter (p-value of 0.006). We draw similar conclusions with respect to the estimated population means of the η^+ and η^- parameters: we cannot reject the hypothesis that the estimated population mean of η^+ is temporally stable (p-value $= 0.651$), whereas we reject the hypothesis of temporal stability for the η^- parameter (p-value $= 0.010$). A joint test of the four estimated population mean coefficients in the probability weighting function for gains and losses, φ^+, φ^-, η^+, and η^-, the two population standard deviations, σ_φ^+ and σ_φ^-, and the correlation coefficient, $\rho_{\varphi^+\varphi^-}$, between the two waves allows us to evaluate whether the joint population distribution of the probability weighting function is temporally stable. The $\chi^2(7)$ test statistic has a p-value < 0.001, so we reject the hypothesis of temporal stability. Finally, we find that the estimated between-wave correlation of the φ^+ parameter, $\rho_{\varphi 1^+ \varphi 2^+}$, is equal to 0.824, and it is equal to 0.688 for the φ^- parameter (both correlation coefficients have p-values < 0.001). These results thus suggests that there is a strong degree of temporal stability at the individual level in the shape of the probability weighting function over gains and losses.

The results for the MTB data thus suggest that every risk preference parameter in the CPT model shows a large and positive within-individual correlation over time. We nevertheless reject temporal stability at the population level when we test whether the joint distribution of all the parameters is stable, and also when we separately test whether the marginal distribution of each parameter is stable; the only exception is the marginal distributions of the probability weighting parameters associated with gains, for which we cannot reject temporal stability. We also observe that the population standard deviation of each parameter's marginal distribution tends to increase over time; all estimated standard deviations are larger in wave 2 than wave 1, and the between-wave changes are statistically significant at the 5% or 10% level, except for the utility curvature parameter in the gain domain and the probability weighting parameter in the loss domain.

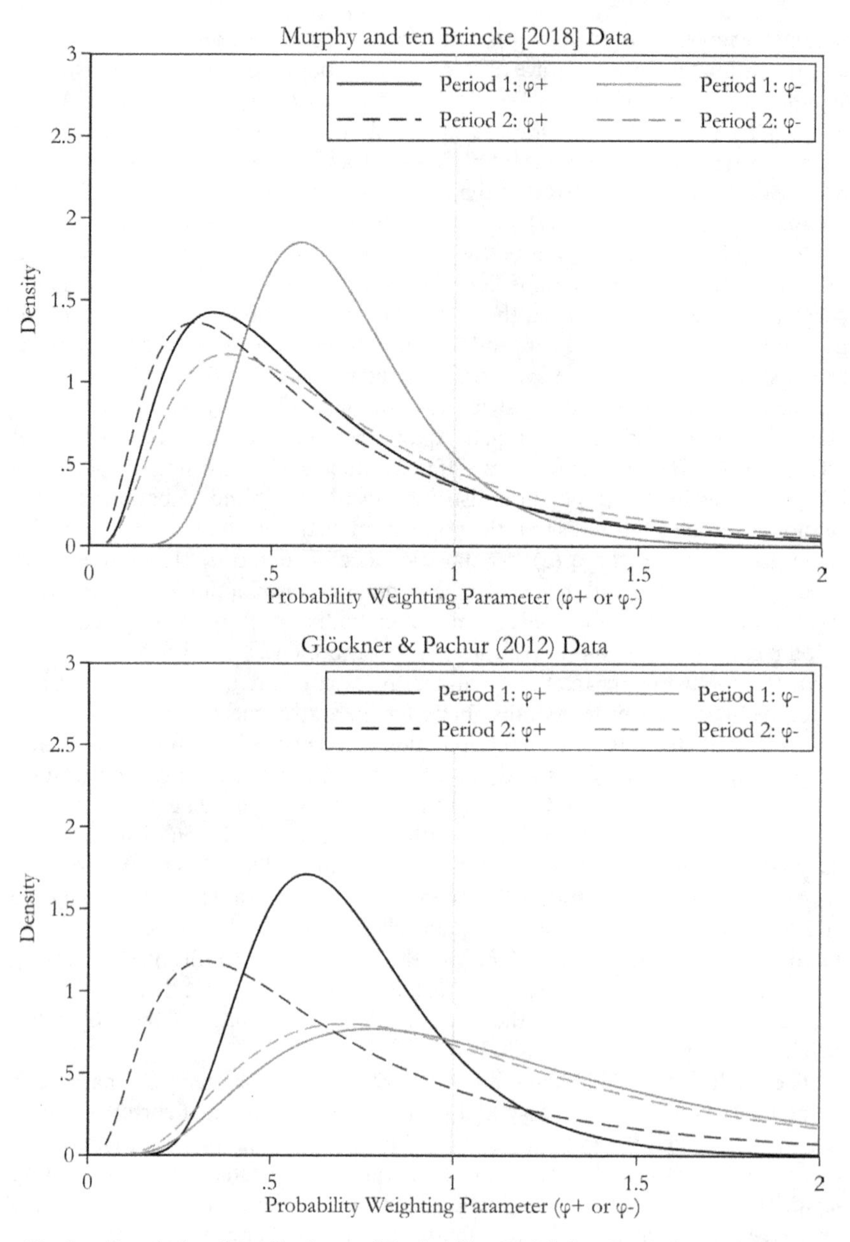

Fig. 3. Population Distributions of Probability Weighting for Gains and Losses.

We find different results for the GP data. At the population level, although we reject temporal stability in the joint distribution of all risk preference parameters in the CPT model (p-value < 0.001), we cannot reject temporal stability in the marginal distribution of any parameter.[16] The estimated standard deviations of all marginal distributions, except for the loss aversion parameter, are larger in wave 2. However, none of the between-wave changes are statistically significant.

We also find weaker empirical support for temporal stability at the individual level compared to the MTB data. For the MTB data, each of the within-individual correlation coefficients ($\rho_{\alpha1^+\alpha2^+}$, $\rho_{\alpha1^-\alpha2^-}$, $\rho_{\lambda1\lambda2}$, $\rho_{\rho1^+\rho2^+}$, and $\rho_{\rho1^-\rho2^-}$) is estimated to be positive, numerically large and statistically significant. For the GP data, each corresponding estimate is much smaller in absolute magnitude and statistically insignificant, though we still reject the hypothesis that the five correlation coefficients are jointly equal to 0 (p-value < 0.001). In case of the utility curvature and probability weighting parameters in the loss domain ($\rho_{\alpha1^-\alpha2^-}$ and $\rho_{\rho1^-\rho2^-}$) and the loss aversion parameter ($\rho_{\lambda1\lambda2}$), we even obtain negative point estimates.

4.2 CPT Without Sign-dependent Parameters

It is common in the literature on prospect theory to assume identical utility curvature and probability weighting functions for gains and losses, mostly to simplify algebraic analyses or to reduce the number of estimated parameters. One simplification offered by these restrictions is that all well-known definitions of loss aversion that are based on the shape of the utility function (see Abdellaoui, Bleichrodt, & Paraschiv, 2007 and references therein) can be expressed as a question of whether the λ parameter takes a value greater than 1.

Using a constrained model that does not allow for sign dependence in the utility curvature and probability weighting parameters, we again draw mixed conclusions on temporal stability of inferred risk attitudes under CPT that depend on which aspect of temporal stability that one is interested in. In the constrained model, risk preferences are characterized by the α parameter, the loss aversion parameter, λ, and the two probability weighting parameters, φ and η. The entire population distribution of risk preferences may be said to be stable when the joint distribution of the four parameters in the model is stable. We reject this type of temporal stability in both the MTB and GP experiment; the associated $\chi^2(10)$ test statistics have p-values < 0.001.

Tables 3 and 4 report the estimated coefficients of the constrained CPT model for the MTB and GP data, respectively. The results in Table 3 show that the estimated mean coefficient of utility curvature in the MTB experiment is equal to 0.717 in wave 1 and 0.728 in wave 2, and the estimated difference in the two mean population coefficients is equal to 0.011, which is not significantly different from 0 (p-value of 0.653). We also find that the estimated population standard deviation of utility curvature is temporally stable; the estimated difference of 0.024 between the two coefficients is not significantly different from 0 (p-value $= 0.371$). A joint test of estimated differences in population mean and standard deviation coefficients allows us to evaluate whether the population distribution of α is temporally stable, and we cannot reject this hypothesis (the $\chi^2(2)$ test statistic has a

Table 3. Estimates of CPT Parameters in Constrained Model: Murphy and ten Brincke (2018) Data.

Variable	Estimate	SE	*p*-value	95% Confidence Interval	
A. Estimated population means in wave 1 and wave 2					
α_1	0.717	0.037	<0.001	0.645	0.790
α_2	0.728	0.046	<0.001	0.637	0.819
λ_1	1.180	0.097	<0.001	0.989	1.370
λ_2	1.319	0.223	<0.001	0.882	1.756
φ_1	0.705	0.097	<0.001	0.515	0.895
φ_2	0.823	0.097	<0.001	0.633	1.012
η_1	0.818	0.029	<0.001	0.761	0.874
η_2	0.770	0.026	<0.001	0.719	0.822
B. Tests for temporal stability of population means					
$\alpha_2 - \alpha_1$	0.011	0.024	0.653	−0.036	0.058
$\lambda_2 - \lambda_1$	0.139	0.145	0.335	−0.144	0.423
$\varphi_2 - \varphi_1$	0.118	0.041	0.004	0.038	0.198
$\eta_2 - \eta_1$	−0.047	0.023	0.045	−0.093	−0.001
C. Estimated population standard deviations in wave 1 and wave 2					
$\sigma_{\alpha 1}$	0.217	0.020	<0.001	0.178	0.256
$\sigma_{\alpha 2}$	0.241	0.021	<0.001	0.199	0.283
$\sigma_{\lambda 1}$	0.543	0.077	<0.001	0.392	0.693
$\sigma_{\lambda 2}$	0.740	0.174	<0.001	0.398	1.081
$\sigma_{\varphi 1}$	0.480	0.153	0.002	0.180	0.779
$\sigma_{\varphi 2}$	0.730	0.159	<0.001	0.419	1.041
D. Tests for temporal stability of population standard deviations					
$\sigma_{\alpha 2} - \sigma_{\alpha 1}$	0.024	0.027	0.371	−0.029	0.077
$\sigma_{\lambda 2} - \sigma_{\lambda 1}$	0.197	0.171	0.250	−0.139	0.533
$\sigma_{\varphi 2} - \sigma_{\varphi 1}$	0.250	0.137	0.067	−0.018	0.518
E. Estimated correlation coefficients					
$\rho_{\alpha 1\,\alpha 2}$	0.962	0.064	<0.001	0.837	1.088
$\rho_{\lambda 1\,\lambda 2}$	0.897	0.048	<0.001	0.803	0.990
$\rho_{\varphi 1\,\varphi 2}$	0.893	0.064	<0.001	0.767	1.019
$\rho_{\alpha 1\,\varphi 1}$	0.277	0.177	0.118	−0.070	0.623
$\rho_{\alpha 1\,\varphi 2}$	0.142	0.087	0.102	−0.028	0.312
$\rho_{\alpha 2\,\varphi 1}$	0.058	0.198	0.770	−0.331	0.447
$\rho_{\alpha 2\,\varphi 2}$	−0.084	0.015	0.000	−0.113	−0.055
$\rho_{\lambda 1\,\alpha 1}$	−0.217	0.084	0.010	−0.382	−0.052
$\rho_{\lambda 1\,\alpha 2}$	−0.292	0.204	0.152	−0.691	0.107
$\rho_{\lambda 1\,\varphi 1}$	0.177	0.149	0.234	−0.114	0.468
$\rho_{\lambda 1\,\varphi 2}$	0.124	0.111	0.264	−0.093	0.340
$\rho_{\lambda 2\,\alpha 1}$	−0.219	0.208	0.292	−0.626	0.188
$\rho_{\lambda 2\,\alpha 2}$	−0.285	0.149	0.055	−0.577	0.006
$\rho_{\lambda 2\,\varphi 1}$	0.081	0.033	0.016	0.015	0.147
$\rho_{\lambda 2\,\varphi 2}$	0.028	0.074	0.705	−0.117	0.173

Log-simulated likelihood = −13,824.815 for 25,844 observations on 142 subjects in waves 1 and 2 using 100 Halton draws.

Table 4. Estimates of CPT Parameters in Constrained Model: Glöckner and Pachur (2012) Data.

Variable	Estimate	SE	*p*-value	95% Confidence Interval	
A. Estimated population means in wave 1 and wave 2					
α_1	0.614	0.032	<0.001	0.551	0.676
α_2	0.668	0.025	<0.001	0.620	0.716
λ_1	1.960	0.153	<0.001	1.660	2.261
λ_2	1.976	0.153	<0.001	1.675	2.276
φ_1	0.730	0.036	<0.001	0.661	0.800
φ_2	0.782	0.043	<0.001	0.699	0.866
η_1	0.969	0.034	<0.001	0.903	1.036
η_2	1.016	0.037	<0.001	0.944	1.087
B. Tests for temporal stability of population means					
$\alpha_2 - \alpha_1$	0.054	0.038	0.149	−0.020	0.128
$\lambda_2 - \lambda_1$	0.015	0.172	0.930	−0.323	0.353
$\varphi_2 - \varphi_1$	0.052	0.055	0.344	−0.056	0.160
$\eta_2 - \eta_1$	0.046	0.046	0.315	−0.044	0.137
C. Estimated population standard deviations in wave 1 and wave 2					
$\sigma_{\alpha 1}$	0.179	0.027	<0.001	0.127	0.231
$\sigma_{\alpha 2}$	0.187	0.013	<0.001	0.161	0.212
$\sigma_{\lambda 1}$	0.264	0.172	0.124	−0.072	0.600
$\sigma_{\lambda 2}$	0.730	0.176	<0.001	0.384	1.076
$\sigma_{\varphi 1}$	0.281	0.041	<0.001	0.201	0.361
$\sigma_{\varphi 2}$	0.566	0.077	<0.001	0.414	0.718
D. Tests for temporal stability of population standard deviations					
$\sigma_{\alpha 2} - \sigma_{\alpha 1}$	0.007	0.031	0.813	−0.053	0.068
$\sigma_{\lambda 2} - \sigma_{\lambda 1}$	0.466	0.277	0.092	−0.076	1.009
$\sigma_{\varphi 2} - \sigma_{\varphi 1}$	0.285	0.083	0.001	0.122	0.448
E. Estimated correlation coefficients					
$\rho_{\alpha 1\, \alpha 2}$	0.127	0.135	0.348	−0.138	0.391
$\rho_{\lambda 1\, \lambda 2}$	−0.214	0.258	0.407	−0.719	0.291
$\rho_{\varphi 1\, \varphi 2}$	−0.000	0.036	1.000	−0.070	0.070
$\rho_{\alpha 1\, \varphi 1}$	0.225	0.090	0.013	0.048	0.402
$\rho_{\alpha 1\, \varphi 2}$	−0.004	0.046	0.926	−0.094	0.086
$\rho_{\alpha 2\, \varphi 1}$	0.119	0.141	0.399	−0.158	0.397
$\rho_{\alpha 2\, \varphi 2}$	0.010	0.050	0.839	−0.088	0.108
$\rho_{\lambda 1\, \alpha 1}$	−0.907	0.274	0.001	−1.443	−0.370
$\rho_{\lambda 1\, \alpha 2}$	−0.076	0.125	0.541	−0.321	0.168
$\rho_{\lambda 1\, \varphi 1}$	−0.522	0.436	0.232	−1.376	0.333
$\rho_{\lambda 1\, \varphi 2}$	−0.056	0.066	0.391	−0.186	0.073
$\rho_{\lambda 2\, \alpha 1}$	0.439	0.095	<0.001	0.252	0.626
$\rho_{\lambda 2\, \alpha 2}$	−0.223	0.068	0.001	−0.357	−0.089
$\rho_{\lambda 2\, \varphi 1}$	−0.181	0.177	0.305	−0.528	0.165
$\rho_{\lambda 2\, \varphi 2}$	−0.238	0.097	0.014	−0.428	−0.048

Log-simulated likelihood = −9,135.878 for 17,940 observations on 66 subjects in wave 1 and 64 subjects in wave 2 using 100 Halton draws.

p-value of 0.619). The results are similar for the GP data, and we cannot reject the hypothesis that the population distribution of utility curvature is temporally stable in the constrained CPT model for both data sets.

The upper panel in Fig. 4 shows the estimated population distributions of utility curvature across the two waves for the MTB data, and the lower panel shows the same distributions for the GP data. The population distribution of utility curvature is remarkably stable over time and across the two data sets, as noted above. Looking at temporal stability in utility curvature at the individual level, we draw different conclusions across the two data sets. There is a strong positive correlation in utility curvature between the two waves for the MTB data (the estimated coefficient, $\rho_{\alpha1\alpha2}$, is equal to 0.962 with a p-value < 0.001), but we find a smaller positive correlation coefficient for the GP data that is statistically insignificant (it is equal to 0.127 with a p-value of 0.348).

Fig. 5 displays the estimated population distributions of the loss aversion parameter for each wave and data set. We observe that the estimated population distributions of the λ parameter for the MTB data are almost identical over the two-week time interval with population means of 1.180 and 1.319 in the first and second wave, respectively, and the between-wave difference in the estimated population distributions is statistically insignificant (p-value of 0.501).[17] The estimated correlation coefficient between the two population distributions of the λ parameter, $\rho_{\lambda1\lambda2}$, is equal to 0.897, and we reject the hypothesis that the two marginal distributions of the loss aversion parameter are independent over time.

The results are somewhat different for the GP data, and we now find a high degree of loss aversion in both waves of the experiment. The population distribution of the λ parameter in wave 1 has an estimated mean of 1.960 and standard deviation of 0.264, whereas the estimated population distribution in wave 2 has a mean of 1.976 and a standard deviation of 0.730. Despite these differences in the estimated population distributions we cannot reject the hypothesis that the loss aversion parameter is temporally stable (p-value of 0.141). The estimated correlation coefficient between the two population distributions of the λ parameter, $\rho_{\lambda1\lambda2}$, is now negative and equal to -0.214 with a p-value of 0.407, and we cannot reject the hypothesis that the population distribution of the loss aversion parameter is independent between waves.

The estimated population distributions of the probability weighting parameter φ are displayed in Fig. 6. We reject the hypothesis that the population distribution of the φ parameter is temporally stable for the MTB data (the $\chi^2(2)$ test statistic has a p-value of 0.014) as well as the GP data (p-value < 0.001). We draw opposite conclusions with respect to the population mean of the η parameter: we reject the hypothesis that the population mean of η is temporally stable for the MTB data (p-value $= 0.045$), but we cannot reject the hypothesis for the GP data (p-value $= 0.315$). Finally, we find that the estimated between-wave correlation of the φ parameter is equal to 0.893 for the MTB data (p-value < 0.001), and equal to 0 for the GP data (p-value of 1.000). Hence, there is a strong degree of temporal stability at the individual level in φ parameter of the probability weighting function for the MTB data, but no such correlation between waves for the GP data.

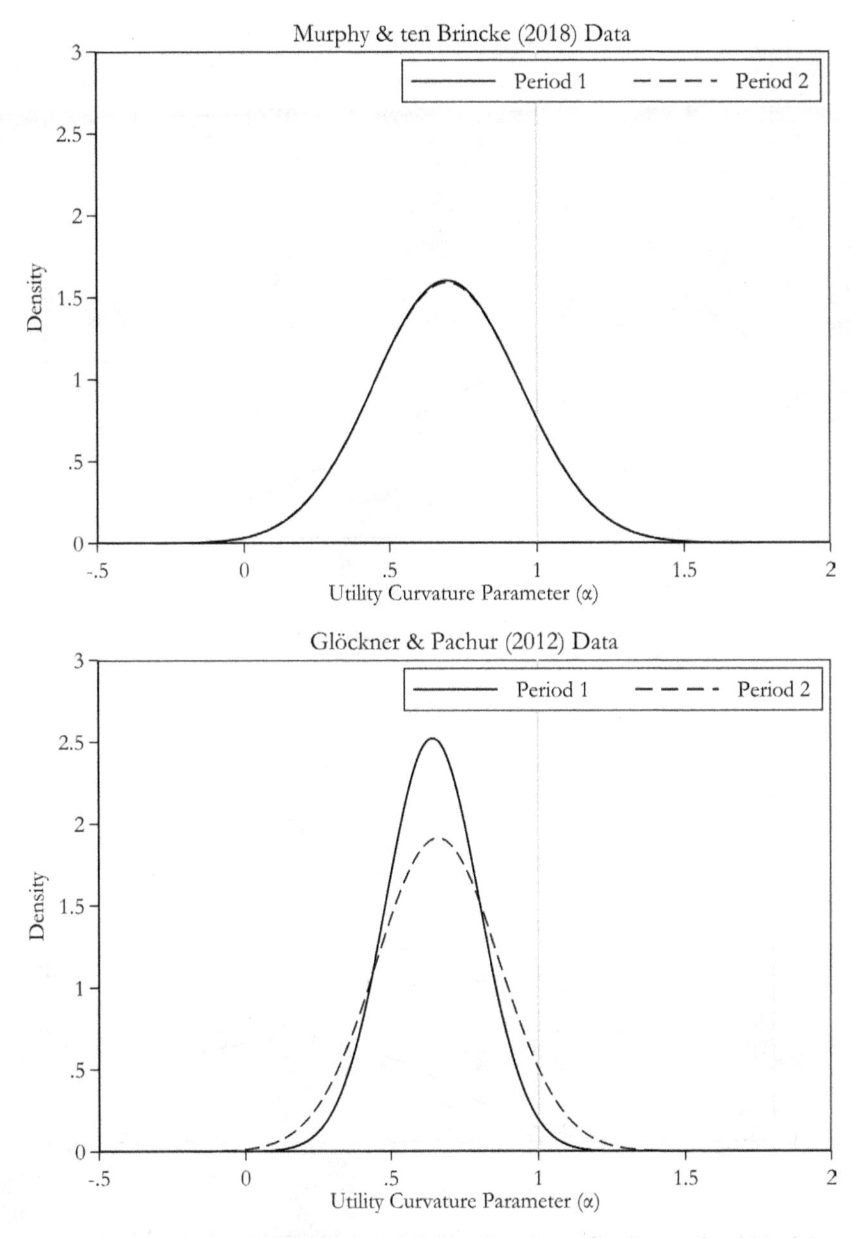

Fig. 4. Population Distributions of Utility Curvature for Constrained Model.

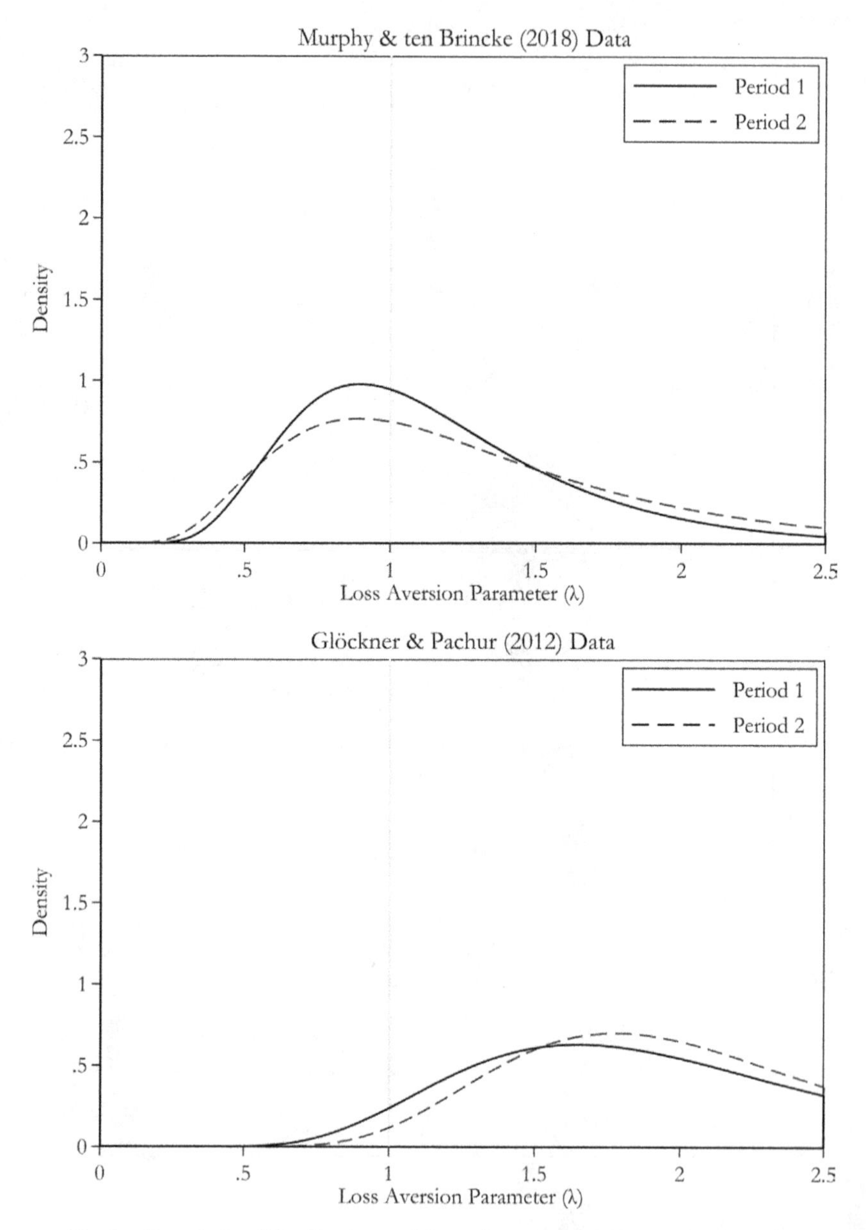

Fig. 5. Population Distributions of Loss Aversion for Constrained Model.

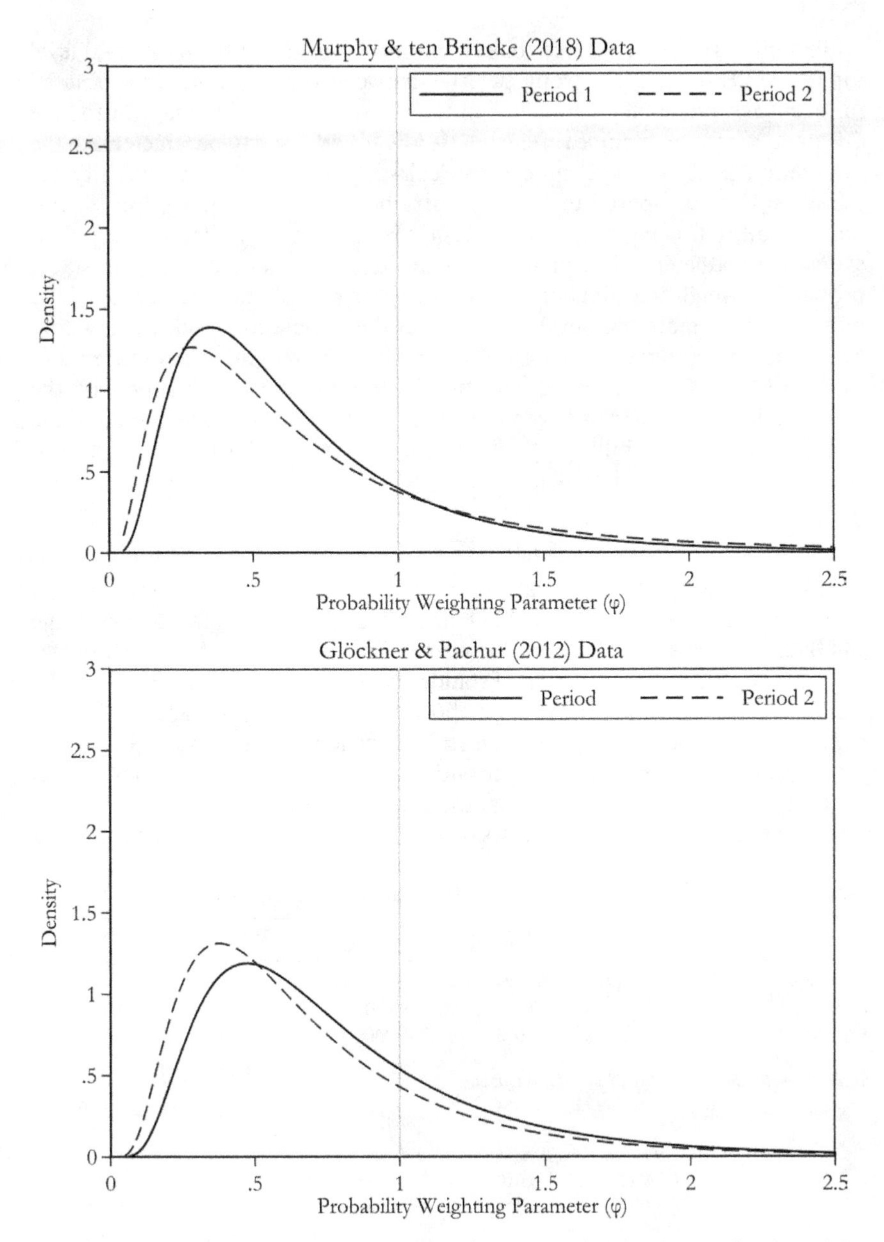

Fig. 6. Population Distributions of Probability Weighting for Constrained Model.

To summarize, we continue to find temporal stability at the individual level for the MTB data, with strong positive between-wave correlation estimated for each risk preference parameter in the constrained model, and not for the GP data, where no significant correlation is found for any parameter. At the population level, we find more empirical support of temporal stability for the MTB data compared to the unconstrained model; we now observe temporal stability for the marginal distributions of the utility curvature and loss aversion parameters, though we continue to observe a temporally unstable probability weighting function. In contrast, for the GP data, the constrained model leads to more temporal *instability* at the population level; we now find an unstable marginal distribution of the probability weighting parameter, and observe greater between-wave variation in the marginal distribution of the loss aversion parameter in Fig. 5 than Fig. 2. For both data sets, we continue to reject temporal stability in the joint population distribution of all parameters in the constrained model.

4.3 EUT Specification

We consider next temporal stability of inferred risk attitudes under EUT. Tables 5 and 6 contain these results for the MTB and GP data, respectively. Looking at the MTB data in Table 5, we find that the population distribution of the r parameter has an estimated mean of 0.817 and standard deviation of 0.247 in wave 1, and a mean of 0.836 and standard deviation of 0.278 in wave 2, and we cannot reject the hypothesis that the two population distributions are similar (*p*-value of 0.084). We also find that the population distribution of the r parameter is temporally stable for the GP data. Fig. 7 shows that the two estimated population distributions for the r parameter overlap almost entirely, but the estimated mean coefficients

Table 5. Estimates of EUT Parameters: Murphy and ten Brincke (2018) Data.

Variable	Estimate	SE	*p*-value	95% Confidence Interval	
A. Estimated population means in wave 1 and wave 2					
r_1	0.817	0.030	<0.001	0.759	0.875
r_2	0.836	0.033	<0.001	0.771	0.902
B. Tests for temporal stability of population means					
$r_2 - r_1$	0.020	0.016	0.204	−0.011	0.050
C. Estimated population standard deviations in wave 1 and wave 2					
σ_{r1}	0.247	0.019	<0.001	0.210	0.284
σ_{r2}	0.278	0.024	<0.001	0.231	0.324
D. Tests for temporal stability of population standard deviations					
$\sigma_{r2} - \sigma_{r1}$	0.031	0.020	0.127	−0.009	0.070
E. Estimated correlation coefficients					
$\rho_{r1\,r2}$	0.943	0.021	<0.001	0.902	0.984

Log-simulated likelihood = −14,715.527 for 25,844 observations on 142 subjects in waves 1 and 2 using 100 Halton draws.

Table 6. Estimates of EUT Parameters: Glöckner and Pachur (2012) Data.

Variable	Estimate	SE	*p*-value	95% Confidence Interval	
A. Estimated population means in wave 1 and wave 2					
r_1	−0.077	0.071	0.279	−0.217	0.063
r_2	−0.084	0.072	0.244	−0.225	0.057
B. Tests for temporal stability of population means					
$r_2 - r_1$	−0.006	0.019	0.733	−0.044	0.031
C. Estimated population standard deviations in wave 1 and wave 2					
σ_{r1}	0.107	0.018	<0.001	0.071	0.143
σ_{r2}	0.104	0.015	0.004	0.075	0.133
D. Tests for temporal stability of population standard deviations					
$\sigma_{r2} - \sigma_{r1}$	−0.002	0.023	0.924	−0.046	0.042
E. Estimated correlation coefficients					
$\rho_{r1\,r2}$	0.476	0.131	<0.001	0.219	0.733

Log-simulated likelihood = −10,269.642 for 17,940 observations on 66 subjects in wave 1 and 64 subjects in wave 2 using 100 Halton draws.

are significantly lower than those observed for the MTB data. We also find a significant between-wave correlation of the r parameter in both data sets: it is equal to 0.943 for the MTB data (p-value < 0.001), and equal to 0.476 for the GP data (p-value < 0.001). Hence, risk preferences under EUT are temporally stable at both the population level and individual level for both data sets.

4.4 Comparison to Previous Literature

We are aware of three studies that consider temporal stability of risk preferences under CPT: Glöckner and Pachur (2012) (GP), Murphy and ten Brincke (2018) (MTB), and Zeisberger et al. (2012) (ZVL). All three studies focus on analyzing temporal stability at the individual level, and apply the maximum likelihood (ML) estimator (GP and ZVL), or an asymptotically equivalent approach known as the maximum *a posteriori* (MAP) estimator (MTB), to compute one set of preference parameters per subject in each session. None of the three studies tests hypotheses concerning the population distribution of risk preferences.

Two of these studies (GP and MTB), impose *a priori* parametric constraints on their CPT specifications. GP restrict potential variability in the preference parameters, by constraining the utility function to be concave in gains and convex in losses, and the probability weighting function to take inverse-S shapes in both gain and loss domains. In the context of our own functional form specification, these constraints correspond to $\alpha^+ < 1$, $\alpha^- < 1$, $\varphi^+ < 1$, and $\varphi^- < 1$. GP take each subject- and session-specific ML estimate as a data point, and compute within-individual correlation in the estimated preference parameters over time. In their most flexible specification, they find three significant within-individual correlation coefficients: 0.59 for utility curvature over gains, 0.32 for utility curvature over losses, and 0.44 for the shape of the probability weighting function in the

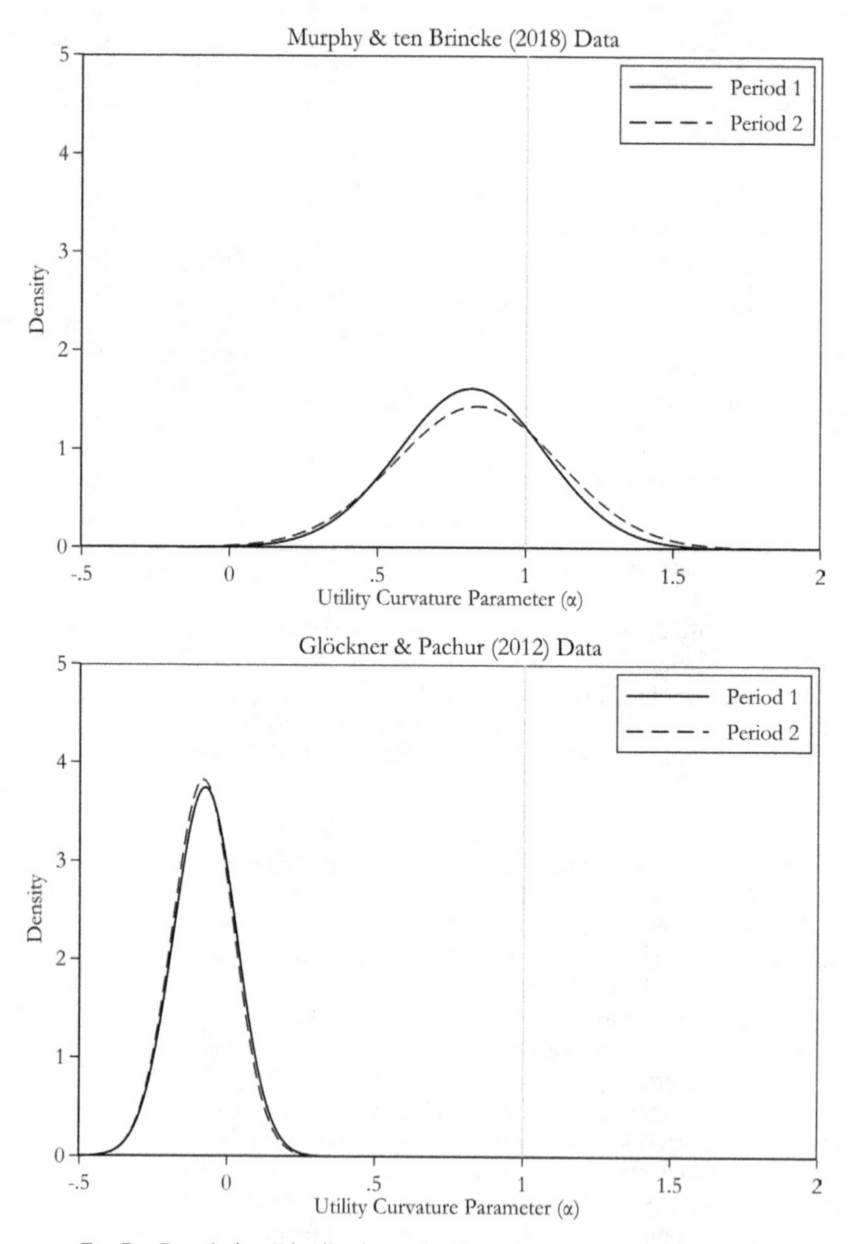

Fig. 7. Population Distributions of Utility Curvature for EUT Model.

gain domain.[18] For the same types of parameters, we obtain statistically insignificant estimates of 0.307 (p-value = 0.110), −0.259 (p-value = 0.729), and 0.029 (p-value = 0.828) instead, albeit direct comparisons should be made with caution because we adopt different functional forms, do not restrict the range of parameter values, and do not follow their two-step procedure that may underestimate standard errors of estimated parameters.

MTB reduce the number of free parameters in their decision model by assuming away sign dependence in the utility curvature and probability weighting parameters. To obtain the prior distribution for the MAP estimator, they estimate a random coefficient model which is more restrictive than our constrained specification in Section 4.B and at odds with their subsequent use of the MAP estimates; they assume that each random coefficient is distributed independently of one another, thereby constraining any type of within-individual correlation coefficient to zero in the prior distribution, and yet they proceed to use the MAP estimates to compute within-individual correlation coefficients, in an analogous manner to what GP have done with the ML estimates. MTB report within-individual correlation coefficients of 0.46 for utility curvature, 0.56 for loss aversion, and 0.67 for the shape of the probability weighting function, which are smaller than the corresponding estimates of 0.96, 0.90, and 0.89 from our constrained specification. They do not subject their results to formal hypothesis tests.

ZVL impose no *a priori* constraints on parameter values, and employ an alternative approach to evaluate temporal stability. Instead of using the subject- and session-specific ML (or MAP) estimates to compute within-individual correlation coefficients, they test the joint hypothesis that each subject's utility and probability weighting functions in a particular domain remain stable over time. Temporal stability is rejected in the gain domain for 12 out of 73 subjects, and in the loss domain for 27 subjects. Overall, for 33 subjects, temporal stability is rejected in at least one domain. Unlike GP and MTB who analyze pairwise lottery choices, ZVL consider certainty equivalents of lotteries, which have been elicited by the Becker–DeGroot–Marchak method. Modeling choice probabilities and expected values of certainty equivalents require different types of statistical models, and we therefore do not include the ZVL data in our study.

5. CONCLUSIONS

We evaluate the temporal stability of risk preferences under CPT, using two data sets from past lab experiments that elicited each subject's risk preferences twice over an interval of one or two weeks. We contribute to the literature by modeling risk preferences under CPT in a random coefficient framework that accounts for unobserved preference heterogeneity across individuals, within-individual correlation in risk preferences across gain and loss domains, and within-individual correlation in risk preferences over time. The flexible modeling approach allows us to evaluate both population-level and individual-level stability in a coherent manner based on the estimates of a single econometric model, instead of basing each level of analysis on a different set of estimates.

By estimating each within-individual correlation coefficient jointly with other parameters in the model, the modeling approach also generates an asymptotic standard error of each correlation coefficient that correctly accounts for sampling variations in estimated preferences.

The risk premium under CPT can be attributed to three sources: utility curvature parameters that vary across gain and loss domains, probability weighting parameters that also vary across gain and loss domains, and a loss aversion parameter that becomes relevant when the decision-maker compares outcomes across the two domains. We do not find that one source of the risk premium is more stable than another, or that the evaluation of lotteries in one domain is more stable than in the other domain. Instead, our findings vary across the two data sets, and also with which aspect of temporal stability we analyze.

In terms of experimental design, we cannot find an obvious explanation for the different results across the two data sets. Both data sets originate from lab experiments which were similar in many aspects. The experiments recruited university students in Germany, asked each student to make a series of choices from lottery pairs with outcomes with similar monetary incentives (–€10 to €12 in GP, and –€10 to €10 in MTB), and adopted a random lottery incentive scheme that selected one of those choices for payment at the end of the experiment. While the time period over which temporal stability is evaluated varies between one and two weeks, we find individual-level stability in the MTB data set that spans two weeks, and not in the GP data set that spans just one week. The GP experiment involved 138 decision tasks per session and paid a show-up fee of €22, whereas the MTB experiment involved 91 decision tasks per session and paid a show-up fee of €10. But the GP experiment recruited 66 subjects whereas the MTB experiment recruited 142 subjects, so the overall sample size is smaller for the former (17,940 choice observations) than the latter (25,844 choice observations). We observe that the estimated standard deviations of the structural parameters in the unconstrained and constrained CPT models tend to increase from the first to the second wave for both data sets, but we do not see any systematic between-wave differences in standard errors of the estimated parameters that can explain the different inferences we draw on temporal stability in the CPT models.

Perhaps a more important issue is a normative question that follows from our findings. How much weight should one place on quantitative predictions based on CPT? Recommendations from quantitative evaluations of policy reforms based on structural economic models are conditional on the assumption that a specific selection of parameter values, which has been used to furnish a theory of interest, remains relevant over time. In the two data sets that we have re-evaluated, we observe that risk preferences estimated under CPT may be unstable over a time span of one or two weeks, which is discomforting from an analytical perspective.[19] However, our results on temporal instability in risk preferences are not invariant to maintained theory. Under EUT, for example, we do not reject temporal stability for the same two data sets, at both the population level and the individual level.

One may suspect that the different inferences on temporal stability of risk preferences are due to finite sample bias, which is aggravated by the richer decomposition of the risk premium into alternative sources under CPT. Stahl (2018) shows that over-fitting of laboratory data by structural decision models of choice under risk may lead to poor forecast performance. He finds that RDU models with one- and two-parameter specifications of the probability weighting function (PWF) are more prone to forecasting errors than the simple EUT model with a single utility curvature parameter. In particular, the RDU model with the two-parameter Prelec function, which is known for flexibility in capturing alternative shapes of the PWF, shows the worst forecast performance. Adding free parameters in structural decision models of choice under risk may improve the likelihood of observed choices, but increase the risk of over-fitting and poor predictive validity.

NOTES

1. These four studies are Harrison, Johnson, McInnes, and Rutström (2005), Andersen, Harrison, Lau, and Rutström (2008), Wölbert and Riedl (2013), and an early version of Harrison, Lau, and Yoo (2020).

2. The unique feature of Harrison et al. (2020) is that their econometric model explicitly controls for the effects of non-random sample selection and panel attrition. They find that corrections for endogenous sample selection and attrition bias may have significant economic effects, although the same corrections do not lead to different qualitative inferences on temporal stability.

3. Hey and Orme (1994) were the first to consider individual level estimation of latent risk attitudes, which requires a relatively large number of observations per subject; they had a sample of 80 subjects with 100 observations per subject. Later applications of individual level estimation of latent preferences also consider individual discount rates (Andersen, Harrison, Lau, & Rutström, 2014) and intertemporal correlation aversion (Andersen, Harrison, Lau, & Rutström, 2017). Harrison and Swarthout (2023) estimate the full set of latent structural parameters for CPT at the individual level and find considerable variation in risk preferences.

4. Murphy and ten Brincke (2018) computed individual-level estimates of structural parameters using what they call "hierarchical ML," a name which may cause some confusion. This method refers to the usual maximum a posteriori (MAP) estimator, which is asymptotically equivalent to the ML estimator. In a finite sample, the MAP and ML estimates may diverge because the MAP estimates are obtained by intentionally tilting the ML estimates towards the mode of some prior distribution that the researcher has in mind for the individual-level parameters. Before applying the MAP procedure at the individual level, Murphy and ten Brincke specified and estimated a random coefficient model, but they used a restrictive population distribution that assumed away correlation between the random coefficients. Our analysis rejects the restrictions that they imposed at this step. It is the point estimates of the restrictive population distribution that they used as a prior distribution in each subsequent MAP estimation run. It is debatable whether tilting individual-level ML estimates towards the *estimated mode* of an implausibly restrictive distribution is a desirable econometric strategy.

5. The exception is the probability weighting function for gains.

6. Zeisberger et al. (2012) used the Becker–DeGroot–Marschak method and asked subjects to state certainty equivalents for each lottery in their experiment. This elicitation format does not preclude structural estimation *per se*, but modeling certainty equivalents requires a fundamentally different behavioral error story, in the form of a stochastic model, from modeling binary choices.

7. The MTB experiment was originally conducted by Pachur, Schulte-Mecklenback, Murphy, and Hertwig (2018).

8. Glöckner and Pachur (2012) estimate an expected utility model with no integration of endowments and prizes, which essentially is a restricted version of CPT with a single utility curvature parameter that applies to both gains and losses, linear probability weighting and no loss aversion.

9. The Arrow–Pratt coefficient of relative risk aversion is given by $(1 - r)M/(M + \kappa)$ which is roughly constant over M for small values of κ.

10. The outcomes and probabilities associated with lottery pairs vary from task to task, and the same subject may make different choices across tasks and waves. Each lottery outcome and its probability are then M_{ijntw} and $p(M_{ijntw})$, leading to the expected utilities EU_{intw} and the index function ∇EU_{ntw}. The indicator y_{ntw} is 1 (0) if subject n chooses lottery B (lottery A) in decision task t of the experiment in wave w.

11. For a Prelec function $\omega(p) = \exp\{-\eta(-\ln p)^{\varphi}\}$ with $\varphi \neq 1$, the fixed point $\omega(p^*) = p^*$ occurs at $p^* = \exp\{-(1/\eta)^{1/(\varphi-1)}\}$. For an inverse-S function that implies overweighting of small probabilities (i.e., $\omega(p) > p$ for $p < p^*$) and underweighting of large probabilities (i.e., $\omega(p) < p$ for $p > p^*$), this means that the threshold for being small versus large, p^*, becomes smaller as η increases. For an S-shaped function that implies underweighting of small probabilities and overweighting of large probabilities, p^* increases in η instead. In addition, the whole function will become more convex when η increases, contributing to stronger underweighting effect at each p, hence η is called the "net index of convexity" (Prelec, 1998). For a power function that arises when $\varphi = 1$, $\eta > 1$ leads to a globally convex function that underweights all interior probabilities and $\eta < 1$ leads to a globally concave function that overweights all interior probabilities.

12. Train (2009, pp. 144–147) provides details on MSL estimation of heterogeneous preference models.

13. The within-individual correlation coefficients of λ, φ^+, and φ^- are computed by applying the usual formula for the correlation coefficient of bivariate log-normal random variables. Other correlation coefficients involving λ, φ^+ and φ^- present cases where we need to compute the correlation between a log-normal random variable and a normal random variable. Garvey, Book, and Covert (2015, p. 443) provide a closed-form formula that can be applied to these cases.

14. In total, temporal stability in the joint distribution of the seven parameters in the CPT model, where we treat five of those seven parameters as random coefficients, entails 22 between-wave equality restrictions: 12 restrictions (7 mean coefficients and 5 standard deviations) on the marginal distributions and 10 restrictions on the correlation coefficients between the five random coefficients.

15. Fig. 1 is generated from the *point estimates* of the population mean and population standard deviation of the utility curvature parameter. It reflects neither the *standard errors* around those point estimates nor the covariance between them. Our statistical tests do take the sampling distribution of the estimated coefficients into account.

16. The $\chi^2(2)$ test of temporal stability in the marginal distribution has a *p*-value of 0.358, 0.439, 0.729, 0.513, and 0.318 for α^+, α^-, λ, φ^+, and φ^-, respectively.

17. We cannot reject the hypothesis that each of the two estimated λ parameters is equal to 1 at the 5% significance level.

18. They find smaller correlation coefficients of 0.28 and 0.15 for the shape of the probability weighting function in the loss domain and the loss aversion parameter, respectively. They do not report what adjustment has been made to standard errors to account for the fact that their analysis computes correlation coefficients for ML estimates, instead of true parameter values.

19. Harrison, Lau, and Rutström (2015) illustrate the importance of correcting for risk attitudes in welfare evaluations of policy reforms using a Computable General Equilibrium (CGE) model of the Danish economy. They consider illustrative examples with revenue-neutral reforms of indirect taxes that lead to uncertain predicted income effects across households, and show that corrections for risk aversion in the gain domain may lead to substantially lower welfare effects from those predicted under risk neutrality. Of course, policy reforms may also end up with some individuals suffering economic losses, in which case CPT is a relevant theory to consider. Policy analyses based on CGE models typically assume that the behavioral parameters in the model are stable over relatively long time periods, which is a strong assumption considering our findings here.

ACKNOWLEDGEMENTS

We thank the Danish Council for Independent Research | Social Sciences (project number: DFF-7015-00054) for financial support. We also thank Andreas Glöckner, Ryan Murphy, Thorsten Pachur, and Robert ten Brincke for making their data available to us.

REFERENCES

Abdellaoui, M., Bleichrodt, H., & Paraschiv, C. (2007). Loss Aversion under prospect theory: A parameter-free measurement. *Management Science*, *53*(10), 1659–1674.

Andersen, S., Harrison, G. W., Lau, M. I., & Rutström, E. E. (2008). Lost in state space: Are preferences stable? *International Economic Review*, *49*(3), 1091–1112.

Andersen, S., Harrison, G. W., Lau, M. I., & Rutström, E. E. (2014). Discounting behavior: A reconsideration. *European Economic Review*, *71*, 15–33.

Barberis, N., Mukherjee, A., & Wang, B. (2016). Prospect theory and stock returns: An empirical test. *Review of Financial Studies*, *29*, 3068–3107.

Chuang, Y., & Schechter, L. (2015). Stability of experimental and survey measures of risk, time, and social preferences: A review and some new results. *Journal of Development Economics*, *117*, 151–170.

Garvey, P. R., Book, S. A., & Covert, R. P. (2015). *Probability methods for cost uncertainty analysis: A systems engineering perspective* (2nd ed.). Boca Raton, FL: CRC Press.

Glöckner, A., & Pachur, T. (2012). Cognitive models of risky choice: Parameter stability and predictive accuracy of prospect theory. *Cognition*, *123*, 21–32.

Harrison, G. W., Johnson, E., McInnes, M. M. & Rutström, E. E. (2005). Temporal stability of estimates of risk aversion. *Applied Financial Economics Letters*, *1*(1), 31–35.

Harrison, G. W., Lau, M. I., & Rutström, E. E. (2015). Theory, experimental design and econometrics are complementary. In G. Frechette & A. Schotter (Eds.), *Handbook of experimental economics methodology* (pp. 296–338). Oxford: Oxford University Press.

Harrison, G. W., Lau, M. I., & Yoo, H. I. (2020). Risk attitudes, sample selection and attrition in a longitudinal field experiment. *Review of Economics and Statistics*, *102*, 552–568.

Harrison, G. W., & Swarthout, J. T. (2023). Cumulative prospect theory in the laboratory: A reconsideration. In G. W. Harrison & D. Ross (Eds.), *Models of risk preferences: Descriptive and normative challenges* (pp. 107–192). Bingley: Emerald.

Hey, J. D., & Orme, C. (1994). Investigating generalizations of expected utility theory using experimental data. *Econometrica*, *62*(6), 1291–1326.

Kaustia, M. (2010). Prospect theory and the disposition effect. *Journal of Financial and Quantitative Analysis*, *45*, 791–812.

Murphy, R. O.. & ten Brincke, R. H. W. (2018). Hierarchical maximum likelihood parameter estimation for cumulative prospect theory: Improving the reliability of individual risk parameter estimates. *Management Science*, *64*(1), 308–326.

Pachur, T., Schulte-Mecklenbeck, M., Murphy R. O., & Hertwig, R. (2018). Prospect theory tracks selective allocation of attention. *Journal of Experimental Psychology*, *147*(2), 147–169.

Prelec, D. (1998). The probability weighting function. *Econometrica*, *66*, 497–527.

Stahl, D. O. (2018). Assessing the forecast performance of models of choice. *Journal of Behavioral and Experimental Economics*, *73*, 86–92.

Train, K. (2019). *Discrete choice models with simulation* (2nd ed). Cambridge: Cambridge University Press.

Tversky, A., & Kahneman, D. (1992). Advances in prospect theory: Cumulative representations of uncertainty. *Journal of Risk & Uncertainty*, *5*, 297–323.

Wilcox, N. T. (2008). Stochastic models for binary discrete choice under risk: A critical primer and econometric comparison. In J. Cox & G. W. Harrison (Eds.), *Risk aversion in experiments* (Vol. 12, pp. 197–292). Bingley: Emerald.

Wölbert, E., & Riedl, A. M. (2013). *Measuring time and risk preferences: Reliability, stability, domain specificity*. CESifo Working Paper Series No. 4339. https://dx.doi.org/10.2139/ssrn.2302494

Zeisberger, S., Vrecko, D., & Langer, T. (2012). Measuring the time stability of prospect theory preferences. *Theory and Decision, 72*, 359–386.

CHAPTER 5

THE WELFARE CONSEQUENCES OF INDIVIDUAL-LEVEL RISK PREFERENCE ESTIMATION

Brian Albert Monroe

ABSTRACT

Risk preferences play a critical role in almost every facet of economic activity. Experimental economists have sought to infer the risk preferences of subjects from choice behavior over lotteries. To help mitigate the influence of observable, and unobservable, heterogeneity in their samples, risk preferences have been estimated at the level of the individual subject. Recent work has detailed the lack of statistical power in descriptively classifying individual subjects as conforming to Expected Utility Theory (EUT) or Rank Dependent Utility (RDU). I discuss the normative consequences of this lack of power and provide some suggestions to improve the accuracy of normative inferences about individual-level choice behavior.

Keywords: Rank Dependent Utility; Expected Utility Theory; risk preferences; welfare; statistical power; model selection

1 INTRODUCTION

Risk preferences estimation is critical to evaluating models of discounting (Andersen, Harrison, Lau, & Rutström, 2014), subjective beliefs (Andersen, Fountain, Harrison, & Rutström, 2014), and other aspects of economic choice.

Models of Risk Preferences: Descriptive and Normative Challenges
Research in Experimental Economics, Volume 22, 227–254

ISSN: 0193-2306/doi:10.1108/S0193-230620230000022005

To eliminate complications arising from both observed and unobserved heterogeneity in risk preferences when drawing inferences from experimental data, preferences can be estimated at the individual level. Examples of estimating these risk preferences at the individual level include Hey and Orme (1994) (HO), with the *descriptive* purpose of classifying subjects as conforming to one model or another, and Harrison and Ng (2016), with the *normative* purpose of calculating the expected consumer surplus (ECS) of an individual's choices.

HO elicited risk preferences from subjects using an instrument comprising 100 lottery pairs. For each pair, subjects were asked to select one lottery in the pair for possible payment. HO estimated 11 risk preference specifications and selected a "winning" model for each subject on the basis of these estimates. HN similarly collected data from subjects over 80 lottery pairs and estimated 4 risk preference specifications for each subject and selected a "winning" model. The primary inferential objective of HO was to determine if there was significant descriptive evidence that subjects in economic experiments regularly deviate from EUT, and found that although their EUT specification was a winning model for more subjects than any other, it did not win for a majority of subjects. On other hand, HN was primarily concerned with the normative calculation of ECS in an insurance task that their subjects also completed. The classification of individual subjects as EUT or an alternative model plays a key role in both studies.[1]

While both inferential objectives are well-posed, subsequent power analyses of the classification processes used by HO and HN have shown that the probability of correctly classifying a subject as one model or another is much lower than expected. Monroe (2020) shows that the classification process HN used to select a winning model for each subject, produced high rates of type I and type II errors in classifying subjects as either EUT or RDU, due to Quiggin (1982).[2] When the HN classification process is used with the HO lottery battery, similar rates of error in classifying subjects are observed.

In this chapter, I explore a *normative* consequence of this lack of statistical power by evaluating the ECS of simulated agents' choices over the insurance task used by HN, and calculating the extent to which the actual ECS of the simulated agents differs from the estimated ECS implied by the subject's winning model. Just as Monroe (2020) found that there were large rates of error in the classification of subjects as one model or the other, the analysis here shows that these errors propagate to inferences about ECS. However, if one is not interested in the *descriptive* veracity of whether a subject conforms to one model or another, I find that, in certain circumstances, the veracity of *normative* inferences about ECS can be improved by abandoning attempts to classify subjects at all.[3]

Section 2 begins by discussing the two models of choice under risk used to calculate the ECS of simulated agents, Section 3 discusses the simulation process used to classify subjects and calculate the ECS. Section 4 presents the key results of this simulation analysis, Section 5 discusses the accuracy of ECS estimates in a hypothetical sample, and an approach to improve accuracy, and Section 6 concludes.

2 MODELS OF CHOICE UNDER RISK AND CONSUMER SURPLUS

To reduce the complexity of the following analyses, only an EUT model and an RDU model will be used for classification. The RDU model nests EUT as a special case, which allows us to describe the utility of a lottery for both models as:

$$\text{RDU} = \sum_{c}^{C} w_c(p) \times u(x_c) \tag{1}$$

where $w_c(p)$ is the decision weight applied to outcome x_c given the distribution of probabilities across all outcomes, p, and $u(x_c)$ is the utility of outcome x_c. Following HN, I use the constant relative risk aversion (CRRA) utility function throughout:

$$u(x) = \frac{x^{1-r}}{1-r} \tag{2}$$

Decision weights for the RDU model are defined by first specifying a probability weighting function (PWF) that weights cumulative probabilities based on the ordinal rank of the outcomes:

$$w_c(p) = \begin{cases} \omega\left(\sum_{i=c}^{C} p_i\right) - \omega\left(\sum_{j=i+1}^{C} p_j\right) & \text{for } c < C \\ \omega(p_c) & \text{for } c = C \end{cases} \tag{3}$$

where $\omega(\cdot)$ is the PWF, and $c \in C$ indexes the rank-ordered outcomes from lowest to greatest. For the special case of EUT, the PWF collapses to the objective probabilities:

$$\omega(p_c) = p_c \tag{4}$$

For the non-EUT case, I follow HN by using the two-parameter PWF developed by Prelec (1998) to allow for flexibility in probability weighting:

$$\omega(p) = exp\left(-\eta(-ln(p))^{\phi}\right) \tag{5}$$

where $0 < p < 1$, $\phi, \eta > 0$, and set $\omega(0) = 0$ and $\omega(1) = 1$.

The Contextual Utility (CU) stochastic model of Wilcox (2011) is used to relate the RDU of an option to the likelihood of it being chosen. Thus, the probability that option A is chosen is:

$$\begin{aligned} Pr(A) &= Pr\left(\varepsilon \geq \frac{1}{\lambda}[\text{RDU}(A) - \text{RDU}(B)]\right) \\ &= F\left(\frac{\text{RDU}(A) - \text{RDU}(B)}{D(A,B)\lambda}\right) \end{aligned} \tag{6}$$

where ε is a mean 0 error term, F is a symmetric cumulative distribution function (cdf), and λ is a precision parameter. The logistic cdf is used here for F for all calculations. The λ parameter scales the difference in the RDU of the two options, with smaller values of λ making the difference large, and larger values of λ making the difference small. Large differences in RDU lead to choice probabilities closer to 0 and 1, and small differences in RDU lead to choice probabilities closer to 0.5.

The function $D(\cdot)$ provides the "contextualization" that gives CU its name, and is defined as the difference between the utility of the maximum outcome, $\overline{x}$, and minimum outcome, $\underline{x}$, *across* lotteries A and B:

$$D(A,B) = u(\overline{x}) - u(\underline{x}) \tag{7}$$

Given that each choice considered here only involves two options, the probability of choosing option A can be defined as a multinomial logit function:

$$Pr(A) = \frac{exp\left(\frac{\text{RDU}(A)}{D(A,B)\lambda}\right)}{exp\left(\frac{\text{RDU}(A)}{D(A,B)\lambda}\right) + exp\left(\frac{\text{RDU}(B)}{D(A,B)\lambda}\right)} \tag{8}$$

The two data generating processes (DGP) to be evaluated therefore consist of an EUT model and an RDU model which have the utility function and stochastic specification in common, and differ only by the treatment of decision weights in (1).

2.1 Consumer Surplus Calculation

HN define the ECS of the chosen lottery as the difference in the certainty equivalent (CE) of the lottery that was chosen and the CE of the lottery that was not chosen.[4] The CE of a lottery is the amount of money received with certainty that provides the same utility as the lottery itself, and thus an agent is indifferent between the lottery and the CE. The CE is calculated explicitly using Eqs. (1) and (2). The RDU of lottery A, calculated with Eq. (1), is set equal to the utility of the CE, and then solved for the CE[5]:

$$\frac{\text{CE}^{(1-r)}}{1-r} = \sum_c^C w_c(p) \times \frac{x_c^{1-r}}{1-r} \tag{9}$$

$$\text{CE} = \left[(1-r) \times \sum_c^C w_c(p) \times \frac{x_c^{1-r}}{1-r}\right]^{\frac{1}{1-r}} \tag{10}$$

The ECS is therefore:

$$\text{ECS} = \text{CE}_{\text{chosen}} - \text{CE}_{\text{not chosen}} \tag{11}$$

HN additionally define an "efficiency" statistic (EF), following Plott and Smith (1978), which is the proportion of the *realized* consumer surplus to the maximum *possible* consumer surplus CE:

$$\mathrm{EF} = \frac{\mathrm{CE}_{\text{chosen}} - \mathrm{CE}_{\text{not chosen}}}{max\left(\mathrm{CE}_{\text{chosen}}, \mathrm{CE}_{\text{not chosen}}\right)} \tag{12}$$

where EF is bound between $[-1,1)$, with 1being perfectly efficient and -1 being perfectly inefficient.

When assessing the ECS of observed choices of subjects, different estimated models may result in different calculated values of ECS. HN classify subjects to determine which model's calculated ECS to use to describe each subject's choices. However, as shown in Monroe (2020), there is considerable variability in the probability of an agent being classified as one model or another. For the subsequent simulation analysis, it will be useful to have a metric that characterizes the ECS that is expected to be estimated for an agent, given the different models that will be applied to the subject's data. The model weighted surplus (MWS) uses the weighted CEs of the model the subject is classified as to calculate the ECS:

$$\mathrm{MWS} = E\left(y \times \mathrm{ECS}_{EUT} + (1-y) \times \mathrm{ECS}_{RDU}\right) \tag{13}$$

where y is equal to 1, if the simulated agent is classified as EUT and 0, if the simulated agent is classified as RDU. The metric in (13) accounts for the probability of a subject being classified as one model or another, and for the possibility that ECS will differ for correctly and incorrectly classified subjects.

The CE of a lottery depends on both the utility and probability weighting parameters that define the RDU of the lottery. The insight of HN is that different individual subjects will have different values of these parameters, and potentially not weight probabilities at all. Differences in these parameters lead to different inferences about the ECS of subjects when making decisions in the insurance task to buy insurance or not.

3 SIMULATION PROCESS

To be able to assess the statistical power of normative inferences, the degree to which estimated ECS deviates from actual ECS needs to be calculated. However, calculating actual ECS requires knowledge of the preferences of an agent, which can only be inferred through choice behavior.[6] This predicament is avoided by simulating agents. With simulated agents, preferences are directly observed because they are assigned in the simulation process.

Simulated agents are defined by the set of parameters that determine their DGP, either the EUT model or the RDU model. The simulated EUT agents are defined by $\{r, \lambda\}$, the CRRA parameter from Eq. (2) and the precision parameter from Eq. (6). The simulated RDU agents are defined by $\{r, \phi, \eta, \lambda\}$, which additionally includes the probability weighting parameters from (5).[7]

Each simulated agent makes choices over both the battery of lottery pairs, and insurance task of HN. The insurance task consists of 24 pairs of one risky lottery and a degenerate lottery where a given amount of money is provided with certainty. This certain amount of money is framed as the premium paid to insure oneself against risk, and the lottery is framed as the distribution of possible outcomes without insurance.

The lottery task consists of 80 lottery pairs chosen to provide increased statistical power when distinguishing between EUT and RDU subjects. Of the 80 pairs in the lottery task, 40 pairs were in the interior of a Marschak–Machina (MM) triangle (Machina, 1987), and 40 corresponding pairs with common ratios at the edge of the triangle. Following the insights of Loomes and Sugden (1998), HN vary the slopes of the chords connecting the lotteries in each pair. For any lottery pair, the chord connecting the lotteries in the MM triangle maps the indifference curve of the common ratio pair. If an agent is indifferent, or close to indifferent, between two lotteries in a pair, the subject will also be indifferent to other lottery pairs with common ratios. Thus, by varying the slopes of the chords, there are more opportunities for subjects to display a strict preference for one lottery over another. HN also note the mixed evidence about "border effects," wherein subjects who make choices across common ratio pairs in the interior of the MM triangle are more likely to be classified as behaving consistently with EUT than if the pairs were on an edge of a MM triangle. HN therefore chose 40 lotteries in the interior, and 40 lotteries of common ratios on the edge of the MM triangle to help control for the possibility of border effects when classifying subjects.

Following HN, the choices made in the lottery task are used to estimate the EUT and RDU models for each simulated agent.[8] The agent is then classified as either RDU or EUT on the basis of a joint non-linear Wald test that $\phi = \eta = 1$ at the 5% confidence level. The EUT and RDU models are estimated with initial values set to the real parameters assigned to the simulated agent, thus maximizing the likelihood of model convergence. However, if a model does not converge, a new set of initial parameters is selected at random and the estimation is attempted again. This process of randomly selecting new initial values is repeated up to five times, after which the model is designated as having failed to converge for that simulated agent. For simulated agents where the EUT model does not converge, but the RDU model does, the agent is classified as RDU, and likewise the agent is classified as EUT if the RDU model does not converge but the EUT model does. If neither model converged for the agent, the agent's data are discarded.[9]

The results of the classification process used here are discussed at length by Monroe (2020), and Appendix A recreates the relevant figures of Monroe (2020) that show the statistical power of the HN lottery battery. Fig. A1 shows the probability of an EUT agent being correctly classified as EUT, and Fig. A2 shows the probability of an RDU agent being correctly classified as RDU. Given the null hypothesis of $\phi = \eta = 1$, a type I error occurs when an EUT agent is incorrectly classified as RDU, and a type II error occurs when an RDU agent is incorrectly classified as EUT. Fig. A1 shows that the probability of a type I error is generally well above the 5% level typically targeted in the economics literature, and Fig. A2 shows that the probability of a type II error is almost always (substantially) higher than 20%.

The classification process discussed here relies on the EUT model being nested in the RDU model, but in general, any classification process can have its power assessed using the same simulation process described above. For example, of the three RDU specifications tested by HN, the specification with a "Inverse-S" PWF, popularized by Tversky and Kahneman (1992), is not exactly nested by the other two. HN use the log-likelihood of the estimated models to determine if the agent should be classified as Inverse-S or one of the other two RDU specifications. Likewise, HO use a likelihood ratio test for differences between EUT and any of the eight models they tested which nest EUT as a special case, and use the Akaike information criterion (AIC)[10] to distinguish between non-nested models.[11] Both processes have their merits and drawbacks. The proper way to adjudicate between classification processes is through power analysis. Simulated data would be classified using competing classification processes and the process that produces the greatest inferential accuracy for the sample you expect to draw is the better process.

However, the classification process is merely a *descriptive* exercise for the inferential objectives of HO and HN. The *normative* consequence of this exercise must be assessed separately. The next section assesses these normative consequences by calculating the ECS of the simulated agents.

4 CONSUMER SURPLUS AT THE INDIVIDUAL LEVEL

Unlike HO, who sought to provide descriptive evidence about the extent to which individual subjects can be said to deviate from EUT, the normative inferential objective of HN was to determine the ECS of individual subjects implied by an estimated model of risk preferences. The objective of HN is therefore informed both by the power of the classification process to correctly select a model used to classify an individual subject, and the degree to which the selected model accurately characterizes that subject's ECS.

For each simulated agent, there are two estimates of ECS, one for each model, one MWS which takes into account the probability that agent is classified as either model, and the agent's actual ECS, which uses the parameter values assigned to the agent to calculate the ECS. To assess the degree to which inaccurate risk preference estimates can result in inaccurate estimates of ECS, the agent's estimated ECS for a given model can be compared to the agent's actual ECS. To assess the degree to which inaccuracy in the classification process can result in inaccurate estimates of ECS, the MWS is compared to the agent's actual ECS. These calculations are performed for each of the EUT and RDU models and displayed graphically below. These analyses are only possible with simulated agents. With simulated agents, the *actual* ECS of the observed choices are known, because their preferences are assumed.

I discuss the accuracy of the estimation of ECS in terms of the differences in ECS, rather than in differences of the efficiency metric proposed by HN. If negative, the ECS metric tells us the maximum amount of money the subject should be willing to pay to change their choices; if positive, the ECS metric tells us the minimum amount of money they would be willing to accept to change their choices.

4.1 EUT Subjects

I begin with the simulated EUT agents. Agents were simulated following the procedure described in Section 3, with the CRRA parameter, r, ranging from 0 to 1, and the precision parameter, λ, ranging from 0.05 to 0.30. Both the EUT and RDU models are estimated on the simulated agent's choice data, and a winning model was selected using the classification approach of HN at a 5% significance level.[12]

Figures showing the actual and potential ECS of subjects are provided in Appendix B. Fig. B1 shows the maximum potential ECS for EUT agents, and Fig. B2 shows the *actual* ECS of the simulated agents. Fig. B2 shows that the actual ECS of an agent's choices depends on the parameters of the model that characterizes that agent. In the case of EUT agents, the ECS of the agents *increases* as the agent becomes less risk averse, viz., as r approaches 0, and the ECS *decreases* as the agent's precision decreases, viz., as λ increases. This is not surprising. If an agent makes choices which deviate from the choice that would be predicted by their risk preferences, the agent forgoes the ECS they would have gained by "choosing correctly." The probability of these deviations increases with the λ precision parameter.

Of greater concern, however, are the comparisons of the estimated ECS to the actual ECS of the simulated agents. The difference between the ECS implied by the estimated EUT model and the actual ECS of the simulated EUT agents is shown in Fig. 1. From Fig. 1, the accuracy of the EUT model in characterizing data generated by EUT agents can be assessed. Estimates of ECS that are closer to the actual ECS are more accurate than estimates of ECS that are very different from the actual ECS. In general, the EUT model provides fairly accurate estimates of ECS for EUT agents. The maximum deviation from the actual ECS is only −\$2.39, the minimum deviation is \$0, and the mean deviation is −\$0.9.[13] The accuracy of the estimated ECS depends on the actual values of the parameters of the agents. The estimated ECS is more accurate for agents with small values of λ and larger values of r. In other words, the more risk averse an EUT agent is, and the less noisy their data, the more accurate the ECS estimates produced by the estimated EUT model will be.

Interestingly, the ECS estimates implied by the RDU model estimated on the EUT agents share this same *pattern* of accuracy. Fig. 2 displays the ECS estimates from the RDU model. The maximum deviation from the actual ECS is −\$2.54, the minimum deviation is −\$0.03, and the mean deviation is −\$1.02.[14] As with the EUT estimates, the ECS estimates implied by the RDU model are more accurate when EUT agents are more risk averse and when they have greater precision. In general, the RDU estimates are less accurate than the EUT estimates, which is to be expected since EUT agents do not probability weight.

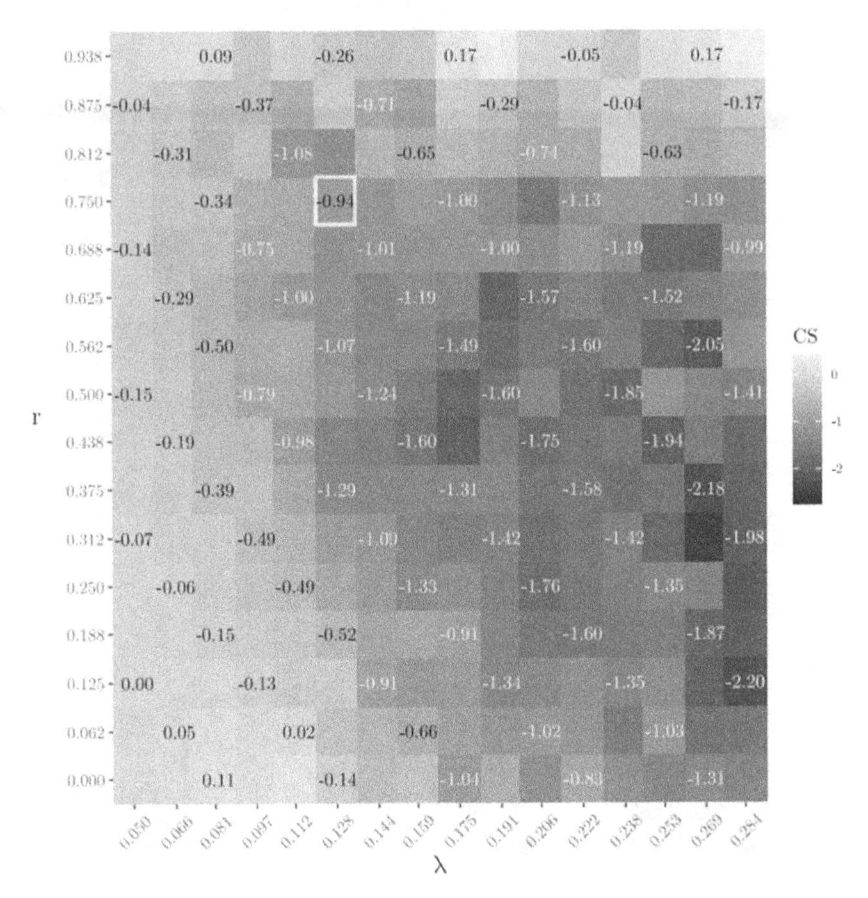

Fig. 1. Difference Between EUT Estimated ECS and Actual ECS for EUT Agents.

Finally, I turn to the difference between the MWS estimates and the actual ECS shown in Fig. 3. The MWS estimates weight the ECS implied by the EUT model by the probability of an agent being classified as EUT, and likewise weight the ECS implied by the RDU model by the probability of an agent being classified as RDU. Fig. 3 shows the overall expected accuracy of ECS estimation as the difference between the MWS and the actual ECS. This difference takes into account the inaccuracy of the classification process.

Fig. 3 shows that the expected estimated ECS of EUT agents remains relatively accurate when agents are classified at the 5% level. This is because EUT agents are relatively likely to be correctly classified, and even when incorrectly classified, the ECS implied by using the RDU model for that agent is not very different from the agent's actual ECS. The maximum expected deviation from the actual ECS is −$1.65, and the minimum expected deviation is $0. The mean deviation from the actual ECS over the given set of possible parameter values is −$0.59.

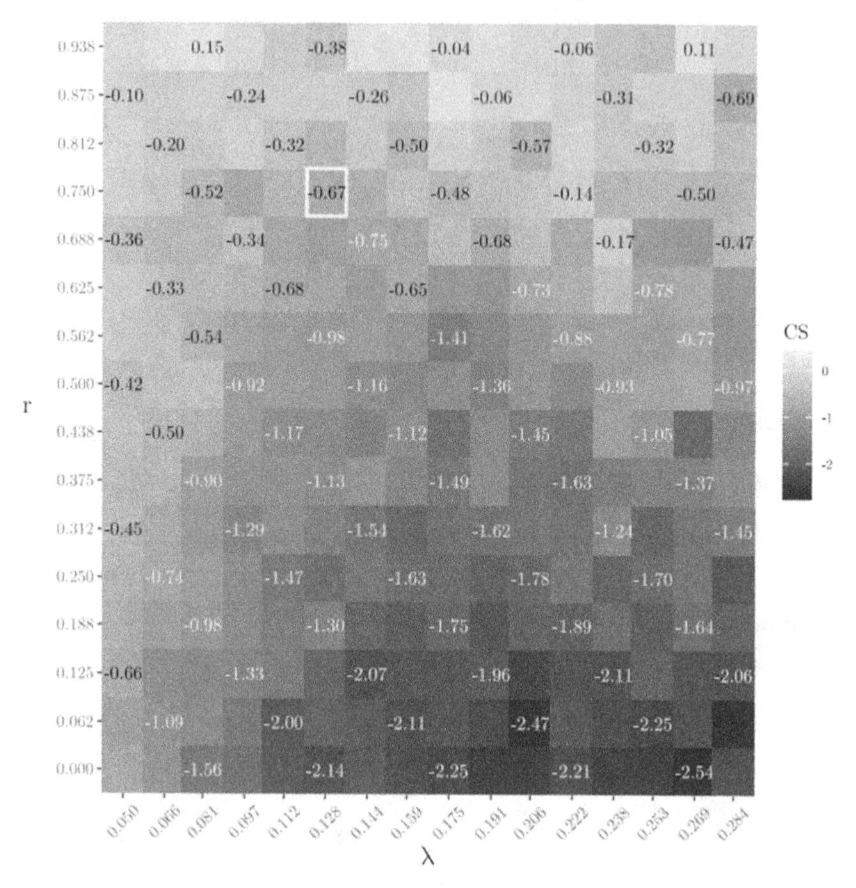

Fig. 2. Difference Between RDU Estimated ECS and Actual ECS for EUT Agents.

To further illustrate the differences in estimated and actual ECS, consider subject 76 from the actual data of HN.[15] This subject was classified as EUT by HN. The estimated CRRA parameter for subject 76 using the EUT model is 0.780, and the estimated λ value is 0.138. The cell this subject would fall into is outlined in white in Figs. 1–3. For simulated agents in this range of parameters, the difference between the EUT estimate of ECS and the actual ECS is $-\$0.94$ and the difference between the RDU estimate of ECS and the actual ECS is $-\$0.67$. For agents in this range of parameters, the RDU model, on average, produces *slightly* more accurate estimates of ECS, even though the agent is known to be EUT. The average actual ECS for agents in this parameter range is \$7.85, and so the EUT model estimated ECS was only 88.0% of the actual ECS, while the RDU model was 91.5% of the actual ECS. In this case, on average, it is actually *better* in terms of ECS to incorrectly classify an EUT agent with parameters in this range as RDU. However, since EUT agents with more accurate ECS estimates are more likely to be correctly classified as EUT,

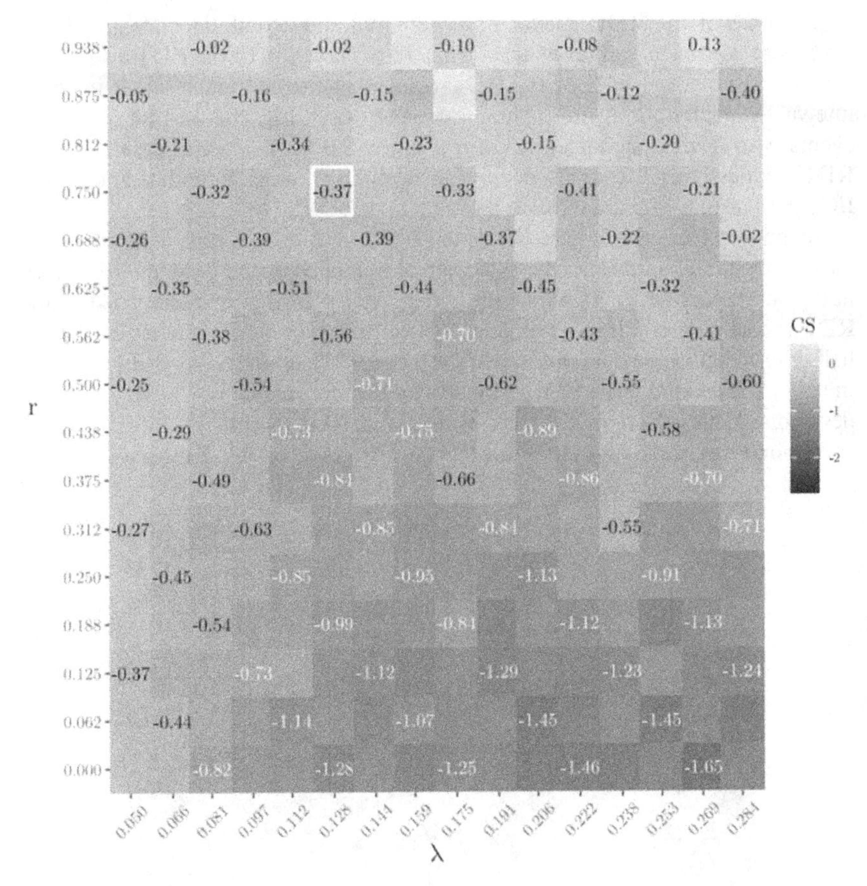

Fig. 3. Difference Between MWS and Actual ECS for EUT Agents.

the MWS for subjects in this range is even closer to the true value, at 95.3% of actual ECS.

4.2 RDU Agents

I now turn to the simulated RDU agents. Agents were again simulated following the approach described in Section 3. Recall that simulated RDU agents are assigned the set of parameters $\{r, \phi, \eta, \lambda\}$. For the simulated RDU agents, the CRRA parameter, r is fixed at 0.50 and the precision parameter, λ, is fixed at 0.10. The probability weighting parameters ϕ and η are both sampled from a uniform distribution between 0.5 and 2.5. These parameter values are typical of the individual-level estimates found by HN. It is the variation in ECS caused by the probability weighting parameters, ϕ and η, which are of interest here. As before, both the EUT and RDU models are estimated over each simulated agent's choice data, and a winning model is selected using the classification process of HN at a 5% significance level.[16]

The ECS of the RDU agents, both potential and actual, depends greatly on the actual parameter values of the agents. In comparison to the EUT agents, the actual and potential ECS of the RDU agents is generally much larger in absolute values for the parameter values considered here. Figs. B3 and B4 show that agents who deviate significantly from a linear PWF, the special case in which RDU reduces to EUT, when $\phi = \eta = 1$, have much larger potential and actual ECS than agents who are close to having a linear PWF.

As might be expected, since the actual ECS varies considerably with the probability weighting parameters, the ECS estimates implied by the EUT model, shown in Fig. 4, are far less accurate than the corresponding ECS estimates implied by the RDU model, shown in Fig. 5. For agents with a value of $\phi > 1.5$, representing the top half of each figure, the minimum deviation for the EUT estimates is –\$8.05 while the minimum deviation for the RDU estimates for the same region is –\$0.87. The mean deviation in this region for the EUT estimates of RDU agents is –\$19.31 and the corresponding mean deviation for the RDU estimates of RDU agents is –\$1.42.[17]

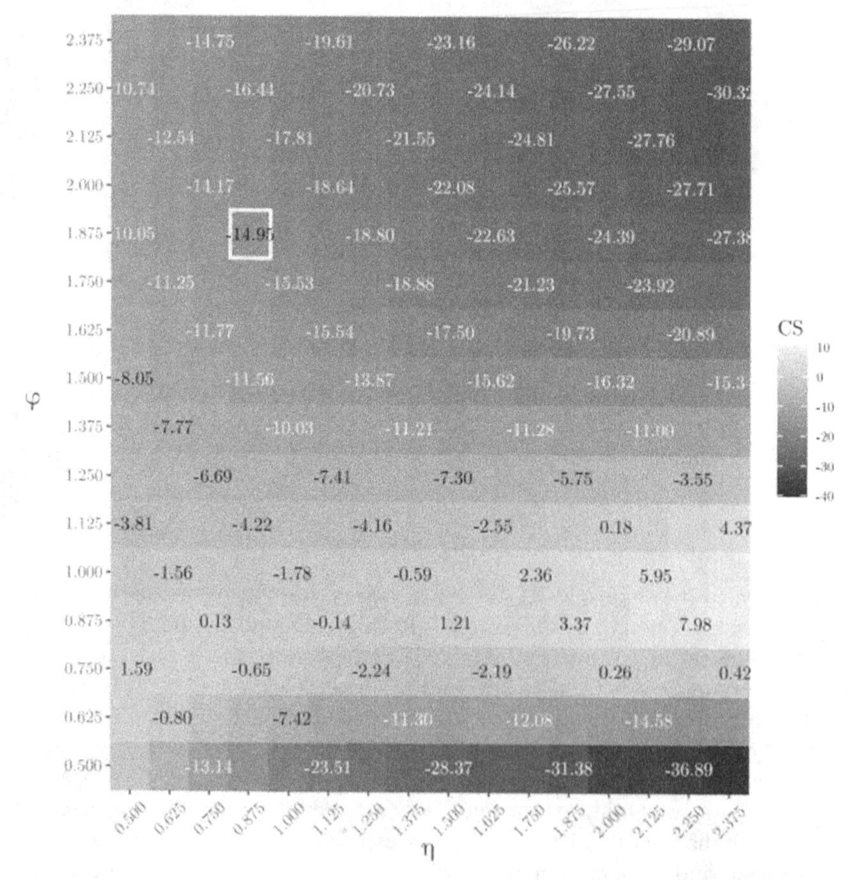

Fig. 4. Difference Between EUT Estimated ECS and Actual ECS for RDU Agents.

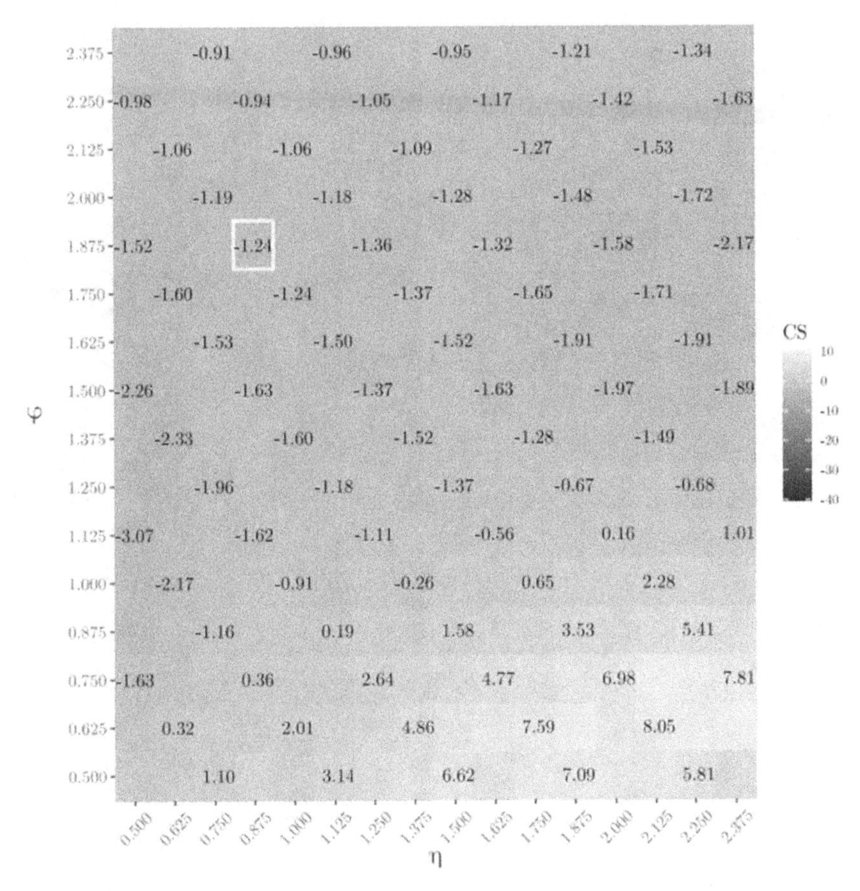

Fig. 5. Difference Between RDU Estimated ECS and Actual ECS for RDU Agents.

Consider subject 77 from the actual data of HN, who was classified as RDU with the Prelec (1998) PWF. The estimated ϕ parameter for subject 77 using the RDU model is 1.940, and the estimated η value is 0.935. The cell this subject would fall into is outlined in white in Figs. 4–6. For simulated agents in this range of parameters, the difference between the EUT estimate of ECS and the actual ECS is –$14.95 and the difference between the RDU estimate of ECS and the actual ECS is –$1.24. For agents with parameters in this range, the RDU model, on average, clearly produces more accurate estimates of ECS. The average actual ECS for agents in this parameter range is $34.99, and so the estimated ECS using the RDU model was 96.5% of the actual ECS, while the estimated ECS using the EUT model was only 57.3% of the actual ECS. In this case, it is extremely costly in terms of ECS to incorrectly classify an RDU agent with parameters in this range as EUT. Since the probability of correctly classifying an RDU agent in this range is so low, the MWS for agents in

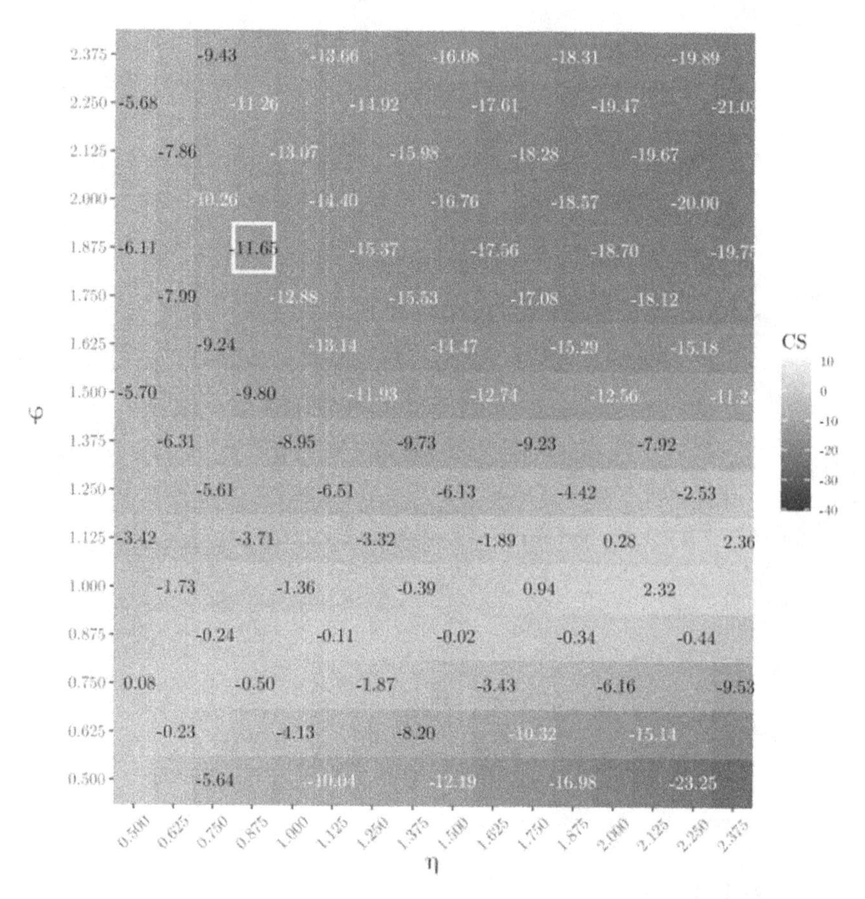

Fig. 6. Difference Between MWS and Actual ECS for RDU Agents.

this range is only 66.7%. Thus, in expectation, the ECS of an RDU agent in this range of parameters is substantially underestimated.

5 WELFARE COST IN A HYPOTHETICAL SAMPLE

In Section 4, I discuss the ECS of simulated EUT and RDU agents for ranges of parameters that might be expected to describe the preferences of real, human subjects. This is a useful exercise because it helps highlight the extent of individual-level heterogeneity in actual and estimated ECS, and the accuracy of estimated of ECS. For EUT subjects with parameters similar to subject 76 in the HN dataset, being correctly classified as EUT or RDU makes very little difference in terms of the accuracy of estimated ECS. For RDU subjects similar to subject 77 in the HN dataset, however, being incorrectly classified as EUT results in a substantial underestimation of the subject's ECS. Figs. 4–6 show that RDU subjects with probability weighting parameters far from the special case of $\phi = \eta = 1$ have very inaccurate estimates of ECS when they are incorrectly classified as EUT, and are likely to have inaccurate estimates of ECS because they are so likely to be incorrectly classified as EUT. For RDU subjects with probability weighting parameters near the special case of $\phi = \eta = 1$, estimated ECS is fairly accurate, regardless of whether the EUT or RDU model is used to calculate ECS. The degree to which the classification process results in inaccurate estimated ECS, for both EUT and RDU subjects, therefore depends on the actual risk preferences of the subjects.[18]

The effect of the heterogeneity of subjects' risk preferences on the accuracy of ECS estimates in a sample can be observed more clearly by considering a hypothetical sample of EUT and RDU agents, and calculating the accuracy of the ECS estimates for the sample. To anchor this exercise in real data, I calculated the median values of the estimated parameters of each model reported by HN and use these values to inform the distribution of parameters in the hypothetical sample. The median value of r for the EUT model was 0.41, and the median value of r for the RDU model was 0.45. The median values of ϕ and η for the RDU model were 1.31 and 0.96, respectively.

Now consider a sample comprised of EUT and RDU agents. In this sample, suppose that the CRRA parameter is distributed normally with a mean of 0.41 for the EUT agents, 0.45 for the RDU agents, and a standard deviation of 0.2 for both models. For both models, assume the λ parameter is distributed log-normal with a mean of 0.12 and a standard deviation of 0.02. For the RDU agents, the ϕ parameter is distributed log-normal with a mean of 1.31 and a standard deviation of 0.2, and the η parameter is also distributed log-normal with a mean of 0.96 and a standard deviation of 0.2. The means of these distributions track the median values of the individual-level estimates of the HN data described above. The standard deviations of these distributions were selected to provide some variation in the preferences of the hypothetical sample, and are not based on the estimates from the HN data.

For the EUT and RDU models, I assume none of the marginal distributions of the parameters are correlated. I draw 100,000 simulated EUT agents and 100,000 simulated RDU agents, 200,000 in total, and simulate responses to the HN lottery task as done previously. Each simulated agent is then classified as EUT or RDU using the HN classification approach, and the actual ECS, the ECS implied by the estimated EUT model, and the ECS implied by the estimated RDU model are calculated for each simulated agent. For each estimated model, the difference between the estimated ECS and the actual ECS, ΔECS, represents the accuracy of the ECS estimate. The p(EUT) and p(RDU) columns of Table 1 show the probability that an agent will be classified as either EUT or RDU, respectively. The ΔECS_{EUT} and ΔECS_{RDU} columns show the average difference between the estimated ECS and the actual ECS implied by the EUT and RDU models, respectively. The MWS column shows the average difference between the estimated ECS of the model the agent was classified as and the agent's actual ECS.

The first two columns of Table 1 show that the probability of correctly classifying a simulated EUT agent using the HN classification process is 0.88, and the probability of correctly classifying an RDU agent is 0.12.[19] This table also shows, as expected, that correctly classified agents have more accurate ECS estimates compared to incorrectly classified agents.[20] The MWS column shows that EUT agents fare better than RDU agents when they are classified because they are much more likely to be correctly classified, correctly classified EUT agents have accurate ECS estimates, and incorrectly classified EUT agents still have more accurate ECS estimates than correctly classified RDU agents.[21]

5.1 Improving Normative Inference by Discarding Descriptive Inference

Since normative inferences about ECS are the primary objective of HN, the accuracy of the ECS estimates are critically important, and the descriptive accuracy of correctly classifying agents as either EUT or RDU is only a secondary concern. The inferential process of HN can be modified to improve the accuracy of ECS estimation, given its relative importance. Monroe (2020, pp. 181–86) shows that increasing the number of lottery pairs in the risk preference task from 80 to 400 substantially increases the probability of correctly classifying an agent for both models. It is clear that increasing the probability of correctly classifying EUT or RDU agents would improve the expected accuracy of the ECS estimates. However, such a large increase in the number of lottery pairs presented to experimental agents may be considered infeasible experimentally.

An alternative approach is to disregard the classification process altogether, and use a "default" model for every agent that produces the most accurate estimates of ECS for the sample. The classification rule would change to: "If the default model has converged, then the agent is classified as that model, otherwise, they are classified as the alternative model." The ECS estimates presented in Table 1 are recalculated using this updated rule assuming EUT as the default model in Table 2, and assuming RDU as the default model in Table 3.

The final column of Table 2 shows that the expected difference in estimated ECS and actual ECS is closer to 0 for EUT subjects when the EUT model is used by default compared to when EUT subjects are classified using the HN rule. Likewise, the final column of Table 3 shows that the expected difference in estimated ECS and actual ECS is closer to 0 for RDU subjects when the RDU model is used by default. This is intuitive: EUT (RDU) agents are less likely to be misclassified when the EUT (RDU) model is used by default. Correctly classified

Table 1. Hypothetical Sample, $N = 200{,}000$.

	p(EUT)	p(RDU)	ΔECS_{EUT}	ΔECS_{RDU}	MWS
EUT agents	0.88	0.12	−0.59	−1.10	−0.65
RDU agents	0.88	0.12	−6.16	−2.07	−5.66

Table 2. Hypothetical Sample, EUT Default, $N = 200{,}000$.

	p(EUT)	p(RDU)	ΔECS_{EUT}	ΔECS_{RDU}	MWS
EUT agents	0.98	0.02	−0.59	−4.02	−0.64
RDU agents	0.98	0.02	−6.16	−2.78	−6.10

Table 3. Hypothetical Sample, RDU Default, $N = 200{,}000$.

	p(EUT)	p(RDU)	ΔECS_{EUT}	ΔECS_{RDU}	MWS
EUT agents	0.02	0.98	−3.91	−1.10	−1.16
RDU agents	0.02	0.98	−8.85	−2.07	−2.18

agents in the parameter ranges given by this hypothetical sample have more accurate estimates of ECS than incorrectly classified agents. Equally intuitive is that when assuming every subject is EUT, RDU agents are worse off in terms of ECS accuracy than if classification is attempted,[22] and when assuming every agent is RDU, EUT agents are worse off in terms of ECS accuracy than if classification was attempted.[23]

The two defaults are not equal, however. For the hypothetical sample described here, 88% of the sample would need to be EUT for the gain to EUT agents in MWS accuracy to outweigh the loss to RDU agents. Even given the difficulty in classifying agents as either EUT or RDU at the individual level, it is unlikely that more than 88% of the agents in the sample collected by HN were EUT, and so a useful rule of thumb for similar samples would be to classify every agent as RDU for the purposes of ECS calculation.

While it is the case that for the hypothetical example shown here, choosing a "default" model, rather than attempting to classify agents as one model or another, results in more accurate ECS estimates, this should not be considered a general result. Rather, the exercise here demonstrates how the composition of the sample interacts with the classification process when assessing the accuracy of normative inferences.

Several key pieces of information need to be identified to make an informed decision about whether the "default" approach described here is appropriate; namely, which types of agents the experimenter wishes to model as present in the sample, such as the EUT and RDU agents discussed here, the proportion of each type of agent in the sample, and the joint distribution of preference parameters for each type of agent.

The experimenter does not need to conduct this exercise blindly. For example, Harrison and Rutström (2009) demonstrate how mixture models at the pooled level can provide information about the proportion of subjects who conform to one model or another.[24] Maximum simulated likelihood estimation (Andersen, Harrison, Hole, Lau, & Rutström, 2012), or Bayesian hierarchical models (Gao, Harrison, & Tchernis, 2023) can provide information about the distributions of parameters of the pooled models.

6 DISCUSSION

The analyses presented here build on the results of Monroe (2020) by providing *ex ante* power analyses of risk preference instruments with respect to their use to make *normative* inferences. Monroe (2020) describes the weakness of experimental procedures used by HN and HO in classifying subjects in economic experiments as conforming to one model of risk preferences over another, a well-posed inferential objective in *descriptive* behavioral economics. As suspected by HO, there is a significant lack of power to correctly classify individual subjects.[25] The focus here, has been to evaluate the ECS of choices made by individual agents over the HN insurance task, leading to several conclusions.

First, the simulation analyses allow us to gain insight about the *actual* ECS of the individual agents irrespective of the estimation process. Fig. B2 shows that there is a dramatic difference in realized ECS as agents' utility functions become less "precise," reflected in an increasing value of the precision parameter, λ. The direction of this effect is not surprising, but the magnitude of differences across values of λ *is* surprising. As the difference in utilities of the lotteries is exacerbated by λ, the probability of correctly classifying an agent also increases. This relationship is particularly important because λ does not reflect a "preference" as defined in economics; there is no value of λ that would change the ordinal ranking of any option in a set of alternatives. The precision parameter, λ, is largely an extension of theory to accommodate data which deviate from the predictions of the utility function. It is clear, however, that these deviations have normative significance in the characterization of ECS.

It may be the case that the precision parameter is directly related to the mechanism that links an agent's choices to outcomes. In particular, the choices presented to the subject may not be sufficiently different to the subject for them to overcome the cognitive burden of making the choice. The "dominance" precept of Smith (1982) requires that the relative difference in rewards between options must "dominate" any costs the subject may incur when choosing between options.[26]

If large values of λ reflect a subject's lack of dominance, experimenters may wish to improve the experimental environment in order to increase the probability of correctly classifying individual agents as well as increase the accuracy of ECS estimates. This may entail different experimental instructions to make clear the differences in options, different presentations of the choice problem, or potentially different kinds of tasks. Whether large values of λ are the result of a lack of dominance, or simply due to random noise in the choice process, the conclusion of HO (p. 1322) seems apt: "Perhaps we should now spend some time on thinking about the noise, rather than about even more alternatives to EU?"

The primary focus of this chapter, however, is the accuracy of the estimated ECS compared to the actual ECS. What is made clear by Figs. 1, 2, 4 and 5, is that accuracy in the classification process matters for both EUT and RDU agents, but far less so for EUT agents. The RDU model nests the EUT model as a special case, which may explain why the estimates of ECS for EUT agents are not wildly different from the real values even when EUT agents are incorrectly characterized as weighting probabilities. The reverse, however, cannot be said of RDU agents. *For RDU agents, the estimated ECS implied by the EUT model generally provides a poor characterization of the welfare of the agents.*

The simulation exercise in Section 5 highlights the process to determine how much these differences matter for the EUT and RDU models, and what can be done about them. For a hypothetical sample, but with parameter values informed by estimation over real agent data, I find that EUT agents are more likely to be correctly classified than RDU agents using the HN classification process, and the estimates of their ECS are closer to the actual ECS of the agents.

However, since normative inferences about welfare are the focus here, not the accuracy of descriptively classifying an agent as one model or another, the classification rule can be modified to improve the accuracy of the ECS estimates. A simple rule is proposed to classify every agent as either EUT or RDU by default if that model converged, and otherwise classify them as the other model. This rule outperforms the HN classification rule in terms of the accuracy of ECS estimates, for EUT agents when the EUT model is used by default, and for RDU agents when the RDU model is used by default. That is not to say both are equally useful as default models.

If EUT is used as a default model, the sample would need to be comprised of approximately 88% EUT agents for the cost to RDU agents to be outweighed by gain in accuracy of ECS estimates for EUT agents. This proportion of EUT agents seems unlikely given the available evidence, even with the caveat that there is low power to classify subjects as one model or another at the individual level. Instead, a useful rule of thumb is to classify all agents as RDU, *when considering only EUT and RDU models as possibilities*. When different models are considered, different rules of thumb may apply.

Fortunately, the exercise performed in Section 5 is generalizable to a wide variety of settings. While only the EUT model and an RDU model with a Prelec (1998) PWF were analyzed here, the same process can easily be applied to non-nested models, and to more than two models. First one needs to define which specifications to estimate for each subject in the sample. For HO there were 11 specifications considered, 8 of which were "top-level" specifications, meaning they were not nested in any other model. HN considered four specifications, two of which were top-level specifications, an RDU model with a Prelec (1998) PWF, and an RDU model with an "Inverse-S" PWF. With the model specifications under consideration defined, one needs a classification process to classify each agent as conforming to one of the given specifications. HO used the AIC to decide amongst top-level models, and a likelihood ratio test to decide amongst top-level and lower-level models. Likewise, HN used the joint Wald test described here to determine if the subject deviated from EUT, and chose the specification with the greatest log-likelihood among the RDU models that were statistically significantly different from EUT.

With proposed models and classification rules in hand, one can simulate the parameter space and agent choices, and calculate the ECS as illustrated here. *Ex ante* power analyses of existing normative inferential objectives are as feasible, and demanding, as power analyses concerned with descriptive inferential objectives. In addition to showing some of the limitations of normative inferences about individual-level risk preference estimation, guidance is provided as to how to conduct normative power analyses, given their importance to economics.

NOTES

1. HO use a likelihood ratio test and the Akaike information criterion to choose "winning" models, while HN use a Wald test. Both methods will be discussed in more detail subsequently.

2. The rate of error typically deemed acceptable for a type I error is 5%, and 20% for a type II error. These acceptable error rates are somewhat arbitrary. Fisher (1956) argues against using the same 5% error rate in every application. Cohen (1988) and Gelman and Loken (2014) refer to 20% as a generally accepted threshold for type II errors when performing *ex ante* power analyses.

3. While the subsequent analyses focus on normative inferences about ECS, the methods discussed can be used to investigate how the lack of descriptive power to classify subjects as one model or another influences the power to make other normative inferences, for example, whether or not a subject conforms to the reduction of compound lottery axiom.

4. If there are more than two lotteries in the choice set, the ECS is the difference between the CE of the chosen lottery, and the CE of the lottery not chosen that provides the greatest utility.

5. In general, the CE of a lottery can easily be solved using numerical methods even if the utility function is not as easily invertible as the CRRA function above. This is because the CE of a lottery must lie between the smallest and largest outcome in a lottery.

6. In economics, preferences are virtual objects used to rationalize observed behavior, that is, they are determined by choices, not *vice versa*. In subsequent discussions, "preferences" refer to a summary of an agent's choice behavior. An "EUT agent," therefore, is an agent who, in the limit, makes choices consistent with EUT; analogous logic applies to an "RDU agent."

7. The parameters r and λ are used in both the EUT and RDU models, but the estimates of these parameters do not need to be the same across models.

8. Harrison and Ng (2016, pp. 101–102) stress that separate tasks are needed to identify risk preferences and to make statements about ECS to be able to declare *any* choices as mistakes. This methodological point, of great significance for normative analysis, is also made by Harrison and Ross (2018, 2023) and Harrison (2019).

9. HN were able to reach convergence for at least one of the four specifications they estimate for 102 out of 111 experimental subjects. Thus, all models failed to converge for 9 subjects, 8.1% of their sample. Instead of discarding data, Gao, Harrison, and Tchernis (2023) revisit the HN dataset and estimate a Bayesian hierarchical model (BHM). They use the predicted posterior distribution to make normative inferences about *all* subjects. BHM methods do not depend on the convergence criteria of maximum likelihood estimation (MLE) for and so inferences can be made for subjects that would fail to provide any useful information using MLE.

10. The AIC is defined as $\text{AIC} = -2lnL\left(\hat{\beta}\right)/T + 2k/T$, where $L\left(\hat{\beta}\right)$ is the likelihood evaluated at the maximum, k is the number of estimated parameters in the specification, and T is the number of observations.

11. The method of ranking described here corresponds to the exercise HO performed to produce their Tables VIII and IX, which they discuss at length. HO (p. 1312) also discuss ranking *all* models on the basis of the AIC, reporting the full results in their Appendix III. For both exercises, the majority of subjects are classified as being best described by a model other than EUT.

12. The probability of correctly classifying an EUT agent as EUT is shown in Fig. A1 of Appendix A.

13. The median is –\$0.96, and the interquartile range spans –\$0.31 to –\$1.37.

14. The median is –\$0.96, and the interquartile range spans –\$0.42 to –\$1.55.

15. HN present the estimates for all subjects in their appendices.

16. The probability of correctly classifying an RDU agent as RDU is shown in Fig. A2 of Appendix A.

17. The median deviation for the EUT estimates of RDU agents is –\$19.25 and the corresponding median deviation for the RDU estimates is –\$1.38.

18. To reiterate, people do not have values of r, ϕ, η, and λ in their brains: the values of these parameters represent summaries of choice behavior. By "actual risk preferences," I mean the risk preferences that would be estimated from an asymptotically large amount of choice data for an individual.

19. See Monroe (2020) for a discussion of the statistical power of the *descriptive* exercise of classifying a subject as one model or another.

20. ΔECS_{EUT} is closer to 0 than ΔECS_{RDU} for EUT agents, and likewise ΔECS_{RDU} is closer to 0 than ΔECS_{EUT} for RDU agents.

21. It is worth noting that these "estimates" are reported without standard errors. In this simulation exercise, the sample size can be chosen to make standard errors arbitrarily small. For the inferences made here, the comparison of the accuracy of ECS estimates, the qualitative conclusions would be unchanged with many more simulated agents.

22. This is seen by comparing the final column of the second row of Tables 2 and 1.

23. This is seen by comparing the final column of the first row of Tables 3 and 1.

24. However, computational complexity increases rapidly when considering more than 2 possible models.

25. Hey and Orme (1994, p. 1315) note that type I errors may be frequent in their analyses, and later note that "it could be argued that the lack of significance for some of the top-level functionals for some of the subjects in our study could simply result from this noise, combined with rather uninformative data" (pp. 1321–1322). Both sentiments are borne out by the analyses conducted by Monroe (2020).

26. See Harrison (1989, 1992) for a further discussion of the dominance precept.

REFERENCES

Andersen, S., Fountain, J., Harrison, G. W., & Rutström, E. E. (2014). Estimating subjective probabilities. *Journal of Risk and Uncertainty*, *48*(3): 207–229.

Andersen, S., Harrison, G. W., Hole, A. R., Lau, M., & Rutström, E. E. (2012). Non-linear mixed logit. *Theory and Decision*, *73*, 77–96.

Andersen, S., Harrison, G. W., Lau, M. I., & Rutström, E. E. (2014). Discounting behavior: A reconsideration. *European Economic Review*, *71*, 15–33.

Cohen, J. (1988). *Statistical power analysis for the behavioral sciences* (Vol. 2). New York, NY: Academic Press.

Fisher, R. (1956). *Statistical methods and scientific inference*. Edinburgh: Oliver & Boyd.

Gao, X. S., Harrison, G. W., & Tchernis, R. (2023). Behavioral welfare economics and risk preferences: A Bayesian approach. *Experimental Economics*, *26*, 273–303. https://doi.org/10.1007/s10683-022-09751-0.

Gelman, A., & Loken, E. (2014). The statistical crisis in science. *American Scientist*, *102*, 460–465.

Harrison, G. W. (1989). Theory and misbehavior of first-price auctions. *American Economic Review*, *79*(4), 749–762.

Harrison, G. W. (1992). Theory and misbehavior of first price auctions: Reply. *American Economic Review*, *79*(4), 1426–1443.

Harrison, G. W. (2019). The behavioral welfare economics of insurance. *Geneva Risk and Insurance Review*, *44*(2), 137–175.

Harrison, G. W., & Ng, J. M. (2016). Evaluating the expected welfare gain from insurance. *Journal of Risk and Insurance*, *83*(1), 91–120.

Harrison, G. W., & Ross, D. (2018). Varieties of paternalism and the heterogeneity of utility structures. *Journal of Economic Methodology*, *25*(1), 42–67.

Harrison, G. W., & Ross, D. (2023). Behavioral welfare economics and the quantitative intentional stance. In G. W. Harrison & D. Ross (Eds.), *Models of risk preferences: Descriptive and normative challenges*, (pp. 7–62). Bingley: Emerald.

Harrison, G. W., & Rutström, E. E. (2009). Expected utility theory and prospect theory: One wedding and a decent funeral. *Experimental Economics*, *12*(2), 133–158.

Hey, J. D., & Orme, C. (1994). Investigating generalizations of expected utility theory using experimental data. *Econometrica*, *62*(6), 1291–1326.

Loomes, G., & Sugden, R. (1998). Testing different stochastic specifications of risky choice. *Economica, 65*, 581–598.

Machina, M. J. (1987). Choice under uncertainty – Problems solved and unsolved. *Economic Perspectives, 1*(1), 121–154.

Monroe, B. A. (2020). The statistical power of individual-level risk preference estimation. *Journal of the Economic Science Association, 6*, 168–188.

Plott, C. R., & Smith, V. L. (1978). An experimental examination of two exchange institutions. *Review of Economic Studies, 45*(1): 133–153.

Prelec, D. (1998). The probability weighting function. *Econometrica, 66*(3), 497–527.

Quiggin, J. (1982). A theory of anticipated utility. *Journal of Economic Behavior & Organization, 3*, 323–343.

Smith, V. L. (1982). Microeconomic systems as an experimental science. *American Economic Review, 72*(5), 923–955.

Tversky, A., & Kahneman, D. (1992). Advances in prospect theory: Cumulative representation of uncertainty. *Journal of Risk and Uncertainty, 5*(4), 297–323.

Wilcox, N. T. (2011). 'Stochastically more risk averse:' A contextual theory of stochastic discrete choice under risk. *Journal of Econometrics, 162*(1), 89–104.

APPENDIX A: POWER PLOTS

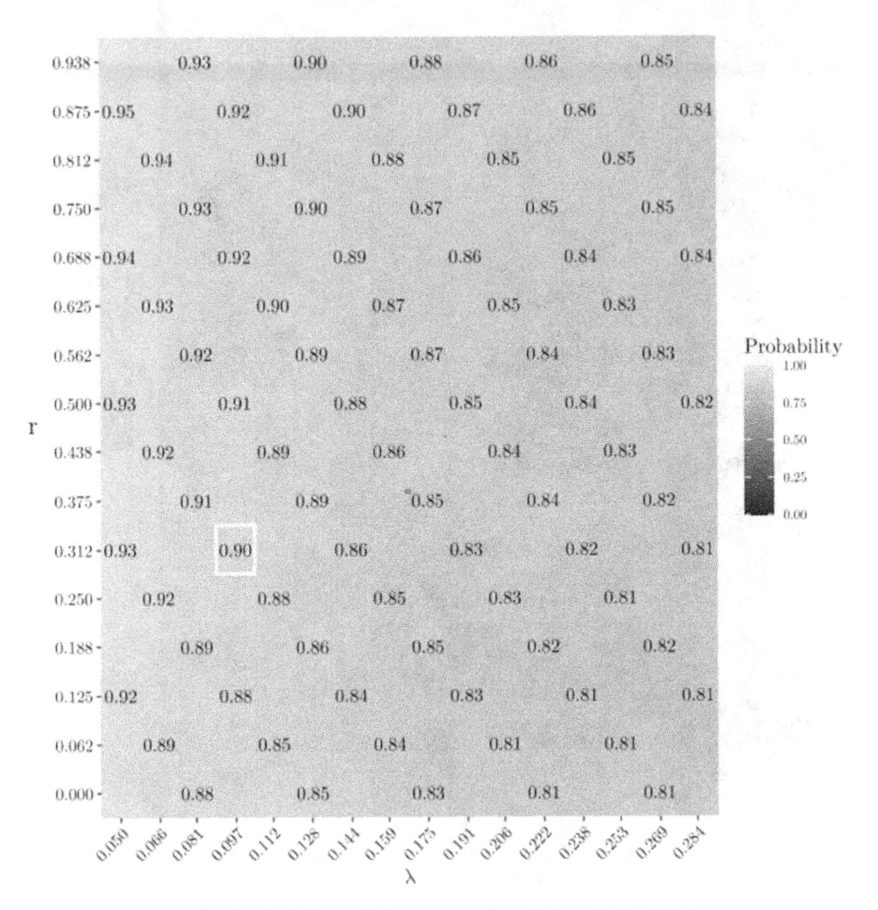

Fig. A1. Probability of Correctly Classifying EUT, 5% Level.

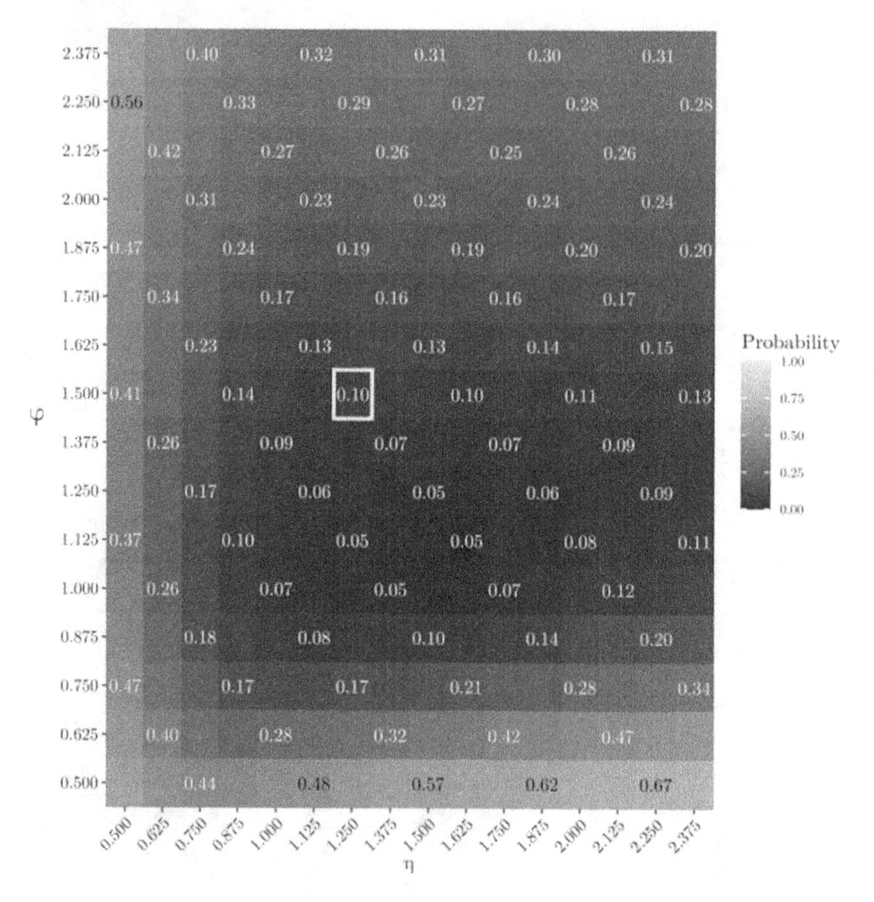

Fig. A2. Probability of Correctly Classifying RDU, 5% Level.

APPENDIX B: POTENTIAL AND ACTUAL ECS

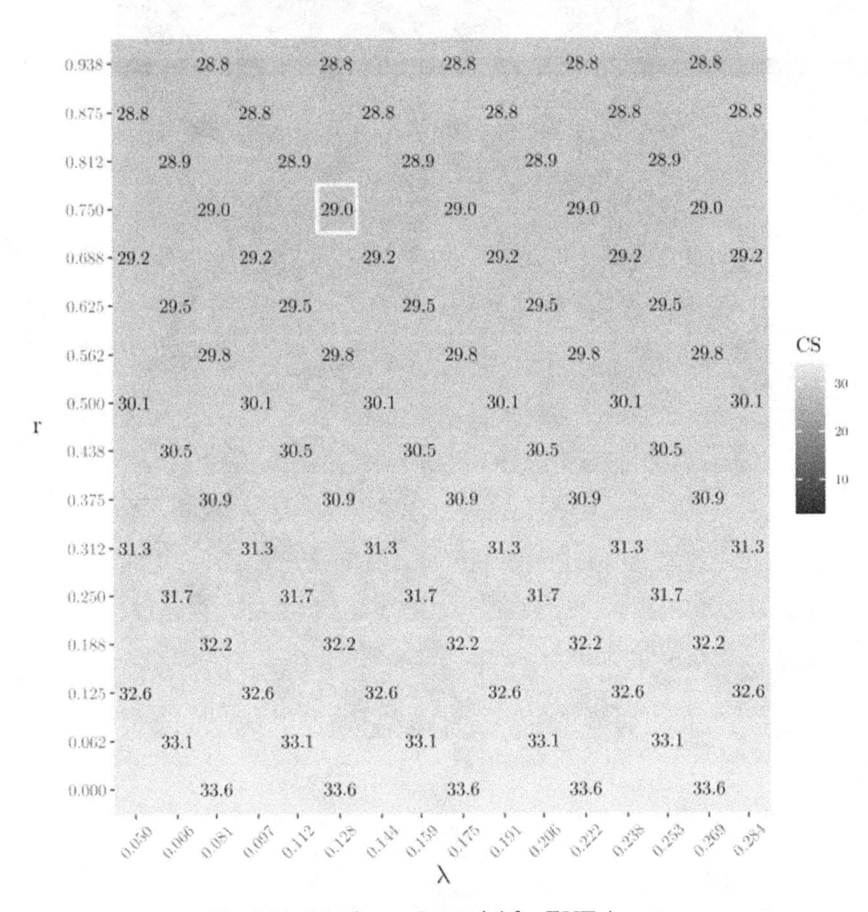

Fig. B1. Maximum Potential for EUT Agents.

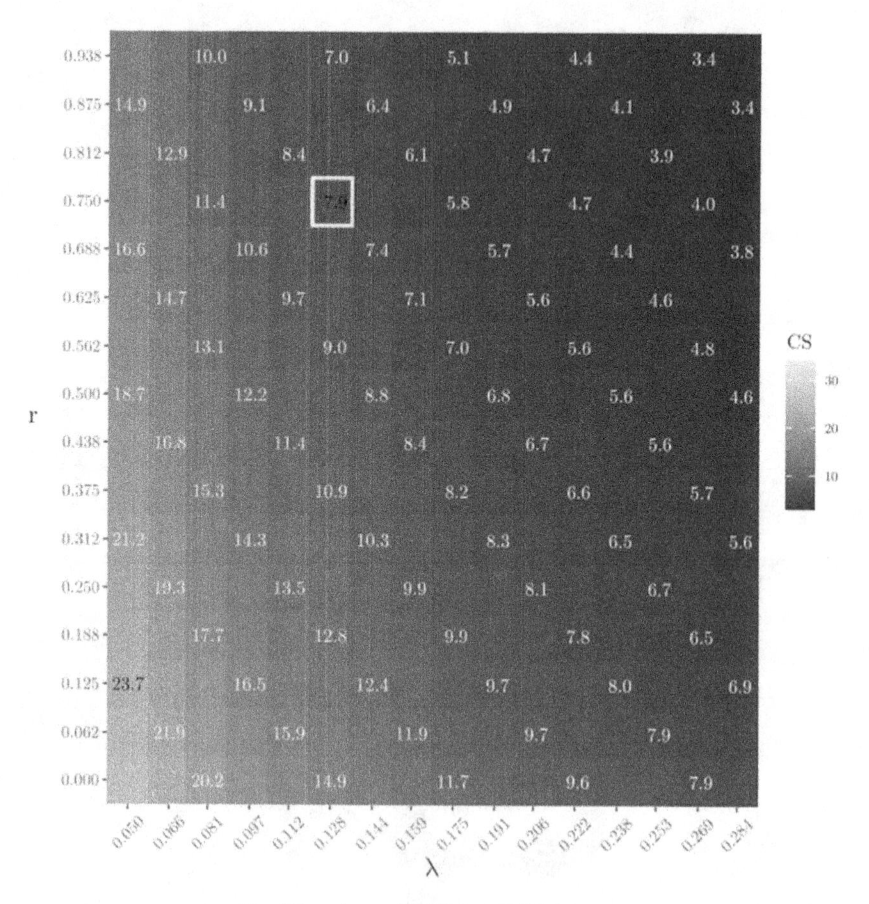

Fig. B2. Actual ECS for EUT Agents.

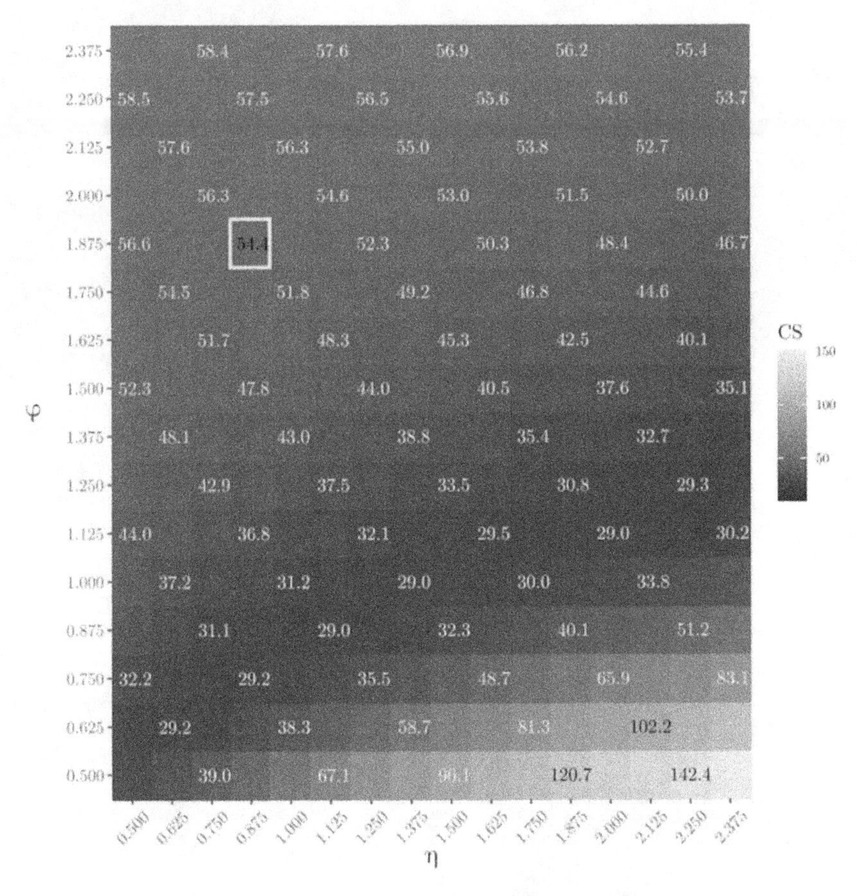

Fig. B3. Maximum Potential ECS for RDU Agents.

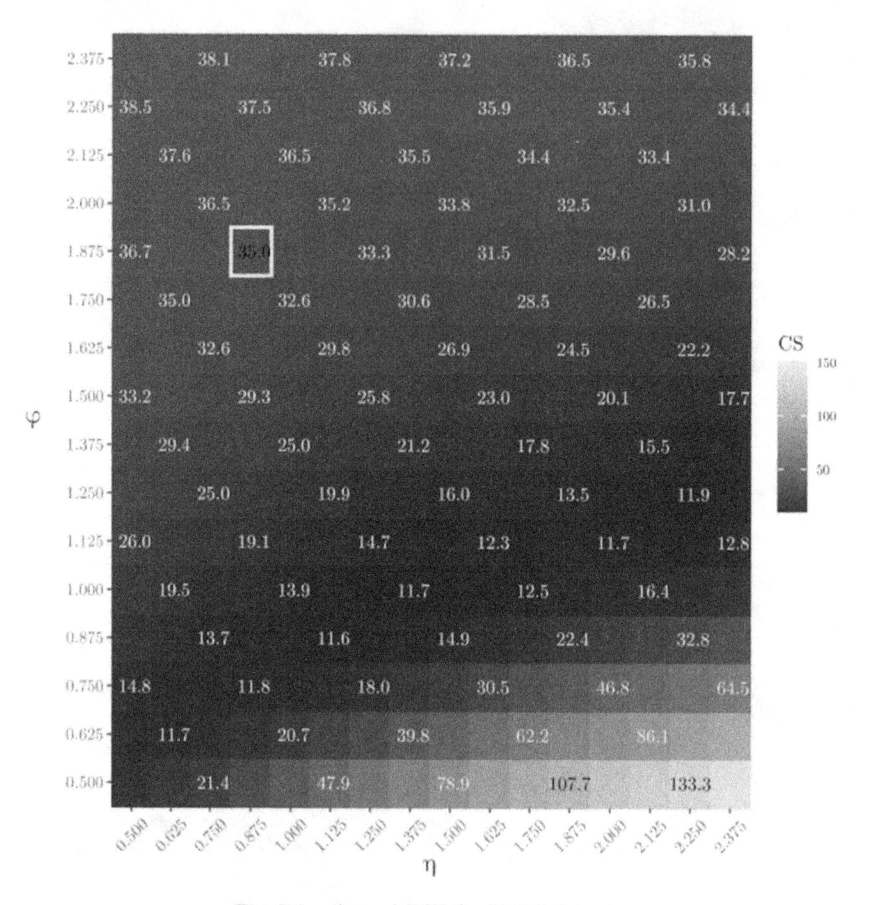

Fig. B4. Actual ECS for RDU Agents.

Printed in the USA
CPSIA information can be obtained
at www.ICGtesting.com
JSHW011458150923
48598JS00003B/6